The Peter Martyr Library
Volume Eight

Predestination

and

Justification

The Peter Martyr Library
Volume Eight

Predestination and Justification

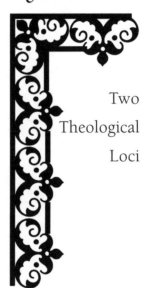

Two
Theological
Loci

Peter Martyr Vermigli

Translated and Edited with Introduction and Notes
by Frank A. James III

VOLUME LXVIII
SIXTEENTH CENTURY ESSAYS & STUDIES
KIRKSVILLE, MISSOURI USA ◆ 2003

Habent sua fata libeli

Library of Congress Cataloging-in-Publication Data

Vermigli, Pietro Martire, 1499–1562.
  [In Epistolam S. Pavli apostoli ad Romanos. English]
  Predestination and justification : two theological loci / Peter Martyr Vermigli ; translated and edited with introduction and notes by Frank A. James III.
    p.   cm. — (Sixteenth century essays & studies ; v. 68) (The Peter Martyr library ; ser. 1, v. 8)
  Includes bibliographical references and indexes.
  ISBN 1-931112-27-4 (Cloth : alk. paper)
    1. Bible. N.T. Romans—Commentaries. I. James, Frank A. II. Title. III. Series.
BS2665.53V4713 2003
234'.9—dc21   2003007963

Cover art and title page by Teresa Wheeler, Truman State University designer
Printed by Thomson-Shore, Dexter, Michigan, USA
Text is set in Adobe Minion 10/13; display in Hadfield-DTC

This volume is dedicated to my colleagues

John Patrick Donnelly, S.J.
and Joseph C. McLelland

—Giants on whose shoulders I stand

Contents

Abbreviations Used in This Volume ix

General Editors' Preface xi

Translator's Preface xii

Translator's Introduction xv

PART ONE ✌ LOCUS ON PREDESTINATION

Prolegomena.. 3
    Should Predestination Be Taught?........................... 3
    Does Predestination Exist? 10

Article 1: The Nature and Definition of Predestination 15
    The Nature of Predestination.............................. 15
    The Definition of Predestination........................... 19
    The Definition of Reprobation............................. 23

Article 2: The Cause of Predestination............................... 25
    The Fourfold Cause of Predestination....................... 26
    Are Foreseen Good Works the Cause of Predestination? 27
    Testimony from the Church Fathers......................... 40
    Contra Pighius... 40

Article 3: The Effects of Predestination 51
    Is Grace Universal? 53
    Is Grace Sufficient? 58
    Arguments to the Contrary 60

Article 4: The Necessity of Predestination 68
    Is Necessity Imposed upon Us? 69
    Does Necessity Hinder Free Will? 73
    Does Foreknowledge Cancel God's Justice? 82

Part Two 🙵 Locus on Justification

Prolegomena 87
    Justification 87
    Faith 88
    Works 95

Proposition 1: Justification Is Not by Works 96
    Proof from Paul's Letter to the Romans 97
    Proof from Paul's Other Letters 106
    Proof from Other Scriptures 111
    Objections to Proposition 1 115
    Proof from the Church Fathers 143
    Proof from Church Councils 152

Proposition 2: Justification Is by Faith 160
    Proof from Paul's Letter to the Romans 160
    Proof from Paul's Other Letters 165
    Proof from Other Scriptures 169
    Objections to Proposition 2 172
    Proof from the Church Fathers 205
    Proof from the Church Councils 217

Proposition 3: Justification Is by Faith Alone 218
    Contra Richard Smith 218
    Proof from the Church Fathers 228

About the Editor and Translator 231

Scripture References 232

Classical Patristic, and Medieval References 237

Index 239

Abbreviations Used in This Volume

CAS   *Calvinism and Scholasticism in Vermigli's Doctrine of Man and Grace.* John Patrick Donnelly. Leiden: Brill, 1976.

COR   *In Selectissimam D. Pauli Priorem ad Corinth. epistolam Commentarii.* Zurich: C. Froschauer, 1551.

DIAL   *Dialogue on the Two Natures in Christ.* Trans. and ed. John Patrick Donnelly, S.J. Peter Martyr Library, vol. 2. Kirksville, Mo.: Sixteenth Century Journal Publishers, 1995.

EW   *Early Writings: Creed, Scripture, Church.* Trans. Mario Di Gangi and Joseph C. McLelland. Ed. Joseph C. McLelland. Peter Martyr Library, vol. 1. Kirksville, Mo.: Sixteenth Century Journal Publishers, 1994.

HRR   *Peter Martyr Vermigli: Humanism, Republicanism, Reformation / Petrus Martyr Vermigli: Humanismus, Republikanismus, Reformation.* Ed. Emidio Campi in cooperation with Frank A. James III and Peter Opitz. Geneva: Droz, 2002.

LC   *Loci Communes of Peter Martyr Vermigli.* London: R. Masson, 1576; Basle: P. Perna, 1580–82 (3 vols.).

LLS   *Life, Letters, and Sermons.* Trans. John Patrick Donnelly, S.J. Peter Martyr Library, vol. 5. Kirksville, Mo.: Thomas Jefferson University Press, 1998.

LPJ   *Commentary on the Lamentations of the Prophet Jeremiah.* Trans. and ed. Daniel Shute. Peter Martyr Library, vol. 6. Kirksville, Mo.: Truman State University Press, 2002.

OL   *Original Letters Relative to the English Reformation.* 2 vols. Trans. and ed. Hastings Robinson. Cambridge: Cambridge University Press for the Parker Society, 1846–47.

OTD   *Oxford Treatise and Disputation on the Eucharist, 1549.* Trans. and ed. Joseph C. McLelland. Peter Martyr Library, vol. 7. Kirksville, Mo.: Truman State University Press, 1995.

PG   *Patralogiae cursus completus ... series Graeca.* 161 vols. Ed. J. P. Migne. Paris, 1857–96. Indices 1912.

PL   *Patralogiae cursus completus ... series Latina.* 221 vols. Ed. J. P. Migne. Paris, 1844–64. Supplements 1–5, Paris, 1958–74.

PMI   *Peter Martyr in Italy: An Anatomy of Apostasy.* Phillip M. J. McNair. Oxford: Oxford University Press, 1967.

PMRE   *Peter Martyr: A Reformer in Exile (1542–1562): A Chronology of Biblical Writings in England and Europe.* Marvin W. Anderson. Nieuwkoop: De Graaf, 1975.

PPRED   *Peter Martyr Vermigli and Predestination: The Augustinian Inheritance of an Italian Reformer.* Frank A. James III. Oxford: Oxford University Press, 1998.

PW   *Philosophical Works: On the Relation of Philosophy to Theology.* Trans. and ed. Joseph C. McLelland. Peter Martyr Library, vol. 4. Kirksville, Mo.: Sixteenth Century Journal Publishers, 1996.

ROM   *In Epistolam S. Pauli Apostoli ad Romanos commentarij doctissimi.* Peter Martyr Vermigli. Basel: P. Perna, 1558.

VWG   *The Visible Words of God: An Exposition of the Sacramental Theology of Peter Martyr Vermigli.* Joseph C. McLelland. Edinburgh: Oliver & Boyd, 1957; Grand Rapids: Eerdmans, 1965.

General Editors' Preface

$\mathcal{T}$he reputation of Peter Martyr Vermigli (1499–1562) rests largely on his role in the Sacramentarian controversies of his time. This partial perception distorts his career as biblical exegete. Volume 6 in our Library, *Commentary on the Lamentations of the Prophet Jeremiah*, presents one of Vermigli's lecture series presented after he left Italy to join Martin Bucer at Strasbourg. The present volume turns to Vermigli's next academic appointment, as regius professor of divinity at Oxford. He chose to lecture on Romans to address the ills of church and society, a fitting complement to his lectures on 1 Corinthians.

The present book consists of only two of the treatises contained in Martyr's large and influential Romans commentary; they are among the longest of his loci—those "commonplace" devices in vogue from the later Middle Ages and used increasingly by Martyr in his lectures, at least in their published form. These two are full-blown tracts, methodically developed and seeking to cover the chief "heads of doctrine."

The doctrines of predestination and justification are familiar shorthand for the Reformed faith. Each formed the center of a minor war of words and conferences, pitting the Reformed against Roman, Lutheran, and Anabaptist opponents. It is fortunate that in Frank James we have a scholar well acquainted with both topics and with Vermigli's texts. Dr. James has studied and commented on them through many years and two doctorates; we are proud to introduce his first contribution to our Library through two of Vermigli's substantive texts on disputed questions. As Dr. James's introduction makes clear, the polemical context informs Vermigli's teaching and provides foils for his attack. Here we meet such adversaries as Richard Smith of Oxford and Calvin's old foe Albert Pighius as well as the Tridentine doctors.

With this volume, series 1 of our Library is two-thirds complete. The remaining books are commentaries, on Aristotle's *Nicomachean Ethics* and on the biblical books of Genesis, Romans, and 1 Corinthians. Series 2 is in the planning stage. We hope that these translations of Martyr's writings will encourage scholars to engage this admirable theologian and will show why he is a significant if neglected player on the complex stage of the Reformation.

John Patrick Donnelly, S.J.
Joseph C. McLelland

Translator's Preface

Predestination and justification are two of the most distinctive doctrines associated with the Protestant Reformation of the sixteenth century. This volume presents Peter Martyr Vermigli's most extensive discussions on these controversial theological principles, drawn from his monumental commentary on the Apostle Paul's letter to the Romans. It has long been my goal to understand the theological dynamics in Vermigli's ecclesiastical transformation from a Roman Catholic theologian to a Protestant theologian. Two theological loci, one on predestination and the other on justification, provide important avenues by which one may gain insight into that profound transformation.

Not only did these two doctrines play a significant role in Vermigli's decision to abandon Rome; they also became the theological realms (besides sacramental theology) in which Vermigli made his most important contributions to the theology of the Reformed branch of Protestantism. Having access to these two loci will enable scholars of the sixteenth century to gain additional insight into the theological and biblical thinking of one of the formative thinkers of the Reformation and, perhaps most importantly, allow a glimpse into the theological diversity among the early Reformers. My early scholarly effort on Vermigli, a doctoral dissertation at Oxford University on the historical origins of his doctrine of predestination, brought unconventional conclusions. I expected to find a viewpoint that mirrored Calvin's, but found instead a theological perspective largely inspired by a fourteenth-century Augustinian, Gregory of Rimini. It seemed that Heiko A. Oberman's quest for a theological link between the early reformation and the late medieval *schola Augustiniana moderna* had been found in Vermigli.

My interest in Vermigli was sufficient to inspire yet another doctoral dissertation, this time in theology at Westminster Theological Seminary in Philadelphia. The goal was to delve deeply into one of the most distinctive Protestant doctrines—justification—and to measure Vermigli's understanding against other great theological views of his day—Catholic, Lutheran, and Reformed. Again, expectations as to what Vermigli would say on the topic had to be reconfigured. I anticipated that he would be in conformity with the Lutherans and Reformed against the Catholics. Instead, what emerged from the research was a much more nuanced understanding of justification. Vermigli did retain some of the features of the Catholic Reform movement in Italy, especially those of the group associated with Juan de Valdés. It may sound obvious from the distance of nearly five centuries, but Vermigli, while clearly indebted to Luther, was not a Lutheran on the matter of justification, nor for that matter, were many of his Reformed colleagues such as Calvin, Bullinger, and Bucer. The doctrinal divide that became apparent over time was evident early on in Vermigli's doctrine of justification.

One of the lasting impressions gained from research into Vermigli's thought is his profound biblical orientation. In some ways, that is his lasting legacy. If one had asked Peter Martyr how he would like to be remembered, he might have pointed to his Bible and stated that he wanted only to promulgate the teaching of Scripture. More work needs to be done on his theology, especially on his biblical commentaries. To that end, the Peter Martyr Library editorial committee is now focusing on translations of his commentaries.

Special thanks to the managing editor of the Peter Martyr Library, Paula Presley, whose untiring efforts and high standards make this a superb series. Finally, I thank my graduate assistant Kate Maynard for her efforts on behalf of this project and Daniel Timmerman of the Theologische Universiteit Apeldoorn for help in identifying obscure references.

I owe a great debt to my colleagues Pat Donnelly and Joe McLelland, who have provided enormous assistance in the preparation of this volume. I am overcome with gratitude for the generosity and support of this American Jesuit and Canadian Presbyterian. I am especially grateful for their assistance in composition of footnote references. This dedication is a small token of my affection and appreciation for these two extraordinary colleagues.

Frank A. James III

Orlando, Florida
Feast Day of St. Nino
15 December 2002

Peter Martyr Vermigli (1499–1562) by Hans Asper (1499–1571), painted 1560.
Courtesy National Portrait Gallery, London

Translator's Introduction

Prologue

ℐt is a measure of Peter Martyr Vermigli's influence in England that his regal portrait by Hans Asper is included in the National Portrait Gallery in London.[1] The piercing brown eyes of a rather handsome Peter Martyr look beyond the confines of his gilded frame as he points to his Bible. This portrait captures something of the true spirit of this Italian theologian. It is as if, in full academic regalia, he is instructing his students to concentrate their undivided attention upon this book alone, much as he urged in his Oxford oration: "Let us immerse ourselves constantly in the sacred Scriptures, let us work at reading them, and by the gift of Christ's Spirit the things that are necessary for salvation will be for us clear, direct, and completely open."[2]

Vermigli's fame rested in large part on his erudite biblical commentaries. Wherever his journey led him, he could be found lecturing on the biblical text, whether in his earlier career as a Catholic theologian lecturing monks in Naples and Lucca, or later in Protestant academies in Strasbourg, Zurich, or Oxford. During his lifetime his lectures on 1 Corinthians, Romans, and Judges were published; his lectures on Genesis, Lamentations, 1 and 2 Samuel, and 1 and 2 Kings were published posthumously.[3] Although Vermigli had wide-ranging theological and polemical interests to which he devoted many pages, there is little doubt that his primary calling was as a biblical commentator.[4] Along with Calvin and Bullinger, Vermigli was among the leading representatives of the Reformed tradition of

---

[1]Torrance Kirby, "*Vermilius Absconditus*? The Iconography of Peter Martyr Vermigli," HRR, 295–303; painting is reproduced on facing page.

[2]From Martyr's "Exhortation for Youths to Study Sacred Letters," LLS, 281.

[3]Cf. Klaus Sturm, *Die Theologie Peter Martyr Vermiglis während seines ersten Aufenthalts in Strasburg 1542–1547* (Neukirchen: Neukirchener Verlag, 1971), 30–37.

[4]Frank A. James III, "Peter Martyr Vermigli (1499–1562)" in *Historical Handbook of Major Biblical Interpreters*, ed. Donald McKim (Downers Grove, Ill.: InterVarsity Press, 1998), 239–45. Cf. John L. Thompson, "The Survival of Allegorical Argumentation in Peter Martyr Vermigli's Old Testament Exegesis," in *Biblical Interpretation in the Era of the Reformation*, ed. Richard A. Muller and John L. Thompson (Grand Rapids: Eerdmans, 1996), 255–58.

Protestant biblical commentators.[5] To begin to understand Martyr one must appreciate that he was first and foremost a man of the book—a biblical scholar.

Peter Martyr Vermigli in England

Vermigli's success in England left a bitter taste in the mouths of Catholics. When his wife, Catherine Dampmartin of Metz, died in Oxford in February of 1553, Catholic hostility directed at her husband unfortunately found its mark in her. Even while alive, Catherine was the brunt of brutal sarcasm, orally and in print.[6] Because she was a corpulent woman, the Catholics at Oxford nicknamed her "flaps" and "fusteluggs." Shortly after Catherine's death, Mary Tudor ascended to the English throne, and a widowed Vermigli returned to Strasbourg. However, hatred for Vermigli ran so high among Catholics that they sought to cause him distress by desecrating the body of his late wife.[7] Archbishop Reginald Pole, once a close friend of Vermigli in Italy, had Catherine's body exhumed and cast upon the city dung heap,[8] ostensibly because she had been buried in close proximity to the grave of St. Frideswyde, the patron saint of Oxford, in the Cathedral Church.[9] But the Catholics did not have the final word on Catherine's remains. After Elizabeth's ascension in 1558 and the return of the Marian exiles, Catherine's bones were recovered from the dung heap and deliberately mingled with the bones of St. Frideswyde. Any desecration thereafter would risk desecrating the bones of St. Frideswyde—a risk most Catholics would be unwilling to take.

The deplorable episode dramatically illustrates the range of emotions the English felt for the Italian immigrant theologian: detractors and advocates alike viewed Vermigli as a particularly important symbol of Edwardian reform. C. H. Smyth writes, "Oxford, which had not taken kindly to the Renaissance, was

---

[5]LPJ, xli–xliv. See also Peter A. Lillback, "The Early Reformed Covenant Paradigm: Peter Martyr vis-à-vis Zwingli, Bullinger, Luther, and Calvin" (paper presented at Sixteenth Century Studies Conference, St. Louis, Mo., 28–31 October 1999).

[6]See George C. Gorham, *Gleanings of a Few Scattered Ears during the Period of the Reformation in England and of the Times Immediately Succeeding, A.D. 1533 to A.D. 1588* (London, 1857), 154 (Vermigli's letter to Bucer, 10 June 1550). See also Jennifer Loach, "Reformation Controversies," in *The Collegiate University*, ed. James McConica, vol. 3 of *The History of the University of Oxford*, gen. ed. T. H. Aston (Oxford: Clarendon, 1986), 374; C. H. Smyth, *Cranmer and the Reformation under Edward VI* (1926; repr., London: S.P.C.K., 1973), 120.

[7]LLS, 311.

[8]Josiah Simler, *Oratio de vita et obitu viri optimi praestantissimi Theologi D. Peteri Martyris Vermilii, Sacrarum literarum in schola Tigurina Professoris* (Zurich: C. Froschauer, 1563), 7. For the English, see LLS, 32. See also Dermot Fenlon, *Heresy and Obedience in Tridentine Italy: Cardinal Pole and the Counter-Reformation* (Cambridge: Cambridge University Press, 1972), 219, and PMI, 96–98, 284.

[9]John Blair, ed., *St. Frideswide: Patron of Oxford* (Oxford: Perpetua Press, 1989), 21–23.

violently hostile to the Reformation.... the whole of Peter Martyr's work was an almost single-handed struggle against overwhelming odds."[10] Whether Vermigli inspired intense animosity or devoted affection, it cannot be doubted that during his nearly six years in England (1547–53), he exercised a decisive influence upon its Reformation.

Of course, the earliest Protestant theological influence was that of Luther, whose books and pamphlets were smuggled into England by German merchants and read in Cambridge by 1520. By March of 1521, Luther's books were publicly burned for the first time in England.[11] Even before the death of Henry VIII on 28 January 1547, a new kind of Protestant influence began to take root on English soil—a theological outlook more Swiss and Reformed than German and Lutheran.[12] Archbishop Thomas Cranmer of Canterbury had been in correspondence with the Swiss Reformer of Basel, Simon Grynaeus, since 1531, and through Grynaeus, Cranmer became a frequent correspondent of Martin Bucer of Strasbourg.[13] This relationship with the Swiss manifested itself in an abortive plan to form a theological alliance between the English church and the Swiss and South German Protestants on the continent.[14] For some years, Cranmer had desired to improve ties between the English church and continental Protestantism.[15] With much of continental Protestantism in disarray after the victory of Charles V in the Schmalkald war, Cranmer believed England could be the rallying point for a resurgent Protestantism. He even made plans to compose a common doctrinal statement and to hold a "godly synod" of continental and English Protestants to counter the effects of the Council of Trent (1545–63), conferring with such theologians as John Calvin, Philip Melanchthon, and Heinrich Bullinger about the proposal.[16] When Edward VI succumbed to tuberculosis, Cranmer's dreams were deferred.

[10]Smyth, *Cranmer and the Reformation,* 108.

[11]Basil Hall, "The Early Rise and Gradual Decline of Lutheranism in England (1520–1600)," in *Reform and Reformation: England and the Continent c. 1500–c. 1750,* ed. Derek Baker (Oxford: Basil Blackwell, 1979), 103–31.

[12]Diarmaid MacCulloch, *The Later Reformation in England 1547–1603* (London: Macmillan, 1990), 67; A. G. Dickens, *The English Reformation,* 2d ed. (University Park: Pennsylvania University Press, 1992), 222–26.

[13]Diarmaid MacCulloch, *Thomas Cranmer: A Life* (New Haven: Yale University Press, 1996), 60–67.

[14]MacCulloch, *Cranmer,* 404–9.

[15]Dickens, *English Reformation,* 257.

[16]*Works of Archbishop Cranmer,* ed. J. E. Cox (Cambridge: Cambridge University Press for the Parker Society, 1844), 2:431–32. See Gorham, *Gleanings,* 42–46; MacCulloch, *Cranmer,* 174–76; 394–96.

It is almost certain that Vermigli first came to the attention of Cranmer through the archbishop's long-standing relationship with Bucer.[17] As part of Cranmer's desire to foster continental associations that would give impetus to a reformation of the English church, he invited Vermigli and his fellow Italian refugee, Bernardino Ochino, to England. Cranmer's warm welcome to Vermigli in the winter of 1547 was followed by decisive support in the Oxford Disputation[18] and further involvement in formulating English church policy.[19] Of all the continental Reformers, Martyr exerted the greatest influence.[20]

This impression is reinforced by Cranmer's response to the new Catholic regime. Immediately after Mary's ascension, when Cranmer's reformation was under severe attack, he bravely threw down the gauntlet and publicly declared on 5 September 1553: "I with Peter Martyr and … others of my choosing" will defend the Prayer Book as "more pure and more agreeable to the word of God than what has been in England for the past thousand years."[21] Cranmer and Vermigli began preparing for a public disputation that never happened. Instead, Cranmer was charged with treason and, on 14 September, the two friends shared a last supper, after which the archbishop told his friend that a trial was inevitable and that they would never meet again. Cranmer was soon sent to the Tower, and Vermigli, after entreaties by his famulus Giulio Santerenziano and William Whittingham, was granted permission to leave the country.[22] The last known letter (1555) from the hand of Cranmer, as he languished in the Bocardo jail awaiting martyrdom, was to his dear friend Peter Martyr.[23] The growing scholarly consensus is that

---

[17]MacCulloch, *Cranmer*, 381, cites a letter of 28 November 1547 from Paris, Bibliothèque Ste-Geneviève MSS 1458, fols. 173v–75r, which reveals that Bucer specifically recommended to Cranmer the Italian exile Emmanuel Tremelli (1510–80), who arrived the next year (1548) and was appointed king's reader in Hebrew at Cambridge. If Bucer was recommending scholars to Cranmer, then it is easy to surmise that Bucer also recommended the Italian Vermigli, for whom he had even greater esteem.

[18]Translated in OTD.

[19]VWG, 23.

[20]MacCulloch, *Cranmer*, 435–36, points out that Cranmer's crucial sermon on rebellion at St. Paul's Cathedral in London on 21 July 1549 was, in fact, the result of a collaboration with Vermigli. More specifically, MacCulloch maintains that Vermigli was involved to a greater extent in church affairs than Bucer. See Diarmaid MacCulloch, "Peter Martyr and Thomas Cranmer," HRR, 178, 192. This echoes the earlier view of C. H. Smyth, who judged that "of all the foreigners [in England], Ochino had probably the least influence: and Peter Martyr probably the most"; Smyth, *Cranmer and the Reformation*, 117. Two years after Vermigli's arrival in Oxford and after the 1548 Augsburg interim made life impossible for Bucer, he too accepted Cranmer's invitation to that city.

[21]Gilbert Burnet, *The History of the Reformation of the Church of England* (London: Lewis Cordell, 1681), 2:249–50. See also *Thomas Cranmer: Churchman and Scholar*, ed. P. Ayris and D. Selwyn (Woodbridge, Suffolk: Boydell & Brewer, 1993), 285.

[22]See OL.

[23]*Works of Archbishop Cranmer*, 2:457–58. See also C. H. Garrett, *The Marian Exiles: A Study in the Origins of Elizabethan Puritanism* (Cambridge: Cambridge University Press, 1938), 198.

Vermigli was one of the most important, if unheralded, theological influences upon Cranmer and, through Cranmer, on the Edwardian Reformation.

When Vermigli left England for good in October 1553, he carried with him not only affection and deep concern for Cranmer and the English church, but an international reputation as a Reformed theologian. When he arrived in Strasbourg to revive his role as a leading Reformed theologian on yet another stage, he deplored in his inaugural address the loss of King Edward and the England that might have been.

> A harsh and lamentable death took away Edward, king of England, the bright light among the monarchs of the Christian world, the rightful student of godliness and a stout defender of Christ's Gospel. Light was changed into darkness, ungodliness replaced godliness, and cruel wolves invaded the new and recent church. Good men were wickedly oppressed; I cannot think about, still less recount, how the providence of the one God delivered me from their dangers and troubles.[24]

Monarchs die and other monarchs, hell-bent on burning heretics, ascend to thrones, but for Vermigli the truth was unassailable. In tribute to the boy-king and his archbishop, Vermigli published his Romans lectures. His dedicatory epistle to Sir Anthony Cooke,[25] Edward's tutor and a Marian exile, is in effect a dedication to the English church. In this dedication is a highly developed sense of belonging to a circle of like-minded continental theologians. Vermigli specifically names Melanchthon, Bucer, Bullinger, and Calvin, and indicates that he has not only read their commentaries on Romans, but has been "greatly helped" by them.[26] This underscores the growing theological affinity, particularly with Swiss Protestantism, reflected in his own commentary on Romans.

Of the many contributions to the Reformation in England, perhaps the most cherished and natural for Martyr were his lectures at Oxford. After completing his first series of lectures on 1 Corinthians in 1549, Martyr turned to Paul's epistle to the Romans in 1550, as he earlier had promised.[27] Martyr's Romans lectures began in March 1550, were completed in Zurich, and finally published in 1558.[28]

---

[24]LLS, 310–11.

[25]For background on Cooke, see Garrett, *Marian Exiles*, 124–26.

[26]ROM, dedicatory epistle.

[27]COR, fol. 39r.

[28]Loach, "Reformation Controversies," 373. See also James McConica, "The Rise of the Undergraduate College," in *Collegiate University*, ed. McConica, 41; John ab Ulmis's letter of 1 March 1552 says he attended Martyr's Romans lectures at 9:00 A.M. According to S. L. Greenslade, "The Faculty of Theology," in *Collegiate University*, ed. McConica, 307, Cardinal Wolsey established the practice for regius professors of divinity. See *Statutes of the Colleges of Oxford* (London: Royal Commission, 1853), 2/2:127.

THE ROMANS COMMENTARY

Of his biblical writings, Vermigli's commentary on Romans was the most influential.[29] It also was the most republished of his biblical writings—going through eight editions from 1558 to 1613.[30] The historical evidence indicates that Vermigli lectured on this epistle in at least three locations during his long career and possibly four. Vermigli had long enjoyed an intimate knowledge of Paul's epistle to the Romans well before crossing the Alps to Protestantism in 1542. Although Philip McNair thinks the evidence inconclusive, he does enumerate cogent reasons for the possibility that Vermigli lectured on Romans as early as his triennium in Naples (1537–40).[31] Whatever doubts remain about Naples, there is an eyewitness to his lectures on Romans in Lucca (1541–42). Girolamo Zanchi, who was a novitiate in the Lucchese monastery at S. Frediano and was converted under the ministry of Vermigli, specifically notes that he heard Vermigli lecture on Romans in Lucca.[32]

Recent evidence indicates that Vermigli also lectured on Paul's epistle to the Romans in Strasbourg in 1545–46. A young Frenchman from Lille, Hubert de Bapasme, who had come to Strasbourg to study theology, revealed in a letter dated 10 March 1546 that he had attended Vermigli's lectures on Paul's epistle to the Romans: "This week, I have listened to one of his [Vermigli's] lectures on the New Testament, the epistle to the Romans, chapter twelve."[33] This places Vermigli's lectures on Romans in his fourth year at Strasbourg, that is, the 1545–46

---

[29]CAS, 18 n. 36. See also Joan Simon, *Education and Society in Tudor England* (Cambridge: Cambridge University Press, 1966), 380, and H. S. Bennett, *English Books and Readers, 1550–1603* (Cambridge: Cambridge University Press, 1965), 88.

[30]*Bibliography of the Writings of Peter Martyr Vermigli*, ed. John Patrick Donnelly and Robert M. Kingdon, with Marvin W. Anderson (Kirksville, Mo.: Sixteenth Century Journal Publishers, 1990), 18–30.

[31]PMI, 152–53.

[32]Girolamo Zanchi, *Operum Theologicorum* ... (Geneva, 1605), vii, 4, writing to Philip, Landgrave of Hesse, on 15 October 1565, specifically mentions that Vermigli lectured on Paul's letter to the Romans in Lucca. "ambo denique simul, cum Martyrem Lucae, Epistolam ad Romanos publice interpretantem...."

[33]Philip Denis, "La correspondance d'Hubert de Bapasme, réfugié lillois à Strasbourg (1545–47)," *Bulletin de la Société de l'Histoire du Protestantisme Français* 124 (1978): 103–4: "J'ay ouy ceste sepmaine une de ses [Vermigli's] leschons qu'il faict au Nouvaux Testament en l'épistre à Romains, douziesme chapitre...." We add two further considerations. First, there is no doubt about the identification of the lecturer: it is Vermigli. Second, de Bapasme's letter ostensibly speaks of lectures, not lecture, so it appears that Vermigli was giving a lecture series on the epistle to the Romans. This is also the opinion of Denis (104n).

term.[34] Finally, as regius professor of divinity at Oxford, Vermigli again lectured on Romans from 1550 to 1552.

There can be little doubt that his Romans lectures were strategically chosen and employed to further his goal of bringing reformation to England, which had been his charge from Cranmer.[35] Vermigli had already survived the ecclesiastical eruptions that came from his lectures on 1 Corinthians, with the controversy on the Eucharist, and it was time to engage on other doctrinal fronts. Oxford in 1550 was by no means Protestant territory, as Vermigli declared in his sermon: "the Oxford men … are still pertinaciously sticking in the mud of popery."[36] But Vermigli judged that he had the ultimate weapon in this war of ideas: Paul's epistle to the Romans. Clearly, he set out to expound not only the text, but also to draw out the full theological implications in two extended loci, departing from his usual plan of many shorter loci on a wide range of topics.[37] This time around he concentrated on only two, predestination and justification, doctrines he believed were taught explicitly by Paul in the epistle to the Romans. Hence, he seized the opportunity, which he regarded as a responsibility, to expound in great detail and with full scriptural citations these two distinctively Protestant doctrines. By this time, Vermigli saw himself as England's chief articulator of continental Reformed theology. There is the implicit suggestion that he, like other leading Protestant theologians, should comment on Romans, as if a commentary on Romans were a rite of passage. The Romans commentary marks Vermigli's self-conscious emergence onto the historical stage of mainstream Reformed theologians. This self-perception reflects something of Cranmer's plan to create theological alliances with continental Protestantism, perhaps with England at the helm, which remained a live option until the demise of the Edwardian regime in 1553.[38]

---

[34]PPRED, 45–49. It would appear that Martyr's lecture sequence began with the Minor Prophets in 1542–43, Genesis in 1543–44, and Exodus in 1544–45. He then moved out of his Old Testament sequence to lecture on Romans in 1545–46, and in his last term at Strasbourg (1546–47) he returned to the scheduled sequence with lectures on Leviticus. According to Dan Shute, the five short chapters of Lamentations were delivered immediately after his lectures on the Minor Prophets in 1543; see LPJ, xlvii.

[35]John Strype, *Ecclesiastical Memorials … of the Church of England under King Henry VIII* (Oxford: Clarendon, 1822), 2:197. See VWG, 16.

[36]Philip McNair, "Peter Martyr in England," in *Peter Martyr Vermigli and Italian Reform*, ed. J. C. McLelland (Waterloo, Ont.: Wilfrid Laurier University Press, 1980), 95. See also OL, 2:464.

[37]*Bibliography of … Vermigli*, ed. Donnelly et al., 18, mentions the only two loci in the Romans commentary, *de praedestinatione* and *de iustificatione*.

[38]MacCulloch, *Cranmer*, 501–2.

Loci Communes

One of the more significant methodological developments of the sixteenth century was emergence of the loci method. *Loci communes* (commonplaces) are in the most basic sense additional explanations of the biblical text. Like Protestant theologians such as Melanchthon and Bucer, Vermigli employed these commonplaces to elaborate on the biblical text.[39] They are, for the most part, learned discussions on especially important theological doctrines or their practical implications. It is worth noting that Melanchthon's 1520 exposition of the *loci theologici* of Paul's epistle to the Romans included three fundamental themes arising from the text: justification, predestination, and morals.[40] Vermigli may have followed somewhat the pattern of Melanchthon in his Romans commentary.[41]

As regius professor of divinity, Vermigli was obliged not only to give lectures at the divinity school, but also to officiate at theological disputations.[42] Whether there was a direct connection between these disputations and his two Romans loci has generated some scholarly wrangling. S. L. Greenslade has argued that the published version of Martyr's Romans lectures was in fact an "expansion" of his Oxford lectures.[43] Greenslade seems to suggest that the two loci were significant revisions or even later additions to the expanded commentary and therefore bear no direct relationship to the theological disputations. If this reconstruction is accurate, the loci would have no direct connection to the disputations since they would have been composed primarily in Strasbourg and Zurich between 1553 and 1557 instead of in Oxford. However, Jennifer Loach disputes Greenslade's

---

[39]CAS 64, states: "The scholia [or loci] were an implicit confession that the theological process must go beyond an exposition of the biblical text. Martyr has taken the important step of introducing systematic, highly speculative and rather scholastic theology right into the citadel of biblical exegesis." In my judgment, Martyr's loci are no departure from the biblical text, but are an integral part of the exposition itself. Martyr's purpose in using the loci is not to go beyond the text, but to go back to the text, summarize it, and clarify the meaning of the text. One might suggest that Martyr had a systematic bent or even a "tidy-mindedness," which is evident in his use of loci, but these do not make him a scholastic nor do the loci take him beyond the text.

[40]T. H. L. Parker, *Calvin's New Testament Commentaries*, 2d ed. (Louisville: Westminster/John Knox press, 1993), 68.

[41]Erika Rummel, *The Humanist-Scholastic Debate in the Renaissance and Reformation* (Cambridge, Mass.: Harvard University Press, 1995), 143ff. Furthermore, Simler mentions that Vermigli read Erasmus, but does not specify which work; see LLS, 20. Could it be that Erasmus's *Ratio* (1519) or *Methodus* (1516) served Martyr in devising his own approach to commentary writing?

[42]Loach, "Reformation Controversies," 368. Cf. OL, 2:420, 481 (Martyr's letter to Bucer, 1 June 1550).

[43]Greenslade, "Faculty of Theology," 319.

analysis, arguing instead that Martyr's theological loci had their source in the regular student disputations and were "part of the original lectures."[44] Loach believes that although Martyr polished the Romans lectures and loci in Zurich, he did not alter them substantially for publication. This perspective maintains the original Oxford context for the composition of the commentary and the loci. In assessing these theories, there are several factors that bear upon the matter. First, it had been Vermigli's practice in Strasbourg to coordinate his student disputations with his lectures. The evidence indicates, for example, that the locus on justification from his published Genesis lectures corresponds exactly with his theses for disputation, which implies that one was derived from the other.[45] Apparently it had been Vermigli's custom to obtain the loci of his commentaries from the student disputations. Second, it is a matter of historical record that his Oxford lectures on Romans were intertwined with formal theological disputations as part of the regular divinity school curriculum.[46] Indeed, the polemical flavor of the loci reflects the climate of disputation.[47] When the details are factored in, it seems that the commentary and the loci are intimately connected and that both had their origins in Oxford, although Vermigli may have made refinements for publications.

PREDESTINATION

CONTEXT

Although Calvin is most often identified with the doctrine of predestination, he was not its only Protestant advocate. Charles Schmidt, a nineteenth-century historian, concluded that, besides Calvin, Vermigli did more than any other Protestant theologian to establish the doctrine of predestination.[48] It was not the central spoke of Vermigli's theological system, as some have argued of Calvin, but it was a conviction he was willing to defend—something he did repeatedly. At three

---

[44]Loach, "Reformation Controversies," 373.

[45]EW, 106–7.

[46]Greenslade, "Faculty of Theology," 308–9, notes that the university disputations were held every other Thursday during term from 1:00 to 3:00 P.M. and were to be presided over by the regius professor of divinity. See G. D. Duncan, "Public Lectures and Professorial Chairs," in *Collegiate University,* ed. McConica, 352.

[47]Further confirmation is found in a letter dated 31 March 1550 in which Vermigli refers specifically to a "late disputation" in which the issue of merit and reward arose. This particular disputation occurred during the same time he was lecturing on Romans at Oxford, and both of these theological issues are addressed in the locus on justification, which strongly suggests that the doctrine in the locus was disputed at the same time the lectures were delivered; Gorham, *Gleanings,* 141. See also CAS, 141.

[48]Charles Schmidt, *Peter Martyr Vermigli, Leben und ausgewählte Schriften nach handschriftlichen und gleichzeitigen Quellen* (Elberfeld: R. L. Friderichs, 1858), 106.

junctures during his Protestant sojourn he became embroiled in controversy on predestination.

In 1553, Vermigli fled the reign of Mary Tudor to a Strasbourg increasingly dominated by scrupulous hard-boiled Lutherans. Although the Strasbourg senate was quite anxious for Vermigli to assume his former position at the academy as professor of theology, the Lutheran faction, led by John Marbach, strenuously objected to Vermigli's reappointment.[49] In taking the Strasbourg post, Vermigli anticipated the Lutheran opposition to his sacramental theology, as indicated in his letters to Calvin and Bullinger just a few days after arriving in Strasbourg,[50] but he did not expect his view of predestination also to become a bone of contention. In May 1554, Vermigli wrote to Calvin:

> I want you to know that this sadly grieves me, along with others, that they [the Lutherans] spread very foul and false reports concerning the eternal election of God, against the truth and against your name…. We here, especially Zanchi and I, defend your part and the truth as far as we can….[51]

Despite the tensions, Vermigli remained in Strasbourg until 1556, when he accepted Bullinger's offer to succeed Conrad Pellican at Zurich.[52] Although warmly welcomed to Zurich by Bullinger, Vermigli found less enthusiasm from one of his new colleagues, Theodore Bibliander.[53] As much as Vermigli wished to avoid it, controversy was brewing yet again. He began lectures on 1 Samuel in August 1556, and by June 1557 Bibliander had begun openly to attack Vermigli's

---

[49]On 15 December 1553, Vermigli wrote to Bullinger: "My own affairs are in this condition. Our friend Sturmius, and the principal professors, with the greater portion of the clergy, have made strenuous exertions for my remaining here, and they had the governors of the school sufficiently favorable to this arrangement. But two or three of the ministers, who possess some influence, object to it on account of my opinions respecting the sacrament and have raised such an opposition that the matter cannot yet be resolved." OL, 2:509.

[50]Vermigli had arrived in Strasbourg on 30 October 1553. On 3 November, he wrote to Bullinger: "Hence it is that I am now here, but I do not yet know whether I shall again be received in this church and school; for, as I suspect, the sacramentary controversy will occasion some difficulties; however, I am not very anxious about it." OL, 2:505.

[51]Vermigli's letter to Calvin is found in *Locorum Communium Theologicorum ex ipsius scriptis sincere decerptorum* (Basel: P. Perna, 1582), 231–32.

[52]The controversies in Strasbourg escalated until May 1556, when Vermigli accepted the invitation from Zurich. The formal request from Zurich is found in Garrett, *Marian Exiles*, 367. On 13 July 1556, Vermigli, accompanied by his English disciple John Jewel, departed for Zurich.

[53]Theodore Bibliander, professor of Old Testament at Zurich, had long been an opponent of Calvin, but had restrained himself from public attack. Bibliander held to a view of predestination much like that of Erasmus. See Schmidt, *Leben*, 215.

doctrine of predestination.[54] According to Joachim Staedtke, a full-blown *Prädestinationsstreit* erupted in Zurich.[55] The Zurich faculty sided with Vermigli, and Bibliander was dismissed from his duties in February 1560. Even with Bibliander's dismissal, Vermigli still was to see a third controversy over predestination. In Strasbourg, John Marbach went on the warpath again in 1561—this time Zanchi's doctrine of predestination was the object of Marbach's ire. Vermigli could not stand idle when Marbach brought charges of heresy against his fellow Italian exile Zanchi.[56] Not only did Vermigli display his personal support in a letter to the Strasbourg senate,[57] but he also rallied support from his Zurich colleagues.[58] Unfortunately, when Vermigli had departed from Strasbourg in 1556, Zanchi inherited the Reformed cause against Marbach and the Lutherans.[59]

CONTOURS

Vermigli lectured on Romans in Strasbourg in the school year 1545–46, but those lectures have not survived; there is no way to determine how he understood predestination in those lectures. Vermigli did, however, address the subject the previous academic year (1543–44), when he devoted an entire locus to predestination in his Genesis lectures.[60] This is the earliest substantial extant expression of his teaching on predestination. Although it is brief in comparison to the later

---

[54]Bullinger's diary specifies the date that Vermigli began lecturing on 1 Samuel as 24 August 1556. Emil Egli, ed., *Heinrich Bullingers Diarium (Annales vita) der Jahre 1504–1574* (Basel, 1904), 48, cited in PMRE, 380. On 1 July 1557, Vermigli wrote to Calvin: "I have read your book (the two works against Castellio) with the greatest delight; God redounded your defense unto honor and to the defense of the orthodox faith—so I hold for my own part, I concur with you in all points. I have begun to treat of predestination, and shall continue with it the whole week. Not only does the inducement of the passage move me to declare it, but also because my college, as you know, is widely separate from me in regard to this, and has spoken against the doctrine in lectures this past week." Johann H. Hottinger, *Historiae Ecclesiasticae Novi Testamenti* (Zurich, 1667), 8:829. The English translation is found in Joseph C. McLelland, "The Reformed Doctrine of Predestination according to Peter Martyr," *Scottish Journal of Theology* 8 (1955): 266. From Vermigli's letter, one can conclude that Bibliander's attacks began no later than June 1557.

[55]Joachim Staedtke, "Der Züricher Prädestinationsstreit von 1560," in *Zwingliana* 9 (1953): 536–46.

[56]J. Wayne Baker, *Heinrich Bullinger and the Covenant: The Other Reformed Tradition* (Athens: Ohio State University Press, 1980), 42.

[57]Schmidt, *Leben*, 277, writes: "Er schrieb sofort an den Scholarchen Peter Sturm, hat ihn Zanchi in Schutz zu nehmen und versicherte, dieser lehre nichts als was Augustin, Luther, und Butzer auch gelehrt hätten."

[58] Schmidt, *Leben*, 277–78.

[59]On the controversy in Strasbourg see James M. Kittelson, "Marbach vs. Zanchi: The Resolution of Controversy in Late Reformation Strasbourg," *Sixteenth Century Journal* 8 (1977): 31–44. Cf. Jürgen Moltmann, *Prädestination und Perseveranz: Geschichte und Bedeutung der reformierten Lehre "de perseverantia sanctorum"* (Neukirchen: Neukirchener Verlag, 1961), 72–109.

[60]Vermigli, *In Primum Librum Mosis, qui vulgo Genesis dicitur Commentarii doctissimi …* (Zurich: C. Froschauer, 1569), fols. 99v–101r. For an explanation of the dates, see PPRED, 49.

locus on predestination in his Romans commentary, one finds there a coherent understanding of the doctrine that differs little from the more substantial locus in the Romans commentary. The earlier treatment arose in connection with the Old Testament text of Genesis 25 and was narrowly concerned with a single question, that is, to explain the different destinies of Jacob and Esau. But in the Romans locus, Vermigli aims to provide a full exposition of the doctrine of predestination.[61] It is significant that he places his locus *De praedestinatione* immediately after his exegesis of Romans 9.[62] This is Vermigli's way of suggesting, not so subtly, that St. Paul himself was an advocate of this doctrine. The commentary on Romans was not published until 1558, but the lectures on which it is based were delivered in Oxford between 1550 and 1552.[63] One would be remiss not to presume that these Oxford lectures bear some relationship to previous lectures on Romans in Lucca and Strasbourg.[64]

Like most Protestant theologians in the turbulent sixteenth century, Vermigli unfolds his doctrine of predestination against a Catholic opponent; in this case, the object of his theological antipathy is the Dutch theologian Albert Pighius.[65]

---

[61]The preeminence of the Jacob and Esau story in the Romans locus is identical to that in the earlier Genesis locus.

[62]The treatments in Genesis and Romans are the only two formal loci on predestination. In the index to Vermigli's commentary on Samuel, derived from his lectures in Zurich (1556–62), the impression is conveyed that it contains a formal locus on *De praedestinatione;* however, there is no formal locus devoted to predestination. The index refers to the passing comments on predestination clustered at various points. The same is true of Vermigli's commentary on 1 Corinthians. There he does make passing comments on predestination (1 Cor. 8:14), but does not devote a formal locus to the subject.

[63]CAS, 125, states: "It [locus on predestination] very likely dates from not later than 1552, perhaps from 1551"; PMRE, 333, concurs. There is no doubt that what Vermigli published in 1558 reflects earlier lectures.

[64]Vermigli devoted special attention to Paul's epistle to the Romans in three significant venues: Lucca, Strasbourg, and Oxford. Even before these terminus points, he may have lectured on this epistle as early as 1537 in Naples. PMI, 152–53, entertains the possibility that Vermigli gave lectures as the abbot of S. Pietro ad Aram. There is no question that he lectured on 1 Corinthians, apparently following the pattern of Valdés. What is not certain, however, is whether he followed in the footsteps of the Spaniard and also lectured on Romans. While the evidence is inconclusive, it may be noted that four Neapolitan historians describe Vermigli as having lectured on more than one of Paul's epistles; see Nicolao Balbani, *Historia della vita di Galeazzo Caracciolo, chiamato il Signor Marcheze* (Geneva, 1587); Antonino Castaldo, *Dell'istoria di notar Antonino Castaldo libri quattro* (Naples, 1769); Scipione Miccio, "Vita di Don Pietro di Toledo," in *Archivio Storio Italiano* 9, ed. F. Palermo (Florence, 1846), 27–28; and Antonio Canacciolo, "Collectanea Historica" (unpublished paper, n.p., n.d.).

[65]For background on Pighius see, Hubert Jedin, *Studien über die Schriftstellertätigkeit Albert Pigges*, Reformationsgeschichtliche Studien und Texte, vol. 55 (Münster: Aschendorffschen, 1931); Ludwig Pfeifer, *Ursprung der kathol. Kirche und Zugehörigkeit zur Kirche nach Albert Pigge* (Würzburg: Rita Verlag, 1938); Remigius Bäumer, "Albert Pigge (d. 1542)," in *Katholische Theologen der Reformationszeit* (Münster: Aschdorff, 1984), 98–106. In 1542, Pighius published *De libero hominis arbitrio et*

This was probably not Vermigli's first encounter with the Dutchman, for as McNair suggests, it is likely that the two men met in Bologna in 1533.[66] It is possible that Vermigli harbored some animus against Pighius because of his strong opposition to Calvin on free will and predestination.[67] Pighius seems to have been selected as a foil in the Romans locus because Vermigli saw him as the champion of contemporary Pelagians.[68] Vermigli's tone throughout the locus suggests that he is engaged in the ongoing historical battle with Pelagianism, of which Pighius was only the latest and one of the best representatives. Vermigli did not see himself as a theological innovator,[69] but as belonging to a theological tradition that was inspired by Augustine, which approached Paul and Scripture in much the same way.[70] As one who belonged to the Augustinian tradition, Vermigli was dutybound to defend the bishop's doctrine of predestination against Pelagianism.

As an heir to Augustine's soteriological legacy, Vermigli embraced and defended a thoroughgoing doctrine of *gemina praedestinatio* (double predestination).[71] It is "double" in that both election and reprobation issue from the one will of God. Vermigli does not hesitate to interpret the story of Jacob and Esau in Romans 9 as a manifestation of Jacob's election and Esau's reprobation according the sovereign free will of the Deity. It is viewed as a twofold preordination arising

---

divina gratia (Cologne: M. Movesianus, 1542). It is clear from Vermigli's citations of Pighius that this is the primary work with which Vermigli is contending. PMRE, 270, offers the suggestion that Vermigli may also have been contending against Richard Smith's use of Pighius in his 1550 *Diatriba de hominis iustificatione ... adversus Petrum Martyrem Vermelinum ...* (Louvain, 1550). PMI, 126, contemplates the possibility that Pighius and Vermigli may have met in Bologna in early 1533.

[66]PMI, 126.

[67]PMRE, 270, offers the suggestion that Vermigli may have been stimulated to attack Pighius because of his 1542 attack on Calvin. In any event, Calvin too judged Pighius to be a worthy Catholic opponent writing two books against him: John Calvin, *Defensio sanae et orthodoxae doctrinae de servitute et liberatione humani arbitrii adversus calumnias Alberti Pighii Campensis* (Geneva: Jean Crispin, 1543), and *De aeterna Dei praedestinatione, qua in salutem alios ex hominibus elegit, alios suo exitio reliquit; item de providentia qua res humanas gubernat, Consensus pastorum Genevensis ecclesiae, a Io. Calvino expositus.* (Geneva: Jean Crispin, 1552).

[68]Vermigli concentrates on Pighius's views at two points in his extended treatment: ROM, 407–9 and 421–26. Vermigli also dubs Pighius the "Achilles of the Papists" (Achilles Papistarum), ROM, 539.

[69]Sturm, *Die Theologie Peter Martyr*, 56: "Seine Theologie ist eine absichtlich unoriginelle Durchschnittstheologie...."

[70]PMRE, 273–75: "Martyr's commentary of 1558 stands in a Catholic genre of the sixteenth century ... and rests on a catholic exegetical tradition." Anderson adds: "Martyr did not abandon orthodoxy when he fled persecution; he joined Bucer in Strasbourg, Cranmer in England, and Bullinger in Zurich to defend the Gospel."

[71]There is a general consensus among Vermigli scholars that his doctrine of predestination should be designated as double, there is at least one dissenting judgment; see McLelland, "Reformed Doctrine of Predestination according to Peter Martyr," 259.

out of the one *propositum Dei,* which inevitably results in eternal salvation and eternal damnation.

Vermigli develops the doctrine within a causal construct. That is to say, on the matter of election (which he identifies with predestination), God's will in eternity is seen to be the exclusive cause. The effect of this election assumes Augustine's anthropology by viewing all humanity as a *massa perditionis,* doomed to eternal condemnation unless God intercedes. Divine election is portrayed positively as the rescue of the doomed sinner, who can do nothing to secure his own deliverance. After being elected from the mass of fallen sinners in eternity past, prompted by the Holy Spirit, and granted the gift of faith, the elect embrace Christ in time and thus inherit eternal life. In sum, Vermigli taught what was subsequently termed unconditional election.

Like his Geneva colleague, Vermigli did not shy away from the thorny matter of reprobation. Two important features disclose his view of reprobation. First, he sees reprobation as a passive expression of the sovereign will of God. By passive willing, Vermigli intends readers to understand something more than mere divine permission, but less than an active willing. For him, God is not to be pictured as sitting back and simply permitting humans to reap what they sow. Rather, God orchestrates events, yet without compulsion, to produce his predetermined salvific result. "To reprobate," is characteristically described as "not to have mercy" or "to pass over." Throughout his discussion, Vermigli is careful to avoid any suggestion of a detached Deity capriciously heaving helpless victims into a lake of hellfire. His view of reprobation is much more nuanced: it portrays God as actively rescuing some sinners, but deliberately and mysteriously bypassing others, knowing full well the inevitable consequence.

Another major feature of Vermigli's view of reprobation is the distinction between reprobation and condemnation. Reprobation refers to the decision not to have mercy in eternity past, and its cause lies in the inscrutable sovereign will of God. Condemnation, on the other hand, has a temporal referent, where causality lies within the matrix of original and actual sins. For Vermigli, "sins are the cause of damnation but not the cause of reprobation."[72] God's role in condemnation centers on the intention and execution of the general principle that sins must be punished. Condemnation, however, is the expression of divine justice. So then, the true cause of condemnation is found in sinful individuals, but the true cause of reprobation lies in the unfathomable purpose of God (*propositum Dei*).

Vermigli's doctrine is an unequivocal double predestination, but he differs from other Reformers, such as Ulrich Zwingli.[73] The latter advocates a strict sym-

---

[72]ROM, 414.
[73]PPRED, 191–222.

metrical double predestination, but Vermigli constructs an asymmetrical version of this doctrine. According to Vermigli, God does not deal with the elect in precisely the same way he deals with the nonelect. For the elect, God is not only the ultimate eternal cause for the attainment of eternal life, but by granting the gift of faith through the Holy Spirit, he is also the temporal cause of the reward of eternal life. Vermigli, however, does not maintain that parallel with regard to reprobation and condemnation. Although the ultimate eternal cause of election and rejection is precisely the same (the inscrutable will of God), the cause for condemnation does not correspond to the cause for eternal blessing. Those who finally are condemned have only themselves to blame.

Scholars have been divided as to the proper categorization of Vermigli's doctrine of predestination. Reinhold Seeberg describes it as "extreme supralapsarian."[74] More recently, Richard Muller has challenged this characterization of Vermigli's doctrine of predestination. While acknowledging the absolute sovereignty of the *propositum Dei*, Muller insists that Vermigli exhibits an "essentially infralapsarian definition of predestination."[75] It is, however, difficult to deny that Vermigli does at times seem to reflect a supralapsarian view, while at other points he seems to be an infralapsarian. The ambiguity can be resolved by recognizing the medieval distinction between *sub specie aeternitatis* (from the perspective of eternity) and *sub specie temporis* (from the perspective of time).[76] When addressing the ultimate cause of predestination or reprobation, Vermigli tends to express himself from the vantage point of eternity (*propositum Dei aeternum*). From the perspective of *sub specie aeternitatis,* the divine will acts prior to anything temporal, including the fall and its consequences, thus implying a supralapsarian orientation. However, the eternal divine will (*propositum Dei aeternum*) is manifested in history, and this is the principal sphere in which Vermigli articulates his doctrine of double predestination. Therefore, when addressing the question of predestination and reprobation *sub specie temporis,* the fall of Adam is the fundamental presupposition of all soteriological activity. In this sense, which is most often the case in the locus, there is a distinctly infralapsarian cast to Vermigli's thought.

---

[74]Reinhold Seeberg, *The History of Doctrines,* trans. Charles E. Hay (Grand Rapids: Baker, 1977), 2:421. Donnelly concurs in this assessment; see CAS, 137.

[75]Richard A. Muller, *Christ and the Decree: Christology and Predestination in Reformed Theology from Calvin to Perkins* (Grand Rapids: Baker, 1988), 65.

[76]See Frank A. James III, "A Late Medieval Parallel in Reformation Thought: *Gemina Praedestinatio* in Gregory of Rimini and Peter Martyr Vermigli," *Via Augustini: Augustine in the Later Middle Ages, Renaissance and Reformation,* ed. Heiko A. Oberman and Frank A. James III (Leiden: Brill, 1991), 183–84.

ORIGINS

Scholars generally assume that Vermigli's doctrine of predestination derives principally from interaction with Protestant theologians, among whom Bucer is acknowledged as probably the most influential.[77] There is a cogency to this line of thinking, especially in view of the close personal relationship between the two in Strasbourg (1542–47) and then again in England (1549–51). It is surmised that Vermigli, a Protestant neophyte, would have fallen under the sway of Bucer, whose predestinarian views were well known.[78] Vermigli was indebted in many ways to Bucer, but there is such divergence in their respective conceptions of predestination that it is unlikely he exercised decisive influence on Vermigli's predestinarianism.[79] Further, it is impossible that Vermigli had come under the spell of Calvin, whose full articulation of double predestination would not take place until nearly a decade later. Neither is Luther a likely source of Vermigli's doctrine; Luther seems never to have held much appeal for the Italian.[80]

While it is true that the Spanish Reformer Juan de Valdés was espousing a full-fledged doctrine of *gemina praedestinatio* to his followers in Naples in early 1538, he was probably not a key influence on Vermigli. In all likelihood Vermigli was the teacher and Valdés the student when it came to the matter of predestination.[81] If neither Vermigli's encounter with northern Reformers nor the influence of Valdés can adequately explain the intellectual origins of Vermigli's doctrine of double predestination, then two medieval options remain: the views of Thomas Aquinas or Gregory of Rimini. Aquinas was a more rigorous predestinarian than many admit, but the differences between his predestinarian vision and that of Vermigli suggest that Aquinas, although an intellectual contributor, is unlikely to have been a primary source. Gregory of Rimini, however, drew out the full implications of Augustine's doctrine of predestination and concluded with the most rigorous doctrine of double predestination in the later Middle Ages. Josiah Simler informs us that the young Vermigli read and approved of the writings of Gregory while a student at the University of Padua in the early 1520s.[82] A comparison of Vermigli's doctrine and that of Gregory reveals an extraordinary degree of

---

[77]CAS, 129. See also Schmidt, *Leben*, 62–63.

[78]For Bucer's strongest predestinarian statements, see his *Metaphrasis et Enarratio in Epistolam D. Pauli Apostoli ad Romanos* (Basel, 1536), 409–13. The fact that Calvin's doctrine of predestination is often traced to the influence of Bucer has contributed to the view that Bucer was the key influence on Vermigli's doctrine.

[79]PPRED, 223–44.

[80]CAS 39, 126–27; see appendix 1.

[81]See Frank A. James III, "Juan de Valdés before and after Peter Martyr Vermigli: The Reception of *Gemina Praedestinatio* in Valdés' Later Thought," *Archiv für Reformationsgeschichte* 83 (1992): 180–208.

[82]Simler, *Oratio*, 4.

compatibility. Linguistic and conceptual parallels abound. Time and again, the same issues are isolated and resolved with the same theological conclusions, often employing the same terms, and always based on the twin sources of Scripture and Augustine. Despite differences in historical circumstances and in degree of treatment, there is extraordinary continuity between the two Italian Augustinians. When all the evidence is taken into account, it becomes almost certain that Vermigli was an heir to Gregory's late medieval intensification of Augustine's doctrine of predestination.[83]

SIGNIFICANCE

Vermigli's adoption of the distinctive doctrine of *gemina praedestinatio* illustrates that soteriological continuity between late medieval and Reformation thought could obtain. The intellectual origins of Vermigli's thought suggest that his predestinarianism was derived in significant measure from his encounter with the academic Augustinianism of Gregory of Rimini. Thus, with regard to *gemina praedestinatio,* Peter Martyr Vermigli, one of the codifiers of Reformed theology, appears to have been a kind of intellectual offspring of late medieval Augustinianism. This is not to suggest that this doctrine underwent no development at the hands of Vermigli or in the intellectual exchanges between Vermigli and his Protestant conferees after his apostasy from Catholicism. It does suggest, however, that Vermigli's predestinarianism, inspired by Gregory, was one of the intellectual tributaries that flowed into the broader current of Reformed theology. It was the absorption of this intensified Augustinian theology of Gregory of Rimini that perhaps explains the speed with which Vermigli was received into the upper ranks of Reformed Protestantism. It would seem that the Reformers at Strasbourg in 1542 recognized in Vermigli a kindred spirit and a ready-made Protestant.[84]

JUSTIFICATION

CONTEXT

The "Italian Stranger," as John Strype christened Vermigli, first set foot on British soil in late 1547.[85] Vermigli was not invited to Oxford merely for his academic reputation and achievements, but rather because he was needed to

---

[83]PPRED, 245–50.

[84]PMI, xiii.

[85]Strype, *Ecclesiastical Memorials*, 2:336. Cf. R. W. Dixon, *History of the Church of England from the Abolition of the Roman Jurisdiction* (London, 1881), 2:521, wrote: "But even from the beginning of Edward's reign, the prospect of England had drawn an invasion of learned strangers." Bodleian Library, Oxford MSS, Ashmole 826, "Expenses of the Journey of Peter Martyr and Bernardinus Ochino to England in 1547," records a detailed account of expenses incurred by John Abell.

promote Protestantism in England.[86] As Simler surmised, Vermigli was "the one person most suited for this task [of reformation] because of his singular learning and incredible skill at many things."[87] To fortify Vermigli for the mission ahead, the honor of doctor of divinity was bestowed in February and he was formally appointed regius professor of divinity in March of 1548.[88] Greenslade concludes that of the early holders of the regius chair in theology, "Peter Martyr was unquestionably the most learned."[89]

A crucial Protestant doctrine to be disseminated to the English church was justification.[90] The Italian stranger wasted little time in pressing the matter with his students. Soon after beginning his lectures on Paul's first epistle to the Corinthians, he devoted a locus to justification at the end of the first chapter. This locus is thoughtfully crafted and one of the clearest and most concise articulations of an early Reformed doctrine of justification.[91] Vermigli had already proffered a brief introductory exposition in his Genesis lectures, which is his earliest extant treatment of the doctrine.[92] As with the doctrine of predestination, it was not until the Romans commentary that Vermigli took the opportunity to present his definitive articulation of the doctrine of justification.

It may well have been that Vermigli was prompted to return to this doctrine yet a third time in his Protestant career, when he got wind of a quarrel in Cambridge concerning Bucer's teaching on the same subject. The difficulty arose in June 1550 when Dr. John Young, fellow at Trinity College Cambridge, challenged Bucer to a public disputation.[93] There were three theses to be disputed, the last of which dealt with justification: "We are so justified freely by God, that, before justification, whatsoever good works we seem to do, it is sin, and provokes God's wrath against us. But being justified, we necessarily do good works."[94] After the public disputation, Young continued to attack Bucer's view of justification, saying

---

[86]Strype, *Ecclesiastical Memorials*, 2:197, wrote: "It was especially thought necessary, that the corrupt opinions about the Eucharist should be rectified in the Universities as well as elsewhere, and both these foreigners [Vermigli and Bucer] thought aught [worthily] in this great point, though differing in their judgements in the expression to be used about them." Cited in VWG, 16.

[87]LLS, 33.

[88]Philip McNair, "Biographical Introduction," EW, 9.

[89]Greenslade, "Faculty of Theology," 315.

[90]Dickens, *English Reformation*, 82–85.

[91]See "Justification and Faith" (from Vermigli's 1579 commentary on 1 Cor.), in PMR, 121–36.

[92]Sturm, *Die Theologie Peter Martyr Vermiglis*, 58–70, examines the locus on justification from Vermigli's Genesis commentary.

[93]Gorham, *Gleanings*, 163.

[94]Gorham, *Gleanings*, 163. The other two theses were: "1. The canonical books of Holy Scripture alone abundantly teach the regenerated all things belonging to salvation," and "2. There is no Church on earth which errs not, in manners as well as in faith."

that he was in "serious error."[95] Bucer responded to Young in his own public lectures and in the university pulpit, defending "this chief article of religion."[96] This controversy was short-lived, largely because Bucer succumbed to the winter chill and died. The Cambridge debate was a sober reminder to Vermigli that doctrinal reform was still an urgent necessity in England.

Having decided to address the topic again, Vermigli went all out. His most extensive treatment of justification occurs in his Romans locus following his exegesis in the first eleven chapters of his commentary on Romans.[97] By this placement, he means to suggest to the reader that Paul is the primary source for this doctrine; it is, according to Vermigli, "the scope and aim of all that Paul has said so far."[98] Further confirmation that his doctrine is Pauline is his repeated reliance upon the first eleven chapters of Romans throughout his exposition.[99]

The polemical tone in the Romans locus should be seen against the larger backdrop of the Council of Trent. This locus affords him the opportunity to engage in his first extensive interaction with the council.[100] Five years had passed since the Council formally addressed the doctrine of justification, and Vermigli had time to reflect upon its canons and decrees and upon their theological implications. This locus is, in many respects, his response to that important council.

Throughout his Romans locus, two other antagonists were in view. Although he makes fewer direct references, Vermigli's sharpest jibes are reserved for Richard Smith, the only adversary who actually wrote a book against Vermigli, contesting his doctrine of justification.[101] Smith's *Diatriba de hominis iustificatione ... adversus P. M. Vermelinum* clearly targets Vermigli in the title, but in the book itself, Smith is primarily concerned to attack Luther and Melanchthon.[102] Because he had been ousted from his regius professorship at Oxford in order to make room for the Italian Protestant, Smith had reason to be upset with Vermigli.[103] As for

---

[95]This is clear from Vermigli's letter to Bucer on 31 August 1550, cited in Gorham, *Gleanings,* 168. Cf. letter from Bucer to Grindall on the same day, ibid., 165.

[96]Gorham, *Gleanings,* 166.

[97]ROM, 517–75.

[98]ROM, 517: "(de iustificatione) quae scopus est et finis omnium quae attulit Paulus tractare."

[99]CAS, 125, indicates that the Romans lectures "very likely" date from "not later than 1552, perhaps from 1551"; PMRE, 333, concurs. There is no doubt that what Vermigli published in 1558 reflects earlier lectures. This locus was probably given in an early form in Oxford, but certainly it reflects the Zurich years as well, for it was in Zurich that he made final corrections, finished editing the commentary, and made final revision of the locus.

[100]ROM, 546–48.

[101]Andreas Löwe, "Peter Martyr Vermigli and Richard Smith's *De votis monasticis,*" HRR, 143–72.

[102]CAS, 150.

[103]Shortly after Smith's sudden departure from Oxford in 1549, his bitterness at being demoted prompted him to pen two treatises against Vermigli. Both works by Smith were published together as *De Coelibatu sacerdotium Liber unus. Eiusdem de votis Monasticis liber alter, nunc primum typis excusi*

Vermigli, he felt the sting of Smith's personal attacks for he wrote to Bucer that Smith's book was "stuffed so full with maledictions, accusations, and the bitterest contempt, that I think I never have heard before of any tongue so unbridled in abuse."[104] For his part, Vermigli is quite dismissive of Smith, whom he charges with plagiarizing from Johannes Eck and Pighius.[105]

The Dutchman Albert Pighius resurfaces in the locus on justification. For Vermigli, the Dutchman was a much more formidable opponent than Smith, because more than other Catholic theologians Pighius offered a substantive biblical defense of the Catholic position.[106] Vermigli gives primary attention to Pighius's *Controuersiaru[m] praecipuarum in Comitiis Ratisponensis tractatarum.*[107] Vermigli may have selected Pighius because of his notable reputation as a defender of papal authority.[108] Indeed, Pighius was cited as a theological authority by Cardinal Seripando during the intensive debates on justification at the Council of Trent.[109] What makes Pighius particularly interesting, however, is that he is a moderate Catholic who was a noted advocate of the doctrine of double justification, explicitly rejected at Trent.[110]

(Louvain: Ioannem Waen, 1550). The title page of the second treatise adds a specific reference to Vermigli: *Eiusdem D. Richardi Smythei confutation quorundam articulorum de votis monasticis Petri Martyris, Itali, Oxoniae in anglia theologiam profitentis.* A second edition was published the same year in Paris, which also makes specific reference to Vermigli: *Defensio sacri Episcoporum et sacerdotum Coelibatus, contra impies et indoctas Petri Martyris Vermelii nugas, et calumnias, quas ille Oxoniae in Anglia, duobus retro annis in sacerdotalium nuptiarum assertionem tenere effutiuit* (Paris: Reginaldi Calderii, 1550). Vermigli makes a brief reference only to *De votis Monasticis*, in ROM, 576.

[104]Gorham, *Gleanings*, 153–54. The letter is dated 10 June 1550. The animosity was exacerbated by the fact that Smith described Vermigli's wife as a "dirty whore." See Löwe, "Vermigli and Smith's *De votis monasticis*," 4.

[105]ROM, 520. See also 557, 568, 574–75; Donnelly, *Calvinism and Scholasticism*, 150.

[106]Vermigli concentrates on Pighius's views at two main points in his extended treatment, ROM, 407–9 and 421–26.

[107]Albert Pighius, *Controversiaru[m] praecipuarum in comitiis Ratisponensis tractatarum, & quibus nunc potissimum exagitatur Christi fides & religio, diligens, & luculenta explicatio,* 3 vols. (Paris 1542).

[108]Remigius Bäumer, "Das Kirchenverständnis Albert Pigges ein Beitrag zur Ekklesiologie der Vortridentinischen Kontroverstheologie," in *Volkes Gottes: Zum Kirchenverständnis der Katholischen, Evangelischen und Anglikanischen Theologie,* ed. Remigius Bäumer and Heimo Dolch (Freiburg: Herder, 1967), 306–22. Cf. Remigius Bäumer, "Albert Pighius," in *Oxford Encyclopedia of the Reformation* (1996), 3:271.

[109]Hubert Jedin, *A History of the Council of Trent* (Frieburg: Herder, 1961), 2:247. Cf. Edward Yarnold, "*Duplex Iustitia*: The Sixteenth Century and the Twentieth," in *Christian Authority: Essays in Honour of Henry Chadwick,* ed. G. R. Evans (Oxford: Clarendon, 1988), 216.

[110]See Alister E. McGrath, *Iustitia Dei: A History of the Christian Doctrine of Justification,* 2d ed. (Cambridge: Cambridge University Press, 1998), 245; Frank A. James III, "The Complex of Justification: Vermigli versus Pighius," HRR, 45–58; and Bäumer, "Albert Pigge," 102–3.

CONTOURS

It is evident that Vermigli continued to think carefully about the doctrine of justification after his earlier lectures on the subject in Oxford. One of the notable features to emerge in his outlook was the ethical orientation of the doctrine of justification. For him, if justification was to be rightly understood it must be directly related to godliness.[111] In this regard, Vermigli was in lockstep with the Swiss Protestants, who tended to stress the positive relationship between justification and piety (or sanctification), although they were careful not to fuse the two doctrines. This pastoral insight is reflected clearly in the Romans locus, for Vermigli wastes no time in declaring that justification "is the head, fountain and summit of all piety"; therefore, "one ought to be certain of it above all things."[112]

Vermigli develops his doctrine of justification under three propositions: that good works do not justify, that faith justifies, and that faith alone justifies.[113] From the start, Vermigli sets his jaw against the perceived Pelagianism of the Catholic church.[114] For an Augustinian like Vermigli, whose most basic theological presupposition was that all humanity after Adam's fall is *massa perditionis* (a mass of perdition), Pelagianism was intolerable.[115] Crucial for understanding Vermigli is the fact that the whole edifice of his doctrine of justification is built upon the foundation of an intensive Augustinian anthropology.[116] For him, this was not simply a clash between individual theologians, but of theological systems.

In many respects, Vermigli provides a conventional Protestant understanding of justification. It is obvious from the opening section of his locus that justification in the strict sense is a legal pronouncement of God. Vermigli specifically employs the legal term "forensic" (*forense*) to describe this judicial proceeding.[117] Justification, then, as he makes clear, belongs to the legal domain and, as such, addresses the theological problem of the legal guilt inherited by all of Adam's progeny and how it is that a righteous divine judge reaches a verdict of "not guilty."

If justification is fundamentally a legal or forensic matter for Vermigli, then the question of how the guilty sinner is legally absolved of the deserved punishment comes to the fore. To describe this divine judicial proceeding, he employs the

---

[111]ROM, 521. Calvin refers to justification as the "sum of all piety." See McGrath, *Iustitia Dei*, 2:36.

[112]ROM, 521: "Cum hoc dogma caput sit, fons et columen totius pietatis, et propterea oporteret de illo omnium maxime constare."

[113]ROM, 520.

[114] James, "Complex of Justification," 55–56.

[115]ROM, 523.

[116]One finds the same intense Augustinianism in his doctrine of predestination; see PPRED, 245ff.

[117]ROM, 517.

concept of imputation (*imputatio*).[118] In general, he sees two movements of imputation. First is the imputation of Christ's righteousness to the elect sinner. When the divine verdict is rendered, it will not be on the basis of the sinner, but on the basis of the imputed righteousness of Christ that the sinner is judged.[119] Second, Vermigli speaks of the nonimputation of sins, by which he means that sins are not counted against the sinner because they have been imputed or transferred to Christ. Thus he states: "He [Christ] justifies those whom he takes to himself, and bears their iniquities."[120]

This double imputation brings a dual legal benefit—acquittal and the right to eternal life.[121] Because Christ has taken their sins and transferred his righteousness to them, sinners are thereby pronounced forgiven, hence justified. The second benefit is entrance into a new relationship with the divine judge.[122] Vermigli remarks that the "chief and principal part" of forgiveness of our sins is "that we are received into the favor of God."[123] For him, this acceptance into the favor of God is particularly identified with adoption, which also has a legal connotation.[124] With the idea of adoption, Vermigli's understanding of justification is not merely forensic, but also entails a relational component.

It is significant that Vermigli's forensic understanding of imputation necessarily requires an extrinsic view of justification, which is to say, the act in which Christ's righteousness is imputed to an elect sinner only has reference to the sinner's legal status. Such an act is external to the sinner and does not itself bring inner renewal. The imputed righteousness of Christ, technically speaking, does not penetrate and transform the soul of the sinner as is required in the Catholic notion of *gratia inhaerens*, but remains external to the sinner. Justification, then, in the forensic sense, is not *iustitia in nobis* but *iustitia extra nos*.

It has been noted that Vermigli never actually employs the distinctively Protestant phrase *simul iustus et peccator* (simultaneously righteous and sinful).[125] However, close examination reveals that the idea (if not the terminology)

---

[118]ROM, 517. Alister McGrath has argued that this legal term "imputation" has its origins in Erasmus's *Novum instrumentum omne* of 1516 where he replaced the term "*reputatum*" of the Vulgate translation of Rom. 4:5 with "*imputatum*." Cf. McGrath, *Iustitia Dei*, 218.

[119]ROM, 565.

[120]ROM, 553.

[121]ROM, 558.

[122]COR, fols. 16r, 18v.

[123]ROM, 558.

[124]ROM, 525. He writes: "there is no doubt that justification [brings] … the favor of God by which men are received into grace, adopted as his children and made heirs of eternal life."

[125]CAS, 154: "Martyr never uses Luther's phrase *simul iustus et peccator*, not only because this paradoxical expression is foreign to his mentality, but also because it does not square with his understanding of justification by faith alone."

is clearly present in the locus. This is not necessarily significant, in view of the fact that Calvin fails to employ the phrase in the definitive 1559 edition of the *Institutes*, yet he unmistakably embraces the idea.[126] It is difficult to avoid the idea of *simul iustus et peccator* when Vermigli writes: "'to justify' means to ascribe righteousness to one by judgment or declaration [and] does not make him righteous in reality."[127] Vermigli's intensive Augustinian anthropology, with its stress on the radical impact of sin on all humanity (including infants)[128] presses him to conclude that even the Christian is both fully a sinner in himself and fully righteous in Christ. Augustinian anthropology again seems to determine Vermigli's stance on this question.

Vermigli's understanding of forensic justification is not particularly unusual. Indeed, it corresponds generally with the Reformed branch of Protestantism. What is unusual is the inclusion of regeneration and sanctification under the rubric of justification. Like his friend and mentor Bucer, Vermigli had long espoused a threefold justification, which includes three distinguishable but inseparable components: regeneration, justification, and sanctification. This threefold character of his doctrine of justification was explicit in his earliest treatment of this doctrine in his Strasbourg exposition of Genesis in 1543[129] and his 1548 lectures on 1 Corinthians in Oxford. Perhaps the most surprising feature of the Romans locus is that, unlike both previous loci on justification, he does not speak explicitly of a threefold righteousness. Apparently, Vermigli has continued to read and think on this subject and has concluded that there are better ways to say what he means. He has not substantially altered his view, but he has reconfigured somewhat the relation of justification to regeneration.[130] Vermigli had always held that regeneration and justification are distinct but not separate. In previous treatments, regeneration had been construed as a constitutive part of justification, but in the Romans locus it undergoes a change of status from a constitutive element to a necessary precursor. In the Genesis commentary, regeneration is explicitly identified as belonging to forensic justification.[131] In his commentary on 1 Corinthians, regeneration is still viewed as belonging to justification, but in

---

[126]John Calvin, *Institutes of the Christian Religion*, ed. John T. McNeill, trans. Ford Lewis Battles (Philadelphia: Westminster Press, 1960), 3.14.9 (1:776).

[127]ROM, 517: "ut iustificare est iudicio ac existimatione iustitiam alicui tribuere, non autem reipsa efficere ut sit iustus."

[128]ROM, 523. Vermigli follows Augustine by including infants under the Adamic fall.

[129]PPRED, 49.

[130]ROM, 79.

[131]Peter Martyr Vermigli, *In Primum Librum Mosis Qui Vulgo Genesis Dicitur Commentarii* (Zurich: C. Froschauer, 1569), fols. 59r–61v.

a different category.[132] In the Romans commentary, regeneration no longer comes under the aegis of justification. Now regeneration provides the context but is not the cause for justification. This progression in the relationship between regeneration and justification is a departure from Vermigli's early Augustinian training, but a movement toward a more self-consciously Protestant understanding of the relationship between regeneration and justification. This development reflects the trend in Protestantism to distinguish more sharply sanctification from justification.[133]

It would seem, then, that Vermigli embraces both a strict forensic understanding of justification and a broader moral understanding, which stresses the necessary relationship between forensic justification and its accompanying benefits of regeneration and sanctification. When speaking of justification in the strict or proper sense *(propria significatione)*, he has in view only the divine acquittal and its basis.[134] But when speaking more broadly of justification, he considers both the cause and the effect of the divine acquittal. Forensic justification, which is based on the imputed righteousness of Christ alone, is necessarily preceded by the regenerative work of the Holy Spirit, who then produces sanctification or moral transformation in the sinner. It is one of the hallmarks of his understanding that these three blessings may be distinguished, but never separated.

Vermigli still retains the crucial distinctives of a Protestant understanding of justification—original sin, a dynamic view of faith *(fides apprehensiva)*, forensic justification based exclusively on the imputed righteousness of Christ, and *simul iustus et peccator*. But his particular conception of justification includes both regeneration and sanctification under the general meaning of justification. While it is his clear conviction that justification, properly speaking, is forensic, he is not content to speak of forensic justification alone. In Vermigli's mind, one cannot properly deal with the immense problem of original sin by considering only the legal dimension; one must also deal with the moral implications. Adam's fall, according to Vermigli, brought legal guilt, spiritual death, and moral corruption. The redemptive work of Christ countered each of these three effects, bringing forensic justification, regeneration, and sanctification into close accord. Certainly he would argue that to break the law of God is not only a legal violation, but a

---

[132]COR, fol. 33v.

[133]Peter Toon, *Justification and Sanctification* (Westchester, Ill.: Crossway Books, 1983), 63, notes: "for Melanchthon (and the majority of orthodox Lutheran and Reformed Protestants after him) justification came to be seen as only the declaration by God that a sinner is reckoned righteous." Cf. McGrath, *Iustitia Dei*, 226ff.

[134]ROM, 548.

moral infraction as well. In essence, Vermigli invests justification with a comprehensiveness equal to the magnitude of original sin.

Vermigli certainly saw himself as a Protestant and as an opponent of Catholicism, as his rejection of the decrees of Trent suggests. He does indeed differ from Lutheranism by placing the principle of "distinct but not separate" at the forefront of his formulation rather than stressing the discontinuity of justification and sanctification.[135] While his formulation differs from the later Lutheranism, Vermigli is generally in accord with Protestant theologians of his day, such as Bucer, Oecolampadius, Zwingli, and later, Melanchthon.[136]

The evolution in Vermigli's thought issued from his continued study of the Scriptures, but cannot be separated from his deep involvement in the English Reformation. There was in Vermigli a Cranmer-inspired sense of responsibility to display, as much as possible, his doctrinal uniformity with continental Protestantism. Apparently there was a growing recognition that he belonged to a distinctive branch of Protestantism—the Reformed branch. With this recognition comes a sense of duty to present his teachings in such a way that the Reformed uniformity is evident. This is not to suggest that he simply imitated Reformed theologians, but that there is a basic theological commonality. Vermigli came to see himself as England's chief spokesman for continental Reformed theology, and Paul's epistle was the ideal vehicle to fulfill his responsibility.[137] One may conjecture that Vermigli's understanding of his role as a representative of the Reformed tradition may explain the polemical tone of the locus. A proper understanding of his Romans commentary, then, signifies Vermigli's emergence as a mainstream Reformed theologian.

Origins

The sixteenth-century Reformed theologian Josiah Simler informs us that sometime during Peter Martyr Vermigli's three years in Naples (1537–40) "the greater light of God's truth" dawned upon him.[138] This "greater light" was the

---

[135]Luther's dynamic understanding of justification undergoes a shift after 1535, when he is much more inclined to stress the difference between justification and sanctification. This shift is clearly manifested first in his commentary on Galatians (1535). There seems to be scholarly consensus that Philip Melanchthon was the main impetus behind the reorientation of the doctrine of justification toward a distinctively legal formulation.

[136]McGrath, *Iustitia Dei*, 207ff.

[137]In the preface to his commentary, Vermigli generally identifies his theological outlook with that of Bucer, Luther, Calvin, and Melanchthon, all of whose Romans commentaries he had consulted in preparation for his own commentary; see ROM, preface. While identifying himself with continental theologians, Vermigli also acknowledges that differences remain.

[138]Simler, *Oratio*, 9.

doctrine of justification by faith alone. In Naples, Vermigli found himself in the company of the Spanish Reformer Juan de Valdés, who had gathered around him a small flock of high-ranking Italian prelates, noblewomen, and literati. To these eager disciples, Valdés clandestinely taught a Protestant-inspired doctrine of justification by faith alone.[139] To the inner circle, Valdés gave books from the pens of Protestants; [140] to Vermigli, he gave books by Bucer and Zwingli, with the result that by the time Vermigli departed from Naples in the spring of 1540, he was, in the words of Philip McNair, "wholly justified by faith."[141]

After arriving in Zurich from Italy in 1542, Vermigli's understanding of the doctrine of justification underwent a maturation process.[142] To be sure, he had already embraced the distinctive elements of a Protestant view, but over the course of the next twenty years he refined and clarified his understanding of this important doctrine. Certainly his intensive Augustinian soteriology initially put him in good stead with other Protestants.[143] The Augustinian anthropology, which directly informed his view of justification, was compatible with the views of Protestant theologians, most of whom were deeply indebted to the same anti-Pelagian writings of the North African bishop. In a sense all the Protestant theologians stood on the shoulders of Augustine. Even while in Italy, having entered the clandestine world of Italian Evangelism and in a close association with Juan de Valdés, Vermigli had encountered and imbibed the teachings of the Protestants, including the doctrine of justification by faith alone. By the time he arrived in Zurich in 1542, he had already crossed the theological Rubicon.

If his Augustinian theological heritage accounts for Vermigli's early view of justification, how might one account for the distinctively Protestant conceptions also present? The answer lies principally with Bucer. Vermigli's early thought is virtually a replica of Bucer's.[144] Both share soteriological indebtedness to

---

[139]Carlos Gilly, "Juan de Valdés: Übersetzer und Bearbeiter von Luthers Schriften in seinem *Diálogo de Doctrina*," *Archiv für Reformationsgeschichte*, 74 (1983): 257–58. José Nieto, "The Changing Image of Valdés" in *Juan de Valdés: Two Catechisms*, trans. William B. and Carol D. Jones (Lawrence, Kan.: Coronado Press, 1993), 51–125.

[140]Schmidt, *Leben*, 28, argues that after his stay in Naples and while in Lucca, Vermigli read more of Bucer and expanded his Protestant reading to include Melanchthon, Calvin, and Bullinger.

[141]Simler, *Oratio*, 4. Schmidt, *Leben*, 20, presumes that it was Valdés who gave Vermigli the Protestant books. See also PMI, 179.

[142]François Wendel, *Calvin: The Origins and Development of His Religious Thought*, trans. Philip Mairet (New York: Collins, 1965), 257–58, seems to suggest that Calvin too undergoes a maturation process with regard to the doctrine of justification.

[143]Simler, *Oratio*, 5. For the English, see LLS, 27–31.

[144]On the matter of justification, Bucer, like Vermigli, has been judged to be beyond the pale of Protestantism. Eduard Ellwein, *Vom neuen Leben. De novitiate vitae* (Munich, 1932), 63–66, 109–17, 132–33, 166–68, concludes that Bucer was not really a Protestant. Walther Köhler, *Dogmengeschichte*

Augustine[145] and to the standard Protestant elements such as *sola fide, imputatio,* and the forensic character of justification. But there are also distinctive parallels: the most distinctive is their threefold conception of righteousness.[146] There is little doubt that those years with Bucer in Strasbourg (1542–47) go a long way to explain Vermigli's conception of justification.[147] Bucer and Augustine seem to share the honor of being the greatest theological influence on Vermigli in Strasbourg, but it seems that Bucer's influence grew significantly in the early years of Vermigli's Oxford sojourn. Of course, this is not to imply that Augustine's theological stature declined for Vermigli. Rather, it is to suggest something more subtle, namely, that Bucer's Protestant insights into this doctrine increasingly govern Vermigli's appropriation of the Augustinian soteriological perspective.

Significance

Vermigli's doctrinal development with regard to justification generally mirrors the evolution of the doctrine in Protestantism. One important historiographical insight garnered from Vermigli is the fact that the Protestant doctrine of justification was not static, but went through a process of theological amelioration. To be sure, Luther blazed a path that others would follow, but it must be recognized that Luther's initial insights provoked decades of Protestant refinement, both from Lutheran and Reformed theologians.[148] One of the more significant developments of the doctrine concerned the relationship between forensic justification, regeneration, and sanctification. Alister McGrath observes that there was a

---

als Geschichte des christlichen Selbstbewusstseins, vol. 2, *Das Zeitalter der Reformation* (Zurich: Max Niehans, 1951), 362–64, 418, reaches the opposite conclusion. See W. P. Stephens, *The Holy Spirit in the Theology of Martin Bucer* (Cambridge: Cambridge University Press, 1970), 48–49.

[145]Bucer, like Vermigli, affirms an Augustinian view of merit and rewards. See Bucer, *Metaphrasis et enarratio in epist. D. Pauli ad Romanos* (Basel, 1562), fol. 13. Bucer also shared with Vermigli and Augustine an intellectualist view of faith. See D. L. Wright, ed. and trans., *Common Places of Martin Bucer,* Courtenay Library of Reformation Classics, vol. 4 (Appleford, Abington: Sutton Courtenay Press, 1972), 171.

[146]Stephens, *Holy Spirit in the Theology of Martin Bucer,* 48–70. As far as can be determined, Vermigli and Bucer were the only two early Reformed theologians to develop this explicitly three-tiered understanding of justification.

[147]James, "Complex of Justification," HRR, 57–58.

[148]McGrath, *Iustitia Dei,* 197–207. According to Toon, *Justification,* 63, up to the 1530s Luther understood that "justification included regeneration and renewal." Bromiley, "The Doctrine of Justification in Luther," *Evangelical Quarterly* 24 (1952): 95–96, makes a similar judgment: "Luther makes no final distinction between justification and sanctification." Bromiley observes that the relationship between justification and sanctification was "so close" that "Luther does not scruple to use the one word justification to cover the process of sanctification as well as justification in the narrower and stricter sense."

definitive movement within early Protestantism, from a dynamic view of justification that stressed the unity (but not identification) of justification and sanctification to a more constrictive understanding that stressed the distinction between justification and sanctification.[149] This same general trend is evident in Vermigli's doctrine of justification.

Although the Reformed church did not give the same prominence to the doctrine as the Lutherans, the same general trajectory is evident in the Reformed branch.[150] The earliest Reformed conceptions of justification tended to place great emphasis on an ethical conception of justification, so that regeneration and sanctification are seen as constitutive elements of justification. Zwingli, Bucer, Bullinger, and Oecolampadius all envisaged a very close relationship between regeneration and justification, although their understanding was nuanced differently than Luther's. Calvin seems to have undergone some development on this matter early in his Protestant career, but by 1540 the main lines of his new configuration are in place.[151] Instead of giving priority to either regeneration or justification, Calvin turned his attention to their common source, the union with Christ *(insitio in Christum)*, which granted them equal standing, distinct, but not separate. This is precisely what Calvin maintains in the 1559 edition of the *Institutes*, namely, that "the grace of justification is not separated from regeneration although they are things distinct."[152]

A proper understanding of the Reformation doctrine of justification is impossible without the recognition that it articulated this view during a period of intensive theological transition. Vermigli, like other Protestant scholars, was a theological pioneer who was in the process of casting off his Catholic theological training and braving the new world of Protestant theological exegesis. In the midst of this intellectual transition period, there was theological diversity among Protestants with regard to the doctrine of justification, and particularly its relationship to regeneration and sanctification. Despite the diversity, there seems to have been an irreducible core of a genuine Protestant doctrine of justification,

---

[149]McGrath, *Iustitia Dei*, 219ff. Cf. Toon, *Justification*, 55–66, 75–88.

[150]McGrath, *Iustitia Dei*, 237–38.

[151]The 1536 edition of Calvin's *Institutes* says almost nothing about justification. However, in the *Genevan Confession* of 1536 (sec. 8), Calvin explicitly places justification before regeneration, and the same is true in the *Consensus Tigurinus* of 1549 (chap. 3). The *Genevan Confession* is found in Arthur Cochrane, ed., *Reformed Confessions of the Sixteenth Century* (Philadelphia: Westminster Press, 1966), and the *Consensus Tigurinus* in A. A. Hodge, *Outlines of Theology* (Grand Rapids: Zondervan, 1977), appendix. See also Wendel, *Calvin*, 257–58.

[152]Calvin, *Institutes*, 3.11.11. It has not escaped the notice of scholars that Calvin treats sanctification before justification in the 1559 edition. McGrath, *Iustitia Dei*, 219–26, argues that this chronology is not significant except to show that Calvin's real interest was the believer's union with Christ and that justification and sanctification are merely two consequences of that signal event.

which centered on the imputed righteousness of Christ for the forgiveness of sins. It is probably more historically accurate to speak of the perimeters of a Protestant doctrine of justification, and within those perimeters are considerable differences among early Protestant theologians. Muller, referring to the earliest period of Reformed theology, is correct when he characterizes this as "a period of great variety in theological formulation despite general doctrinal consensus."[153] The crucial distinction between Roman Catholics and Protestants was that the latter saw the grounds of justification to lie exclusively in the imputed righteousness of Christ. From Vermigli's perspective, the decrees of Trent could not make the same claim. When the war of words finally settled down, one fact remained: Vermigli's portrait in London is that of a Protestant.

TEXT AND TRANSLATION

In a sense these two loci on predestination and justification are taken out of their original context. Vermigli intended these two loci to be understood as having been generated directly from the theology of the Pauline letter to the Romans. However, these texts, which represent Vermigli's most mature and extensive understanding of these pivotal doctrines, warrant special treatment. They are full-fledged treatises and each stands on its own merit. One might also argue that the very enormity of each locus represents an interruption of Vermigli's exegesis and commentary. Admittedly, separating the loci from the biblical commentary was a difficult decision, but in the final analysis, judicious.

The base text for this translation is from the first edition of Vermigli's Romans commentary, *In Epistolam S. Pauli ad Romanos commentarii doctissimi…*, published in Basel by Peter Perna in 1558. The locus on predestination is located after Vermigli's exegesis of Romans 9, and the locus on justification is found after his exposition of Romans 11. The two loci are included in every subsequent edition of the Romans commentary: Zurich edition (1559); Basel editions (1560, 1568, and 1570), Heidelberg editions (1612, 1613); and the English edition, with the title *Most Learned and Fruitfull Commentaries upon the Epistle of S. Paul to the Romanes …* was translated by Sir Henry Billlingsley and published by John Daye in London (1568).[154]

The two loci also appear in every edition of *Loci Communes: Ex variis ipsius Aucthoris libris in unum volumen, collecti,& quatuor classes distributi*, edited by the

---

[153]Richard A. Muller, *Post-Reformation Reformed Dogmatics* (Grand Rapids: Baker, 1987), 1:28.

[154]*A Short Title Catalog of Books Printed in England, Scotland and Ireland, 1475–1640*, 2d ed., rev. and enlarged by W. A. Jackson and F. S. Ferguson, completed by Katherine F. Pantzer, 2 vols. (London: Bibliographic Society, 1976–86) (hereafter STC), 24672, II (sig. Q2), p. 422.

French pastor Robert Masson and published by John Kyngston in London (1576). Subsequent editions appeared as follows: Zurich (1580, 1587), Basel (1580, 1581, 1582), London (1583), Heidelberg (1603, 1613, 1622), Geneva (1623, 1624, 1626, 1627), and Amsterdam and Frankfurt (1656). There is also an English edition titled *The common places of ... Peter Martyr ... with a large addition of manie theologicall and necessarie discourses, some never extant before,* edited and translated by Anthony Marten and published by H. Denham and H. Middleton in London (1583).[155]

It is well known that Vermigli's Latin can be cumbersome and complex. Consequently, this translation subdivides his very long sentences into shorter ones, to enhance the readability of the text. His penchant for connectives and superlatives does not make for a smooth translation, and it seemed the better part of wisdom to scale down these infelicities while retaining the author's intent. In every sense, this has been a collaborative translation. Although I have carefully worked through the Latin text, I have benefited from and relied upon the superb sixteenth-century English translation of the loci from the Billingsley edition of the commentary. The translation was subjected to appraisal and correction not once, but twice, by each of my colleagues John Patrick Donnelly and Joseph C. McLelland, who invested enormous effort to ensure the accuracy and clarity of the translation. To facilitate reading and comprehension, I have inserted topical headings throughout both loci.

As a biblical commentator with a theological agenda, Vermigli cites a great many biblical texts, either directly or by allusion. In almost every case, the citation has been successfully identified and the citation included in a footnote. Vermigli typically employed the Latin Vulgate for his biblical references. Sometimes he cites from the Hebrew and often from memory. We have translated them with due regard for his own words. Where there is a significant difference from the Latin Vulgate, that is indicated in the footnote.

Writings of the church fathers play a significant role in both loci. Every effort has been made to identify all classical and patristic citations, but in some cases, no matter how heroic the effort, certain references or allusions remain unidentified. References to the church fathers are generally to the Migne editions of the *Patrologia Graeca* or the *Patrologia Latina.*

---

[155]STC, 24669.

PART ONE

Locus on Predestination

Predestination

1. *[404]* In case our reasoning should stray too far, which might easily happen in so large a field as God's predestination, a subject full of twists and turns, we intend to divide the subject into four principal parts.[1]

First, I will examine carefully the nature and definition of predestination. Second, I will ask what the cause of predestination is, since nothing can be known adequately unless its cause is known. Third, I will consider the effects that predestination brings forth in men; there are many things that are most plainly understood from their effects. Last, I will ask whether its power is such that it brings necessity to man, whether it takes away or hinders the freedom of the human will, and whether it can be changed. After each of these parts has been discussed, we will end this discourse.

Yet I will not promise to say all that can be said, for there are innumerable things that present themselves to those considering this matter. For the moment, I will touch only those things that seem most necessary and are most controversial. Since my treatment is so compact, it will not be hard for others to gather many things elsewhere.

Before we proceed to the definition of predestination, there are two things I must answer: first, whether it befits true Christian religion to dispute or to preach about predestination: if it is not lawful, we would seem to be acting wickedly by writing on the topic. Second, Logicians first pose the question of whether a thing *log.* exists naturally goes before the question of what it is. Lest we go against that *order* order, let us consider whether or not there is such a thing as predestination, so that afterward we may define it more certainly.

Should Predestination be Taught?

Touching the first question, it is to be understood that God makes various choices, for there are some that serve to perform specific duties, such as election

---

[1] The locus on predestination follows Martyr's commentary on Paul's letter to the Romans, chap. 9, *In Epistolam S. Pauli ad Romanos commentarii doctissimi...* (Basel: Peter Perna, 1558). It begins on p. 404; numerals in square brackets indicate page numbers in the 1558 Basel edition. Section divisions are from the *Loci Communes ... ex variis ipsius authoris scriptis, in unum librum collecti & in quatuor Classes distributi* (London: Thomas Vautrollerius, 1583), bk. 3, sec. 4, are included for convenience. Subject headings are given by this editor.

to the office of king or the office of apostle; there are other elections to eternal life. These are sometimes distinguished from one another, for it often happens that someone elected to a kingdom is not automatically elected to eternal life. This also happens regarding the office of an apostle, as in the case of Judas. Sometimes they are joined together, so that when it is spoken of temporal election, we may understand that the same applies to eternal election. Thus Paul says that he was "called to be an apostle and set apart from his mother's womb,"[2] that is, to be an apostle and to preach the gospel. Yet together with this, we may understand that he was predestined to eternal salvation. Christ also said: "You did not choose me, but I chose you and appointed you that you should go and bear fruit and that your fruit should remain."[3] Together with that, he commanded them to be of good comfort, for their names were written in heaven.[4] Therefore, between these elections there is a great difference and also a great connection, so that often the one is taken for the other. So by his wonderful wisdom Paul made spiritual those things foretold of Jacob and Esau in Genesis and Malachi that seemed to be temporal.[5]

2. As to this latter [eternal] election, I see that there have been many who judged that this question should not even be raised. Their reasons, which are given by Prosper and Hilary (bishop of Arles and sometime disciple of Augustine)[6] are stated in two letters prefixed to the book *The Predestination of the Saints.*[7] These letters were written for this reason, that when Augustine was writing against the Pelagians about the grace of Christ, he taught many things about predestination in this book. Many of the brethren in France, and not minor figures, were greatly troubled and offended with this doctrine. They claimed *[405]* that this doctrine takes away from the fallen the opportunity to rise up again; and for those who are standing firm, it encourages slothfulness. The opposing parties [in France] judged that diligence is in vain if God's predestination had already determined that the reprobate could not be restored and if there was no way the

---

[2]Gal. 1:15.
[3]John 15:16.
[4]Luke 10:20.
[5]Gen. 25:21; Mal. 1:2; Rom. 9:10.
[6]Prosper of Aquitaine (ca. 390–ca. 463) was a vigorous defender of Augustine's theology in southern Gaul. There was also an otherwise unidentified Augustinian advocate named Hilary, who may have been associated with Sicily. See Gerald Bonner, *St. Augustine of Hippo: Life and Controversies,* rev. ed. (Norwich: Canterbury Press, 1986), 324. Traditionally, this Hilary, to whom Augustine addressed one of his letters, was thought to have been the bishop of Arles, and Vermigli seems to have made the same assumption here. For more on this problem see Owen Chadwick, "Euladius of Arles," *Journal of Theological Studies* 44 (1945): 200–205.
[7]Augustine *Praed,* (PL 44.947ff.).

elect could fall away, even when they could not maintain a constant and firm course because they were uncertain of their predestination. Seeing then that this doctrine takes away industry and leaves only a kind of fatal necessity, it is much better that one should not speak of this matter.

They also add that it is superfluous to debate something that is beyond comprehension, for it is written "Who has known the mind of the Lord, or who has become his counselor?"[8] Therefore, they thought that we should teach that God in his goodness wishes all men to be saved, but since all men are not saved, it is because all men do not want to be saved. This, they say, is a safe doctrine. On the other side, the doctrine of predestination takes away all the power and usefulness of both preaching and admonitions as well as corrections, for if a certain number of the elect is appointed, which can neither be diminished nor increased, then preachers will labor in vain. If God's decision is immovable, there will be an impenetrable confusion between elect and reprobate, so that no one can go from this group to that, nor can any pass over from that group to this. Therefore, all effort of teachers is vain and useless.

This doctrine also seems new to them, for the early fathers wrote nothing or very little about this matter, or else handled it in another way. Up to Augustine's time the church defended the doctrines of the faith against heretics without this doctrine, and was content to be without it. They assert that those who teach it do nothing else than call men to uncertainty about God's will, which accomplishes nothing except to drive them to despair. All these things were raised as objections to Augustine. If they were true, then we are now proceeding rashly and imprudently to treat predestination.

The reasoning with which Augustine defended himself can also defend our undertaking. Therefore, those things of which we wish to speak we will gather from two books of his, *The Gift of Perseverance*, chapters 14, 15, and 20, where Augustine refutes those objections we mention, and *Rebuke and Grace*, chapters 14, 15, and 16, where he treats the same issues.[9]

3. First, it is a wonder that they should think that the doctrine of predestination would subvert the good effect of preaching, especially since Paul, teacher of the Gentiles and preacher to the whole world, inculcates this doctrine in his letters, often clearly and explicitly, for instance in his letters to the Romans, the Ephesians, and Timothy. Also, Luke in the book of Acts[10] and Christ himself in his sermons mention this doctrine. Christ says: "No one is able to snatch out of

[8]Rom. 11:34.
[9]Augustine *Persev.* 14, 15, 20 (PL 45.1013ff.); *Corrept.* 14–16 (PL 44.924ff.).
[10]Acts 2:23.

my hand those whom my Father gave me."[11] Christ also says, "For many are
called, but few are chosen." And in the last days he will answer the faithful: "Come
you blessed of my Father, inherit the kingdom prepared for you from the foundation of the world."[12] He gives thanks to the Father that he has hidden those things
from the wise and revealed them to children, "for it was well-pleasing in his sight."
In another place he said: "I know the ones I have chosen"; also "You did not
choose me, but I chose you."[13] If Christ and the apostles often spoke of predestination in their sermons, he is saying that no one should consider this doctrine of
ours to be opposed to good preaching.

Paul also affirms that it does not follow that if our will, salvation, and good
works depend on the will and decision of God, we should therefore cast away all
our diligence, effort, and care. When Paul said that God works all things together
in us both to will and to perform, he did not stop encouraging upright behavior.[14] And when he wrote to the Philippians that God, who had begun a good
work in them, would complete the work he had begun, so that they might be
blameless in the day of the Lord (words that he attributes to God both the beginning and success of good works), in the same letter he strongly exhorts them to
holiness.[15]

Christ also commanded his apostles to believe, but on the other hand, he said
"No one can come to me, unless the Father who sent me draws him."[16] Christ also
said, "He who has ears, let him hear." Yet God said in the Scriptures that he would
give them a heart from above to understand, eyes to see, and ears to hear.[17] These
things are not repugnant to one another, namely, that the appointment of good
works lies in God and that the gift of good works is to be hoped for only from
God's hands, and that we must also devote our zeal, care, and efforts to upright
and holy living. As was said, the Scriptures teach both.

Further, if we should deny predestination for this reason, then because God's
foreknowledge is similarly certain and cannot be deceived, shall we deny that God
foreknows all things? In his book *The Perseverance of the Saints*, chapter 15,
[Augustine] cites this example, which happened in his time. In the same monastery there was a certain man who was not upright in his life. When admonished,
he used to say, "I shall be as God has foreknown me to be." Augustine argued that

[11]John 10:29.
[12]Matt. 22:14; 25:34.
[13]Matt. 11:25–26; John 13:18; 15:16.
[14]Phil. 2:12–13.
[15]Phil. 1:6, 27ff.
[16]John 14:1; 6:44.
[17]Matt. 13:9; Deut. 6:6.

he spoke the truth indeed. Although his judgment was true, yet every day he became worse and worse, *[406]* and finally he returned to his own vomit.[18] What kind of man he will become, only God knows.[19] Though this man abused the truth, yet none of the faithful will deny that God foreknows all things.

Christ showed that this foreknowledge of God does not impede good works when he commanded his disciples to pray, and yet told them also that God knew very well what things they required.[20] Therefore, God's foreknowledge does not call us back from a zeal for praying, for the things both profitable and necessary that God has decreed to give us, he has decreed to give them by this means of prayer.

They are also deceived who think that this doctrine is an unprofitable one; they do not understand its profit. To the godly, it is very profitable, to the end that they should not put any confidence either in themselves or in others, but should place all their hope and assurance in God alone. This is something that no one can do truly from the heart unless he is fully persuaded that his salvation and good works depend not on himself but on God.

We cannot acknowledge the gifts of God unless we understand from what fountain they spring, and that fountain is the free purpose and mercy of God given to those whom he has elected before the foundation of the world.[21] Those who do not see this do not see the goodness of God towards them. By this doctrine men may be brought to glory not in themselves but in the Lord. They cannot do this who ascribe to their own free will even the tiniest bit of why they say they are chosen by God, for they have in themselves the basis of their boasting. Further, the Scriptures would have us mortify ourselves and act humbly; nothing brings this about more easily than this doctrine. The certainty of salvation also, which we defend, is better established by this argument than by any other. In 2 Thessalonians Paul orders us to give thanks to God, that we are elected by God,[22] but we cannot do this unless election is seen and understood by us. Without this doctrine the grace of God cannot be defended against the Pelagians, for they taught that the election of God comes by our merits. The doctrine of free justification would also perish unless we understand predestination rightly. Therefore, since this doctrine, when soundly understood, is so profitable in so many ways, no one should count it unfruitful. When it is set forth in the Holy Scriptures, it can hardly be called a new doctrine.

[18]Prov. 26:11; 2 Pet. 2:22.
[19]Augustine *Persev.* 15.38 (PL 45.1017).
[20]Matt. 6:9, 32.
[21]Eph. 1:4.
[22]2 Thess. 2:13.

4. If the fathers before Augustine did not devote much effort to speaking about predestination, it should not surprise us, for when doctrines were more earnestly discussed and searched out, they provided occasions for new heresies, which often sprang up in the church. In the time before Pelagius, no one had spoken against the grace of God and so there was no need to defend it, but when there arose a new error, it was necessary that this doctrine should be examined more carefully.

Still, the fathers who came before Augustine did not always ignore predestination. Augustine himself proves it in his book *The Gift of Perseverance*, chapter 19.[23] Ambrose, commenting on the Gospel of Luke said "God could if he wished make ungodly persons godly." He also said, "God calls them whom he has promised and those whom he will make religious." He writes these things on that passage where it was written that the Samaritans would not receive Christ.[24] Augustine also cites Gregory of Nazianzus, who said "God gives to the faithful both to believe in the Trinity and also to confess it."[25]

When it was objected that this doctrine is very obscure and cannot be understood, and that it makes men uncertain of the will of God, Augustine answered: "It is indeed obscure and unsearchable if one should seek reasons for the judgments of God, for why some are rejected and why this or that one is chosen, but if all that Scripture transmits about predestination is taught, then those things are not so obscure but obvious to our faith."[26]

We do not counsel that when someone does something he should deliberate about his own predestination; rather, he should refer to the will of God expressed in the Scriptures. Everyone should trust that he is not excluded from predestination. Nor is it any obstacle to preaching that the number of the elect is certain and fixed, as it really is, for by preaching we do not go about trying to transfer men from the number of the reprobate into the number of the elect, but rather affirm that the elect, by the ministry of the Word, might be brought to their appointed end. As this ministry is profitable to the one, it brings destruction to the other, and takes away all their excuse. As to whether predestination and election to salvation may be said to pertain to all men, so that God "will have all men to be saved,"[27] we will speak to this later, in the proper place.

Meanwhile, Augustine tells us not to keep silent about the truth of predestination, for there is a danger that an evil understanding of predestination would

---

[23]Augustine *Persev.* 19.49 (PL 45.1025).
[24]Luke 9:53; Ambrose *Exp. Luc.* 7.27 (PL 15.1706).
[25]Gregory of Nazianzus, *Oratio* 41.8 *Pent.* (PG 36.440–41).
[26]Augustine *Persev.* 9.21 (PL 44.928–29), paraphrase.
[27]1 Tim. 2:4.

corrupt the true doctrine. Moreover, those who have the capacity to understand should not be defrauded because others cannot understand it properly. Because this doctrine can bring so many consolations, it should be universally set forth to both the learned and the unlearned, although not always in the same way. Some people need milk, others need solid food.[28] This doctrine can be handled so that it will satisfy both learned and unlearned. Augustine accomplished this wisely, not only in his learned controversies against the Pelagians on this subject, but also in his homilies and sermons, in which he plainly and gently presented the subject to [407] the people. He asks, "What is more profound than the saying of John, 'in the beginning was the Word' or his other statement, 'and the Word was made flesh?'"[29] Reading these sentences, many men fall and err fatally, and yet we must not cease to set them forth to the learned and the unlearned, only using different ways of speaking.

We should not preach predestination to the people of God in such a way as to say that whether you do this or that, you cannot alter the determination of God, and if you are of the elect, whatever you do cannot remove you from salvation, for this could easily hurt the weak and unlearned. An unskillful, or rather a malicious, physician who foolishly and unwisely applies a medicine that is otherwise good, may hurt someone's health. To set forth this doctrine profitably and with fruit, the ends and utilities that we spoke of earlier ought to be regarded.

Let all our speech be directed to this, namely, that those who are of Christ should not put confidence in their own power and strength, but in God; that they should acknowledge his gifts and glory in God and not in themselves, and feel the grace and mercy that are given them, and that they are freely justified by Christ. Let them understand also that they are predestined to be made into the image of the Son of God, into the adoption of children, and to walk in good works.[30] Last, they have a testimony of the certainty of God's goodwill toward them.[31]

Further, everything has handles by which it may be held effectively; if it should be taken by any of the other parts it would either slip from the hands or hurt the one who holds it. We have gathered this out of those books of Augustine which we just cited, and in which he answered the objections of Hilary and Prosper.

5. Now two doubts remain to be resolved: first, opponents argue that we approve a certain fatal necessity; second, they think that predestination drives

---

[28]1 Cor. 3:2.
[29]John 1:1, 14. Augustine *Conf.* 7.9, 13 (PL 32.741).
[30]Eph. 1:5; 2:10.
[31]2 Cor. 1:12.

men to despair. Concerning the first issue, if by fate or destiny one understands a certain force proceeding from the stars, and that an invincible connection of causes by which God himself is brought to order, then quite rightly we reject utterly the idea of fate. But if by that name one understands the order of causes governed by God's will, then it cannot be seen as against piety. Still, in my judgment I think it best to abstain from that name, lest the unlearned think we approve the ideas of the pagans.[32]

Augustine has written excellently on the matter in book 5, chapter 8 of *The City of God*.[33] According to predestination, neither are the natures of things changed, nor what happens by necessity or by chance, as we have said in our comments on providence.[34] Rather, by the effect of predestination, that is, by grace, we are made free from sin and made slaves of righteousness, which is a holy service and one to be loved in the Lord.

So far is predestination from breaking or diminishing our hope; it rather strengthens it to the greatest degree, for Paul in Romans 8 says: "Hope does not confound," and then adds, "we know that God causes all things to work together for good to those who love God."[35] He confirms this from predestination: "For whom he foreknew, he also predestined," and adds, "Who shall separate us from the love of God? Shall tribulation, or distress?" He then adds, "Neither death nor life, nor angels nor principalities," and so on.[36] Therefore, we are not driven to despair by this doctrine, but rather greatly confirmed in hope, and by it we receive great comfort. Certainly it is much safer to commit our salvation to the care and providence of God than to our own judgment, for we are changeable every day and every hour, but insofar as our salvation lies in the hand of God, it is quite safe and sure. To conclude, the doctrine of predestination also greatly advances the glory of God; therefore, we should not shrink from it, especially since it is part of the Gospel, which is not to be received in part but fully and wholly. This ends the first part of our exordium.

DOES PREDESTINATION EXIST?

6.   In the second part, we will consider whether predestination exists, lest we should seem to define something that is not real—not that anyone has ever openly and intentionally dared to deny God's predestination, but there have been

[32] See Martyr on fate, "Providence," PW, 180ff., §4.

[33] Augustine *Civ. Dei* 5.9 [*sic*], 2 (PL 41.149).

[34] Apparently Vermigli is referring to his comments in ROM, 410–11. See also Vermigli, "Providence," PW, 187ff., §§8ff.

[35] Rom. 8:28–29.

[36] Rom. 8:29, 35.

some who proposed grounds on which, if granted, predestination could not stand.

Some say, especially Pighius, that in God there is neither past nor future, and therefore, God is always predestining and foreknowing in the present.[37] They argue that we are deceived if we think that God predestined some previously, that is, in the past. From this they draw many absurd conclusions, namely, since all things are present to God, he is always foreknowing and predestining. Pighius infers from this that it lies in every man how he will be foreknown by God. That is, it is in our own power to be predestined as we wish.

Pighius strays far from the truth. Although in God there is no course of time nor any past or future, that creature whom God foreknows and predestines is not without a beginning; it is not coeternal with God the creator. It follows of necessity that God predestined it before it was born, for predestination is one of those divine actions that looks to other things. Therefore, we must not fly to the eternity of God, for in it men have no participation with God the creator.

This may be more clearly understood of the past. One might say, "Certain men are now dead *[408]* and gone, but to God all things are present; therefore, God now predestined them and also it is now in their power how to be predestined." On this point no one is so foolish that he cannot see the absurdity. They are not now predestined when they come to their end, nor does it lie in their power whether they exist or how they exist. If their argument is so weak concerning the past, how firm can it be with regard to the future?

Let us leave this argument, even though it is quite solid, and let us consider what the Scriptures say. Paul states that although the twins Jacob and Esau "were not yet born, and had done nothing either good or bad, in order that God's purpose of election might stand (not because of works) but because of him who calls, it was said, 'the elder will serve the younger,'" and does he not assert to the Ephesians, "He chose us in him before the foundation of the world"?[38] These and many other passages clearly declare that men are predestined before they begin to have their being. He who takes this away from us takes from us a great consolation, for from this we know that God predestines us to glory in eternity.

Let us now see how Pighius twists these things back and forth so that he can refute this, that our doings are determined and appointed by God before they take place. Pighius thinks that man's free will would fall away and we would be left under necessity. This evil, as Pighius sees it, can be remedied if we say that God

---

[37]Vermigli is referring to Albert Pighius, *De libero hominis arbitrio et divina gratia* (Cologne: M. Movesianus, 1542), fol. 125r–v (hereafter Pighius, *De libero*).

[38]Rom. 9:11–12; Eph. 1:4.

does all things in the present; but he should have remembered that in the Prophets and other Scriptures there are many prophecies in which many things were determined and appointed long before they were done. What shall we say? Should we think that those prophecies were not given before those things which were to come? Christ says, "It was so that the Scriptures should be fulfilled."[39] Therefore, these fond imaginations serve no purpose. With their lying inventions these men strive only to obscure things that are plain and clear, lest they be found out in how they pour out their black ink.

7. Pighius also goes further and says that the providence of God has not allowed men to know the time or manner of either life or death. Indeed, he says, there have been many in God's providence who might have lived longer if they had not shortened their lives through negligence or intemperance, for if these things were so determined, a murderer who has killed someone may be excused because he has done the will of God.

I wonder how such a great theologian could let such an old wives' tale come out of his mouth, as if when the murderer kills someone he wishes to please God. He considers this alone, how to play the thief and carry out his hatred and hostility. How could he understand that this is the will of God, when God has commanded the opposite in his law? Does he think that Judas can be excused for his wicked treason because he had heard the Lord foretell his mischievous act? Or shall Pharaoh be excused because God had foretold that his heart would be hardened? Therefore, it is foolish to infer from God's ordering of things that sins are excused.

Pighius adds still another argument: If our actions should be determined by God in this way, then all our care, diligence, and effort would be removed, for what profit is there to avoid unsafe and dangerous journeys or winter sailings, or drunkenness, or unhealthy food, if both the manner and time of death and other such things already have been appointed by God with certainty?

Here comes to my mind what Origen said, in the second book against Celsus, where he mentions a subtle argument among those writing about fate.[40] A certain man advised a sick man not to send for the physician because it is already appointed by destiny either that he will recover of this disease or not. If it is his destiny to recover, then he will not need the physician, and if not, the physician cannot help; therefore, whether fate has decreed that he will recover or not, it is useless to send for the physician. In another illustration a man dissuaded his

---

[39]John 7:42.
[40]Origen *Cels.* 2.20 (PG 11.838–39).

friend from marriage. He told the friend that he takes a wife in order to have children, but if he is fated to have children, then he shall have them even without a wife. If it is not your destiny, it will profit you nothing to get married for that purpose; whatever fate has decreed, you will take a wife in vain. Thus they deride and scorn fate or destiny, for they intended to show the absurdities into which men fall if they wish to defend fate.

On the other hand, those who defend fate dissolved these reasons and showed that they should not trouble us. They said that the sick man should have answered: If by fate I shall recover, I will send for the physician, since he claims to restore health to the sick, so that by his industry I may obtain what destiny has determined. Concerning that other who deliberated about marriage, they felt he should have answered: If it is appointed that I will have children, and since children come by no other means than intercourse of man and woman, I want to marry a wife so that destiny can take place.

Let Pighius think that these answers may also serve against him, for the Scriptures also go against him. Fifteen years were added to the life of Ezekiel, and seventy years were prescribed for the Babylonian captivity.[41] Christ said: "The very hairs on your head are all numbered" and "Not one sparrow will fall to the ground apart from the Father."[42]

8. Pighius adds another childish argument, namely, that our prayers *[409]* are in vain if things happen by certain appointment. We have spoken of this in another place, that God not only decreed what he wants to give us, but also has determined the means by which he will have us attain them.[43] Thus Christ says that God knows what we have need of, yet nevertheless admonishes us to pray.[44] This argument of Pighius does nothing else but lead one away from the providence of God, for God's providence is not new, but an eternal disposition of all things. Concerning the death of Christ, the place, time, and manner were so prescribed and revealed in the predictions of the prophets that it could not have come to pass in any other way. Christ himself said, "My hour has not yet come."[45] And what is true in Christ, how can it be denied in others?

We grant that the reasons and causes for wind, flowers, tempests, calm weather, and drought may be discerned long before in the stars. Shall we not state that those causes are in God, who in his infinite ways comprehends more than the

[41] 2 Kings 20:5; Jer. 25:11.
[42] Matt. 10:29–30.
[43] See Martyr, "Providence," PW, 195–96.
[44] Matt. 6:32.
[45] John 2:4.

heavens? As we said a moment ago, the Scriptures speak clearly about the twins: although "not yet born, and had done nothing either good or bad, in order that God's purpose of election might continue (not because of works) but because of him who calls it was said, 'the elder will serve the younger': Jacob have I loved but Esau have I hated." It [Scripture] also speaks of the time to come: "I will have mercy on whom I will have mercy."[46] This is not because of works but because of him who calls so that the proposition about election may endure. And in Deuteronomy, "He chose their seed after them."[47] A posterity was appointed to David, even to the coming of Christ, and when he committed sin he was told that "The sword will not depart from your house," and that his wives would openly be raped by his nearest kin. In Jeremiah, "Before I formed you in the womb I knew you."[48] Christ also says, "They will show great signs to mislead even the elect, if possible," and "as many as were given me by my Father, no one is able to pluck them out of his hand."[49] In Acts, "and as many as had been appointed to eternal life believed."[50]

God is compared to a potter who surely before he begins to work determines in his mind what kind of vessel he will make.[51] A little before, "for whom he foreknew, he also predestined to become conformed to the image of his Son."[52] Predestination is put in the first place, followed by the conformity to the image of the Son of God. We read in Acts, "The Jews took Christ and crucified him, according to the foreknowledge and determinate counsel of God."[53] How many more testimonies do we need? Paul says to the Ephesians that "He chose us in him before the foundations of the world."[54] These things declare sufficiently that we are not deceived when we teach that the foreknowledge and predestination of God precedes those things that are foreknown and predestined. This determination in no way impedes or prohibits the notion that in God's act there is no past or future. The Scriptures are clear that there is a predestination of God. They also teach what we will say later.

Meanwhile, I will confirm it by a reason, which in my judgment amounts to a demonstration. The purpose for which we are made surpasses nature by far, so that by our own power and strength we cannot attain it; therefore, we have need

---

[46]Rom. 9:11–13, 15.
[47]Deut. 4:37.
[48]Ps. 83:37; 2 Sam. 12:10; Jer. 1:5.
[49]Matt. 24:24; John 10:28.
[50]Acts 13:48.
[51]Rom. 9:21.
[52]Rom. 8:29.
[53]Acts 2:23.
[54]Eph. 1:4.

of God to prepare us and to lead us to it. So Paul says to the Corinthians, "Things which the eye has not seen and ear has not heard, and which have not entered the heart of man, the things God has prepared for those who love him."[55] Seeing, therefore, that it is necessary that we must be brought by God to this end, this cannot be done by chance or rashly, but by the counsel of God, which is appointed and determined, even before all worlds.

ARTICLE 1: THE NATURE AND DEFINITION OF PREDESTINATION

THE NATURE OF PREDESTINATION

9. Now when we can safely come to a definition, I think it best to begin with what the Logicians call *quid nominis,* that is, what the word signifies. The Greeks call predestination *proorismon,* from the verb *proorizein,* which signifies "to determine and appoint beforehand," for [the root] *orth* is terminus, that is, a boundary or limit. Therefore, the elect are separated from those that are not elect. The Latins call this *praedestinatio,* for *destinare* is nothing else than to determine firmly in mind and constantly appoint anything, or by some firm decree of the mind to direct something to some purpose.

We may speak of predestination in two ways: either by its bringing something to effect (such as Paul's going to Damascus and being converted to Christ, and thereby separated from unbelievers) or in its being with God from eternity, before men are born (Paul speaks of this to the Galatians when he writes, "When he who set me apart even from my mother's womb" which was long before he was converted). To the Ephesians Paul says, "We were predestined before the foundations of the world were laid," and to the Romans he writes of the twins, "Before they had done either good or evil … [God said] Jacob have I loved, Esau have I hated."[56] At present we will speak of this eternal predestination of God, of which the other is nothing but a declaration of this predestination. Therefore, predestination (*ab aeterno*) can be distinguished in two ways: commonly (*communiter*) and properly (*proprie*).

(1) Common Predestination

Since God does all things by an appointed counsel, and nothing by chance or fortune, doubtless whatever he creates or does, he appoints it to some end or use. In this way, neither the wicked, nor the devil himself, nor sins can be excluded from predestination, for God uses all these things according to his will. Therefore,

---

[55] 1 Cor. 2:9.
[56] Gal.1:15; Eph. 1:4; Rom. 9:11.

Paul calls wicked men appointed to utter damnation *skeuê*, that is, "vessels of God on whom he manifests wrath."[57] In Proverbs, Solomon says that God "made all things for himself and the wicked for the evil day"; and of Pharaoh, "Even to this end I have raised you *[410]* up to show forth my power."[58] If predestination is taken in this way, then it is common to all things.

(2) Predestination Proper

This word predestination will signify nothing else than the eternal ordinance of God regarding his creatures (*Dei de creaturis suis aeternam dispositionem*), relating to a certain use. The Scriptures do not often use the word predestination in this sense except with reference to the elect alone. Although in Acts 4 we read "they assembled together to do whatever your hand and purpose predested to happen."[59] If these words refer to the death of Christ and the redemption of mankind, they do not pass beyond the bounds of election to salvation; if they include those who gathered together against the Lord, they also include the reprobate. Let us make our judgments based on how the Scriptures most often use the term predestination.

The Scholastic theologians also affirm that the elect alone and not the reprobate are predested. We will also follow that sense for now, but not for the same reason, since their argument is very weak, as we will show in due course. We follow this understanding of predestination [of the elect alone], because the Scriptures speak this way for the most part. Therefore, in this treatise predestination will comprehend the saints only. It is for this reason I think Augustine entitled his book *De praedestinatione sanctorum*, that is, the predestination of saints, which signifies the decree of God by which the saints are appointed to communion of salvation. By antithesis or in contrast to predestination we set reprobation. So much for the name.

(3) Foreknowledge and Predestination

10. Before we come to the true and proper definition, we must presuppose certain things. The first pertains to the foreknowledge of God which, as Paul testifies, is joined with predestination: "For whom he has foreknown, he has predestined."[60] Although in God all things are one and the same, yet because of our capacity and understanding, those things that are attributed to him should be distinguished in some way. We should understand that the knowledge of God

[57] Rom. 9:23.
[58] Prov. 16:4; Exod. 9:16.
[59] Acts 4:28.
[60] Rom. 8:28.

extends farther than his foreknowledge, or his knowledge does not reach only to things present, past, or future, but also to those things that will never happen, whether possible (as they say) or impossible.[61] God's foreknowledge pertains to those things that will come about, so that foreknowledge requires a will that precedes, for nothing will happen unless God wills it; otherwise, he would prevent it. Therefore, God foreknows those things that he wills to come to pass.

Furthermore, God does not also predestine all those whom he foreknows, for he foreknows the reprobate, who he knows will be damned. Even though the foreknowledge of God is joined with his will and yet pertains primarily to the knowledge and understanding of God, so on the contrary, although predestination cannot be without foreknowledge, yet it properly pertains to the will. Paul makes this point to the Ephesians when he teaches that "we are predestined according to his purpose by the power by which God works all things according to the decree of his will."[62] By these things we may see in a sense how predestination is joined with foreknowledge and how it differs from it.

(4) Providence and Predestination

Now let us see what predestination has in common with providence and how it differs.[63] It has in common with providence that both require knowledge and are referred to the will; both have respect to things to come. They differ in this, that providence comprehends all creatures, while predestination pertains only to the saints and the elect. Besides this, providence directs things to their natural ends, but predestination leads to those ends that are above nature, such as adoption into the Son of God, to be regenerated, to be endowed with grace, to live uprightly, and finally to come to glory. Therefore, we do not say that animals are predestined, for they are not able to receive this supernatural end. Neither are angels predestined, for they have already attained their end. Predestination refers to the future.

When we said that providence pertains to all things, this may be proved because nothing is hidden from God; otherwise he would not be most wise. And if he knows all things, either he governs all those things or else he disregards the care of many things. If he disregards the care of anything, he does it either because he cannot or will not take on the care of those things. If he cannot, then he is not all-powerful; if he will not, then he is not the supreme good. To deny that God is

---

[61]Martyr has in mind the debate on future contingencies. See his "Providence," PW, 192ff.

[62]Eph. 1:11.

[63]On the problem of the relation between the two, see Martyr's loci on "Providence" and "Free Will and Predestination," PW, xxxiii ff., 171ff., 265ff.

most wise, most powerful, and most good is to deny that he is God.[64] So then, it remains that God's providence is over all things, which the Scriptures clearly teach in many places, for they teach that God's care extends even to the leaves of trees, even to the hairs of the head, even to sparrows.[65]

Providence may be defined, meanwhile, as follows: God's appointed, unmovable, and perpetual administration of all things.[66] When I speak of God, I mean that he is endowed with great authority and that he is mighty. Administration signifies that his government is not tyrannical, but quiet, gentle, and fatherly. Tyrants violently oppress their subjects and relate everything to their own advantage and lust, but God does not violently press any person, either by this government, getting any advantage for himself, but only communicates his goodness to creatures. And this administration extends to all things, for nothing is free from it, nor can anything endure without it. It is called appointed because it is joined with most excellent wisdom, so that it admits no *[411]* confusion. It is immovable because the knowledge of this governor is not deceived, nor can his power be frustrated. It is also perpetual because God himself is present with things, for when he had created things, he did not leave them to themselves; rather he himself is in them and perpetually moves them. "For in him we live and move and exist."[67] So much for providence.

(5) Fate and Predestination

Fate also resembles these matters: if it is a word (as said before) taken for a certain inevitable necessity that depends upon the power of the stars, then the fathers have not without just cause abstained from its use. If fate signifies nothing else but a certain connection of causes, which is not carried rashly or by chance, but is governed by the providence of God and may at his will be changed, I see no cause why the thing itself should be rejected by any. However, because there is a danger that error might sometimes creep in, Augustine thinks it best that we refrain completely from using that term.[68]

---

[64]The classic dilemma of theodicy was put by David Hume: "Epicurus's old questions are yet unanswered: Is he willing to prevent evil, but not able? Then is he impotent. Is he able, but not willing? Then is he malevolent. Is he both able and willing? whence then is evil?" See David Hume, *Dialogues concerning Natural Religion* (1761; repr., London: Thomas Nelson & Sons, 1947), 10:198.

[65]Matt. 10: 29–30.

[66]*Providentia est Dei ordinata immobilis et perpetua universarum rerum administratio*; cf. Martyr's definition in "Providence": "It is the power or faculty of God by which he directs all things and brings them to their ends," PW, 185; cf. the fuller definition, PW, 178.

[67]Acts 17:28.

[68]Augustine *Civ. Dei* 5.9, 3 (PL 41.150).

(6) Love, Election, and Predestination

We should also remember that the love, election, and predestination of God are so ordered together that they follow one another in a certain course. First, the knowledge of God is offered to all who are not in a happy state, indeed being needy and miserable. In his pure and singular mercy God loves those he cares for and sets apart others whom he passes over *[praterit]* and does not embrace with his benevolence. By this separation they are said to be elected, and those so elected are appointed to a purpose.

THE DEFINITION OF PREDESTINATION

11. In his book *The Predestination of the Saints*, chapter 12, Augustine defines predestination as a "preparation of grace." He says that it is a foreknowledge, and a preparation of the gifts of God, by which those who are delivered are delivered with certainty. The rest are left in the mass or lump of perdition.[69] In another place he calls it the purpose of mercy.[70] The Master of the Sentences [Peter Lombard], book 1, distinction 40, defines it as a preparation of grace in this world, and of glory in the world to come.[71]

I do not reject these definitions. However, because they do not comprehend the whole matter, I will (as much as I can) introduce another, fuller definition. I say, therefore, that predestination is *the most wise purpose of God by which he has from eternity constantly decreed to call all those whom he has loved in Christ to the adoption of his children, to justification by faith, and at last to glory through good works, that they may be made like the image of the Son of God, and that in them may be declared the glory and mercy of the creator.*[72] I think that this definition comprehends all things relating to the nature of predestination, and all its parts may be proved by Holy Scripture.

[69] Augustine *Praed.* 10 [*sic*], 19 (PL 44.974). Cf. Augustine *Serm.* 293.8: "the mass of the entire human race which is alienated from him through Adam"; Augustine *Ad simp.* 1, Q. 2.19: "Una est ex Adam massa peccatorum et impiorum." In fact the *massa redempta* has priority over the *massa damnata*; see Johannes Quasten, *Patrology*, vol. 4, *The Golden Age of Latin Patristic Literature from the Council of Nicea to the Council of Chalcedon,* ed. Angelo di Bernardino, trans. Placid Solari (Westminster, Md.: Newman Press, 1960), 434–35.

[70] Augustine *Praed.* 6.11 (PL 44.964).

[71] Peter Lombard *Sent.* 1.40.4 (PL 192.632).

[72] Italics added. Cf. the Church of England's *Articles of Religion*, art. 17 "Of Predestination and Election" in *Creeds of Christendom: With a History and Critical Notes*, ed. Philip Schaff, rev. by David Schaff (1931; repr., Grand Rapids: Baker, 1983), 3:497–98. See CAS, 176–77.

(1)Elaboration of the Definition of Predestination

First, we take "purpose" as the general term, for the word is common to both predestination and reprobation. Paul says to the Ephesians: "we are predestined according to the purpose of God," and in Romans he says "the purpose might abide according to election."[73] We understand what the "purpose" is by the first chapter of Ephesians, for there it is written "God has predestined according to his good pleasure."[74] By these words it is clear that this is called good pleasure (*beneplacitum*), which Paul later called "purpose" (*propositum*), and that this purpose pertains to the will, which is declared by what follows: "having been predestined according to his purpose who works all things according to the counsel of his will."[75] By this will we should understand that will that is effective, which they call consequent; through this it happens that God's predestination is not frustrated.[76] We call this purpose most wise, because God does nothing rashly or by chance, but does all things with the greatest wisdom. Therefore, the apostle joined predestination with foreknowledge, saying: "those whom he has foreknown, he has predestined."[77]

The purpose of God from eternity. This is added because predestination is no new thing, nor does it fail to come first before things happen (as many pretend). Paul says in his second letter to Timothy: "Who has called us with his holy calling, not according to our works, but according to his purpose and grace, which was given us in Christ Jesus before the world was."[78] Here we clearly see that eternity is joined with the predestination of God. In the letter to the Ephesians we are said to be elect "before the foundations of the world were laid."[79]

Constantly decreed. By these words we are taught that the predestination of God is immutable. Paul says in the later letter to Timothy, "The foundation stands firm; the Lord knows who are his."[80] In chapter 8, where the apostle sought to teach that hope does not make us ashamed, and that those who had a sure hope would be saved, he proves it by predestination: "For whom he foreknew, he also predestined," adding, "who shall separate us from the love of God?

---

[73]Eph.1:11; Rom. 9:11.

[74]Eph. 1:5.

[75]Eph. 1:11.

[76]The *necessitas absoluta* or *consequentis* is an absolute necessity, applicable to creation but not to God. The *necessitas ex suppositione* or *consequentiae* is conditional, dependent on God's commitment to his own decrees, *de potentia ordinata*: Heiko A. Oberman, *The Harvest of Medieval Theology* (Grand Rapids: Eerdmans, 1967), glossary, 472. Cf. Martyr, "Free Will," PW, 279–80.

[77]Rom. 8:28.

[78]2 Tim. 1:9.

[79]Eph. 1:4.

[80]2 Tim. 2:19.

Shall tribulation, or distress, or persecution…?"[81] James says: "With God there is no change or variation." And in Isaiah God cries, "I am God and there is no other; I am God and there is no one like Me," and in the letter to the Romans 11, where Paul treats of predestination, he says, "The gifts and calling of God are without repentance."[82] But when Jeremiah, in chapter 18, says that God would change his judgment with which he had threatened many nations *[412]* so that they would repent, this is not to be understood of predestination, but of those things that are foretold to occur by that will of God which they call "the signified will."[83] This is when God declared to men by his prophets either what their sins deserved or what hangs over their heads by reason of natural causes.

12. *Whom he has loved in Christ.* We add this because whatever God gives or decrees to give, he gives and will give through Christ. As we have often stated, Paul says to the Ephesians that we are elected and predestinated in Christ, for he is the prince and the head of all the predestined; indeed none is predestined except to this end, namely to be a member of Christ.

To call into the adoption of children. In one sense Paul speaks of this [adoption] everywhere, and especially in Ephesians 1, for he says there, "We are predestined to the adoption of children." And calling follows immediately after predestination, as those words we have already cited declare: "those whom he has predestined, he also called."[84]

To justification by faith. By these same words Paul teaches that justification is joined to calling: "those he called, these he also justified."[85] Because we have already clearly declared that we have been justified by faith, we shall not need further declaration.

Unto glory by good works. This is something Paul also teaches in the same place: "those whom he has justified, these he also glorified."[86] That glory follows good works and that we are predestined unto those good works is clearly proved by that passage to the Ephesians we have often cited. First he says: "We are predestined, that

---

[81]Rom. 8:29, 35.

[82]James 1:17; Isa. 46:9; Rom. 11:19.

[83]In William of Occam's distinctions within divine willing, the voluntas signi corresponds to the manifest will *(potentia ordi*nata), and the *voluntas beneplaciti* to the absolute will *(potentia absoluta)*; William of Occam, *In IV Sententiarum* (1483), d. 16, q. 1. In the latter, God does what he wants; in the former, "he wills only in accordance with the commands he has given." See *Cambridge History of Later Medieval Philosophy*, ed. N. Kretzmann (Cambridge: Cambridge University Press, 1988), 640; cf. §31, p. 45, below. Vermigli cites John of Damascus for similar distinctions regarding providence: "Whether God is the Author of Sin," PW, 260–61.

[84]Eph. 1:5; Rom. 8:29.

[85]Rom. 8:29.

[86]Rom. 8:29.

we should be holy and blameless before God"; afterwards he says, "God has prepared good works, in which we should walk."[87]

That they may be made like the image of the Son of God. This image is begun in us by regeneration when we are justified; in those of full age it grows daily into perfection by good works and is completely finished in eternal glory, but in infants this likeness begins with regeneration and is finished in that last glory, but because of their age good works are not required of them.

That in them might be declared the mercy and goodness of the Creator. This is the final goal of predestination, signified to us by Paul's simile of the potter who has the power to make one vessel to honor and another vessel to dishonor. So God has prepared his vessels for glory so that in them he might declare his glory. By this definition, we gather that God has ordained to the elect not only glory but also good works, that is, the means by which he will have his elect come to glory. By this we may see how terribly deceived they are who live wickedly and yet boast that they are predestined, for the Scriptures teach that according to God's predestination, men are not brought to glory by wicked acts and evil deeds, but by a virtuous living and manners. Nor are they to be listened to who cry out, "No matter how I live, the predestination of God will have its effect." This is to be utterly ignorant of what predestination is, and to abuse it horribly.

(2) Implications of the Definition of Predestination

13. Now that we have generally examined this definition by its parts, let us bring out certain things that are profitable. First, predestination is a work of God and is to be placed in the purpose of God; for though men are said to be predestined, yet we must not attribute predestination to them. Likewise, things are said to be perceived and known when neither knowledge nor perception is in them, but only in the one that knows them. Just as we can foresee either rain, or cold, or fruit before they come, so God predestines men who have no existence as yet. For instance, some relatives exist out of necessity because the one cannot exist without the other, such as father and son; and there are some relatives in whom one may exist even though the other [relative] may not exist with it at the same time, such as before and after, or knowing and the thing to be known. Predestination belongs to the latter kind of relatives.

Insofar as it is in the mind of him who predestines (as we have said), those things to which the predestined are directed, namely grace, justification, good works, and glorification, are in those whom he predestines; for these have no place except in the saints. It is not be marveled at that we have put the effects of

---

[87]Eph. 1:4, 10.

predestination in the definition, for this definition cannot be given unless the correlatives (as they call them) are also expressed. Predestination is indeed defined, but it is necessary to express and declare the ends to which men are directed by it. Therefore, they are joined with foreknowledge because God knows both the beginning, the means and the ends of our salvation.

This moreover should be known, that when the fathers (as sometimes happened) called predestination foreknowledge, it signifies not only a bare knowledge *[notitiam]*, but also approval, which (as we have declared) pertains to purpose. Therefore, we did what we could to speak properly, so that these things would not be confused.

Lastly this should be also considered, how the goodness, wisdom, and the power of God, which are his chief properties,*[413]* are knitted together in predestination. Purpose, which comes from his goodness, is placed in the will of God. Foreknowledge shows a wise preparation, for the will purposes nothing that is not known before. Finally, when it comes to execution, then power is present.

The Definition of Reprobation

14. Now, because opposite things relate to the same knowledge, and the one serves the knowledge of the other, we also will define reprobation just as we have defined predestination. I said before that I was of the same mind with the Scholastics, that is to say, the reprobate are not predestined; not that I judge their reasons to be sound, but because the Scriptures for the most part speak this way. This is their reason, that predestination directs not only to the end, but also to the means which lead to the end. Since sins are the means by which men are damned, they argue that God cannot be the cause of sins.[88]

Certainly, if we speak correctly and properly, God cannot be said to be the cause of sins, yet we cannot utterly exclude him from the government and ordering of sins, for he is the cause of those actions which to us are sins; although since they are from God, they are simple justice, for God punishes sins by sins. Therefore, sins as punishments are laid upon men by God, as by a just judge.[89]

Further, it is God who withdraws his grace from men. When withdrawn, it cannot be otherwise than that they fall, since through his motion or stirring we both live and move. Doubtless it is of necessity that all the works we do, are in a sense done by his impulse. Although it does not follow that he pours into us any new malice. We have enough malice in ourselves, both by reason of original sin,

---

[88]Syllogism: *major premise:* God ordains the means of salvation; *minor premise:* sins are the means of damnation; *conclusion:* therefore, God is not the cause of sins (QED).

[89]See Martyr, "Whether God is the Author of Sin," PW, 241, §22, referring to Augustine *Grat.* 41 (20) (PL 44.906).

and also because, if the creature is not helped by God, it will by itself decline without measure and end, to a worse and worse state.

Moreover, with justice, God provides occasions for sinning to the reprobate and the wicked, and wonderfully inclines the hearts of men not only to the good but also (as Augustine says) to evil by his just judgment. Indeed, he also uses the malice of men (whether they will or not) to those ends he has purposed in himself. And the Holy Scriptures do not hesitate to say that "God delivers men into a reprobate sense," and makes them blind and seduces them, and many other such things.[90] Yet for all this, he cannot truly be called the cause of sins, since we have the true cause of sins sufficiently in ourselves. Therefore, the reasoning of the Scholastics is not sound, nor does it stand on a very sure foundation.

I separate the reprobate from the predestined because the Scriptures nowhere (that I know of) call men that are damned predestined. This sentence, even if I saw no reason why, I would judge is to be followed because of the authority of the word of God. Yet I do think that the Holy Scriptures speak like this; since (as we said before) predestination has a regard for those ends which we cannot achieve by nature, such as justification, good life, and glorification—things by which God exalts us far above all strength and power of nature. But the sins for which we are damned, although they are not excluded from the government of God in the way we have already taught, yet they do not surpass our natural strength, for everyone is in himself prone enough to sin.

15. Reprobation is [defined as] *the most wise purpose of God by which he has before all eternity constantly decreed, without any injustice, not to have mercy on those whom he has not loved, but passes over them, that by their just condemnation he might declare his wrath towards sins and also his glory.*[91]

The early parts of this definition were already declared when we explained predestination, down to the part "without any injustice," which is added because God does no injury to anyone, although he does not bestow his mercy on some, for he is not bound to any man by any law, nor is he compelled by duty to have mercy on anyone. Thus God answers in the Gospel, "Is your eye wicked because I am good? Is it not lawful for me to do with my own what I will?"[92] Paul taught the same thing by the power of the potter. Yet he affirms that there is no injustice with God.[93] In Exodus it was answered to Moses, "I will have mercy on whom I will

---

[90]Rom. 1:24, 28; Isa. 6:10; Ezek. 14:9.
[91]Italics added; cf. the definition of predestination in §11, p. 19 above.
[92]Matt. 20:15, Vulg.
[93]Rom. 9:23–24.

have mercy … and I will not have mercy on them…."[94] By those words it is signified that all men are in misery through their own nature.

God delivers some out of this misery; those he is said to love. Others he passes over, and these he is said to hate, since he has not had mercy on them, so that by their just condemnation he might declare his anger against sins and also his justice. The damnation of these men is said to be just because it is inflicted upon them for their sins. Yet we should not infer from this that foreseen sins are the cause of a man's reprobation. Sins do not cause God to intend not to have mercy; however, they are the cause of damnation, which follows in the last judgment, that was prepared from the beginning.

The last goal of reprobation *[414]* is the declaration of the mighty justice of God, as Paul has taught, namely, that "these vessels are prepared to wrath," because God would show his power in them.[95] And God answers Pharaoh, "for this very reason I have raised you up, to demonstrate my power in you."[96] The final end is damnation, which is just and is allowed by God, but the next end concerns sins, for God commanded that the people should be made blind so that they would not understand and that they should not hear, "lest they should be converted and I would heal them,"[97] for sins, although they are sins, are condemned by God in his laws. Yet, sins are just punishments imposed by God as the wicked deserts of the ungodly, but we must not stay in these nearer ends. We must go farther, so that at length we come to the end that Paul has set forth, namely, that the justice of God should be declared.[98] This concludes the first article.

ARTICLE 2: THE CAUSE OF PREDESTINATION

16. Now let us come to the second article, where the cause of predestination must be addressed. Just as predestination is the purpose or the will of God, and the same will of God is the first cause of all things and is one and the same with the essence of God; therefore, it is impossible that it should have a cause. We do not deny that sometimes some reason for God's will may be evident. Although such may be called reasons, they should not be called causes, especially efficient causes. That the Scriptures sometimes assign reasons for the will of God may be seen in many places. The Lord says that he led the children of Israel through the desert instead of the shorter routes through which he could have led them, so that

---

[94]Rom. 9:18.
[95]Rom. 9:22.
[96]Exod. 9:16.
[97]Isa. 6:10.
[98]Rom. 2:5.

they would not suddenly meet their enemies.[99] Adam was put in paradise to take care of it.[100] And God testified that he did not yet wish to expel the Canaanites from the land of Canaan, because they had not yet fulfilled the full measure of their sins.[101]

Although we have said that the Scriptures sometimes give reasons for the will of God, yet no one should take it upon himself to render reasons for that certain will of God, except what he gathers from the Scriptures. Since we are dull of understanding, we might easily seize on our own dreams instead of true reasons.

THE FOURFOLD CAUSE OF PREDESTINATION [102]

We do not deny that there are final causes of God's predestination, for they are expressly set down by Paul, especially when he cites the example of Pharaoh: "even for this purpose have I raised you up, that I might show my power in you," but of the elect he says, "God would show forth his glory in them."[103]

The material cause also may be assigned in a sense, for those who are predestined as well as those things that God has decreed to give to the elect by predestination (vocation, justification, and glorification) may be called the matter with which predestination is concerned.

Moreover, it should be noted that the end (final cause) sometimes may be understood as it is conceived by us in the mind and will. Then it has the mark of an efficient cause, for being thus conceived in the mind, it drives men to act. Sometimes it is understood as it is in things and as we reach it after our labors. Then it is properly called the end, because the work is then finished and we are at peace, having obtained the goal of our purpose.

We put forward this distinction, that if at any time we should be asked whether God predestines men because of works or not, we should not rashly give an answer, either by affirming or denying. There is ambiguity in this word ["for"]. How is it to be understood? If good works are taken as they are in fact and in deed (because God predestined us to this end that we should live uprightly, as we read in the letter to the Ephesians, namely that "We are elected to be holy and blameless," and that "God has prepared good works that we should walk in them"),[104] then this is the meaning of the proposition and it is to be affirmed. If, however,

[99]Exod. 13:17.
[100]Gen. 2:8.
[101]Gen. 15:16.
[102]For Aristotle's fourfold causality (formal, material, efficient, final), see *An. post.* 2.11, p4a20ff., etc. This is a familiar usage by Vermigli; e.g., introduction to Aristotle's *Eth. nic.*, PW, 7ff., and "Miracles," PW, 199.
[103]Rom. 9:17, 23.
[104]Eph. 1:4; 2:10.

the word "for" has reference to the efficient cause, as though the good works God foresaw that we would do are like merits and causes which move God to predestine us, then this meaning is not in any way to be admitted.

It is possible that the effects of predestination may be compared so that one effect may be the cause of another, but they cannot be causes of the purpose of God, for calling, which is the effect of predestination, is the reason we are justified; justification also is the cause of good works; and good works, although they are not causes, are the means by which God brings us to eternal life. Yet none of these is the cause or the means by which we are chosen by God. On the other hand, sins are indeed the causes why we are damned, but not why we are reprobate of God. If they were the cause of our reprobation, no one could be chosen, for the condition and estate of all men is the same—all are born in sin.

When Augustine says at times that men are justly reprobate for their sins, he understands this as the last effect, together with reprobation, namely damnation; but we will not speak that way, if by reprobation we understand the purpose of God not to have mercy, for that purpose is no less free *[415]* than the other purpose of showing mercy.

ARE FORESEEN GOOD WORKS THE CAUSE OF PREDESTINATION?

17. Now that we have set forth these things, we will assign reasons why we deny that foreseen good works are the cause of predestination. First, the Scriptures nowhere teach it, and on such a weighty matter we should affirm nothing without Scripture. I am aware, however, that some have labored to gather support for this assertion from the second letter to Timothy, where it is written: "In a great house there are vessels of gold, silver, and wood; and if a man cleanses himself from these he will be a vessel of honor, fit for every good work."[105] They conclude from this that some are destined to be vessels of honor because they have cleansed themselves from the filthiness of sin and from corrupt doctrine. And because they are said here to have power to do so, they say that it lies in everyone to be predestined by God to felicity.

They do not reach a valid conclusion, for Paul's meaning in that passage is to be understood in view of the previous verse: "Nevertheless God's foundation stands firm, the Lord knows who are his."[106] It is as if he had said that men may sometimes be deceived, for they often judge those to be godly who are far from godliness. In these words he reproved Hymenaeus and Philetus; he had just spoken of their perverse doctrine, for they taught that the resurrection was already

---

[105] 2 Tim. 2:20–21.
[106] 2 Tim. 2:19.

passed.[107] Paul would not have such men judged as they appear at first sight, for God has in this world, as it were, in a great house, some vessels of gold, some of silver, some of wood, and some of clay. He knows best which of these vessels are honorable and which are made for dishonor. But we, who do not know or understand God's secret will, can judge only by the effects, that is, those who are cleansed from corrupt doctrine and live godly lives are vessels of honor.

This does not prove that men can cleanse themselves or make themselves vessels of honor. Paul has taught us in the letter to the Romans that it is God alone who brings this about, for God is, as it were, a potter who has the power to make from the same lump of clay one vessel for honor and another for dishonor.[108] This passage interprets the other. Therefore, we should not conclude anything more from those words of Paul than that such cleansing is a token by which we judge the worthiness or unworthiness of the vessels in the church. It is God who truly knows which kind [of vessel] each one is. His foundation stands firm, for it cannot be deceived; but we can judge others only by some tokens and results. This is what Christ admonishes: "By their fruits you will know them."[109]

Nor do they understand Paul correctly when they teach from these words, "if a man keeps himself clean from these things,"[110] that it lies in our will to make ourselves vessels of honor, for the strength of our free will is not proved by conditional propositions so that we could infer that the Holy Scriptures teach that if you will do this or that, or if you believe, you will have salvation; therefore, we can believe by ourselves, or live a godly life. Such conclusions are weak, [111] for God teaches in another place "He will make us able to walk in his ways."[112] Therefore, precepts and exhortations and conditions are to be added so that we should understand what is required at our hands and what kind of person it will be who relates to God and will obtain eternal life.

Therefore, we should not gather from these passages what our own power and strength is able to do. It is easy to declare why those who are purged by God are still said to purge themselves, for God does not work in men as if they were sticks and stones, things without sense and will.[113] When God regenerates men he so cleanses and renews them that they understand for themselves what they do

---

[107]2 Tim. 2:17–18.

[108]Rom. 9:21.

[109]Matt. 7:16.

[110]2 Tim. 2:21.

[111]The *propositio hypothetica* (if A and B, then C) was part of the Scholastic debate about consequences in syllogistic reasoning; see *Cambridge History of Renaissance Philosophy*, ed. Charles B. Schmitt and Quentin Skinner (Cambridge: Cambridge University Press, 1988), 169ff.

[112]Isa. 42:16.

[113]See Martyr's "syllogism of choosing" in his lecture on free will; see PW, 297.

and also why they desire and choose those things, after they have once received a heart of flesh for their heart of stone. So then, after they are once regenerated they become workers together with God, and of their own accord they bend themselves to holiness and purity of life. God through Moses commanded the Israelites to sanctify themselves; yet in another place he clearly states that it was he who sanctified the people.[114] And Paul says to the Corinthians "Christ became to us wisdom, righteousness, redemption, and sanctification."[115] God also commands us to believe; yet the Scriptures elsewhere declare that faith is "the gift of God."[116]

18. Therefore, by all these things it is quite clear how little this passage supports our adversaries, no matter which way they turn. Besides all this, the Scriptures not only teach that predestination is not based on foreseen works, but quite the contrary, for Paul says of those twins, "Before they were born or had done anything good or bad, in order that God's purpose according to his choice might stand, not because of good works, but because of him who calls ... the elder will serve the younger," and also "Jacob have I loved and Esau have I hated, that it should not be of works, but of him that calls."[117] Therefore, Paul denies that either God's love or hatred comes from works.

They are worthy of scorn who argue that Paul excludes works already done but not those that are to be done. They do not see that here Paul *[416]* strives to remove all differences from those two brothers, so that we might fully understand that in themselves they were completely the same, for when he declared that they were born of the same father and mother, and that they were brought forth at the same birth, Paul's meaning intends no other purpose but this: to show by their equality that the election of God is free, so that it lay in him to elect the one and to reject the other. If the difference had been only in foreseen works, then Paul would have put forth such great equality in vain. Paul makes a universal statement, saying, "not from works." In these words he includes works to be done as well as works already done. To make us understand this more firmly, he adds, "But of him that calls." Therefore, Paul sends us to God and not to works.

If you diligently consider all those things that follow in this chapter [Rom. 9], you will see the apostle gathering what he teaches on predestination into these principal points. First, as concerning *power,* he says, "does not the potter have power?"[118] Second, concerning *purpose* or *good pleasure,* he uses both words with

---

[114]Exod. 12:10; Isa. 8:14.
[115]1 Cor. 1:30.
[116]Mark 1:15; Eph. 2:8.
[117]Rom. 9:11–12.
[118]Rom. 9:21.

reference to the Ephesians: "He predestined us … according to the good pleasure of his will," and "according to his good pleasure which he purposed."[119] Third, concerning *will*, he says, "He has mercy on whom he will and hardens whom he will."[120] Finally, concerning *mercy* or *love*, he says: "it is not of him who wills or him that runs, but of God who has mercy." And [he adds] also: "Jacob have I loved and Esau have I hated."[121] Whatever the causes Paul mentions here or elsewhere, they can be reduced to these four principal points. Can we doubt his meaning or shall we take it on ourselves to give another meaning?

Concerning works, Paul speaks not so much as a word when he treats this matter of predestination, except to exclude them. Further, consider this: nothing is more against the scope and meaning of Paul than to put foreseen works as the causes of predestination. By that means works would be the cause of justification; but that doctrine is opposed by the apostle in every possible way. I can prove the soundness of this reasoning, because the apostle makes predestination the cause of vocation, and vocation the cause of justification.[122] Therefore, if works are the cause of predestination, they must also be the cause of justification, for this is a firm rule among Logicians: whatever is the cause of any cause is also the cause of the effect.[123]

Further, no one can deny that good works proceed from predestination, for we are said to be predestined "that we should be holy and blameless," and by predestination, "God has prepared good works in which we should walk." Paul himself confesses that he "obtained mercy to be faithful."[124] Therefore, if works are the effect of predestination, how can one say they are the causes, and especially the kind called efficient causes? For that use of free will, which they so often boast of, is worth nothing. It is as though free will comes from ourselves and not the mercy of God. However, Paul says, "For it is God who works in us both to will and to work."[125] And in Ezekiel God says, "I will take their heart of stone away from them and give them a heart of flesh." "We cannot" (Paul says) "claim anything as coming from us."[126]

If we had in ourselves that good use of which they speak, what would keep us from being able to glory in ourselves? Clearly, our Lord says, "No one can come to

---

[119]Eph. 1:5, 9.
[120]Rom. 9:15.
[121]Rom. 9:13, 18.
[122]Rom. 8:30.
[123]See Aquinas *S. theol.* 1a–2ae, q. 75, a. 4; cf. Martyr, "Whether God Is the Author of Sin," PW, 250.
[124]Eph. 1:4; 2:10; 1 Cor. 7:25.
[125]Phil. 2:13.
[126]Ezek. 11:19; 1 Cor. 3:5.

me unless my Father draws him."[127] Jerome writes excellently against the Pelagians that those said to be drawn [by God] are understood by that word to have been resisting and unwilling before, and afterward God so works that he changes them.[128] The nature of grace proves the same thing; for Paul says that "the remnant might be saved according to the free election of grace," that is, according to free choice. So we should render the genitive case after the Hebrew phrase.[129]

19. Further, in the definition of predestination we have put first the word "purpose," which signifies nothing else but the good pleasure of God (as we have taught from the letter to the Ephesians). Therefore, it clearly shows that we should not seek the cause of predestination elsewhere.

Moreover, works cannot be the cause of our vocation, much less our predestination, since predestination precedes vocation. The second letter to Timothy shows that works are not the cause of vocation: "... who has saved us and called us with a holy calling, not according to our works, but according to his own purpose and grace, which was granted us in Christ Jesus from all eternity."[130] Here it clearly appears that works are not the cause of our calling. Nor are works the cause of our salvation, which would be far more likely, since by good works God brings us to felicity. Paul says to Titus, "He saved us not on the basis of deeds which we have done in righteousness, but according to his mercy." [131] Further, why did Paul need to cry out after this discussion, "O the depths of the riches of the wisdom and knowledge of God! How unsearchable are his judgments and unfathomable his ways?"[132] Had he followed their opinion he might have resolved the whole matter and said that some are predestined and others rejected because of the works God foresaw would be in them both. In mockery, Augustine [417] called them sharp-witted, because they saw so clearly and easily things that Paul could not see.

They say that in this passage the apostle does not resolve this question, but it is absurd to say this, especially since he brought it in deliberately and the solution served very well what he had in view. How in God's name can he seem not to have resolved the question when he referred it to the highest cause, namely, the will of God, and thus showed that we should not go any farther? When God had appointed limits at the foot of Mount Sinai, anyone who went beyond those limits

---

[127]John 6:44.
[128]Jerome *Pelag.* 3.9 (PL 23.579).
[129]Rom. 11:5, referring to 1 Kings 19:4.
[130]2 Tim. 1:9.
[131]Titus 3:4.
[132]Rom. 11:33.

was punished by the law. Therefore, let them beware when they boldly presume to go farther than Paul thinks they should.

They say that here the apostle rebukes the impudent. So be it, yet this rebuking is a true solution to the question, for by this rebuke Paul prohibits us from inquiring into anything beyond the mercy and will of God. If they want such a solution as human reason may resolve, I will easily grant that the question is not in that sense resolved, but if they seek that solution which faith should embrace and rest in, they are blind if they do not see the answer.

20. Let us see what moved them to say that foreseen works are the cause of predestination. Undoubtedly, it was nothing else but to satisfy human judgment, which they have not yet reached, for they have nothing to answer on the matter of an infant who is grafted into Christ and dies in infancy. If they will have him saved, they must confess that it was predestined, but since no good works follow in him, God certainly could not foresee them. Rather, he foresaw that by his free will he would do nothing.

To object that God foresaw what the infant would have done if he had lived longer is even more absurd; human reason will not be satisfied with that. Reason will complain that some are passed over and rejected for sins they have not committed and even more for those sins they would have committed had they lived. Civil judges will not punish people for those faults they might have committed if they had not been prevented. That God is not moved by those good works men might have done, Christ plainly teaches when he deals with Chorazin, Bethsaida, and Capernaum: "If the things which have been done in you had been done in Tyre and Sidon, they would have repented ... and those cities would still exist today."[133] You see that God foresaw that these nations would have repented if they had seen and heard those things that were granted and preached to these cities. Since they perished, it is clear that in predestinating, God did not follow those works men would have done if they had lived.

Nor should anyone gather from this saying of Christ that they could have repented by themselves, even by the power of free will; for repentance is the gift of God. The meaning of that passage is that in their case God did not use those means by which they might have been moved.

They suppose that by nature itself there is a difference in men that God's election follows. They do not consider that all are born the sons of wrath. When considering the mass from which men are taken, no difference at all can be placed in them, since whatever good comes to us certainly comes from God's grace. No

---

[133]Matt. 11:21, 23.

difference may be made in human nature, as the apostle declares; for when he shows that one of two brothers was taken and the other rejected by the free will of God, he first used the example of Isaac and Ishmael.[134] But since it could be objected that there was some difference in these two, because one was born of a free woman and the other a servant, he afterward brought forth two brothers who were twins. Jacob and Esau not only had the same parents but were also brought forth at the same time and in the same birth. Concerning works, there was no difference between them. As the apostle says, "Before they had done either good or ill, it was said the elder will serve the younger … Jacob have I loved and Esau have I hated."[135] What need was there for Paul so diligently to allege these things, except to make these two brothers equal in nature? This would have served no purpose if there still remained so much difference in foreseen works. So then it follows that whatever difference is in men depends on God's will alone, for we are all born under sin.

21. Further, if there is anything in ourselves that might move God to predestine us, it would chiefly be faith. When Augustine was still young and not thoroughly acquainted with this question, he thought God took account of faith and infidelity in predestination and reprobation—a view that both Ambrose and Chrysostom *[418]* embraced before him, [136] but this cannot be attributed to faith, for faith also comes from predestination. It is not from ourselves but is given by God, not rashly but by his deliberate counsel.

This may be easily proved by many places in Scripture. Paul says to the Ephesians, "By grace you are saved through faith and that not of yourself, for it is the gift of God lest any man should boast." And in the same letter he adds, "Love and faith from God the Father and the Lord Jesus Christ."[137] In the letter to the Romans he states, "As God has allotted to each a measure of faith"; to the Corinthians he writes, "I have obtained mercy, that I might be faithful"; to the Philippians he says, "For to you it has been granted for Christ's sake not only to believe in him but also to suffer for his sake"; in the Acts [of the Apostles] it is written, "And the Lord opened the heart of the woman selling purple goods to respond to the things spoken by Paul"; and in chapter 13 it states "and as many as had been appointed to eternal life believed."[138] Christ also said in the Gospel, "I praise you

---

[134]Rom. 9:7.

[135]Rom. 9:11.

[136]Augustine *Quaest. Rom.* 62 (PL 35.2079ff.); cf. Ambrosius *Fide* 5.83 (PL 16.691–92), and Ambrosiaster *Ep. Rom.* (PL 17.133–34); cf. Chrysostom *Hom. Rom.* 16.6 (PG 60.556ff.).

[137]Eph. 2:8; 6:23.

[138]Acts 13:48; 16:14; Rom. 12:3; 1 Cor. 7:25; Phil. 1:29.

O Father, Lord of heaven and earth, that you hid these things from the wise and intelligent and did reveal them to babes. Yea Father, for such was your gracious will," and in another place he stated, "I speak to them in parables because while seeing they do not see and while hearing they do not hear nor do they understand. But to you it has been given to know."[139] He said to Peter, "Blessed are you Simon Bar-Jona because flesh and blood did not reveal this to you."[140] There are many other testimonies in the Scriptures that prove faith is given and distributed by God alone. Therefore, faith cannot be the cause of predestination; and if faith cannot, much less can works be the cause.

22. No one can deny that God's predestination is eternal. Paul says to Timothy, "God saved us … from all eternity," and in Ephesians he adds, "God has elected us before the foundations of the world."[141] But our works are temporal; therefore, that which is eternal cannot come from them. They used to quibble that those works in view of which we are predestined are to be understood as foreseen by God; but by this reasoning they cannot be temporal. Let us admit the argument; let works be taken in this sense. Even so, it cannot be denied that works come after predestination, for works depend on predestination and are the effects of predestination, as we have taught. Therefore, according to their doctrine, what follows would become the efficient cause of what precedes. This is absurd, as anyone can easily see.

Further, the efficient cause is, of its own nature, more worthy and more excellent than its effect, especially since it is this kind of cause. So if works are the cause of predestination, they are more worthy and more excellent than predestination.

Moreover, predestination is sure, constant, and infallible. How then can we make it depend on works of free will that are uncertain, inconstant, and may be swayed hither and yon, if you examine them in themselves? For everyone is prone in the same way to this or that kind of sin as occasions arise. On the contrary, if we speak generally, before regeneration man's free will can do nothing else but sin, because of the sin of our first parents. Therefore, according to their thinking, it follows necessarily that God's predestination, which is certain, depends on human works, which are not only uncertain but are also sins. Nor can they say that they are referring to those works that follow regeneration, for those works (as we have taught) spring from grace and predestination.

---

[139]Matt. 11:25; 13:23.
[140]Matt. 16:17.
[141]Eph. 1:4; 2 Tim. 1:9.

They do not consider that, to satisfy human reason and attribute a freedom to men (I know not what kind), they rob God of his due power and liberty in election. The apostle sets forth this power and liberty, saying that God has no less power over us than has the potter over the vessels he makes, but according to their opinion God can only elect those whom he knows will act well, nor can God reject anyone except those he sees will be evil, but this proceeds to overrule God, and makes him subject to the laws of our reason. Erasmus speaks in vain against this reason, for he says that it is not absurd to take from God that power which he does not attribute to himself, namely to do anything unjustly.[142] We respond to Erasmus that if so, then Paul has in vain, even falsely, proposed this freedom of God, if he does not have it nor will have it attributed to him. But Paul has clearly proved this freedom of God in that passage we have already cited.

They also protest against us in vain concerning the justice of God, for here only his mercy is dealt with. Nor can they deny that they greatly diminish God's love and goodwill towards us. When the Holy Scripture commends to us the fatherly love of God, it affirms that he gave his Son unto death, even while we were yet sinners, enemies, and children of wrath.[143] But they will allow no one to be predestined who has no good works foreseen in the mind of God. So everyone *[419]* may say of himself: if I am predestined, the cause depends on me, but another who truly feels in his heart that he, who was in every way unworthy of his love, yet was freely elected by God for Christ's sake, will be wonderfully inflamed to love God in return.

23. It is also profitable to us that salvation should not depend on our works. We often waver and are not constant in living uprightly. Certainly, if we would put our confidence in our own works, we would utterly despair, but if we believe that our salvation abides in God, fixed and sure for Christ's sake, we cannot but be of good comfort.

Further, if predestination comes to us by our foreseen works, the beginning of our salvation would be from ourselves. The Scriptures everywhere cry out against this, for that would be to erect an idol of ourselves. Moreover the justice of God would then need the external rule of our works, but Christ says: "You have not chosen me, but I have chosen you."[144]

In addition, it is not the same in God as it is in men when we begin to favor someone or to love a friend, for men are moved by excellent gifts which they see adorning a person; but God can find nothing good in us which does not first

---

[142]Desiderius Erasmus, *De libero abitrio: Diatribe seu collatio* 22 (Basel, 1524).

[143]Rom. 5:8.

[144]John 15:16.

proceed from him. Cyprian says (as is often cited by Augustine) that we cannot glory, for we have nothing that is our own. Augustine concludes that we ought not to distribute parts between God and us, giving one part to him and keeping another for ourselves in order to obtain salvation. Clearly everything is to be wholly ascribed to him.[145]

When the apostle writes of predestination he always has this end before him, to confirm our confidence, especially in afflictions, from which he says that God wishes to deliver us. However, if the reason of God's purpose were referred to our works as causes, then we could in no way conceive of such confidence, for we often fall, and the righteousness of our works is so slender that it cannot stand before the judgment seat of God. That the apostle mentions predestination mainly for this reason we can see from Romans 8. When he describes the effects of justification, he says among other things that through it we have obtained the adoption of children, and are moved by the Spirit of God as the sons of God. Therefore, with valiant mind we suffer adversities, and for that reason every creature groans and earnestly desires that we may at last be delivered and the Spirit himself makes intercession for us. At the end he adds, "To those who love God, all things work together for good." And immediately he shows who are the ones that love God, "those who are called according to purpose."[146] Paul is seeking to make them secure, so that they should not think they are hindered when afflicted with adversities, since they are foreknown, predestined, called, and justified. He was concerned with this security, as is shown by what follows: "If God be on our side, who shall be against us? Who will accuse the elect of God?"[147] By this method we conclude first that the adversaries make a grave mistake by supposing that they may infer from this place that predestination comes from foreseen works, for before that sentence Paul wrote, "To those who love God, all things work together for good," as though foreknowledge and predestination, which he mentions afterward, should depend on that statement.

Opponents cite the Proverbs of Solomon in the same sense: "I love those who love me."[148] They do not consider (as we said) that in this place Paul intends to disclose those to whom it is given to love God and for whom all things work for good. These (he says) are those who by predestination are chosen by God.

---

[145]Cf. Cyprian *Test.* 3.4 (PL 4.764). Augustine indeed quotes this saying quite often—fourteen times; cf. Augustine *Persev.* 14.36 (PL 45.1015), 17.43 (PL 45.1020), 19.48–49 (PL 45.1023–24); *Praed.* 3.7–8 (PL 44.964ff.); *C. Pelag.* 4.9.25–26 (PL 44.626ff.); *Corrept.* 7.12 (PL 44.923–24); *Retract.* 2.1.1 (PL 32.630); *C. Jul. op. imp.* 6.18 (PL 45.1541–42).

[146]Rom. 8:27–28.

[147]Rom. 8:31.

[148]Prov. 8:17.

Concerning Solomon, we also acknowledge those who love God are in turn loved by him. What is now in question is this, whether the love of God by which he embraces us springs or grows from our love. John expressly declares this in his letter, saying: "not that we loved God but that he first loved us."[149]

The second thing we gather from these words of Paul is that God's predestination (if it has this power to confirm us by the goodwill and love of God toward us) cannot depend on our works, for our works are both weak and of little righteousness. We should also note that Paul did not hide those causes that might have been assigned, for he expressly states that the final cause is that God's mercy and justice might be made known. But when he comes to the efficient cause, he wants us wholly to rest on the will of God, comparing God to a potter and us to clay. In this comparison he shows that there is nothing further to be investigated.

I know that the adversaries say that the comparison is made only to suppress impudent questions, but in neither case is it true that God elects men on the basis of foreseen works. If it were so, how then shall the mouth of murmurers be stopped? They will say, "If the justice of God requires that election is based on foreseen works, what need did Paul have in saying, 'Before they had done either good or bad it was said, the elder shall serve the younger'"?

And why did he say, "Not of works but of him that calls, that election *[420]* might stand firm according to the purpose"?[150] Why is this simile of the potter introduced, when the thing itself is far otherwise? As a potter, God does not do all things according to his desire, nor are we as clay utterly without distinction. Surely by their reasoning an impudent questioner is not suppressed. Indeed, rather there is offered here an occasion for reproach, since the simile does not serve the purpose.

24. There is another passage in Paul's letter to the Ephesians by which our proposition is strongly confirmed. After he had said: "We are predestined according to the purpose of God," he adds, "by the power through which he works all things according to the counsel of his will."[151] If things were as these men imagine, God would not work all things according to his will but according to the will of another. As we produce our works, so he would adapt his election, but this is to be led by another's will and not by one's own. Paul says this very thing to the Corinthians, saying, "God has chosen the foolish, weak, and vile things of this world to confound the wise, mighty, and noble." "Look, brothers," he says, "at

---

[149]Martyr writes: "non, inquit, quod nos illum dilexerimus: ille rior dilexit nos," which is a conflation of 1 John 4:10 and 19.

[150]Rom. 9:11–13.

[151]Eph. 1:5, 11.

your calling: not many wise, not many mighty, not many noble." And in the same letter, after he has described the former state of the elect and has added up many and grave sins, at length he adds, "Such were you, but you are washed, you are consecrated."[152] And to the Ephesians he says, "You were once without God and without hope in the world."[153] These prove that God's calling and predestination do not depend on our merits.

As Augustine writes to Simplicianus, God passes over many philosophers, men of intellect and exceptional learning.[154] He has also passed over many who with respect to civil manners were innocent and lived an acceptable life. Nor should we wonder at this, for if God predestined so that he might display the riches of his mercy, that is accomplished more quickly if he brings salvation to those who resist more and are farther from him because of the [de]merits of their lives, than if he should choose those that human reason judges more suitable. It happened that Christ gathered his flock of disciples from sinners, publicans, and the humble; nor did he shrink from calling to himself both thieves and prostitutes. In all these, what consideration of merit was present (I ask you)? Paul says to the Corinthians, "We preached Christ crucified, to the Jews an offense and to the Greeks foolishness; but to those who are called, both Jews and Gentiles, Christ the power of God and wisdom of God."[155] We also see here that the apostle makes a distinction when he affirms that some think well of Christ preached, and some ill; all this, he says, comes wholly from their calling: "But to those who are called." This is as if he had said, those who are not called have Christ for an offence and foolishness; but those who are called follow him and embrace him as the power and wisdom of God.

In the prophets also, when God promises that he will deliver his people, he does not say he will do it because of their works or merits, but he says, "I will do it for my name's sake."[156] Paul does not depart from this reasoning, for he shows that by predestination God will open the riches of his glory, that all may know how little the Jews deserved this divine election. Other nations were passed over, but they [the Jews] alone would be counted as the people of God. Stephen makes the same point in the Acts of the Apostles when he says, "They had always resisted God, and were always a stiff-necked people."[157] What good works did God see in them, to prefer that nation over all others? Ezekiel describes how God looked on

[152]1 Cor. 1:26; 6:11.
[153]Eph. 2:12.
[154]Augustine *Ad simp.* 2, Q. 2.3 (PL 40.140).
[155]1 Cor. 1: 23–24.
[156]E.g., 1 Sam. 12:22.
[157]Acts 7:51.

the Jewish people at the beginning, namely as a naked maiden, defiled on every side and shamefully wrapped in blood: "I passed by, says the Lord, and when I saw you like that I had compassion on you."[158]

25. Let us remember the apostle's purpose (*scopus*) in the letter to the Romans, for if we are to judge properly in controversies we must not take our eyes away from the purpose. The apostle attempts to commend by all means possible the grace of Christ. Nothing obstructs this purpose more than to declare that the predestination of God, the head and fountain of grace, comes from human works. If it is counted as a fault in orators when in their orations they perhaps narrate things that greatly hinder the cause they took in hand, how can we suspect that the Holy Spirit does not persist in what he began, but speaks of what is remote from his purpose?

We cannot have a different rationale for the members than for the head, which is Christ Jesus. No one can doubt that the Son of God freely took human nature on himself. (If the question is asked why he rather than any other man took flesh of the virgin Mary, no other reason can be given but that it pleased him. As to works, any other man, born of any other virgin, might have had them, no less than he who was born of Mary, for whoever had possessed divinity as Christ did, in truth could have done the very same works as did Christ.) Seeing then that humanity was taken by the Son of God freely, and out of the pure and exclusive mercy *[421]* of God, in the same way whoever are members of Christ are chosen freely, without any merit of works. Finally, all those arguments that prove that justification is not based on works also prove that predestination does not depend on works.

Now it remains to show whether Christ and his death may be said to be the cause of predestination. Here we answer that Christ and his death is the principal and chief effect of predestination. Among those things God gives to the elect is Christ himself and the fruit of his death. Whatever is given in this way, as through a water pipe, comes to us from God. While it is certain that the effects of predestination may be compared together so that one may be the cause of another, yet none of them is suitable to be the beginning of predestination. Therefore, we deny that Christ is the cause of predestination in terms of his humanity or death, although he is the beginning and cause of all good things, which come to us from the purpose of God.

---

[158]Ezek. 16:6.

26. I am aware that some have tried to reconcile statements of the fathers with this true doctrine we have now proved by many reasons. They say that when the fathers write that predestination is based on foreseen works, they do not understand by the name predestination the work or action of God by which he elects or predestines any person. Rather, they understand the purpose and certain means [of God's works], and in that regard, nothing can prevent works from being causes, for it is certain that the final damnation comes from works as the cause and that good works spring from faith as from their head or fountain.

I see that the intention of those who labor to apply the statements of the fathers to the truth (as far as is possible), is not to be denied. However, I cannot say that what the fathers assert is true, for certain statements of theirs are so harsh that they cannot be drawn to this meaning at all. To defend the freedom of our will they deny that everything depends on God's predestination. They intend to say that everything does not depend on God, that something is also required of us. They say explicitly that God elects some because he foresaw they would believe. Occasionally, they also say many other such things, so that by no means can I see how their statements can agree with our doctrine on this point.

Augustine fully agrees with us, and Jerome does not disagree, although he does agree often with Origen and others, but against the Pelagians he highly commends Augustine's position on this matter and strongly accepts his writings against this heresy.[159] Seeing that Augustine often used this argument against the Pelagians, it must follow that he greatly pleased Jerome in his old age. Cyprian, as we said before, clearly writes that nothing is ours; so that it follows necessarily that it is all of God.[160] However it stands, there is no need for us to debate now regarding the fathers, for when I explained the text of Romans itself, I spoke at length on these matters as the passage taught. As in all other things that pertain to faith, so also in this question, we must speak according to the Scriptures, not according to the fathers. The fathers themselves require the very thing in our hands and so I have, as much as possible, endeavored to advance its arguments.

CONTRA PIGHIUS

27. Among later writers, Pighius is forced by the strength of the Scriptures to grant that works are not causes of predestination.[161] He admits that it consists freely of the mercy of God but in consideration of works, lest he seem to have

---

[159]Jerome *Pelag.* 1.1, etc. (PL 23.497ff.), referring to Augustine *Gest. Pelag.*

[160]Cyprian *Test. Judaeos* 3.4 (PL 4.764). Cf. n. 145 above.

[161]Pighius, *De libero,* fols. 107ff.

argued so diligently in vain. If predestination is free and depends solely on the will and mercy of God, as Scripture testifies, why does he from his own head imagine this new consideration of works? For the Holy Scriptures, and especially Paul, completely exclude works from this matter. In order to satisfy his base desire for controversy, Pighius brings forward some arguments that have nothing at all to do with the issue. What happened with the blessed virgin, the Mother of God (he says), occurred in view of election, and should also take place in others. Yet she was not predestined freely, but rather because of her humility, for she sang: "He has regarded the humility of his handmaiden." Thus the same thing should happen in others.[162] It is a wonder how he failed to see that there is a great difference between *tapeinôsin* and *tapeinophrosynê*, for the latter is a virtue, called *Modestia* by the Latins, and has to do with those who have a lowly and moderate opinion of themselves. Its opposite is pride or arrogance, but *tapeinôsis* is vileness and baseness (*abiectio*) which comes to men either because of poverty or from low breeding or similar things.[163]

Thus the blessed virgin rejoiced and praised God, since he had advanced her to so great an honor, although she was common, obscure, and unworthy; she did not (as he dreams) put forward her own merits and virtues, saying that she was chosen by God because she deserved it through her modesty. If you consider well the burden of that song you will easily see that she ascribes all her good to God: "Your mercy," she says, *[422]* "is from generation to generation," and adds, "he has remembered his mercy." Afterward she joins the promises with mercy: "as he spoke to Abraham our father." Why did this good man not see that the image of our predestination is to be set in Christ rather than in the virgin? Augustine says that the humanity of Christ was predestined, and assumed, quite freely and completely, without any reference to good works.[164]

28. They also raise objections regarding the words of the Lord to Samuel when he was to anoint one of the sons of Jesse as king over Israel, and Eliab, the eldest, was brought to him first. The Lord said to him: "This is not the one I have chosen; do not look at the height of his stature, for men see those things that appear outwardly, but I look at the heart."[165] Pighius says this passage teaches that God is moved by the perfection of the heart, and not by outward conditions. But

---

[162]See Pighius's reference to the virgin from the root of Jesse (*virginem ex radice Iessae*), *De libero,* fol. 138v.

[163]The word in Luke 1:48 is *tapeinôsis;* each stems from *tapeinos,* which has both good and bad connotations.

[164]Augustine *Praed.* 15.31 (PL 44.982).

[165]1 Sam. 16:7; Pighius, *De libero,* fols. 126v–127r.

that ancient text is not concerned with God's eternal predestination by which he has elected us to eternal felicity; it treats only the promoting of a man to kingship. God has given us here a notable example, that when we entrust any office or function to someone, we should attend chiefly to the strength and skill required to execute that office. It is in accord with this principle that Paul, in his letter to Timothy, also puts before us what things are to be required of one who is chosen as elder or bishop.[166] In the Old Testament God has described at length the qualities the person should possess if he were to be appointed king. Peter seems to have considered the same thing when two men were set before him, one of whom was to replace Judas. He called on God, "the searcher of hearts," who alone knew the mind and heart of the one he wished to be chosen.[167] Still, we should not think that God finds in men that heart which he is looking for; rather he changes and renders fitting those whom he will appoint to any office, as we know he did with Saul, of whom we read that he was so changed that he became a completely different man. Whereas before he was plain and rude, afterward he was able to prophesy among the prophets. Because this was new and strange, it gave rise to this proverb: "What! Is Saul also among the prophets?"[168]

Pighius also alleges that it will follow from our teaching that men will seek the causes of their damnation not in themselves but in God, which is both absurd and wicked.[169] Let him ask how this could be inferred from our teaching, since we teach that everyone is subject to sin and, therefore, deserves damnation. I never said to anyone that he does not have in himself a most just cause of his damnation. Indeed, we seek and have always sought to persuade everyone that when they take anything in hand, they should take counsel nowhere else than from the revealed will of God and not from the secret of predestination.

Yet it does not follow that by this sort of teaching the doctrine of predestination is of no use. We should regard it chiefly when we are tossed with adversities and when through the sheer force of afflictions we feel our faith weakened. Paul taught this in Romans 8: "If God is on our side who can be against us? Who shall separate us from the love of God? Shall tribulation, or anguish?" and so forth.[170] So then this doctrine is not to be avoided as though it has no application to ourselves. It is to be retained diligently, until opportunity serves to use it. Nor is it a matter of arrogance, but of spiritual wisdom, for one to use it for himself when need arises.

---

[166]1 Tim. 3:1.
[167]Acts 1:23.
[168]1 Sam. 19:24.
[169]Pighius, *De libero,* fols. 114v–115v, 135r.
[170]Rom. 8:31–35.

29. Moreover, Pighius falsely states that what we are saying is contrary to God's goodness, as if it were unjust that God should choose a few for himself while overlooking countless others. This [he argues] might suggest some cruelty in God, especially when we say that he is offended before anything is done against him.[171] He says it is fitting that God's purpose should be reasonable; yet no other reason can be given for his justice except the works of the predestined. Nor can God's justice be defended in any other way. Such things may have a show of godliness, but do not help overturn what we have proved. First, to deal with the goodness of God, no creature seems to be without it, for God constantly bestows many good things, even on the wicked. "He makes his sun to rise on the good and on the evil, and rains on the just and the unjust."[172] Although he does not distribute his goodness equally to all, yet he cannot for that reason be rightly accused. Christ answers in the Gospel: "May I not do what I wish with my own?"[173] If Pighius thinks it unacceptable that out of the many few are chosen, he does not pick this quarrel with us, but with God, for Scripture teaches clearly that "Many are called, but few are chosen,"[174] and that out of the many nations only the Jews were taken by the Lord to be his particular people. Even among that people, although their number might be compared with the sand of the seashore, only a remnant would be saved.

How can Pighius strive against those evident witnesses? Do we not also see that in natural things the most excellent *[423]* are the rarest? There is an abundance of common stones, but a strange scarcity of precious stones; worthless weeds grow everywhere, but grain is for the most part dear. Why God will have it so, he himself knows best. Perhaps we may suppose that he does it so that the gifts of God to men might be valued more highly. We are so dull that we never wonder at those things that happen regularly, but this is nothing but human conjecture. Since God has not provided a reason for his judgment, I think it is not our part to be curious in seeking one.

I will add this only, that God is not only good and bountiful towards us, but also in him one cannot find so much as a hint or token of cruelty. It is the nature of cruelty to rejoice in the punishment of others, especially if innocent people are afflicted. But to take pleasure in seeing justice exercised against the wicked, or to be distressed if you see them living happily, cannot be ascribed to envy or to cruelty, for in the prophets, and especially in the Psalms, we see many such emotions, which clearly relate to *nemesis*, that is, to zeal, not to cruelty or envy.

[171]Pighius, *De libero,* fol. 128r–v.
[172]Matt. 5:45.
[173]Matt. 20:15.
[174]Matt. 22:14.

Although God's purpose is reasonable, indeed reason itself, yet the reasons are not to be looked for in the elect; they lie hidden in the deepest wisdom of God. Paul recalls us to this when he cries out: "O the depth of the riches of the wisdom and knowledge of God! How unsearchable are his judgments and unfathomable his ways. Who has known the mind of the Lord? Or who has been his counsellor?"[175] By these words Paul teaches nothing else than that by reason of his manifold and infinite wisdom God does not lack reasons, but they are unsearchable by humans because he has not revealed them.

It is odd that Pighius would complain of violating the justice of God, since Paul raises the same question for himself, yet does not change his mind.[176] This is not surprising, for Paul says himself that this whole matter relates to mercy, not to justice. Even so (as Augustine teaches), we may very well defend the claim that God does nothing unjustly.[177] Whatever he gives to the elect, he gives of his own [mercy], not another's; and whatever he requires of the reprobate, he requires it with justice and perfect righteousness. Pighius would not have raised these objections if he had diligently weighed the antithesis that Paul puts between our works and God's purpose, for he says: "not of works, but of him who calls, that election might be according to the purpose."

30. He also thinks it absurd that predestination should be so free, since in that case he supposes that a necessity is laid on us, and so all consideration of blame is removed.[178] This argument refers to our fourth article, where we will treat such necessity.[179] Still, I wonder how this could enter his head, that the consideration of sin is removed if one grants this necessity, as though anyone can avoid original sin; but it does not follow that such a sin is no sin.

He [Pighius] adds that we cannot avoid making God a respecter of persons.[180] If he had considered that this fault is committed when we are moved to render a judgment according to certain circumstances and conditions that have nothing to do with cause, he would never speak like this, for it cannot be so with God. He [God] did not discover such circumstances and conditions in men, but places them in men as he will. Therefore, no one may object to him concerning election, that he failed to attribute to someone what was fitting or appropriate,

---

[175]Rom. 11:33–34.

[176]Rom. 9:19.

[177]Augustine *Div. quaest. Simpl.* 68.6 (PL 40.73–74). Also possibly a reference to *C. Jul. op. imp.* 3.107 (PL 45.1292); *Persev.* 8.16 (PL 45.1002).

[178]Pighius, *De libero.*, fols. 128v–129r.

[179]See §49 below.

[180]Pighius, *De libero.*, fols. 126r–127r.

for God is the creator of all persons and all qualities. He [Pighius] states that the care and effort to live uprightly is taken away, as though by this doctrine we make men worse, and open a window to licentiousness and a profligate life. I think it is clear how strange and false this is, since we always teach that predestination includes not only the end but also the means. Men are predestined not only to happiness but also to good works, that we should walk in them and be conformed to the image of the Son of God. The wicked disregard such things and live evil lives without this doctrine, but the godly, because they have confidence that they are predestined, labor by holy works to make their calling sure. For them this doctrine is a window to modesty, to patience in affliction, to gratitude, and to a singular love towards God; take away this doctrine and one opens not just a window but the widest gate to ignorance of God's gifts, to uncertainty and doubting of salvation in adversity, and the weakening of our love towards God.

31. These men say further that this counts heavily against us, for under predestination and reprobation nothing can happen except what God wills, but for God to will sins is a most absurd and blasphemous teaching. They say, moreover, that God cannot justly punish if we commit those things which he both wills and works, but we must say this if we affirm that not only the ends but also the means to the ends depend on God's purpose.

To solve this dilemma, they should first recall that it cannot be denied but that God in a sense wills or (as some others say) permits sin. Since that happens without *[424]* any compulsion (*coactio*) of our mind, no one can be excused when he sins, for he committed those sins willingly and of his own accord, for which he should be condemned. Such a person has the true cause in himself and so has no need to seek it in God.

Second, the comparison they make between good works and sins is faulty. God so produces good works in us that he grants us his grace and Spirit by which these works are performed. They are the grounds of good works, grounds we do not have in ourselves, but he governs sins in such a way, and wills in such a sense, that even their grounds, that is, the flesh and our corrupt and wicked nature, are not in God but in ourselves. Therefore, there is no need for them to be poured into us by some outward mover.

In one sense, God is said to will sins, either because when he does not prohibit them when he could, or because he does not allow them to burst forth except when and how and for what purpose he will, or so that by them he will punish other sins. They add that God by no means wills sin, for it is written in Ezekiel, "As I live, says the Lord, I have no pleasure in the death of the wicked, but that he be converted and live."[181] We answer that in this passage the prophet is not concerned with the absolute and hidden will of God, but his effective will—that will by which God "works all things as he wills both in heaven and on earth."[182] Rather, he deals with that will which they call "the signified will." By those signs and tokens expressed in the law, no one can conclude that God wills his death or condemnation. For example, the Lord commands that his law should be proclaimed to all; he revealed to everyone whatever would be profitable and healthy; and last, he pours his great benefits upon all indifferently. Therefore, by this will, which we call the signified will, he does not will the sinner's death. Rather he provokes them to repentance. As to the other will, which they call the will of his good pleasure (*beneplacitus*), if by it he wills that no one perish, then surely no one would perish. As Augustine says, there is no will so perverse that if he wishes to, God cannot make it good.[183] According to this will he has done all things he wished. This is a simple and plain interpretation. If our adversaries will not accept it, but insist on contending that the prophet's words are to be understood of the absolute will of God, and the will of his good pleasure, then we answer that the statement does not relate to all sinners universally, only to those who repent. They are the elect and predestined, to whom God, according to his purpose, gives faith and calling, and repentance. So, whichever sense they follow, they shall never absolutely conclude from those words that God wills the death of sinners or wills sin.

32. They put forward certain words from the Book of Wisdom, chapter 1, where it is written, "God does not rejoice in the destruction of the living."[184] They say that if God in any sense wills sin or its punishment, he cannot be said not to rejoice for he rejoices in what he wills to be done. First, I answer that book is not in the canon; therefore, its authority may be denied. However, assuming the book is canonical, those words do not contradict us. Whoever was the author of that book, he meant nothing else than to remove from God the depravity of nature, by which the wicked take pleasure in evil things. It was not his meaning that God punishes wicked acts against his will; otherwise, the author (under the name of Solomon) would be against the true Solomon, for in his Proverbs he writes of the ungodly and unbelievers, under the person of wisdom: "I also will laugh at your calamity."[185] This indicates that with this laughter, that is, with a cheerful mind, God administers justice.

---

[181]Ezek. 33:11.
[182]Ps. 115:3.
[183]Augustine *Enchir. lauren.* 98, 25 (PL 40.277).
[184]Wisd. of Sol. 1:13.
[185]Prov. 1:26.

Concerning the words of Ecclesiasticus 15, it is written that "No one should say of God, *autos me eplanêse*," that is, "He has deceived me," and where the Latin translation has *Me implanavit.* [186] We must explain these words in this way, so that no one should place the blame on God in order to excuse himself. Otherwise, it would contradict many other passages of Scripture, where God is said to have deceived the people by false prophets, to have ordered King Ahab to be deceived, and to have made the hearts of the people blind, so that they should not see. If Ahab was deceived, he justly deserved it, because he condemned the true oracles of God and delighted in false prophets. The infidelity and impiety of the people of Israel caused the vengeance of God, and blindness came upon them, so that when they were deceived, they could by no means be excused.

Our adversaries also seem to be somewhat offended when we say that men have the cause of sin in themselves, that is, a corrupt and wicked nature. In the Book of Wisdom 1, the generations of the world are said to be good, and not to have in them *pharmakon olethrion*, that is "a deadly medicine." [187] This is certainly true, if understood of the first constitution of things, chiefly the creation of man, who was created by God in a good state, but afterwards, through his fall, spoiled both himself and his posterity.

33. Pighius quibbles against our teaching, as though we stir men up to hate God. Christ says this to Judas, "Woe to that man; it would have been better for him never to have been born." [188] Being rejected and a reprobate, it must follow that he hated God, seeing that God first hated him. Since the number of the reprobate is the greater *[425]* number, everyone (they say) might easily suspect that he is one of that number and it would come to pass that many would abhor God. We answer: Christ well said, "it would have been better for him never to have been born"; for each of us would rather more gladly either never have existed, or be brought to nothing, than offend God by committing sin. So Christ said truly and plainly, "it would have been better for him never to have been born." Yet in absolute terms with regard to God it was not better; for through him God's counsel concerning our redemption was fulfilled and also by the punishment laid upon him, the justice and power of God was more clearly displayed. It is vain to say that many could come to suspect their reprobation, for out of Holy Scripture no one can find any effective arguments for his reprobation. Even if God sometimes reveals it by some secret judgment, it cannot be made a common rule.

---

[186] Ecclus. 15:12. The Latin translation is somewhat softer: "non dicas ille me implanavit" (do not say, it was he [God] who hindered me).

[187] Wisd. of Sol. 1:14, "the generative faces of the world."

[188] Matt. 26:14.

In our time a certain man in Italy named Francesco Spiera felt within himself that God had imposed this evil [reprobation] on him, but in my judgment, this happened to induce fear in other people. After he had known the truth of the Gospel and confessed it openly, when brought before the papal legate in Venice he publicly recanted it. Later he was seized with a grave wound of conscience and convinced himself that he had sinned against the Holy Spirit. By this means he was thrown into such great despair that he would never afterward accept any consolation, although famous and pious men attended him, exhorting him to have hope in Christ and his death. He used to say that these things served well when spoken to others, but to him they did not count, for he saw with absolute certainty that he had sinned against the Holy Spirit, and there was no remedy left to deliver him from damnation. He remained in this despair until he died.[189]

Through this man, by a singular and unusual dispensation, God wished to frighten others away from such evil and impiety. This does not happen regularly, as far as we can gather from the histories, nor can anyone discern this despair from Holy Scripture. Perhaps God did not do this to Spiera. Perhaps, once he had renounced godliness, the devil (whose slave he was), used it to drive him to utter despair. So when speaking, we should make a distinction (as we advised before) between the alienated who are quite without any feeling of piety, and the godly and those who are now called. If you speak of the alienated, they do not regard these divine counsels, or else they have already despaired of themselves. If we refer to the godly, they will not allow themselves to be tormented by this suspicion for long, for now they see themselves as called and faithful, and therefore are justified. All this persuades them to have confidence and to hope that their names are entered in the roll of the elect.

34. Finally, Pighius imagines that we speak absurdities because we teach that mankind as a whole was first marred and corrupted by original sin before they were predestined by God.[190] Just as we would validate God's purpose, even though in the counsel of predestination, we put condemnation and eternal

---

[189]Francesco Spiera of Cittadella was an Italian lawyer who embraced and then abjured his Calvinist faith; he died in utter despair in 1549, believing that by denying his true Calvinist convictions he had betrayed Christ. Pier Paolo Vergerio visited Spiera but failed to ease his conscience, although the experience confirmed Vergerio's own Reformed allegiance. See Anne J. Schutte, *Pier Paolo Vergerio: The Making of an Italian Reformer* (Geneva: Droz, 1969), 239–46. Cf. Salvatore Caponetto, *The Protestant Reformation in Sixteenth-Century Italy,* trans. Anne Tedeschi and John Tedeschi (Kirksville, Mo.: Thomas Jefferson University Press, 1999), 48–49.

[190]Pighius, *De libero.,* fol. 122r.

unhappiness before sins and our corrupt nature, and so we validate what is first by what follows. He also adds that by this means, concerning the purpose of God, even by our own doctrine, the end is appointed first as well as those things which bring the end about. Since original sin is one of the means by which we are condemned, it cannot, as we imagine, precede reprobation, since it falls under and is included in it as a means to eternal condemnation. This shows that this man does not understand what we are saying.

Neither Augustine nor we ever said that original sin went before predestination. Predestination is before all eternity, but Adam fell in time. It is not so absurd as he [Pighius] thinks, that sins should fall under reprobation, not as its cause, but as the cause of condemnation and eternal misery. He says that if it were so it would follow logically that God wills sins, but we have explained how this should be answered. He cannot deny that God employs sins, which are committed later, for those purposes he has himself appointed. And since he does not do this rashly, but by his deliberate counsel, how can it be that sins are not somehow comprehended under reprobation? Now if he contends that God does not in the same sense cause (and will) sins and good works, we say the same thing. In the meantime, let him stop speaking of it as an absurdity that both the end and the means either of predestination or of reprobation are comprehended under the purpose of God, though in different ways.

Concerning original sin, we also affirm that it does not go before predestination or reprobation, but of necessity follows it, for God would not produce men out of any other flock or other matter except the progeny of Adam, through whom all are born infected with the stain of corruption. Since this was not hidden from God, Augustine says, and we with him, that God from eternity purposed to have mercy on those whom he loved and not to have mercy on those whom he did not love. Those who lack that mercy bestowed on others are justly and worthily damned if they live their lives in original sin and when they come of age and to the use of reason, add many other sins to it. This may be effectively stated to repel those who perhaps presume to lay the cause of their damnation [426] not on their own faults but on God. Therefore, original sin precedes the birth of all men, so that it relates to every person; it also precedes the damnation of all the wicked, although it could not exist before the eternal purpose of God, except in his foreknowledge.

35. We maintain that to use these things is in no way absurd. They can well be perceived in this way, if we do not depart from the sense of Scripture, a sense that Pighius overlooks because of his own fond invention, as I will show in few words. He makes many decrees or acts in the mind of God, which he orders not

by a distinction of time, but of nature.[191] He calls such acts "signs." Yet Pighius does not get that from the Holy Scriptures, but from Scotus.[192] In the first sign (Pighius says), God appointed to bring all men to eternal salvation, which they might enjoy together with him, and without any difference. He would have Christ to be their head over them. He believed that Christ would have come in the flesh even if the first man had not sinned.

In the second sign, he says, God foresaw the fall of man, so that it was not now possible that men should come to salvation, that is to the end that God had purposed in himself when he determined in the beginning to create man.

In order to have things proceed, he says, God established the third sign, the remedy in Christ, namely grace and the Spirit and such like, by which those who wish to receive them might be helped, and those who refused them would be abandoned.

Finally, in the fourth sign, foreseeing that many would embrace these aids and would use them well and effectively, he predestined them to salvation. Others who he saw would reject these divine benefits, he condemned to utter destruction. He says this about adults, but by this naive imagining he could not satisfy the question of infants who die before they have the use of free will, and so he patches together another fable to this.[193] That is, that after the judgment, they will be happy in this world through a natural blessedness, in which they will continually praise God and thank him for their acceptable state. So this man imagines a doctrine which he cannot prove by one word of Scripture. How did he attribute to God that in the first sign he decided about those things that will not happen, namely, that all men will enjoy happiness? It is the mark of a wise man, I will not say of God, to determine or to will things.

Let him also produce some oracles of God to show us that the Son of God would have assumed human flesh even if man had not sinned. He will not be able to show any such thing, since the Holy Scriptures everywhere teach that Christ was given for our redemption and for the remission of sins. This might have taught him something, if he had realized that original sin went before all the effects of predestination, with the sole exception of creation. Since Christ was

---

[191]For what follows, see Pighius, *De libero.*, fols. 122r–128v passim.

[192]Duns Scotus *Div. nat.* (PL 122.453, 705, 712, 764).

[193]On infants, see Gregory of Rimini, *Gregorii Ariminensis OESA Lectura super primum et secundum Sententiarum*, ed. A. Damasus Trapp and Venicio Marolinio, Spätmittelalter und Reformation Texte und Untersuchungen, vols. 6–12 (Berlin: De Gruyter, 1979–87), 1 sent. dist. 40–41, q. 1, art. 2 (3:326–27); cf. Frank A. James III, "A Late Medieval Parallel in Reformation Thought: *Gemina Praedestinatio* in Gregory of Rimini and Peter Martyr Vermigli" in *Via Augustini: The Recovery of Augustine in the Later Middle Ages, Renaissance and Reformation*, ed. Heiko A. Oberman and Frank A. James III (Leiden: Brill, 1991), 16.

predestined to this end and given to us so that we might have a remedy for our falls (for which original sin is the head and principal fact), Christ would not have assumed human flesh if no sin had been committed. He imagines, without the Scriptures, that it lies in the power of our free will to receive the remedies offered generally, since this is the highest gift of God.

What he brings finally, namely the natural happiness of children, is not only outside Scripture, but clearly against it, since it teaches that all perish in Adam unless they are renewed by the mediator. Everyone understands easily how inconsistent it is with happiness to perish or die. Also, he has not one of the fathers who dares imagine such wild devices. Nor can I be persuaded that Pelagius himself, if he were alive again, would color his opinion more diligently than this man has painted it and beautified it.

36. What we have proved above concerning predestination, namely, that it does not depend on foreseen good works, we also claim for reprobation, for it too does not depend on foreseen sins, if by reprobation you understand not ultimate damnation but that deep eternal purpose of God not to have mercy. Paul says of both Esau and Jacob, "Before they had done any good or ill, it was said: the elder shall serve the younger; Jacob have I loved, but Esau have I hated, that it should not be of works but of him that calls."[194] Pighius strives in vain to have this sentence of Paul understood of only one of them, that is of Jacob, seeing that the apostle joins both together under the same condition. Later he declares it most clearly saying: "He has mercy on whom he will, and whom he will he hardens."[195]

Further, if sin were the true cause of reprobation, then no one would be chosen, since God foreknows that all are defiled with it. Augustine proves the same thing to Simplicanus.

ARTICLE 3: THE EFFECTS OF PREDESTINATION

37. Now we will deal with the third article, so we may see the effects of predestination and of reprobation. We can be briefer, since what is to be said is clear from what has been said before. The first effect of predestination is Christ himself. The elect have none of the gifts of God unless given to them by our Savior. Let us also note those effects that Paul describes in Romans 8, when he says: "Whom he foreknew, those he also predestined; whom he predestined, those he also called; whom he called, those he justified; and whom he justified, those he

---

[194]Rom. 9:11.
[195]Rom. 9:18.

glorified."[196] From this it is clear that calling, justification, and glorification are effects of predestination, to which may be added conformity to the image of the Son of God, since Paul counts it as an effect of predestination. *[427]* Let us also add good works, since God is said to have prepared those who should walk in them.[197] Then follows the certainty or confirmation of our salvation. Last is a declaration of the riches of the glory of God, which Paul mentions explicitly in Romans 9, while to the Ephesians he writes, "That we might be to the praise of his grace and glory."[198]

Concerning reprobation, if it is related to the first man, God decreed from eternity to create him, that by means of free will and the giving of grace he could have stood, if he wished. God could have given him greater grace so that he would not have fallen, but he did not wish to do so. Whether Adam was in the number of the reprobate or the predestined cannot be determined from Scripture, although almost all the fathers agree that he was saved, and so belonged to the number of the predestined. Others who were reprobate appeared before God in a mass of perdition and utterly corrupted, for God decreed to produce them from the seed of Adam and not elsewhere.[199] Since by his free purpose he would not bestow his mercy on many, a complete refusal, and rejection, followed, by which they were left in the sin they were born with.

Furthermore, God does not allow his creatures to be idle; they are constantly prodded forward to work. Since they were not healed, they do everything according to their corrupt nature. Although at times such works seem to be attractive, yet before God they are sins. Moreover, since their evil acts deserve it, God often punishes them with other sins. For example, in the letter to the Romans, many are said to have been delivered to a reprobate mind, "for when they knew God, they did not glorify him as God."[200]

As to the sin of the first man, we should consider that this sin cannot be said to have been the punishment of another sin. If it was the first sin, there was no other sin before it. We cannot say absolutely that God did not will that sin, for how could it be committed against his will? He saw that Adam would fall if not sustained by his Spirit and with more abundant grace, but he did not help him or stretch out his hand to keep him from falling. Moreover, the devil would not have dared to tempt him if God had chosen otherwise. Also, he [God] had planned to declare his goodness and severity through Adam. He presented the opportunity to

[196]Rom. 8:28.
[197]Eph. 2:10.
[198]Rom. 9:12; Eph. 1:6.
[199]On the *massa perditionis*, see §11, p. 19, above.
[200]Rom. 1:21, 25.

sin when he issued a law which he knew would not be kept and also gave him a wife who would tempt him. Finally, the occasion itself (as a subject or event that sustained the lack of righteousness) could not have occurred without the power and might of God. Thus it is evident that in a sense God willed that sin and was in a way its author, even though it was not the punishment for a previous sin. On the other hand, he is said not to have willed it and not to have been its author, since he prohibited and punished it and did not will it absolutely, except for another purpose. He did not suggest it himself, nor inspire the evil; but Adam's will, not being prevented by a stronger grace, fell from righteousness of his own accord.

Isaiah also identifies an effect of reprobation, namely that God will blind and harden the heart of the people, so that they would not understand. God often sends thoughts and offers occasions, by himself or by evil angels, which would be for the best if we were righteous, but since we are not renewed, they drive us to evil, and afterwards, damnation for sins follows, justly and rightly. Finally, the declaration of the power and justice of God is the last effect of reprobation. All these things follow reprobation, although as we stated before, God is not equally the cause of them all.

Is Grace Universal?

38. Since all the benefits of God given to the predestined are referred to grace as to their head and fountain, let us see whether that principal effect of God's predestination is, as some have imagined, established by God as common to all. If it were so, then all would be predestined and it would lie in their own power or their own hands (as the saying is) to be predestined, so that they would receive grace when it is offered.

We do not say that grace is common to all, but is given to some and not to others, according to the pleasure of God. To confirm this point we bring forth the following passages of Scripture. In John 6, it is said, "No one comes to me unless my Father draws him."[201] I wonder why opponents say that all are drawn to God but all will not come? As if to say no one can credit himself with education in fine arts who is not endowed with reason and sense, yet it does not follow that while everyone has reason and sense all should master the fine arts, since besides those principles, study and determination are required.

So they say that all are drawn by God, but besides being drawn by God, it is required that we are willing and give assent; otherwise we are not brought to Christ. Certainly it cannot be that in all those statements there are no exceptions; if so, then the exception should apply to everyone. Christ says to Pilate, "You

---

[201]John 6:44.

would not have power over men unless it were given you from above."[202] Shall we take it on ourselves to say that power over Christ was given to all? And when it is written, "No one shall enter the kingdom of heaven unless he is born again by water and the Spirit,"[203] should we then infer that all are born again of water and the Spirit? And when the Lord said, "You will not have life in you, unless you eat the flesh of the Son of Man, *[428]* and drink his blood,"[204] shall we take it that all men eat the flesh and drink the Lord's blood? If this is not the case, why do these men infer that all are drawn to the Father when we say, "No one comes to me unless my Father draw him?"

If you consider the intent of the text, you will see that this interpretation cannot stand. After he had mentioned the eating of his flesh and drinking of his blood, the Jews were offended by it, and the disciples went their way. Christ said, "No one comes to me unless my Father draws him." He should not have said this if he had meant to reprove only unbelievers. Clearly he should not have mentioned the Father as though he did not draw them, if he gave that gift to everyone. When Augustine interprets this passage he says: "When he draws this man and does not draw that other man, do not judge if you do not want to fall into error."[205] By these words he declares that all are not drawn by God.

It is written in the same chapter, "All that my Father gives me will come to me." If all were drawn they would all come to Christ. In the same place it is written, "Everyone who has heard and learned from my Father comes to me."[206] Since many do not come to Christ, it is said that many have not heard or learned. And in chapter 10, when Christ had said that he is the shepherd and has his own sheep, he says among other things, "Those whom my Father has given me no one can snatch out of my hands."[207] We see that many fall from salvation, and so we must conclude that they are not given by the Father to Christ.

39. Here too the adversaries claim that while no one can draw them away, they may, however, depart of their own accord. It is as if someone with servants, a lord of great power, might say, "No one can take these servants from me, yet on their own they may go away." The futility of their objection is shown by the words that follow. Christ adds: "The Father who gave them to me is greater than all."[208]

---

[202]John 19:11.
[203]John 5:15.
[204]John 6:53.
[205]Augustine *Ad simp.* 1, Q. 2, 12 (PL 40.118–19).
[206]John 6:44, 46.
[207]John 10:28.
[208]John 10:29.

He states here that those he has received from the Father could not be taken away from him, since he is almighty. Therefore, if those who are in Christ cannot be taken away by others, neither are they able to withdraw themselves. It is not that they are compelled by force, but it is necessary by way of persuasion that they remain. The Lord said the same thing regarding the temptation of the latter days: "If it were possible, the elect would be deceived."[209]

In the same John 6, Christ says that no one comes to him except those who are given by the Father, which has the same sense as that other saying, "No one comes to me unless my Father draws him."[210] In John 3, it is written that John the Baptist, on hearing from his disciples that Christ baptized many, answered, "No one can receive anything unless it has been granted from heaven," and in the same chapter, "The Spirit blows where it wills."[211] While this is spoken about the wind, yet it is applied to the Holy Spirit, who regenerates. The simile is taken from the nature of the wind to show the power of the Holy Spirit.

This is more clearly set down in Matthew when it is said: "No one knows the Father except the Son, and anyone to whom the Son wills to reveal him."[212] This passage teaches us that the revelation of Christ is not given to all. Christ repeats this in the same Gospel. Turning to the Father, he said, "I give you thanks O king of heaven and earth, that you have hidden these things from the wise and understanding and have revealed them to babes."[213] This also shows that true doctrine is not revealed to everyone, but if you say that it is not revealed to the wise because they will not receive it, the words that follow do not support you. Rather they declare that God's will has decreed it so, for it follows, "For so it has pleased you." Again, when the apostles asked why he [Christ] spoke to the people in parables, he replied: "To you it has been granted to know the mysteries, but to them it is not given."[214] He said he spoke like this so that seeing they might not see, and hearing they should not understand. He cites a prophecy from Isaiah 6, where it is commanded that the people should be made blind and their heart hard, lest perhaps they should be converted and God should heal them.[215]

Moreover, the apostle cites from the book of Exodus, "I will have mercy on whom I will have mercy and I will have compassion on whom I will have compassion." And in the same chapter, Paul says: "Pharaoh, for this reason I raised you

---

[209]Matt. 24:24.
[210]John 6:37, 44.
[211]John 3:8, 27.
[212]Matt. 11:27.
[213]Matt. 11:25.
[214]Matt. 13:11.
[215]Isa. 6:9.

up, that I might show my power in you." He also says that some vessels are made to honor and some to dishonor.[216] These words quite clearly show that grace is not offered equally to all.

Peter, too, said to Simon Magus in the Acts of the Apostles, "Repent, if perhaps God will forgive you this thought."[217] Opponents say that here Peter did not doubt that grace is common to all, but was uncertain whether Simon would receive it and earnestly repent. This subtle shift is of no help, for as the apostle teaches Timothy, even repentance is the gift of God. He admonishes a bishop to hold fast to sound doctrine and to reprove those who resist, "if perhaps God may grant them repentance."[218] From this we conclude that it does not lie in the hands of all men to return to the right path, unless it is given to them by God.

Further, some sin against the Holy Spirit and are not pardoned either in this world or in the world to come. So it is clear that to them grace is no longer set forth nor is it common. In the Acts of the Apostles God is said to have opened the heart of the woman who sold silk, *[429]* to give heed to those things which Paul said. This is described as something peculiarly given to that woman.[219] This passage makes plain what is written in the Apocalypse, "Behold I stand at the door and knock; if anyone opens to me," and so forth.[220] We are said to open inasmuch as God works this in us, for he makes us open and it is he who moves us to work out our salvation as it is said to the Philippians.[221] And it is often written in the Gospel, "many are called but few are chosen."[222] Paul proclaims the liberty of the Spirit in distributing his gifts when he says to the Corinthians, "One and the same Spirit distributes to all men as it pleases him."[223] Although this may be understood of charisms and free gifts (as they call them), still it may be transferred no less to the grace by which we are renewed unto salvation, since God is as free in the one as in the other.

40. Last, while these men make grace common to all, they convert it into nature, which in no way agrees with the teaching of Scripture. How much they are deceived may be easily proved. From these arguments they wish to establish that it lies in everyone's power to receive grace when it is offered them, which does not agree at all with the Holy Scriptures, for Paul says, "We are unable to think

---

[216]Rom. 9:15 (Exod. 33:19); Rom. 17:22. (Exod. 9:16).
[217]Acts 8:22.
[218]2 Tim. 2:25.
[219]Acts 16:14.
[220]Rev. 3:20.
[221]Phil. 2:13.
[222]Matt. 20:16.
[223]1 Cor. 12:11.

anything in ourselves, but all our sufficiency is of God." To the Philippians he writes, "God works in us both to will and to work according to his goodwill."[224] To the Corinthians, when he had said he had labored much, he added, "Not I, but the grace of God that is in me." He also writes in this letter, "So then it does not depend on the man who wills or the man who runs but on God who has mercy."[225] This could not be true if it lies within our will to receive grace when offered.

Augustine says to Simplicianus, in book 1, question 2, "The meaning of those words is not as though it is not sufficient for us to choose unless God helps us with his grace, for then he might have said on the contrary, 'it is not of God who has mercy but of man who wills,' but the meaning is what is written to the Philippians, that it is God who works in us to will and to work."[226] It is true that we choose in vain unless God has mercy and helps us, but who will say that God has mercy in vain, if we do not choose? In the prophet Ezekiel it is said that God himself would change our hearts and instead of stony hearts would give us hearts of flesh.[227] And David sings in the Psalm, "Incline my heart, O God, to your testimonies," so as to show that bending our wills has to do with God. He asserts the same elsewhere saying, "Create in me a clean heart O God."[228] It is written in the Book of Wisdom, "No one can have a chaste heart, but he to whom God shall give it."[229] Christ taught quite clearly that an evil tree cannot bear good fruit; therefore, so long as men are not regenerate they cannot bring forth fruit good enough to enable them to assent to God's grace when it knocks. It is first necessary that the tree be changed and evil trees turned into good. As in human generation, no one who is procreated contributes anything to it. So also is it in regeneration, for there also we are born again through Christ and in Christ.

If we were to acknowledge the view of these adversaries, then all boasting would not be excluded, because each one might boast of his own actions by which he received grace when it was offered. This apprehension is by faith according to our view, but our opponents think it is by charity. What will they do? Will they deny that faith and love are gifts of God? Augustine also argues that just as in Christ the divine nature took human nature freely, not waiting for its consent, so those who are justified are not justified by their own will or assent. The same father also notes that in the Scriptures eternal life is sometimes called by the name of reward, since good works precede it; but grace and righteousness,

---

[224]2 Cor. 3:5; Phil. 2:12–13.
[225]1 Cor. 15:10; Rom. 9:16.
[226]Phil. 2:13; Augustine *Ad simp.* 1, Q. 2, 12 (PL 40.118).
[227]Ezek. 11:19.
[228]Ps. 51:10; 116:36.
[229]Ecclus. 8:21.

he says, are never called by the name of reward in Scripture, because no good work that precedes is acceptable to God.[230] Paul says to the Romans, "I know that nothing good dwells in me, that is, in my flesh."[231] He understands by "flesh" whatever is in those who are unregenerate. They dare even to attribute to someone unregenerate and still living in the flesh so much good that he is able to apply salvation to himself.

To the Corinthians, Paul says, "What do you have that you did not receive? But if you have received it, why do you boast as if you had not received it?"[232] We will not allow these men to fly to the creation, for we do not speak here of the soul or its powers, that is, of the will or understanding which we have from God in creation. Rather, we refer to that act or work of receiving grace, which they seek to find in free will. Insofar as they say this is of themselves, they speak against the apostle. The Corinthians might have answered: You ask what has separated us and what do we have that we have not received? See, now we show you that act and assent by which we freely, and by our own power, receive the grace which you preach to us. This separates us from others. So Paul would have reproved them for nothing. Moreover, if grace is proposed as common to all, as these men teach, why should we pray to God for the conversion of unbelievers? Certainly, we do so because we believe that it lies in the hand of God to open their hearts, if he will.

Is Grace Sufficient?

41. We must not think, as these men imagine, that God gives to every man so much grace as is sufficient to move them. If that were sufficient, then every man would certainly be moved. *[430]* If some huge weight were set before someone, and if he was willing to move it and had in him as much strength as was sufficient, that is, enough to overcome the weight to be moved, then doubtless movement would follow. So if God (as they say) would move the hearts of the wicked and give enough strength, that is, enough grace, so as to exceed the hardness of the wicked heart, then nothing could prevent the heart from being bent—not by compulsion, but by most effectual persuasion. Augustine writes to Simplicianus in book 1, question 2, that there are two kinds of calling, one by which men are called in common, but not in such a way as to be moved and converted. Others are called as they are inclined to be moved. He says we must not think that God could not have called Esau, for he might have been moved and made ready, but all men are not moved and drawn to God in the same way.[233]

---

[230]Probably a reference to Augustine *Praed.* 7.6 (PL 44.955).
[231]Rom. 7:18.
[232]1 Cor. 4:7.
[233]Augustine *Ad simp.* 1.2.13 (PL 40.118–19), about the elect who are *congruenter vocati*.

Inasmuch as God is omnipotent, he could by his impulse take away the natural hardness. They say that if God wanted he could, but that he will not always do what he is able to do. Let it be so. We say the same thing, that God passes over (*praeteri*) some, and will not have mercy on them. Therefore, he does not give to all men as much [mercy] as is needed for their salvation. As for those he passes over, he attains the end he wills, as it was written about Pharaoh: "For this purpose have I raised you up, to show my power in you, and that my name might be proclaimed throughout the whole earth."[234]

Christ knew very well, as he himself testified, that Tyre, Sidon, and Sodom would have been moved to repentance if he had shown them the miracles and teaching he gave to the Jews.[235] Therefore, since he did not give them those things, they lacked what was necessary for salvation. The Lord also said to the apostles, "You did not choose me, but I have chosen you."[236] But in the opinion of my adversaries, who assume universal grace, no one should be chosen by God, for God should exist in the same way for all, that is, we should choose God by receiving his grace when offered. In that case, we become the shapers of God's election, instead of being shaped by him.

Paul says, "I planted, Apollos has watered, but God gave the increase,"[237] that is, life and Spirit, but if those things are given to everyone, Paul should have said, "you have taken for yourselves the Spirit, life, and grace." The apostle says in the Philippians that God began a good work and would perform it until the day of the Lord.[238] These words plainly declare that all is to be ascribed to God, both the beginning and the completion. And to the Ephesians it is written, "He works all things according to the counsel of his will,"[239] not "according to the counsel of another's will," which he would have said if everyone had it in his power to take salvation or not. Again, to the Galatians he says, "When it seemed good to him, he set me apart even from my mother's womb."[240] If it were as these men say, Paul should have said, "when it seemed good to me," for in respect to God, they hold that grace is always ready and offered to all. By their opinion, conversion should then come when it pleases us.

---

[234]Rom. 9:17.
[235]Matt. 11:21–24.
[236]John 15:16.
[237]1 Cor. 3:6.
[238]Phil. 1:6.
[239]Eph. 1:11.
[240]Gal. 1:15.

42. I think these considerations are enough at this time, although many more might be brought. It remains only to overthrow those reasons which seem to count against us. Before we get into that further, we in no way deny that God calls all men by an outward calling, namely, through his prophets, apostles, preachers, and Scriptures. One man is no more excluded from the promises or warnings than another, for they are set forth to all alike, although all are not predestined to attain to their fruit. This is to be diligently noted if we will answer objections easily. When they charge us, as they often do, that the promises are common and universally proposed, it must be kept back from this or that man, and that God does not toy with men, but acts in earnest.

Concerning universality, I will bring forward other propositions no less general. "All flesh shall see the salvation of God; all shall be taught of God; all shall know me, from the least to the greatest; I will pour out my Spirit on all flesh."[241] Shall we say that these things are true for all men? Not unless Origen's fable be revived, namely, that all men shall be saved in the end.[242] Opponents will answer that these propositions should be confined to believers and those who are willing and who respect the grace of God. We also say that they are to be confined, but we place our confinement farther off, and ascend to the election of God and to reprobation. Which solution, I ask, is the more perfect and which confinement more equitable? We do not say that God toys with men in these universal promises. Insofar as the predestined and the reprobate live their lives together, they are not distinguished from one another. It is right that preaching should be directed to all, lest the elect, who will profit from the preaching of God's Word, should be defrauded because of the reprobate. By this universal preaching God brings about that end which he himself wills, for when the godly see that the reprobate are left to their own senses and do not believe, they understand that it is grace and not nature. They see what would have happened without the mercy of God, whose conversion is a gift and not in human power. The ungodly are made inexcusable when they have not even performed those outward works they might have done, as is declared to the Romans in chapters 1 and 2.

43. First, the adversaries imagine that they are declaring the mercy of God, because they make it common to all, but if we consider the matter more closely, *[431]* we attribute much more to mercy than they do. We affirm that everything

---

[241]Luke 2:6; John 6:45; Jer. 31:34; Joel 2:28.

[242]Origen's doctrine of *apokatastasis,* or the restoration of all things through successive aeons, *Prin.* 2.10.8 (PG 11.240).

depends on it, something they deny, because they think it is in our power to receive God's grace. If we say that mercy is not equally distributed to all, we cannot be reproved, since the Scriptures clearly teach this, but when they say that it lies in our own will to receive grace, even though they qualify it, yet it is surely proved to be of significance. What profit is it to have grace universally set forth to all unless someone by his own power will apply it to himself? Therefore, let them stop adorning their opinion with the name of God's mercy.

Second, they bring another argument: Inasmuch as God provides things necessary for bodily life for everyone, it is unlikely that he will fail to provide them with the preparation for eternal salvation, which would not be the case unless enough of God's grace were offered to everyone. In this reasoning they are rebutted by a simile. Since God gives corporeal life to every mortal without human assent, so they must conclude about the spiritual life, something they refuse to grant at all. We admit indeed that through his mercy God causes the sun to rise on the good and the evil. We also admit that both the predestined and the reprobate are partakers of some of the benefits of God. Just as in this life the commodities of the body and of life are not evenly given to all, so also predestination to eternal happiness is not common to all. Some are born leprous, blind, deaf, foolish, very poor, and quite unfit for all sorts of natural happiness, nor do they achieve it at any time. Thus the comparison they bring counts strongly against them.

Adversaries say that God has created all men in his own image and thus has appointed them all to blessedness. Therefore, we should not say that some are predestined and some are reprobate. We also grant that men are made in the image of God and capable of blessedness; but after the fall nature was corrupted and the image was badly blemished, so that men cannot by themselves attain happiness, but need to be delivered from misery. The Scriptures do not teach that God has decided to deliver all men from misery and to make them blessed through Christ. Therefore, we do not say without just cause that God rightly decreed to deliver some and to leave some others. The causes of this justice are not to be sought by our works, seeing that they are known to God alone through his hidden and unspeakable wisdom.

44. They bring this from John: "He gave them power to become sons of God."[243] They infer from this that everyone may become a son of God if he will. But they pay no attention to what follows, for it is added: "to those who have believed in him, who are born not of blood, nor of the will of the flesh, nor of the will of man, but of God." If these things are rightly understood, they state that this

[243]John 1:12.

dignity and privilege are given to the believer and the regenerate. To have the power to be sons of God means nothing else. Therefore, this dignity is an effect of regeneration and faith, not its beginning as they dream.

They also grant that "Christ died for us all"[244] and infer from this that his benefits are common to everyone. We gladly grant this, too, if we are considering only the worthiness of the death of Christ, for it might be sufficient for all the world's sinners. Yet even if in itself it is enough, yet it did not have, nor has, nor will have effect in all men. The Scholastics also acknowledge the same thing when they affirm that Christ has redeemed all men sufficiently but not effectually.[245] It is necessary that the death of Christ be useful for us and that we take hold of it, which can only be done by faith. We have earlier sufficiently showed it to be the gift of God and not given to all.

It is also objected against us that the apostle compared Adam with Christ and said to the Romans that just as we all die in Adam, so in Christ we are all made alive.[246] By this means they say that the grace of Christ should be open to all universally. If they take this comparison in this way, they will also be compelled to grant that all will be brought to eternal life by Christ, just as all are thrown headlong into sin and death by Adam. Seeing that the subject shows the opposite, they may easily see that this likeness is not to be taken as relevant in all its details, especially since no one falls into original sin of his own consent. They will have it that grace is not accepted except by one's own consent. If they then admit this difference, how dare they claim that things are the same on each side?

The apostle's aim (*scopus*) is to be considered in this comparison; nothing is to be inferred outside his aim. In that comparison, Paul meant nothing else but that to the regenerate Christ is the beginning of life and blessedness, just as Adam is the cause of death and sin to those who came from him. Now whatever else is deduced besides this point, whether it concerns the equality of the many, or the means, it is *per accidens*, that is, by chance, and does not relate to the scope and substance of the simile.

45. They also put forward the statement to Timothy, "God will have all men to be saved."[247] Pighius regularly repeats this passage *[432]* as if it were invincible. Yet Augustine often taught that it may be expounded in such a way that it lends no weight at all to prove their fond invention.[248] First, we take it to be spoken of all

[244]1 Tim. 2:6.

[245]See *Magistri Petri Lombardi Parisiensis episcopi Sententiae in IV libris distinctae 3.20.5* (Grottaferrata: Collegii S. Bonaventurae ad Claras Aquas, 1971–81), 2:128 (PL 192.799).

[246]Rom. 5:17.

[247]1 Tim. 2:4.

states and kinds of men, that is, that God will have some of all kinds of men to be saved. This interpretation agrees perfectly well with the purpose of the apostle. He had instituted that prayers and supplications should be made for all men, especially kings and those in public authority, so that under them we may live a quiet life in all piety and chastity.[249] Therefore, to declare that no state or kind of person is excluded, he added, "God will have all men to be saved." It is as if he had said that no one is prevented by that calling and level in which he is placed, so long as it is not repugnant to the word of God, but that he may come to salvation; therefore, we should pray for all kinds of men. Yet we cannot infer from this that God endows everyone in particular with grace, or predestines everyone to salvation. Similarly, in the time of the flood, all living creatures are said to have been saved in the ark with Noah, but only some of every kind were gathered together in it.

Or we may understand it like this: God will have all men to be saved, for as many as are saved, they are saved by his will. It is as if one should say of a teacher of rhetoric in a city that he teaches all men. This kind of speech does not mean that all the citizens are hearers of rhetoric, but that as many as learn are taught by him. It is also like someone pointing to the gate of a house and saying that everyone enters this way. We must not understand from this that everyone enters that house, but that as many as enter do so by way of that gate alone.

Third, there are some who interpret these words of the apostle as referring to the signified will or antecedent will, that all men are invited since preaching is set forth to all indifferently.[250] No one fails inwardly to feel some spur by which he is continually stirred up to do well. Thus if we relate this to the will of God, we will easily grant that he will have all men to be saved.

They will not have it to be understood of the hidden and effective will which they call the consequent will. In this way one may understand such speech as "God illumines every man who comes into this world" and "Come unto me all who are weary and heavy laden,"[251] for all are provoked by the oracles of God and all are inwardly moved by some spur.

All these interpretations are quite probable and also fitting, yet beside these there is another, both ready and plain. The Holy Scriptures set forth two human societies: one of the godly and the other of the ungodly. Both societies have universal propositions attached which should be restricted to their own category by the careful reader. The prophets say, and Christ cites them: "All shall be taught by

---

[248]Augustine *Corrept.* 14.44 (PL 44.943); idem, *Ep.* 217.6.19 (PL 33.985–86); idem, *C. Jul.* 8.42 (PL 44.759–60), idem, *Praed.* 8.14 (PL 44.971).

[249]1 Tim. 2:1–2.

[250]On divine willing, see §31 above.

[251]John 1:9; Matt. 11:21.

God (*theodidaktos*) and all shall know me from the least to the greatest"; and again he says, "When I shall be lifted up from the earth, I will draw all things to myself."[252] Unless these universal propositions refer to the godly who are elected, they are not true. This is also true of these passages: "I will pour out my Spirit on all flesh" and "All flesh shall come in my sight and shall worship in Jerusalem," and again, "All flesh shall see the salvation of God," and finally, "God lifts up all who fall."[253] Who does not see that these passages are to be understood only of the saints?

In contrast, these following passages refer to the ungodly: "No one receives his testimony" yet many believed, and "You will be hated by all." Again it is stated, "They all seek after their own interests"; and "They have all turned aside together; they have become corrupt. There is no one who does good, not even one."[254] Those who are pious and regenerate are acceptable to God and endeavor to show him some obedience to the law, but these universal sayings should not be extended beyond their own society.

Augustine had this distinction in mind in his book *The City of God*, where he proves that there have always been two cities, one the city of God and the other the city of the devil. Therefore, in these general propositions we must always give due consideration as to which class or group of men they refer. If we do so here, we will apply the statement to the saints and the elect, namely, that "God will have all men to be saved," and so all doubt is removed. Otherwise, it seems that God does not effectively will the salvation of all men, as is demonstrated by the many infants who have perished without Christ and many also which have been born fools, and deaf, and never had the right and proper use of reason. It often happens that some have had long lives, honest and faithful enough, and yet suddenly fall at last and are taken out of the world to perish eternally.

Others, on the contrary, who have perpetually led a life of wickedness, are at the end of their lives endowed with faith and repentance and are saved. Yet they might have been taken away first, so that evil would not have changed their minds. Who will in these examples say that God wills the salvation of all with the same effectiveness?

46. They bring up a saying of Christ's: "How often would I have gathered your children together as a hen gathers her chicks, and you would not?"[255] Here also it is the antecedent will of the sign that is meant. God through his prophets,

---

[252]John 6:45; Jer. 31:33.
[253]Joel 2:28; Isa. 66:23; Luke 3:6; Ps. 145:14.
[254]John 3:32; Matt. 10:22; Phil. 2:21; Ps. 14:3.
[255]Matt. 23:37.

preachers, apostles, and Scriptures invited the Jews to fly to him by repentance time after time, but they refused, but *[433]* by his effective will, which is called consequent, he always drew to himself those who were his.[256] Nor was there any age when he did not gather as many of the Hebrews as he had predestined. Therefore, as Augustine said, those that I would, I have gathered together, although you would not.[257]

They think that what is written at the beginning of the letter to the Romans concerning the Gentiles supports their side. Concerning those who were "without excuse," they say that this could not have been said unless everyone was given enough grace and help as was sufficient for salvation. It should be noted that the apostle is concerned only with knowledge in this passage, that is, the Gentiles could not excuse their sins because they did not have a law given to them from God as had the Jews. Clearly, God had not opened himself to them in the way he had for the Jewish people. "You know God," he says, "by his creatures and by the light of nature: you did not lack the knowledge of right and wrong; therefore, you are without excuse."[258] We must not think that this passage extends farther than Paul intended. If one weighs the matter carefully, he will see that pagans and ungodly men, against whom the apostle writes, did not think they lacked the strength to perform those things they knew to be upright, inasmuch as they ascribed all things to free will. So the apostle well decides against them, as if he had said: Do you think you have enough strength, so that you judge that you have no need of Christ? But since I have proved that you did not lack knowledge and yet have lived wickedly, I conclude that you are without excuse.

Further, infirmity and lack of ability do not excuse, since we do not have strength in ourselves by creation and our original constitution, for it was brought into the human race by the fall and sin through the first man. The pagans also were without excuse, for they did not achieve in civil justice what they had in them to do. Therefore, nothing can be inferred from this passage that can prove the view of the adversaries.

They think that this also supports their view: "Is God the God of the Jews only and not also of the Gentiles? Yes, of the Gentiles also."[259] They work hard to infer from this passage that God gives enough to all men since he is the God of all, but they should consider that in this passage, Paul is reproving the Jews for thinking that God's benevolence and grace was owed to them so that the Gentiles were completely excluded. So he declared that God had not only elected some of the

---

[256]See §11 (1), p. 20, above.
[257]Augustine *Persev.* (PL 44.568/898?) and *Ep.* 186 (PL 33.827?).
[258]Rom. 1:20.
[259]Rom. 3:29.

Jews, but also had his elect among the Gentiles. It does not necessarily follow that all the Gentiles should be given grace sufficient for salvation, when not even all the Jews were partakers of such grace. We do not deny that God is God of all. We know that even the wicked, whether they will or not, are subject to him, nor can they avoid his providence. Although he does not bring them to eternal salvation, at least he punishes them as they deserve, but he is particularly said to be the God of those whom he has allowed to acknowledge him as their God, and having acknowledged him, to worship him.

47. The passage written to Timothy seems more difficult, where God is called the Savior of all, especially of the faithful.[260] Here the word *sotêr*, that is "Savior," is not to be taken as though God gives eternal salvation to everyone, but meaning that God preserves and defends all men from many evils which the devil would otherwise practice against them. So great is the devil's rage against mankind that if not restrained by God he would destroy everything. He would allow no commonwealth or church, but would bring to nothing both goods and all things that pertain to human life. Therefore, God is the Savior of all in that he drives away such great evils from us. Regarding eternal salvation, that is to be understood of the elect alone and so it is added, "especially of the faithful." Since they are predestined, they above all others attain this benefit.

They also twist something from the prophet Isaiah that Paul has cited a little later in the same letter: "All day long I have stretched out my hands to a disobedient and obstinate people."[261] They gain nothing else from this place other than what has been said many times, namely, that God universally invites all men, that the prophets were sent indiscriminately to all, and that the Scriptures are given to all, but this says nothing about the efficacy of grace, of which we speak. We also grant that he stands at the door and knocks, and indeed will enter if any man will let him.[262] They should add that there is no one who can open the door himself. It is first necessary that the goodness of God be given to him who knocks.

To commend the divine mercy they bring forward the words of Isaiah: "Though a mother can forget her children, yet I will not forget you."[263] Surely this passage has little or nothing to do with the issue at hand. No one denies that God is constant of faith and stands by his promises and covenants. In that place God makes the pledge that he will not forget his promise. We have also taught generally that God's predestination is quite certain, so that whether this passage in

---

[260] 1 Tim. 4:10.
[261] Isa. 65:2; Rom. 10:11.
[262] Rev. 3:20.
[263] Isa. 49:15.

Isaiah is understood of predestination or of the covenants and promises, it does not follow that it pertains to all.

Pighius cannot abide what both Augustine and we ourselves say, namely, that the reprobate serve the purpose of God to promote and demonstrate the strength of God's wrath. He says that God has no need of such cruel behavior to exalt his name. He tries to prove his point from a passage in the book of Ecclesiasticus,[264] *[434]* but that should be interpreted to mean that none of us ought to think that God needs human works. God's felicity is perfect and absolute without the aid and help of any creature. Who dares to deny that the justice of God is manifested by the unfaithfulness and wickedness of men, while God takes vengeance on them, when Paul teaches that quite evidently and plainly?

He also cites from the same book of Ecclesiasticus, "God has mercy upon all men, and winks at the sins of all men, because of repentance."[265] The solution to this objection appears clearly by the words cited, that is, the words refer to the universality of the elect. Winking at sins does not lead the wicked to aspire to repentance; rather, they become daily worse and worse, falling headlong into more grievous sins. It is the predestined only who return again to the right way after God has been patient with them.

48. Now I will finish my response to objections and bring an end to the third article. Meanwhile, we bid you recall that the reprobate may sometimes and to some degree produce good works, and on the other hand, the predestined may sometimes fall into grave sins. On the first part, Saul may be for us an example and firm witness. At the outset he was moderate and had a modest opinion of himself, as Scripture says.[266] Solomon also fell grievously in his later years. He fell away from God, but at the beginning he was most holy. When he was consecrated his prayers were most pleasing to God; therefore, his prayers were heard.[267] Ahab also repented, a repentance God commended when speaking with Elijah.[268] And Joash the king, so long as Jehoiada the priest lived, behaved himself well.[269] Ezekiel also teaches this same thing when he writes, "If a righteous man turns away from his righteousness and lives sinfully, I will forget all his righteousness."[270] Experience itself shows that many have lived lives of integrity, yet at length, in the

---

[264]Pighius, *De libero,* fol. 121r–v.
[265]Ecclus. 17:29?
[266]1 Sam. 9:21.
[267]1 Kings 11:4.
[268]1 Kings 21:29.
[269]2 Kings 12:2.
[270]Ezek. 18:24.

last days of their life, they perish. Therefore, it is clear that good works sometimes have a place in the reprobate, yet they do not come from a sincere and perfect faith, but from a faith that endures only for a time. Therefore, they cannot be said simply to be good, nor do they in fact please God, but having only a show of goodness, they are praised for their outward discipline.

David is an example that the predestined sometimes gravely sin, for he committed adultery and murder. Peter is also an example of one who betrayed his Savior. Moses and Aaron also are examples of persons who the Scriptures tell us committed no small sins.[271] We see daily that those who are perhaps in the number of the predestined fall into horrible crimes. Therefore, we may say that good works sometimes serve predestination and sometimes reprobation. Predestination with [good works] brings the elect into eternal life, but with regard to the reprobate, they are sometimes reasons why the fall becomes all the more serious. For those who fall away from God, inasmuch as they were adorned with good works by him, their sin is the greater and so their punishment is more severe.

Sins also serve both predestination and for reprobation. They bring those who are reprobate to eternal destruction, while those who are predestined illustrate the glory of God by their sins, when they are delivered from them. Therefore, their sins provide ample opportunities to know themselves and to acknowledge the benefits that are given to them by God. So they give thanks for them and call on him for help. We should not conclude from these examples that since God by his perfect wisdom uses these things rightly for our salvation, we should then sin. We must follow Holy Scripture which commands that "Evil things are not to be done so that good may come from them."[272]

ARTICLE 4: THE NECESSITY OF PREDESTINATION

49. Now at last let us come to the fourth article, in which we intend to treat three things especially: First, whether any necessity is laid on us by God's predestination or reprobation. Second, if there is any necessity, does it hinder free will? Last, whether God's foreknowledge or predestination takes away his justice, through which Scripture says he renders to every man according to his works.[273] Once these matters are fully discussed, I trust the article will be quite resolved.

---

[271]2 Sam. 11; Matt. 26:74; Exod. 2:12, 32:21.
[272]Rom. 3:8.
[273]Rom. 2:6.

Is Necessity Imposed upon Us?

Earlier in the first part, we said that necessity is to be defined as that which cannot be otherwise; but the principles or grounds of necessity are sometimes intrinsic and sometimes extrinsic. Things that are inherently necessary by an internal principle are either necessary absolutely (*simpliciter*), or are such that they cannot be changed without contradiction (as they say). For example, that four is not an even number or that four and three are not seven: this is called geometrical necessity, for it permits no variety. Other things are of intrinsic necessity, yet not absolutely and simply, unless they follow the regular course of nature. Fire is said to burn necessarily things that are suitable to be burned and it is necessary that the sun moves perpetually, but this is not simple necessity, for God is able to prevent them and to cause physical and natural things at times to cease from their proper operation. This is clear from the three children put in the fiery furnace, who were not burned even though the flame was very great. Also, the sun strayed from its course while Joshua pursued his enemies.[274] And in the time of Elijah it is most likely that moisture was being drawn from the earth and from the sea, yet for all that, for the space of three years, neither dew nor rain came down from the clouds.[275] It is also clear concerning Ezekiel, his disease was by nature terminal.[276] These examples will suffice regarding intrinsic necessity.

Extrinsic necessity (*necessitate exterius*) is of two kinds. *[435]* One is violent, when things are compelled to work against their nature. The other is hypothetical. The Scholastics have said that there is a necessity of consequence and another of the consequent.[277] By this distinction they mean that the connection is sometimes necessary, although what is inferred is not itself necessary. The Logicians have also distinguished them in this way, calling the one a compound sense, the other a divided sense.[278] If you would say that it is impossible for white to be black, that would be granted. If these two are taken in conjunction and together, that is, if the same thing should be both black and

---

[274]Dan. 3; Josh. 10:12.

[275]1 Kings 17:1.

[276]1 Kings 10:1.

[277]*Necessitas consequentiae, necessitas consequentis*: see Martyr, "Does Providence Allow Any Contingency in Things?" PW, 192ff., and "Free Will," PW, 279–80. Cf. CAS, 140ff., "Human Freedom and Predestination," for an excellent summary of Vermigli's logical categories. Donnelly writes, "Martyr feels it necessary to review the various kinds of necessities. His review is intricate and scholastic" (141). To summarize: intrinsic necessity is mathematical/physical; extrinsic necessity is violent/hypothetical; hypothetical necessity is consequence/consequents and composite/divided. "Martyr, however, prefers a distinction of his own as a solution. He distinguishes the necessity of coaction or coercion from the necessity of infallibility or of certainty." Thus the human will "is subject to the hypothetical necessity—it is conditioned by God's foreknowledge and predestination … the necessity lies in the connection of divine predestination with human acts" (142).

[278]*Sensus compositum, sensus divisum.*

white, this is by no means possible, but if they are taken separately, then it may not be impossible, since something now white may be changed and made black. The Scholastics think that the whole difficulty of this controversy consists in the necessity of the consequence and the necessity of the consequent in the compound sense, but to clarify things we will add another distinction: that there is one necessity of certainty and another of compulsion.[279]

50. Now let us more closely search out how those distinctions of necessity may be applied to the present purpose. First, our actions have no intrinsic necessity. Willing is of its own nature (as God created it), mutable and flexible to either side. It has a hypothetical necessity. As soon as you consider the foreknowledge and predestination of God, it follows of necessity that it will come about just as God foreknows and predestines it. Our will does have an aptitude to be bent in either direction, but the act of conversion does not possess it, except in the direction God has foreknown. Therefore, the necessity falls on the connection and conjunction of God's predestination with our works, by which they mean the compound sense and the necessity of consequence, for if our works are considered separately and in regard only to their closest origin, namely, the will, they are necessary.

Here there is also acknowledged a necessity of certainty or of infallibility, for God can never be changed or deceived. Nor do we grant that predestination brings any necessity of compulsion, for compulsion and violence are against the nature of the will. If the will should do anything unwillingly it would not be called will but "nil" (if one may so call it), and it would be destroyed.[280]

I know that the Scholastics quarrel among themselves whether God foreknows the things he foreknows necessarily or contingently. I will not myself meddle in this contention, for no such subject is set forth in Scripture. It is enough for me to prove that God is free from all kinds of change and alteration. The contingency and novelty is in the things themselves; God always and perpetually remains one and the same.

We will bring certain passages to prove it clearly that there is a certain necessity found in the Holy Scriptures, that is [the necessity] of the consequence or the compound sense or infallibility. Lest anyone think it to be an imagined invention, Christ said, "It is necessary that he should be delivered to the Jews to be mocked." This necessity can be inferred from nothing other than the concrete counsel of God, which Peter teaches in his sermon in the Acts of the Apostles.[281] Christ also

---

[279]*Necessitas certitudinis, necessitas coactionis.*
[280]*Non voluntas sed noluntas.*
[281]Matt. 20:19; cf. Acts 2:23.

said, "It is necessary that the Scriptures should be fulfilled." It is written in John, "The Scriptures cannot be broken," that is, it is not possible to be otherwise than fulfilled.[282] To the Hebrews it is written, "It is impossible that those who have once been enlightened," and so forth.[283] In this place the sin against the Holy Spirit is dealt with and the fact that it is impossible for those who are guilty to escape, for God has forever decreed to forsake those who have so sinned.[284] Christ also said of the temptations of the latter days, "The elect also, if it were possible, should be deceived"; again he says, "Heaven and earth shall pass away, but my words shall not pass away."[285] These words signify that all those things God has spoken either in Scripture or in his eternal decree, cannot be frustrated by any means. He also answered his parents, "Did you not know that I must do those things that belong to my Father?"[286] Paul says to Timothy, "The foundation stands firm, God knows who are his." And in John it is written, "Those whom the Father has given me, no one can snatch them out of my hand."[287] Last, the psalmist states, "He has done all things as it pleased him, both in heaven and in earth."[288] So we gather from all this how clearly this necessity of certainty and infallibility is set forth in the Holy Scriptures, for it is not (as some think) a human contrivance.

51. What we have said about foreknowledge also pertains to providence. Although in this totality of things many matters are said to be done by chance (*contingenter*), yet is there nothing, no matter how small, that is not subject to the providence of God. Thus it has the necessity we call the necessity of certainty and others the necessity of consequence. If things may be called partly necessary and also partly contingent or free, as we have claimed, which condition agrees best? I answer: that which most agrees with what is natural and intrinsic.

Inasmuch as the necessity which we treat now comes externally and is only by hypothesis, things should not be valued according to it, but according to those principles or grounds which are understood by us. Thus our works which proceed from our will are said to be free, and those things produced in nature which may or may not come to pass, *[436]* are considered contingent. Now we assert that the necessity of certainty or consequence should never be denied, nor

---

[282]Luke 22:37; John 10:35.
[283]Heb. 6:4.
[284]Cf. Matt. 12:32.
[285]Matt. 24:24, 35.
[286]Luke 2:29.
[287]2 Tim. 2:19; John 10:29.
[288]Ps. 115:3.

must we snatch our works away from nature or from foreknowledge or God's providence.

As for the divine will, we must surely think that it governs and moderates all things, something that everyone acknowledges. Although men perceive and feel that by the exercise of their will they decide and choose those things that they wish, yet if they are faithful, they will always say, "I will do this or that, if God permits." If they are yet without Christ's religion (as were the heathen), they still talk of "fate" or "destiny," of the three sisters called Parcae, or of chance, all of which are often read in the poets.[289] If, as we have said before, by the word "fate" or similar words they understand the connection of causes over which God himself rules, moderating and governing, then there is no harm in that opinion. Although because of the abuse of the word, it is better to abstain from it. There are also some who dream of a kind of fatal necessity (mighty and strong) fixed to the stars and natural causes, which even God cannot change. This is false, impious, and far from the wise men of old. They explicitly declared that by fate they understood the will and governance of God. Cleanthes the Stoic wrote verse on this subject, and Seneca translated it into Latin in book 18 of his letters.

> Lead me, great Lord, king of eternity
> Even where thou wilt, I'll not resist thee.
> Change thou my will yet still I vow subjection,
> Being led, to that is in the good election.
> "Fate leads the willing, hails the obstinate."[290]

Although these verses exalt fate or destiny, yet the governance is placed in the hands of God; for he calls on the Father most high and desires to be led by him, whose will he affirms to be both certain and infallible. Homer seems to mean the same thing by these verses in the *Odyssey*:

> The mind of men upon the earth
> is such as the father of gods and men
> brings on them day by day.[291]

When we speak of foreknowledge we do not exclude the will, for as we admonished at the beginning, God cannot foreknow something will happen unless he chooses that it will happen. Nothing can exist except what God wills,

---

[289]The Parcae were the Fates; see Martyr, "Providence," PW, 195–96.

[290]Cleanthes (ca. 301–252 B.C.E.) succeeded Zeno as head of the Stoic school in Athens. Augustine *Civ. Dei* 5.8, quotes the same passage: "these verses (of Anneus Seneca's, I think)," i.e., Seneca the Younger (ca. 3 B.C.E.–65 C.E.) *Ep.* bk. 18. The lines are in a different order in Martyr's text.

[291]Homer *Odyssey* 18:136ff. These lines are also quoted by Augustine *Civ. Dei* 5.8 as "translated into Latin by Tully" (Cicero). Vermigli quotes the original Greek.

and what God wills he also brings about for us. It is as Paul says, "He works in us both to will and to perform."[292]

DOES NECESSITY HINDER FREE WILL?

52. When joined with foreknowledge, this will neither subverts nor destroys natures, but works in them so that it agrees with them. Therefore, since the nature and property of the human will is to work freely and by choice, God's foreknowledge and will do not take this power or faculty from it, although his predestination is the cause of all good acts done by the elect and in the elect. This is proved not only by the witness of Scripture, but also by the consensus of the Church in their prayers; for it prays, "O God from whom all holy desires, all good counsels, and all just works proceed," and so forth.[293]

Although sins are in one sense subject to the will of God, they are not produced by it in the same way as are good deeds. Yet it should be certain that sins are not done completely apart from any will of God. "Permission," which some acknowledge, is no different from will, for God permits what he will not prevent. Nor should it be said that he permits unwillingly, but willingly, as Augustine said.[294] Therefore, in either kind of works the will and foreknowledge of God employs itself in such a way that it does not overthrow the faculty or power of man's will. In the predestined it provides that nothing will be committed that may defeat their eternal salvation. And from the reprobate it takes away no natural power relating to their substance or nature, nor does it compel them to attempt anything against their will. Yet it does not provide them with enough grace or mercy (as is given to the elect) necessary for their salvation.

A great many stumble at this point, for they think to themselves that if God had foreknown that we will meet together tomorrow, then it must be that our will was quite determined to do this, otherwise it could not have been foreknown. We answer as we have already intimated, that the determination in God is of the kind that agrees with the property or nature of will. It is proper to its nature to will one part in one way and it can also will another part in another way. Therefore, we confess that if we consider God, it is appointed and decreed what we shall do, for his knowledge is not called foreknowledge for nothing, since he does not merely have an opinion of things so that his knowledge might be changed, but he has a certain and sure knowledge. *[437]* There can be no knowledge unless (as we have

---

[292]Phil. 2:13.

[293]Familiar as the morning collect for peace in the Book of Common Prayer, it comes from the Sarum liturgy, and originated in the Sacramentary of Gelasius (494 C.E.), *Deus, a quo sanct desideria, recta consilia, et justa sunt opera...* (thanks to Torrance Kirby for this reference).

[294]Augustine *C. Pelag.* 1.19.37 (PL 44.568).

said) it is certain and sure, but this determination and certainty of his—we have said and say again—does not subvert the nature of things or take away liberty from our nature.

We may prove this as follows: God foreknew that many things were possible that will never be, and although they will never be, the foreknowledge of God does not remove from them the possibility of existence. We will illustrate this by an example from Scripture. When Christ was arrested he said, "I could have asked of my Father and he would have given me more than twelve legions of angels to defend me from these soldiers."[295] Here Christ affirms that it was possible for him to ask that it might be granted him so many legions of angels, yet this was neither done nor was it meant to be done. God foreknew that it might have been done, and although it would never happen, yet it was not hindered by foreknowledge, but was possible. Therefore, since the foreknowledge of God does not exclude possibility, neither does it remove contingency and freedom.

53. This necessity of infallibility is not only declared by the Scriptures and proved by reasons (as we have shown); it is also acknowledged by the fathers. Origen in his book 2 against Celsus records the argument of Celsus where he objected to the Christians: "Your Christ at the last supper foretold that he would be betrayed by one of his disciples. If he were God, as you claim, could he not have kept it from happening?" Origen wonders at this and responds that this objection is quite ridiculous, for he [Christ] foretold that it would happen. If he had prevented it he would not have spoken the truth. So he adds, it was necessary; it could not be otherwise than what was foretold should come about.[296] Because this foretelling did not change the will of Judas, he is justly accused and the blame should not be laid on Christ, who foretold it. In this passage Origen acknowledges both the necessity of certainty and the nature of unimpeded will. When Ambrose interprets these words of Paul, "Jacob have I loved and Esau have I hated," he refers Paul's statement to foreseen works, but adds that it could not happen otherwise, except as God foresaw that it should happen.[297] Chrysostom also, expounding on what is written to the Corinthians where it says, "It is necessary that there must be heresies," declares that this necessity is a necessity of prediction, which does not prejudice the power of our will and our choice.[298]

---

[295]Matt. 26:53.
[296]Origen *Cels.* 2.18 (PG 11.834).
[297]Ambrose *Comm. Rom.* 9.13 (PL 17.134).
[298]1 Cor. 11:19; Chrysostom *Hom. 1 Cor.* 27.2 (PG 61.226).

Nor is this necessity taken away by certain places in Scripture, which at first glance seem to put a change in the mind of God. For instance, when Isaiah threatened King Hezekiah with imminent death, the prophecy of God seemed to change when he prolonged his life fifteen years.[299] It was foretold to the city of Nineveh that it would be destroyed within forty days, which did not come about.[300] Those items do not count against the truth we have taught. God warned Hezekiah that his death was near because of the disease he suffered. It was not a lie.[301] According to foreknowledge, God foreknew that the king would be in danger from that fatal disease and also foreknew that his life would be prolonged fifteen years. God also foreknew that the sins of the Ninevites deserved immediate destruction, but he also foreknew that by his mercy he would lead them to repentance and they would be saved.

The same rule can be applied to Jeremiah 18. God said that he would change his mind about the plague with which he had threatened every city, nation, or kingdom, if they would repent.[302] And what shall we say about Paul, who wrote to the Corinthians, "He chastised his body and brought it into obedience, so that he might not be a reprobate?"[303] Did he intend to change the firm purpose of God? Surely Paul did not mean that he was able to invert the order of God's predestination or reprobation. Thus he did not say, "lest I become a reprobate," but "lest I be reproved.[304] He endeavored with all industry and diligence to be obedient to the predestination of God. Those who are predestined to eternal life labor to mortify the flesh. He said that he would not become reproved, that is, he would not be found and accused of living his life other than he preached, which is a vice which all men criticize, detest, and condemn. Therefore, that passage did not treat God's reprobation, but the kind of crime of which those are guilty who give good advice and meanwhile lead a wicked life. If one must refer these things to the judgment of God, we might well grant the same thing concerning present justice or injustice, but not according to the firm purpose of which we are speaking at present.

54. Cicero, a man otherwise full of wit, well learned, and deserving of praise, was much deceived in this question, as is evident in his second book, *On Divination.* (Augustine refers to this in book 5, chapters 9 and 10, of *The City of*

---

[299]2 Kings 20:1, 5.
[300]Jonah 3:4, 10.
[301]2 Kings 20:1ff.
[302]Jer. 18:8.
[303]1 Cor. 9:27.
[304]*Ne reprobatus efficiar … ne reprobus efficiar.*

God).[305] He [Cicero] thought it impossible that the foreknowledge of things to come would not overthrow the faculty or power of man's will. Therefore, he rejected predestination completely.[306] Everyone knows how repugnant this is to our religion, for it is built on the sure foundation of the oracles of the prophets. And it is written that God never did anything of any weight that he did not first reveal to the prophets.[307] He showed Noah *[438]* the destruction that would come by the flood long before it came about. He showed Abraham beforehand the burning of Sodom and signified the oppression and deliverance of his posterity in Egypt.[308] And he charged those prophets to foretell the captivity of Babylon and the return from there.[309] He also commanded all the prophets to predict the coming of Christ. Therefore, the authority of prophecy is so constant to us, that to deny it would be to completely overthrow all religion. Therefore, not without just cause did Augustine say that those men called "Genethliacs," who taught the fatal necessities of the stars, were more tolerable than Cicero, for they gave some place to God.[310] If it is denied that he foreknew things to come, it must also be denied that he is God.

David says, "The fool says in his heart, there is no God."[311] This statement shows the opinion of the wicked, for when they commit evil deeds they think God does not see them and will never punish them. Cicero has given us occasion to suspect that he was in a sense infected with this impiety, for in his book *On the Nature of the Gods* he introduces Cotta and the high priest into the discussion. Cotta greatly desired to have it proved to him that the gods exist.[312] Yet because he saw that it was odious and hateful and almost infamous to deny that there is a God, towards the end of the book he sided with Balbos, who argued that the gods exist, but he also said to Velleius that the opinion of Cotta seemed the more probable.[313] Truly, a godly man and one confirmed in religion would never say that the proposition calling divinity into doubt is likely to be true. Such are the debates generated from our discussion of what Paul wrote so much about in Romans 1.

[305]Augustine *Civ. Dei* 5.9–10 (PL 41.153).

[306]Omnem praedestinationem penitus sustulit: Cicero *Div.* 2.7; see Martyr, "Providence," PW, 188, for the same reference. In this section Vermigli is following Augustine closely.

[307]Amos 3:7.

[308]Gen. 6:3; 18:17.

[309]Jer. 25:8,12.

[310]"Their opinion is more tolerable, they ascribe fate uno the stars, than his, that rejects all foreknowledge of things to come:" Augustine *Civ. Dei* 5.9. "Genethliacs" seems to be Vermigli's own term.

[311]Ps. 14:1.

[312]Cicero *Nat. Deor.* 1.21–22. Cotta wishes "to have the existence of the gods, which is the principal point in debate, not only fixed in opinion, but proved by demonstration." See Martyr, "Nature and Grace," PW, 20, for the same reference.

[313]Cicero *Nat. Deor.* 3.17.

Afterward, Cicero himself, in his book *On Divination,* under his own name denies that God possesses foreknowledge of things to come and answers his brother Quintus, who had confirmed oracles and prophecies in the whole course of the first book. Why did he deny foreknowledge? He was driven to it, for he saw that he would have to accept an order of causes and effects that is immovable and permanent; otherwise, things to come could not be foretold. Now if such an order is granted, he concludes that nothing would remain in our hands and power; but we must affirm that God is a most singular will joined with a most singular power and, therefore, the knowledge of all things must be attributed to him. Yet let us not fear on that account that what we do is not by our own will and choice.

The Stoics who proposed fate or destiny seem also to have been somewhat moved by Cicero's reasons, for they did not place the motions of the human will under fate or the connection of causes. Not that they understood the human will to be completely free, but only that it lay in the choice to interact or not with some things, which if they did so would at once be enveloped in the necessity of fate. The question may be clarified by an example. They say that it was in the power of Oedipus to join with a woman or to abstain. But if he once joined himself he could not choose but to commit incest, from which children would be born who would pollute themselves by murdering their brother and overthrowing their father's kingdom.[314] Ancient philosophers such as Democritus and Empedocles affirm that the will is subject to fate or the connection of causes, but Chrysippus the Stoic rather inclines to exempt the human will, as does Oenomaris the Cynic, whom Eusebius of Caesarea cites in *The Preparation for the Gospel* as saying that Democritus made men slaves and Chrysippus made them only half slaves.[315]

55. Putting these other matters behind, let us return to Cicero, who said: If there is foreknowledge then things should happen as they were foreknown nor can a foreseen event be avoided; therefore, human liberty is completely lost. Laws, admonitions, rewards, punishments, and such things are in vain. So he offers a choice, that one should choose whether he would rather admit foreknowledge or freedom of the will, since both cannot exist together, as far as he could see. And because he was involved in civil matters dealing with laws and judgments, he rejected the foreknowledge of God rather than lose human free will. For this reason Augustine said of Cicero, "Those who will be free he makes blasphemous," so

---

[314]See the Oedipus trilogy of Sophocles: *Oed. rex (Antigone),* "Oedipus at Colonus."
[315]Eusebius *Praep. ev.* 7 (PG 21.438); see Martyr, "Providence," PW, p. 187, §8, for the same material.

that in defense of their liberty they rob God of his foreknowledge."[316] Cicero's reason was that if the will is free there can be no sure connection of causes, for if it were sure it could not be broken by our will, and if there is no certain connection then foreknowledge cannot stand. Thus, he affirmed that God does not foreknow what will happen. If God foreknows things, there would be a certain and firm order of causes and if this is granted, it leaves nothing for the power of our will.

We should hold both of these. We experience one of these [freedom] by our senses, for everyone may see in himself how he works by counsels and deliberations and chooses what pleases him. For the other, that is, God's foreknowledge, we hold by faith a knowledge of no less force than the apprehension of sense and reason. And so we deny Cicero's conclusion that there is a certain and constant order of causes which God foreknew; therefore, there is nothing in our will. We deny the argument because our wills are also to be placed among the causes of things, and indeed not in the least worthy place. So just as God can foreknow what will happen through other causes, *[439]* similarly is he able to see clearly what our will chooses. And in foreseeing other causes and their effects, in no way does he destroy or change their nature. Here too he has left human wills intact.

This also moved Cicero, for he reasoned that nothing could happen by chance, but since a great many things seem to happen by chance and fortune, there cannot be a sure order and foreknowledge of causes. We answer that those things said to come by chance are so called as they are referred to our understanding, which is weak because of its dullness and cannot see the course or connection of causes; but if they are referred to the mind of God from which nothing is hidden, they cannot be said to come by chance or rashly. The infirmity of our mind has made room for fortune or chance, as is shown by an example. If a master should send his servant to the market and tell him to be there by six o'clock, and if the master should also order his bailiff to do the same, no doubt both bailiff and servant will meet each other, which seems to them to happen by chance, since they did not know of their master's orders. But the master himself, who knew the situation, will not judge this as happening by chance.

Let us consider another example. Suppose I knew that treasure was hidden in a certain place and ordered someone to dig there. When he found the treasure he would cry out, "What good luck!" But since I knew of it I would attribute nothing to luck. Neither would God experience any good luck, since he knows the course and connection of all causes. Therefore, let us submit all things to the providence

---

[316]Augustine *Civ. Dei* 9 (PL 41.152): "and so instead of making men free, makes them blasphemous." See Martyr, "Providence," PW, 188, for the same reference.

of God, including our wills, which we must acknowledge to have only that power which God chooses (who tempers the power and nature of all things).

Augustine says that there is a certain cause that works in such a way that it is not accomplished through any means and God is the cause. And there is another cause that works in such a way that it is also done by another.[317] Our will is of this sort, which wills and works in such a way that it is also done by God. Therefore, we should neither assent to Cicero nor to the Stoics. We must not withdraw anything from the foreknowledge of God; least of all should our wills be exempted, for they relate to the better part of the world. For what should God have care? Or what should he foreknow if he neglects humankind?

"Our wills," says Augustine, "are able to do as much as God chose and foreknew they would be able to do. Therefore, whatever they are able to do, they are able to do most certainly. Whatever they will do, they will doubtless do it, for he, whose foreknowledge cannot be deceived, foreknew what they could do and also do."[318] In chapter 10, book 5, of the book just cited, he distinguished, as did we, two kinds of necessity. There is the kind of necessity through which we are compelled to experience those things we do not want, such as the necessity of death, to which we must yield whether or not we want. The other necessity, he says, is that according to which something is said to be necessary, which will without any doubt occur. Regarding this there is no need to be afraid concerning our will, for the will is not diminished by it.[319] The former is contrary to our will, for it is impossible for it to choose anything unwillingly, but the latter is not at all against the nature of the will. While the life and foreknowledge of God are necessarily attributed to him, yet they do not harm his nature or will. He can neither be deceived nor die, and yet he allows nothing that he does not will. So also we say that when we choose anything, we choose it by necessity, yet we do not think our choice is violated by this.

56. Augustine clearly shows how the foreknowledge of God does not hinder our will, in book 3, chapters 2 and 3, of his *Freedom of the Will*.[320] First, he says that by this question many wicked men are set to work. They either would wish (if the will were free) that God would have no providence or care of mortal affairs, so that they might give themselves to licentiousness and lusts by denying the judgments of both God and man and avoiding them as much as they can. Or if it

---

[317]Augustine *Civ. Dei* 5.9 (PL 41.152) distinguishes "causal" and "voluntary" causes: "The cause then that makes all, and is not made itself, is God. The other causes do both effect and are effected."

[318]Augustine *Civ. Dei* 10.8 (PL 41.168).

[319]Augustine *Civ. Dei* 5.10 (PL 41.152–53).

[320]Augustine *Grat.* 3.2–3 (PL 32.1268–70).

cannot be avoided, it must be granted that God foresees and understands the things we do. At least they would want to keep this, so that his providence should so compel men's wills that they may be excused from blame of wickedness. But how much their devices are deceived, Augustine easily shows by setting forth how God's knowledge may stand along with human will, and that a free will. He asks the person with whom he is arguing whether he knew if tomorrow he would have a righteous or a corrupt will? His opponent answers that he could not tell. "Do you think," says Augustine, "that God knows this?" The other admits that he thinks God knows this. "Therefore" (says Augustine), "since God foreknows this, he also foreknows what he will do with you, that is, whether he will glorify you at the end of your life. And if he foreknows and cannot be deceived, then he will glorify you by necessity. Meanwhile, tell me, will you be glorified against your will or with your will? Truly (he says), it is not against my will for I desire this most dearly." So he concludes that what God will do in us of necessity does not hinder our will.[321]

He also shows that this will be clearer if we consider foreknowledge of the present as though it were our own. Suppose I know beforehand that a certain man will come to me tomorrow, will my foreknowledge take away his will so that if he comes it is not through his own choice? Surely we cannot say this, for he comes willingly. Nor will my foreknowledge diminish his choice in the least. Just as our memory does not compel things past to be past, so foreknowledge does not compel future events to happen. This point can be illustrated further. If someone saw Plato discussing with Socrates or the sun or moon being eclipsed, the sight of the beholder *[440]* does not cause those who are debating to debate by necessity or against their wills, nor does the beholder cause the sun or moon to be eclipsed by chance, since those eclipses of the heavenly lights have their necessary causes. Therefore, he who sees them does not by his sight make what is contingent to be necessary, nor the necessary to be contingent. We should not imagine that God's foreknowledge secures his certainty of the necessity of things, for so great is the perspicuity of the mind of God that it can understand contingent things perfectly.[322] This reason is not hindered by what we often stated earlier, that is, that God's foreknowledge always has his will joined to it, since nothing can be foreknown by God that he himself does not choose to be. Yet this will, by which God works all in all, adapts itself to the natures of things. In meat it nourishes, in the

---

[321] Augustine *Grat.* 3.3.8 (PL 32.1275).

[322] The medieval debate on future contingencies associated with William of Occam was not of special interest to Vermigli; see his "Providence," PW, 192–93, §13. If future contingencies are true/false only indeterminately, i.e., becoming so on the realization or nonrealization of the predicted event, then the divine will is present in indeterminate mode.

sun it shines, in the vine it brings forth wine, and in the human will it causes the willing of those things they choose by their own accord and freely.

We read in Acts that Paul cites the statement of Aratus, "in him we live and move and exist."[323] It follows from this that man's will gets its movement from God, but if one says that it receives such motions from God as it willed before on its own, then he utters an absurdity, for in that case our will would measure and govern the divine influences, which is far from the truth. Rather, let us say that it receives from God such impulses and motions as he wants to give, and meanwhile, let us note that God so works in our will that it gladly, willingly, and of its own accord receives the motions that God puts into us.

57. How does it happen that God foresees things to come with certainty, while human wills and many natural causes are doubtful and work in a contingent manner? It is like this: it is quite true that those who consider things only in terms of their causes are often deceived, for all causes do not necessarily produce their effects; sometimes they are prevented and incline to some other way than was expected. Therefore, men are not deceived when they judge that effects are brought to light; but they are deceived when they pass judgment about effects hidden in their causes. God's foreknowledge not only knows what things will come about by their causes, but also sees them clearly, as if they were already produced and made perfect by their causes. Thus we may infer from the foreknowledge of God the necessity of certainty or infallibility, which we cannot do of secondary causes.[324] When we say that God foreknows that this or that will be tomorrow, we rightly add that it will necessarily be. Necessity is not applied to something already known, except insofar as God knows it beforehand as present and already produced. This is why we can infer the necessity and infallibility from God's foreknowledge, but not from proximate causes, because when we say that God foreknows that this or that will happen tomorrow, we rightly add that it will happen necessarily. This makes not only for clarity, but also necessity. For everything that is necessary, we must not say afterward that the thing was necessary, for it is not taken in the same sense as was the foreknowledge of God.

So far we have defended the power of the human will, yet we would not have this taken universally, but only in relation to foreknowledge and predestination. Although this (as was proved) does not impede free will, yet in other respects it does not lack impediments or blockage, for we are born in sin, and whether we wish it or not we are wrapped in original sin. There is no way we can unravel

---

[323] Acts 17:28; Aratus *Phaenom.* 5.

[324] See §49, p. 68, above: Vermigli's favorite category is this *necessitas certitudinis seu infallibilitas.*

ourselves from sin. Before regeneration, whatever power we ascribe to the human will concerning civil and indifferent matters, we first should think that whichever way the will turns itself, it sins of necessity. Nor can it do anything acceptable to God, or give to civil works the success it intends.

So Augustine well wrote in his *Enchiridion* that by sinning the first man lost the liberty of free will. This is also to be considered: the wills and motions of the mind, even among the unregenerate, are directed by God in such a way that by his providence they are brought to the end prearranged and determined by him. This is also true of the regenerate, while we obtain liberty through Christ in one sense, yet it is not full but only the beginning, for the first motions that stir us up to sin and creep upon us against our wills, we have proved to be sins.[325]

Ambrose plainly confesses that our hearts are not in our own power, nor is there any believer who does not continually fall, when he would stand.[326] So we should all pray, "Forgive us our trespasses."[327] Paul said to the Galatians, "The Spirit fights against the flesh and the flesh against the Spirit, so that you do not the things that you would."[328] And in his letter to the Romans he writes: "The evil which I hate, I do." Again he confesses: "I see a different law in my members, striving against the law of my mind, and making me a prisoner of the law of sin"; these words can be understood only of the regenerate,[329] for he had said, "In my mind I serve the law of God but in the flesh, the law of sin."[330] This last verse cannot refer to someone not yet justified.

We grant indeed that if he wished, God could give men so much aid that they would not sin at all, but so far, he has not done so nor undertaken to do it in the future. Therefore, our will is still subject to some bondage. Since we want to remain certain and without doubt, we affirm on the other side that by the foreknowledge and predestination of God, the will is not impeded.

Does Foreknowledge Cancel God's Justice?

58. We have seen in this third article that necessity comes [from foreknowledge] and that such a necessity is not absolute, but *[441]* hypothetical, which we call a necessity of consequence, of infallibility, and of certainty, but not of compulsion. Since this is so, it is now evident that no injustice is committed by God

---

[325]See ROM, 222–66 (chap. 7).
[326]Ambrose *Fug. saec.* 1, in Augustine *Persev.* 20–21, etc. See also Martyr, "Whether God Is the Author of Sin" and "Free Will," PW, 261, 274.
[327]Matt. 6:12.
[328]Gal. 5:17.
[329]Rom. 7:15, 23.
[330]Rom. 7:22–23.

when he condemns sinners and glorifies the just, for to every person is rendered according to his works, so that no one can say his sins are not his own work, since he is not compelled to commit them, but allows them and wills them with zeal. Nor are laws, admonitions, promises, and punishments in vain, as was objected, for they have as much force as God has decreed they should have, as Augustine writes in his fifth book, *The City of God*, in the chapter cited earlier.[331] God's will is to use them for the salvation of many, and though they are not profitable for some, they do not lack purpose, for they lead to the condemnation of the wicked.

Prayers are not made unprofitable, for by them we obtain those things that God has decreed to give us through them. This is an excellent saying of Gregory in his *Dialogue*, "that by prayers we can obtain only those things that God has predestined to give."[332] Many testimonies of Scripture teach us how it is that sins are not excused by predestination or foreknowledge or predictions. Christ foretold that Judas would betray him. Truly that prediction neither took away wickedness from Judas nor poured it into him. He followed the allure of covetousness; he did not betray the Lord to obey this prophecy. Christ was slain by the will of God, for he said in the garden, "If it is possible, let this cup pass from me; yet not my will but yours be done," and he said of himself beforehand, "I will give my life for my sheep."[333]

Even Herod and Pilate in the Acts of the Apostles are said to have agreed to do those things the counsel of God had decreed.[334] Are either the Jews or those nobles to be acquitted from sin, when they condemned and killed an innocent man? Who will say so? Can anyone discharge the villainy of the brothers of Joseph, when they sold their brother, even though God would bring Joseph to Egypt by that means?[335] Neither will the cruelty of the king of Babylon be excused, although God's justice decreed that the Jews should be punished in this way. One who is killed is said to be delivered into the hands of his enemy.[336] God is also said to deliver a city, when it is won by assault. And Job said that those things taken away from him by the Chaldeans and Sabeans through violence and theft were taken away by God. He says, "The Lord gave and the Lord has taken away."[337] Therefore, we cannot infer any just excuse for sins from that counsel of

---

[331]Augustine *Civ. Dei* 5.10 (PL 41.152–53).
[332]Gregory, *Dial.* (presumably one of Gregory Nazianzen's *Orations*).
[333]Matt. 16:35; John 10:11.
[334]Acts 4:27.
[335]Gen. 45:8.
[336]Isa. 10:7; Exod. 23:31.
[337]Josh. 6:6; Job 1:21.

God that uses sins to their appointed purpose, for evil works are judged and condemned because of the wicked and corrupt heart from which they spring.

Therefore, let no one be offended by the doctrine of predestination, seeing that we are led by it to acknowledge God's benefits and to give thanks to him alone. Let us also learn not to attribute more to our own strength than we ought. Let us have also an assured persuasion of the goodwill of God towards us, by which he would elect his own before the foundations of the world were laid. Let us, moreover, be confirmed in adversities, knowing assuredly that whatever calamity happens, it is done by the counsel and will of God and that it shall at length by the governance of predestination turn to good and to eternal salvation.

Finis

PART TWO

Locus
on Justification

Justification

PROLEGOMENA

1. *[517]* In order for us to put the final touch on the debate, it will be worthwhile to treat more fully the topic of justification, which is the focus and end of all that Paul has been teaching.[1] The question may be posed in these words: "Are men justified by works or by faith?" But first it is important that the words of the proposed question be explained; we will begin with the word justification.

JUSTIFICATION

Tsadac is a Hebrew verb that in the first conjugation means "he was just"; if the word is translated according to the third conjugation, it signifies that justice is transferred to another, for this is the force of the form of those verbs which they call *hiph'il*. Just as *'amad* indicates "to stand," so *he'emid* means "to set up" so that it makes something stand. Therefore, in Hebrew *hitsdiq* would be "to justify," that is, to make someone just.[2]

It is important to understand that when such an act comes from God it is accomplished in two ways. Sometimes, in reality, he brings forth righteousness in men. First, he endows them with his own Spirit and renews them fully by restoring the strength of their minds and by retrieving their human faculties from the greater part of their natural corruption: this idea is first a righteousness (*iustitia*) that is within and clings to our minds by the goodness of God through Christ. Second, when he has fashioned and renewed them in this way he gives right and holy works, and by their frequent and continuing use there is born in our minds a quality or (as they call it) a "habit" by which we are inclined to right and holy living. We do not deny that this type of righteousness is renewed in the hearts of the regenerate.

Sometimes God justifies by forgiving sins, and ascribing and imputing righteousness; consequently, *hitsdiq* is a forensic verb, because it looks to judgments;

---

[1] The locus on justification follows Vermigli's commentary on Paul's letter to the Romans, chap. 11, ROM, 517–75. Section divisions are from the *Loci Communes ... ex variis ipsius authoris scriptis, in unum librum collecti & in quatuor Classes distributi* (London: Thomas Vautrollerius, 1583), bk. 3, §4; they are included for convenience. Subject headings are given by the editor.

[2] Vermigli points out that often in Hebrew a verb that is stative in the qal conjugation is transitive in the hiph'il; in English, verbs undergo similar change; e.g., "I walked to the store," "I walked the dog." Thus, in Hebrew *tsadeq*, "to be just," becomes *hitsdiq*, "to make just"; *'amad*, "to stand," becomes *he'emid*, "to stand [something] up." Cf. n. 3 below.

likewise, this word *hirshiah,* meaning "to declare one wicked."[3] Then "to justify" means that through judgment, words, witness, or assertion one counts the person just. Since there are these two meanings of "to justify," namely, in fact or in judgment or estimation, and since the same God is author of both, which of the two should we follow in the proposed discussion? The latter, in fact, because the renewal imputed by the Spirit of God and our righteousness, that is, the way of life acquired from good works, are still imperfect and incomplete while we live, so that if judgment were to come through them we would not be able to stand before divine judgment. Besides that, when debating the matter, Paul was influenced by the testimony of the history of Abraham in Genesis and by the authority of David; he used the verb "to be reckoned," and, with proper understanding, reasons in light of our present concern and question. I think this is enough discussion concerning the understanding of the first word, namely, justification.

FAITH

2.   Now let us discuss faith. For the Hebrews, *'aman* in the first conjugation means "to be firm."[4] The same verb in the third conjugation, called *hiph'il,* as I said above, signifies "to ascribe stability" to any word or deed. Hence, the Latins say they attribute faith to a person or to words, and they mean "they believe." The Hebrew verb is *he'emin,* which indicates nothing else than "to suppose" or "to think a thing firm and sure."[5]

So far as God is concerned, the one who does not believe in him makes God a liar. For John said in his first letter, chapter 5: "He who does not believe in God, makes him out to be a liar."[6] Let everyone consider for himself how great a sin this is. On the other hand, however, whoever believes in God adorns him with glory and honor. For it is written about Abraham in the letter to the Romans that he did not waver in doubt, though his own body was weakened and the womb of Sarah past childbearing, but gave glory to God, being strong in his faith, and was fully persuaded that God was able to perform whatever he willed.[7] Therefore, there seems to be a certain analogy or proportion between this word "to believe" and that word "to justify," as we take it here. For as "to justify" comes by way of judging or accounting, to ascribe righteousness to someone and not make him just in

---

[3]The verb *rasha,* "to be wicked," in the hiph'il *hirshiah,* means "to declare wicked."

[4]Martyr is following the analysis of Rabbi David Kimhi, *Sefer hashorashi* ("Book of Roots"), entry אמן; *Radicum Liber sive Hebraeum Bibliorum Lexicon,* ed. Biesenthal and Lebrecht (Berlin, 1847), fol. 20.

[5]נאמן (*aman*) in the first conjugation means "to be firm," נאמן (*eemin*) in the hiph'il means "to consider someone firm.'"

[6]1 John 5:10.

[7]Rom. 4:19–21.

reality, so "to believe" is not (in truth) to make the words and promises of anyone sure and firm, but to think and determine within ourselves that they are such.

Moreover, the act of believing, which we now examine, has a twofold certainty and assurance. First, there is the substance: the divine words and promises which remain far more fixed than heaven and earth. Second, regarding the persuasion itself: since it comes from God's power, it is itself most sure and certain; that is, it is never alone but draws along with it many and various motions of the mind. For experience and daily life teach that in civil affairs a man who is fully persuaded of pleasant promises is filled with confidence and joy, displays a happy manner, is glad and pleasant, and clings to the one who made the promise, so that he makes himself respectable in every way. On the other hand, someone who does not believe the persuasion scoffs at it, neglects and condemns it, or grows cold and bears a sour countenance. Therefore, it can never happen that he who believes truly can lack such feelings as usually follow a wholehearted and firm persuasion. Those who are the pure professors of the Gospel, therefore, rightly affirm that "to believe" has a very strong connection with the act or motion of confidence, hope, and similar affections, but most of all with the sincere and firm confidence that faith always brings along with it.

So it happens, as you see in Holy Scripture, that promises are made both to faith and to trust. *[518]* For indeed it is said, "The righteous live by faith" and "he who believes will not be disappointed"; likewise, in the New Testament, "He who believes in the Son has eternal life"; and again, "we believe that a man is justified by faith."[8] So it is written in the Psalm, "Blessed are all those who put their trust in him," and in Isaiah, chapter 26, "You will preserve [our] peace: peace because we have hoped in you."[9] In the New Testament, "Hope does not disappoint," so also Titus, chapter 3, "We are made heirs according to the hope of eternal life."[10] Although in the Old Testament we find that the promises more often are made in regard to hope than to faith, in the New Testament the matter is different. The reason may be this, that in the old era the Hebrews were not wrong in believing that there is only one God; indeed, they professed the worship of him alone. But it was not good that theirs was not a living faith, which drew trust with it; through education they had conceived a certain opinion or knowledge. The Scriptures exhorted them to it, to believe truly and effectually, expressed by the name of trust. But in the New Testament both the Gentiles (who were worshippers of idols and many divinities) and the Jews went astray on this very point. The Jews did so with regard to the

---

[8]Ps. 22:5; Hab. 2:4; John 3:36; Rom. 8:17.
[9]Ps. 2:11; Isa. 26:3. The Vulgate for the latter is "Servabis pacem: pacem, quia in te speravimus."
[10]Rom. 5:5; Titus 3:7.

circumstances related to the coming of the Messiah. For they looked for him to come in glorious pomp, like a king, and magnificent in worldly rule. So faith was often beaten into them by which they might obtain the promises of God. It was quite necessary for them to be rightly taught the chief point of the matter to be believed.

3. Moreover, from the Hebrew verb *'aman* the noun *emuna* is derived, meaning "faith"; it sometimes signifies "firmness and constancy of words and promises." Thus in Holy Scripture God is frequently called faithful and his works faithful, because they are firm and they endure. In the letter to the Romans we read, "What if some of them did not believe? would their unbelief nullify the faithfulness of God?"[11] Moreover, faith—*fides* in Latin, if we may believe Cicero—is derived from *fio* because what was spoken is done in fact.[12] Sometimes it signifies the assent of our mind, by which we accept the statements spoken to us, as it is said concerning Abraham: "He believed God and it was reckoned to him as righteousness."[13] Since in the current discussion we understand faith in this way, it is relevant to define what faith is. Thus *faith is a firm and assured assent of the mind to the words of God, an assent inspired by the Holy Spirit to the salvation of believers.* So it exists in the mind and is occupied with the words of God: from this we take its matter [material cause]. We need not doubt its form [formal cause] because it is defined to be an assent. The efficient cause is set down as the inspiration of the Holy Spirit. The end [final cause] is declared in the last place, when, as we said, this assent is inspired by the Holy Spirit for the salvation of believers.[14]

What is written about faith in chapter 11 of Hebrews is not unlike this definition, namely, that "faith is the assurance of things hoped for, the conviction of things not seen."[15] What the Latin interpreters call *substantia,* in Greek is written *hypostasis,* a word Budé defines with erudition in his commentary as "boldness, fortitude, or valour of mind."[16] It is derived from the verb *hyphistamai,* which signifies "to sustain, receive, not to yield to one rushing blindly." Hence, a soldier is called *hypostatôs* if he is trusting and does not turn his back to the enemy, but goes up

---

[11]Rom. 3:3.

[12]Reference not found; Cicero, however, often relates *fides* to *fiducia,* e.g. Cicero *De Amic.* 15.52, 18.65.

[13]Gen. 15:6.

[14]Martyr is following the familiar fourfold causality (material, formal, efficient, final) of Aristotle, e.g. *An. post.* 2.2, 194a 20ff. Cf. PW, 7.

[15]Heb. 11:1.

[16]Guillaume Budé, *Commentarii linguae graecae* (Paris: Josse Badius, 1529). Budé (1468–1540) was a Parisian Hellenist, legal scholar, and adviser to Francis I. Martyr owned the *Opera Omnia* of Budé, 4 vols. in 3 (Basel: Nicolaus Episcopius, 1556–57). See CAS, 216. Eph. 6:16.

against them and resists them. Thus, in believing there is need of strength and patience on account of the great struggle we experience there. We must resist the flesh, we must overcome reason, which strives much against faith. We must also resist the condemnation of our own conscience, of sin, and the wrath of God; there are many other things besides by which the assent of faith is prevented and hindered. How well are these compared, this *hypostasis* or substance and those things that are hoped for. For God promises resurrection, but to the dead; he promises eternal life, but to the decaying; he calls them blessed, yet they abundantly thirst and hunger and are oppressed on all sides; he pronounces men justified, yet are they covered with sins and filth.

Accordingly, when these things seem so far off from us, we must have boldness, strength, and the assurance of the firmest assent to make them abide and stand with us as ultimate sureties. We must be armed with such a strong shield of defense by which we may quench all the fiery darts of the devil cast against us,[17] and even overcome the world. As John testifies: "This is the victory that conquers the world: our faith."[18] Moreover, it must be noted that the word *argumentum*, in Greek *elegchos*, is defined by some as *demonstratio*, that is, a declaration, because by faith unseen things are shown and declared. Indeed, to me it seems that Augustine, although perhaps not in such good Latin, yet faithfully terms it *convictio*.[19] For indeed by faith our mind is overcome as it assents to those things God either says or promises as true.

4. In his book *De summa Trinitate & fide catholic*, Hostiensis labors in two respects to show that faith is not defined by these words of the apostle, because *hypostasis* or *substantia* also agrees with hope.[20] In light of this, as it is not proper to faith, it cannot be applied to that definition. Further, faith does not only look to future reality and things hoped for, it also refers to the past. For we believe that God created heaven and earth, that Christ was born of a [519] virgin, that he suffered for us, and was raised from the dead; all these things are past; it is not hoped that they will recur. These two reasons of Hostiensis are quite weak, nor do they prove that the words in Hebrews cannot be applied to the definition of faith. Yet I concede that the apostle, or another who is held to be the author of the letter, was not defining faith there, because he spoke chiefly of patience and wished to show that it is closely joined to faith, because faith is *hypostasis* [substance], and so on.

[17]Eph. 6:16.
[18]1 John 5:4.
[19]Augustine *Trin.* 13.1.3 (PL 42.1014–15).
[20]Hostiensis (Henry de Segusio), *S. trin & fide cath.* Hostiensis (ca. 1200–71) was a canon lawyer whose monumental *Summa Copiosa* is a synthesis of canon and Roman law.

His reasoning includes all things that express the nature of faith. As to the first objection, we say that *hypostasis* is indeed applied to hope, namely, what it draws from faith, not what it has of itself.

It should not seem anything new if these things of different natures have something in common in their definitions; for example, lion, dog, and man differ much in nature, yet they agree in being living creatures. Therefore, something is included in their definitions that is common to all, since they are bodies, have life, and are endowed with senses. It should not seem strange if faith and hope agree in that *hypostasis* since they are distinguished by other differences. For in relation to faith hypostasis refers to assent, but in relation to hope it refers to expectation by which we patiently wait until the promises and what we have received by faith are given to us.

We respond to the other reason,[21] that Paul mentioned things past which are made sure and clear to us by faith; for he not only says that faith is the substance of things hoped for, but adds that it is an argument or conviction of things unseen. Even now those things that were past are not seen, for by that word Paul understands whatever is believed and is not visible, whether past, now present, or still to come. Perhaps you will ask why he, or someone else, mentions things hoped for in the first place? We answer that it is done correctly because the things most difficult to believe are put first for good reason. Perhaps there are some who will grant easily enough that all things are created by God, that Christ the Son of God came into the world, was born of a virgin, and such like things; yet they will have grave doubt about the forgiveness of their sins, the future resurrection of the flesh, and the eternal glory granted to the just. Therefore, those things are placed in proper sequence that we find in the letter to the Hebrews.

5.   The prophet Isaiah aptly expresses the nature of faith in chapter 26, where the church is called a city built by God. The prophet writes, "Open the gates and a righteous nation will enter in."[22] He adds the cause of their righteousness, *shomer emunim*, that is, "a keeping or guarding faith," by which you see that believers are justified by faith. Then he adds what that faith consists of, by which the people of God are just, namely, *yetser samuch tittsor shalom*, "with firm mind will you keep the peace." This is the true faith by which we are justified, namely that we believe that God will be to us the author of happiness and peace, and a faithful keeper of his promises. In treatise 40 on John, Augustine wrote, "What is faith except to believe what you do not see?" He wrote the same thing concerning the words of the apostle

---

[21]The second argument of Hostiensis *S. trin & fide cath.* is noted in sec. 4, p. 91, above.
[22]Isa. 26:2.

in sermon 27.[23] But in *The Spirit and the Letter*, chapter 31, he writes, "To believe is nothing except to consent that what is spoken is true."[24] The Master of the Sentences in book 3, distinction 23, says that faith sometimes is that which we believe.[25] In the creed of Athanasius it is written, "Moreover, this is catholic faith that we believe," and so forth.[26]

Sometimes it is the means by which we believe (*quo credimus*); in this discourse we understand faith in this latter sense. This also separates living faith from dead, a distinction acceptable because James makes mention of dead faith.[27] But we should know that a dead faith is faith in name only; nor is it faith any more than a dead man is a man. For just as a dead man is called a man, although he is not, so even though a dead faith is called faith, it does not have the nature of faith.

There is also another kind of faith that serves to work miracles, and differs a great deal from justifying faith; it is common to both faithful and unfaithful. Paul mentions it in 1 Corinthians, "to one is given the word of wisdom, to another the word of knowledge, to another faith."[28] It is unlikely that a different kind of faith would be meant in that list of gifts and graces from that which is the root of miracles, especially when gifts of healing and virtues or powers are immediately added. Of this type of faith, both Chrysostom and Theophylact made mention on the same 1 Corinthians, where in chapter 13 it is written, "If I have all faith so as to remove mountains ..." and so forth.[29]

Moreover, it is stated that this kind of faith is also given to the wicked, as is shown in that they do miracles and prophecies. So Christ may say to them, "I know you not," even though they boast with open mouth, "Lord, Lord, did we not prophesy in your name, and cast out demons in your name, and do many mighty works in your name?"[30] We must separate the faith that is only temporary, which the Lord mentions in the parable of the seed sown in the field.[31] Not all seeds fall on good

---

[23]Augustine *Tract. Ev. Jo.* 40.9; *Serm.* 27.9 (PL 35.1690, 1619).

[24]Augustine *Spir. et litt.* 31.54 (PL 44.235).

[25]Peter Lombard, *Sent.* 3.23.6 (PL 192.806).

[26]Athanasian Creed, 44. See *The Creeds of Christendom: With a History and Critical Notes,* ed. Philip Schaff, rev. by David Schaff (1931; repr., Grand Rapids: Baker, 1983), 2:70. Most contemporary scholars doubt Athanasian authorship. Thus, either St. Vincent or an admirer has been suggested as the author. The earliest known copy of the creed was included in a prefix to a collection of homilies by Caesarius of Arles (d. 542).

[27]James 2:17, 26.

[28]1 Cor. 12:8–9.

[29]1 Cor. 13:2; Chrysostom *Hom. 1 Cor.* 32.4 (PG 61.269); Theophylact *Hom. 1 Cor.* 13.2 (PG 123.726).

[30]Matt. 7:22.

[31]Matt. 13:1–23.

ground; some fall on stony soil and whenever growth springs forth successfully it obviously signifies those who receive the word of God with glad and joyful mind, but when burning and fierce persecutions come they fall off from their conviction *[520]* and are called *proskairoi,* that is, those having faith for a season. Now leaving all these meanings, in this discourse we understand faith to be that firm assent which is of such strength and effectiveness that it brings with it the affections of confidence, hope, and love, and finally, all good works, as much as the weakness of this present life allows.

6. Then there is [Richard] Smith, who wrote a book of justification against me, although he had earlier set it out against Luther and Melanchthon, speaking much against others but seldom mentioning me.[32] He is quite deceived in it, because he judges that they are to be sharply reproved who say that faith is trust. He draws from Ephesians, chapter 3, where it is written, "Through whom," namely, through Christ Jesus, "we have *parrêsian,*" that is, "boldness to speak" and *"prosagôgen,"* that is, "access," *"en pepoithêsei,"* "in trust," "which comes through faith." He says, therefore, since trust comes through faith, it is not itself faith. O fine man and astute theologian, who alone saw that these two, faith and trust, are two things, distinct and different! What else could Philip [Melanchthon] and our other learned doctors mean when they speak of "trust" except the faith by which we are justified. It is not dead, not lazy, not human persuasion, but so powerful an assent it has trust itself joined to it, inwardly and properly. I do not much care to contend with this man; all that he babbles he scrapes from the works of Eck, Pighius, and other rabble of the Roman Antichrist, and markets them as though they were his own.[33]

The faith that does not bring along with it trust, and other holy motions of the mind, draws men into desperation. It is so far removed that it cannot justify, a fact

---

[32]Richard Smith, *Diatriba de Hominis Iustificatione Aedita Oxoniae in Anglia anno a natiuitate Domini Nostri Iesu Christi 1550 Mense Februario aduersus Petrum Martyre[m] Vermelinu[m]...* (Louvain, 1550–51). Smith was Vermigli's predecessor as regius professor of divinity at Oxford, who despite his demotion, continued there as resident critic. Concerning Smith's work against Vermigli, Donnelly remarks: "although the title attacks him by name, [it] was really written against Luther and Melanchthon and seldom mentions him" (CAS, 150).

[33]Johann Eck (1486–1543) was, according to W. L. Moore, "the most important anti-Protestant theologian of his generation"; *Oxford Encyclopedia of the Reformation* (1996), 1:18. Eck wrote a critical response to Luther's Ninety-Five Theses (1517), which led to Luther's participation in the Leipzig Disputation (1519). Eck helped draft the papal bull *Exsurge Domine,* which condemned forty-one propositions of Luther. Albert Pighius (ca. 1490–1542) wrote his *De libero hominis arbitrio et divina gratia* (Cologne: M. Movesianus, 1542), against Calvin. Calvin famously answered Pighius in his *Defensio sanae et orthodoxae doctrinae de servitute et liberatione humani arbitrii adversus calumnias Alberti Pighuii Campensis* (Geneva: Jean Crispin, 1543).

that the miserable ends of both Cain and Judas plainly teach. But a firm faith trusts continually; indeed, in the church our faith is sealed by that common word "Amen," used among the faithful. This word is derived from the Hebrew word *'aman,* as I stated above, and means (as David Kimhi states) "it will be ratified and firm"; thus, the Lord brings it to pass.[34] Those who pray without such a faith lose their labor. Doubtless, in this faith men rest in tranquillity and ineffable peace. They are like the one who found the greatest treasure and precious pearl, with which he was so taken that he sold all that he had to buy it. Hence, in chapter 7 of Isaiah the prophet says to wicked King Ahaz, encouraging him to true faith, *hishshamer vehashket,* that is, "take heed and be quiet."[35] For the prophet wished the king to be aware of his own unbelief and to rest in the word of the Lord, which is the property and nature of faith. On the other hand, it is the nature of unbelief to waver and be inconstant. "For those who do not believe are tossed by every wind of doctrine and opinion and always waver and are in doubt."[36] So in chapter 7 of Joshua the people are reproved because their hearts melt as water, which happened on account of their unbelief.[37]

WORKS

7.　Since our understanding of faith is now clear from the above remarks, and which meaning of this word we adopt from among many in this question, let us now speak about works. There is a certain kind of work that follows action and motion and remains outward, appearing when labor is finished, just as the statue of Phidias is called a work and the Temple in Jerusalem is called the work of Solomon.[38] Likewise, human actions are themselves called works, as are their reasonable and voluntary motions. Let us take works in this way; they are distinguished among themselves in various ways. Some are inward, such as to believe, to love, to favor, to fear, to pity; others are outward, such as to travel abroad, to give alms, to preach, to teach, and so on. Our question is understood in relation to both types of work. They also divide works into those things which pertain to ceremonies and those they call moral; we embrace both kinds. Also the time in which good works are done must be distinguished, for some are done before we are justified and have obtained the benefit of regeneration; others follow, and are counted as the fruit of the new life and the righteousness already begun. Since we cannot treat the latter (works that follow justification), we will speak only of the former, for this alone is

---

[34]See n. 4 above.

[35]Isa. 7:4. This is a puzzling passage. Martyr's argument seems to lead up to Isa. 7:9b: "If you do not believe, surely you shall not be established," instead of the more innocuous Isa. 7:4.

[36]See Eph. 4:14.

[37]Josh. 7:5.

[38]Phidias was a famous Greek sculptor of the fifth century B.C.E.; for the Temple see 1 Kings 5.

called into controversy, as to whether works justify us. Those that follow justification cannot bring justification since it is already present.

Proposition 1: Justification Is Not by Works

8.   Now that we have considered these hypotheses, we will divide this whole question into three propositions. These are: justification is not by works; justification is obtained by faith; justification is given through faith alone.[39] If we establish these three statements with reasons from Holy Scripture and defend them from the opposition and railings of the adversaries, then we think we will have sufficiently addressed the question. May God grant and work with us to bring what we seek to fulfillment.

As to the first proposition, when we assert that men are not justified by works, it must not be thought that good works are destroyed. If those [good works] could be performed by us as the law commands, then we would be justified by them. For since God is just, he does not acquit the wicked, yet by his sentence he would justify those who satisfy the law. There is none, however, who is able to keep *[521]* such works as the law commands. It is as if one were in debt for a thousand gold crowns, but able to give only a thousand lead or brass coins; surely he is not freed from the debt, nor can he be declared absolved. This does not happen through the fault of the gold crowns or his bad money, but because he lacks the gold. So we say that the law is spiritual and just and holy, and one who could do what it demands would live by it, for it is given to us as life. But since none of us can do it as laid down by God, nor do we, we are not justified by works.

Moreover, if faith itself is considered our work, we cannot be justified by it, since as a work it is imperfect and flawed, far beneath what the law requires. But we are said to be justified by it [faith] because through it we take hold (*apprehendimus*) of the promises of God and the righteousness and merits of Christ, and apply them to ourselves. Suppose there were a beggar with a loathsome and leprous hand by which he received alms from one who offered them. Surely that beggar is not helped by the loathsomeness or leprosy of his hand, but by the alms he receives with it, whatever kind of hand he has. No one is so gifted with true piety that he does not need to mourn deeply and feel sorrow when he sees that many who are called Christians are ignorant as to whether works justify. This doctrine is the head, fountain, and mainstay of all religion. Therefore, we should be most

---

[39]"Iustificatio non ex operibus; Iustificatio per fidem habetur; Iustificatio datur sola fide." The first includes §§8–39; the second, §§40–82; the third, §§83–90.

sure and certain of this above all. But nowadays it is not only called into controversy, but many disagree among themselves and wander dangerously from the true doctrine.

If I could prevail a little by complaining, I would complain heartily concerning this indignity. But since we cannot alter the facts of the situation, I will simply do what I can to prevent our falling into these opinions that diminish the glory of God and are repugnant to the Holy Scriptures, and are also harmful to our conscience. Perhaps some will expect me to answer the cursings, slanders, and reproaches by which the adversaries defame us quite wildly and sadly on this matter. But I am not so mad as to think these things are to be preferred to the declaration and defense of the truth.

First, I will deal with the question at hand; then, when I have confirmed our own opinion I will choose those unworthy objections made against us, and will overthrow them through the strength God has given me. So that it will be perfectly clear that men are not justified by works (our first proposition), I will rehearse in due order the explanations Paul has in the letter to the Romans. By this it may be easily understood that I agree with him in all points, nor do I depart from his doctrine in any way.

PROOF FROM PAUL'S LETTER TO THE ROMANS

9. (1)[40] In chapter 1 he began to reprove the Gentiles, because even though before they came to the knowledge of Christ they knew the true God by their philosophy, they did not worship him as they should, nor give thanks to him as the author of all good things. They became fools and were frustrated in their reason and thoughts, and exchanged the glory of God, transferring it from him and giving it not only to human images but to birds, four-footed beasts, and serpents.[41] Therefore, God handed them over to the affections and desires of their own hearts. By this means they lived quite shamefully, and became (as it is written there) full of all iniquity, malice, fornication, avarice, and the vices that follow. If in fact they were like this, and lived so, doubtless they could not be justified by their works. Nor would Paul's reason against the Gentiles be of any force, to prove to them that it was necessary for them to receive the religion of Christ in order to be justified, unless he had thought that they were universally such as he painted them to be in chapter 1. For who would think it a sufficient reason if it appeared to be true only of some, and not of all?

---

[40]The numbers of the reasons appear in the marginalia.
[41]Rom. 1:18ff.

(2) In chapter 2 he writes much the same of the Jews: "Behold" (he says) "you are called a Jew, and trust in the law, and make your boast of God, and know his will, and allow the things that are profitable, being instructed by the law; you boast that you are a guide to the blind, a light to those who are in darkness, a corrector of the foolish, a teacher of the ignorant, an instructor of young children, as one that has the form of doctrine that is in the law. You that teach others, do you not teach yourself? You who preach against stealing, do you steal? You who say that one should not commit adultery, do you commit adultery? You who abhor images, do you rob God of his honor? And you that make your boast in the law, do you dishonor God by breaking the law? For as it is written, the name of God is blasphemed among the Gentiles because of you."[42] Such were the Jews without Christ. Therefore, in no way could they have been justified by their works, or else they might have answered Paul that such a harsh accusation was unjust.

10. (3) The state of mankind before receiving the faith of Christ is displayed more clearly in chapter 3, for there we read: "There is none righteous, there is none that understands or seeks after God, all have turned aside and are become unprofitable, there is none that does good, no not one. Their throat is an open grave, with their tongues they have deceived, the venom of asps is under their lips, their mouth is full of curses and bitterness, their feet are swift to shed blood, in their paths are ruin and misery, they have not known the way of peace, the fear of God is not before their eyes," and so forth.[43] Paul gathered these testimonies out of various places of Holy Scripture, in which human nature, destitute of the grace of God, is set forth in its true colors. *[522]* Lest anyone say that only the idolatrous and wicked Gentiles are meant by these words, the apostle shows, as is quite clear, that these things also apply to the Jews, who above all others thought themselves holy. Therefore, he adds: "We know that whatever the law says, it speaks to those who are under the law." And in order that we should not doubt that his intent was to give a universal principle, he adds: "Because by the works of the law no flesh shall be justified." By flesh he understands the unregenerate.

(4) I know there have been some who understand by "flesh" the lower parts of the mind that are gross and wrapped in filthy lusts.[44] But Paul excludes this meaning when he says, "by the works of the law," that is, by works commanded by God in the law, that must come from reason and not the strength of the inferior soul.

---

[42]Rom. 2:17–24.
[43]Rom. 3:10–18.
[44]Plato's tripartite psyche posited a concupiscent lower part; see e.g. *Resp.* 10.617d.

(5) Further, Scripture understands by "flesh" the whole person, following the sense of the Hebrew, something we have explained more fully elsewhere.[45] Afterwards, in order to better confirm the sentence, he says, "that every mouth might be stopped, and the whole world might be guilty before God."[46] Without doubt, if people were justified by their works their mouths would not be stopped, nor would they be guilty before God, for they would always have something to say, namely, that they are free from sins, because they deserved it by works. But now, when they perceive the opposite, they dare not once open their mouths. Later he says, "But now the righteousness of God has been manifested apart from the law, although the law and the prophets bear witness to it."[47] Who would select that to be the cause of our righteousness, without which righteousness may be obtained? No doubt anyone who is wise would not do so, since the nature of causes is that without them effects cannot be brought about.

(6) What follows serves the same purpose: "Where then is your boasting? It is excluded. By what reason? By reason of works? No, but by that of faith."[48] He wants us to know that every proper cause of glory is excluded and taken away from us, for the whole glory of our righteousness should give place to God. But if we were justified by works it would not be so, for the glory would be ours, and everyone would count himself to be justified because he lived virtuously and justly.

(7) What comes next declares how certain and sure this was to the apostle: "We hold, therefore, that a man is justified by faith without works of the law."[49] Will we then deny what the apostle affirms with such vehemence? This surely would be a most reckless thing to do. Therefore, let us agree with the apostle, and not resist so great a testimony.

(8) Besides these matters, let us weigh and consider the point of Paul's meaning: if we were justified by works (he says) we would not only have something to boast of, but the reason for glorifying God and proclaiming his favor towards us would be removed.[50] For indeed it is something most praiseworthy and glorious for us to acknowledge, that the benevolence and favor of God towards us through Christ is so great that he delivered us miserable creatures from our sins, and receives us unto favor, even though we were covered with such great filth and dregs of sin. If (I say) we were justified by works, then doubtless we could not truly boast, brag, or glory in them.

---

[45]ROM, 222–66, esp. 225–45.
[46]Rom. 3:19.
[47]Rom. 3:21.
[48]Rom. 3:27.
[49]Rom. 3:28.
[50]Rom. 3:27.

11. (9) Let us proceed to hear what the apostle says at the beginning of chapter 4. "What then shall we say about Abraham, our forefather according to the flesh? For if Abraham was justified by works, he has something to boast about, but not before God. For what does the Scripture say? Abraham believed God, and it was reckoned to him as righteousness. Now to one who works, his wages are not reckoned as a gift, but as his due."[51] Therefore, lest so sweet a consolation of God's love and goodwill towards us be snatched away from us, let us constantly affirm with the apostle that we are not justified by works. In order to persuade us the more on this point, he advances this word *logizein,* which we say means to impute, to ascribe righteousness to someone, or to count someone as just. He sets it as an antithesis to merit or debt, so that he to whom something is imputed neither deserves it nor receives it as a debt. Whoever obtains something owed him does not count it as imputed or ascribed to him. Paul did not think it enough to cite Scripture concerning Abraham, but also mentions David: "Blessed are those whose iniquities are forgiven, and whose sins are covered. Blessed is he against whom the Lord will not reckon his sin."[52] From this we gather not only that the righteousness by which we are said to be justified is not from our minds but is imputed by God, and that it is the kind of imputation that consists not of works but of the mercy of God alone.

(10) Moreover, the apostle confirms his statement by another property of good works, namely because works are signs or seals of the righteousness already obtained. Thus he says of Abraham: "He received circumcision as a sign or seal of the righteousness he had by faith, while uncircumcised," and so forth.[53] Since good works are signs and seals, witnessing to a righteousness already received, they cannot be its causes. Not only do ceremonies have that property, but even those works called moral, when they are pleasing and acceptable before God, for they are also signs and tokens of our righteousness. Hence, Peter exhorts us to strive to make our vocation sure, by living uprightly and by good works.[54]

(11) We must also consider the form of that promise that God made to Abraham, for no condition of law or works is added to it. Since God adds "none," it would be presumptuous for us to attempt it. Paul says, "For the promise made to Abraham and his seed that he should inherit the world, did not come through the law but through the righteousness of faith. For if *[523]* the adherents of the law are to be heirs, faith is null and the promise is void, for the law brings wrath."[55] So if we

---

[51]Rom. 4:1–4.
[52]Ps. 32:1–2 (Rom. 4:7–8).
[53]Rom. 4:11.
[54]2 Pet. 1:10.
[55]Rom. 4:13–15.

do not fulfill the law, the promise will not take place; it will be vain to believe a promise that is never to be fulfilled. This must be so if it is given on condition that we should perform the law, when no one can fulfill it perfectly.

(12) But the apostle proceeds further, discerning the most merciful will of God: "Therefore, the inheritance is given by faith, that it might rest on grace, so that the promise might be firm."[56] This is as if to say that our mind would waver continually if the promise depended on works; no one could hold any certainty of his salvation; his conscience would always accuse him of not performing those works for which the promise was made. So that we should not waver like this, God willed that our justification should consist of faith and grace, that the promise might be firm.

(13) The same is seen in what is declared of Abraham: "In hope he believed against hope."[57] One is said to believe in hope against hope, who sees or feels nothing in himself or nature that might persuade him to hope. Abraham was one hundred years old, his body in one sense dead, and his wife both old and barren; all this drove him away from hope. Yet prevailing against them all, he hoped. But if we have merits or good works by which we could obtain righteousness, then we would not hope contrary to hope, but in hope and according to hope. Hence, our justification is to be found in no other way than we read that it was for Abraham: "For he is the father of us all."[58] Just as it was reckoned (*imputatum*) to him, so it will be reckoned (*imputabitur*) also to us.

12. (14) Now let us come to chapter 5. There again Paul explains the state men are in before they are regenerate, for he says, "While we were yet weak, at the right time, Christ died for the ungodly."[59] And just after, "God shows his love towards us, in that while we were yet sinners, Christ died for us." He adds, "For if while we were enemies, we were reconciled to God by the death of his son, much more, now that we are reconciled, shall we be saved by his life."[60] From this we gather that before regeneration, men are weak, sinful, unbelieving, and enemies of God. Who then can ascribe to such men the ability to attain righteousness when they choose, by bringing forth good works? Others may believe it, but the faithful will never be so persuaded.

(15) Here it is further demonstrated that he sets forth the cause of so great an evil, when he says, "Therefore, even as sin came into the world by one man and death through sin, and so death spread to all men because all men have

---

[56]Rom. 4:16.
[57]Rom. 4:18.
[58]Rom. 4:16.
[59]Rom. 5:6.
[60]Rom. 5:8,10.

sinned."[61] It is as if he said that even from the beginning, by the first man, we were lost and condemned. In case you think infants are to be exempted, he says, "Yet death reigned from Adam to Moses, even over those whose sins were not like the transgression of Adam."[62] The mass or lump of perdition includes all those that are born;[63] Holy Scripture teaches that it is not possible for men to escape from this corruption by their works and then claim justification for themselves.

(16) Afterwards, in chapter 6, our apostle speaks as follows: "What fruit did you gain from those things of which you are now ashamed? The end of those things is death. But now that you have been set free from sin and have become slaves of God, the fruit you get is sanctification and its end, eternal life."[64] What else do these words mean but that all things that men do, before they believe in Christ, deserve nothing else but ignominy and shame? There is no fruit of sanctification except what follows regeneration. Who will say that we are justified by those things full of ignominy and shame?

(17) Now let us hear what is said at the beginning of chapter 7: "Do you not know, brethren (for I am speaking to those who know the law) that the law is binding on a man during his life? Thus a married woman is bound by law to the man as long as he lives; but if he dies she is discharged from the law concerning the husband. Accordingly, she will be called an adulteress if she lives with another man while her husband is alive. But if her husband dies she is free from that law, and if she marries another she is not an adulteress. Therefore, my brothers, you too are dead to the law through the body of Christ, so that we might be joined to another, namely to him who was raised from the dead, so that we may bear fruit unto God."[65]

By this reasoning Paul would declare that before our faith in Christ we were like husbands joined to the law and the flesh. No fruit could come from this union, except what is pernicious and deadly. But now, delivered by the grace of God, we are joined with Christ by the Spirit, to Christ himself being raised from the dead. By this union we may bring forth fruit to God, and no more death and damnation. He affirms the same thing, or rather expounds, when he adds, "While

---

[61] Rom. 5:12.

[62] Rom. 5:14.

[63] *Massa perditionis* is the distinctive term consistently employed by Augustine to refer to the mass of the entire human race which is alienated from him through Adam. See, e.g., Augustine *Corrept* 7.16 (PL 44.925). See the excellent discussion by Gerald Bonner, *St. Augustine of Hippo: Life and Controversies*, rev. ed. (Norwich: Canterbury Press, 1986), 326–29.

[64] Rom. 6:21.

[65] Rom. 7:1–4.

we were living in the flesh, our sinful passions, aroused by the law, were at work in our members to bear fruit for death."[66] Let us note here that so long as we were in the flesh we were subject to wicked affections, which were at work in our members by the law: how then could we be justified by our works?

(18) It is written further in the same chapter: "What I do I do not allow. For I do not do what I want, *[524]* but I do the very things I hate. Now if I do what I do not want, then it is not I that do it, but sin that dwells in me. For I know that nothing good dwells in me, that is, in my flesh."[67] In this passage it is clear that human works are discussed. Although in interpreting these words I have effectively shown that they are to be understood of those works performed by believers who have already obtained justification, yet now I leave it to the adversaries to take whichever side they will. If they allow that these things should be understood of works done before justification, then they are neither acceptable nor good. How could they deserve (*merebuntur*) justification? For they are called evil, and no one is justified by an evil action.

If we understand the works described here to be the works of those that are justified, then I will make my argument from the major premise, that is, from the greater.[68] If those works that seem to be acceptable, just, and holy to God, are called evil and not allowed by the judgment of a renewed reason, then how can we say that those works done by sinners are such that they are able to justify?

13. (19) Let no one say that we take our argument only from what happens through human sloth. The debate really concerns what would happen if men were to exercise their goodwill; for it is true that many are not justified by their good works even though they could be justified by them if they chose. We answer this with the apostle, who in chapter 8 says, "For God has done what the law, weakened by the flesh, could not do: sending his own Son in the likeness of sinful flesh and for sin, he condemned sin in the flesh."[69] This passage reminds us that the righteousness of God demonstrated in the commandments could not be performed by the help of the law, because of the corruption and weakness of the flesh. For that reason Christ was sent by the Father to perform what we could not accomplish.

(20) He teaches the same thing a little later, for when he says, "The lust of the flesh is death," and he adds, "the flesh is hostile to God, it does not submit to God's

---

[66]Rom. 7:5.
[67]Rom. 7:15–18.
[68]*A maiori,* from the major premise of the syllogism.
[69]Rom. 8:3.

law—indeed it cannot be."[70] Therefore, whatever we do by our natural strength, called flesh, resists God; for our corrupt nature cannot be subject to God's law. This being the case, we cannot be justified by its works.

(21) In the same chapter we also read, "everything works for good for those who love God, those who are called according to his purpose."[71] In these words the apostle touches on the origin and chief point of all our goodness, namely, the purpose of God, which is so far the cause of our salvation that all our other goodness depends on it, yet it is not moved by any of our goodness. The causes of human felicity are described afterwards clearly and distinctively; among these there is no mention at all of our good works. "For those he foreknew he also predestined; and those he predestined he also called, and those he called he also justified, and those he justified he also glorified."[72] This chain is linked together by all the means and aids by which God leads us to salvation. Since there is no mention of the law or merits, it is shown quite clearly that those in no way justify us.

(22) It is stated further, "Who shall bring any charge against God's elect? It is God who justifies; who is to condemn? Is it Christ who died, yes, who was raised from the dead, who is at the right hand of God, who indeed makes intercession for us?"[73] If according to God's judgment we were justified by works it would have been enough to say that the elect will be accused in vain, since they have good merits and since they will obtain absolution by their virtuous and holy works. He does not say so, "but," he says instead, "it is God who justifies." Another answer could have been given: no one will condemn the elect, since their works are such that they deserve both absolution and reward. He makes no such reply. Rather he says, "It is Christ who died," and so forth. Why then should we take it upon us to mix our works like this, when Scripture explicitly warns against doing so?

14. (23) Now we come to chapter 9, in which he treats God's providence that orders all things. Certainly there is no other reason except that we should think that the nature of providence and that of justification is the same, for both are given freely, and not through works. The apostle writes of two brothers, "though they were not yet born and had done nothing either good or bad, in order that God's purpose of election might continue, not because of works but because of his call, it was said, 'The elder will serve the younger. As it is written, Jacob have I loved, but Esau have I hated.'"[74] We see here quite clearly that works are excluded.

---

[70] Rom. 8:6–7.
[71] Rom. 8:28.
[72] Rom. 8:30.
[73] Rom. 8:33–34.
[74] Rom. 9:11–13.

(24) Moreover, Moses received the reply, "I will have mercy on whom I have mercy, and I will have compassion on whom I have compassion."[75] These words also declare that the forgiveness of sins; the means by which men are received into favor do not depend on their works, but only on the merciful goodness of God. The following words state the same thing: "It depends not on human will or exertion, but on God, who shows mercy." [76]

(25) Again, "He has mercy on whomever he wills, and he hardens the heart of whomever he wills."[77] If justification could be obtained by our will or works, then it would be by both him that wills and him that runs. Nor would those on whom God has compassion be converted, but those who have compassion mainly on themselves. God would not harden anyone, since everyone might promptly, easily, and at their own pleasure be reconciled to God by good works, and also be justified. It is quite otherwise, for those who put their trust in works are far from the true righteousness of which we speak here.

(26) Towards the end of chapter 9 the apostle says, "Israel who pursued the righteousness based on the law did not fulfill that righteousness. Why? Because they did not pursue it through faith, but as if it were based on works of the law."[78] If works of the law were a hindrance to the Jews in obtaining justification, *[525]* what then may we hope for from such works?

(27) The apostle declares the same thing, though in other words, in chapter 10: "Being ignorant of the righteousness that comes from God, and seeking to establish their own righteousness, they did not submit to the righteousness of God."[79] These words mean nothing else but that those who attribute too much to their own righteousness, namely to works, depart from God's righteousness. So great is the contrast between grace and works that the effect that proceeds from the one cannot proceed from the other.

(28) Paul says, "There is a remnant, chosen by grace. But if it is by grace, it is no longer on the basis of works; otherwise grace would no longer be grace."[80] For it is the property of grace to be given freely and out of sheer generosity; but the property of a work is that the reward should be given by duty, and even by right itself.

(29) Finally, what shall we say when the apostle cries out, "O the depth of the riches and wisdom and knowledge of God?"[81] There is no doubt that by this

---

[75]Exod. 33:19.
[76]Rom. 9:16.
[77]Rom. 9:15–18.
[78]Rom. 9:31–32.
[79]Rom. 10:3.
[80]Rom. 11:5–6.
[81]Rom. 11:33.

sentiment Paul declares that it is something very difficult to understand, whether God deals justly, when he predestines whom he will and justifies whom he will, having no regard to condition and merits. In this, human reason is much offended, our flesh forever cries out against it. But if either justification or election should occur through works and merits, there would be no trouble or offense, no stumbling block placed in our way. Since it is far otherwise, and we cannot give a reason for the will of God, Paul thus rightly and with justice cries out, and all who are wise must agree with his judgment.

(30) In chapter 14 it is written, "Blessed is he who has no reason to judge himself for what he approves. But he who has doubts is condemned, if he eats, because he does not eat from faith; for whatever is not of faith is sin."[82] This teaches us that those who lack true faith can perform nothing that is not sin. I know well that the adversaries interpret these words as applying to the conscience, but they cannot prove that faith signifies conscience. While Paul perhaps treats of it at the beginning, namely, that we should not do anything against our conscience, afterwards in a way he introduces a general principle when he writes, "Whatever is not of faith is sin." It is as though he should have said: This is a general rule, when men prepare to do anything they should be persuaded by the Spirit and word of God, that what they propose to do is acceptable to God and pleases him; if they do not have such persuasion then without doubt in doing so they sin. If I were to grant that in this passage faith means conscience, I suppose we should also add that the conscience should not be believed unless it is instructed by the word of God. For there are many who have such a superstitious conscience that, whether they obey it or not, they sin most severely. But at present I do not wish to delay any longer in expounding this passage, since I dealt with it before, and will speak later about it when I come to the place.[83]

PROOF FROM PAUL'S OTHER LETTERS

(31) Let us hear further what is said in 1 Corinthians 4, where it is written, "I know nothing against myself, but I am not thereby acquitted."[84] Paul spoke these words about his ministry, having been converted to Christ and being now an apostle, whom no one could accuse as to his actions. If such a great friend of God pronounced this of himself and his works, can we attribute justification to the works of those not yet regenerate? If the works of the faithful, and of the chief apostle of

---

[82]Rom. 14:22–23.
[83]That is, when he reaches chap. 14 in the Romans commentary.
[84]1 Cor. 4:4.

Christ, could not deserve it [justification]—how then can it be granted to those who are yet strangers from Christ?

15. (32) To the Galatians, chapter 2, Paul repeats that sentence he had written in chapter 3 of Romans, "that no flesh will be justified by the works of the law."[85] This passage is plain enough, and has been cited before, so it needs no further exposition now. But in chapter 3 it is written, "If righteousness comes by the law, then Christ died in vain (*gratis*)."[86] In this place *gratis* signifies nothing else than "in vain" and "to no purpose," which is certainly true. For if true righteousness before God could have been attained by men through any other means, why did he die, and why was he crucified?

(33) Again: "Let me ask you only this: did you receive the Spirit by the works of the law, or by hearing with faith?" and just after, "Does he who supplies the Spirit to you and works miracles among you do so by works of the law, or by hearing with faith?"[87] Those who are justified receive the Holy Spirit, for without him it is quite impossible to be justified; if he is not given through works, neither can justification come through works.

(34) Moreover, no one can doubt that justification comes through the good-will and favor of God, since by it men are received into grace, adopted as his children, and made heirs of eternal life. But those who before justification are busy with works of the law are bound under the curse, which is a long way from having the fruit of God's favor. For the apostle adds, "All who are under the law are under the curse."[88] Lest we think that this is his own invention, he says, as it is written, "Cursed be everyone who does not abide by all things written in the book of the law."

(35) After this, he argues from the progression of time: "To give a human example: no one annuls even a man's will, or adds to it, once it has been ratified. Now the promises were made to Abraham and to his offspring. It does not say, 'And to offsprings,' referring to many, but, referring to one, 'And to your offspring,' which is Christ. This is what I mean: the law, which came four hundred and thirty years afterwards, does not annul a covenant previously [526] ratified by God in relation to Christ, to make the promise void."[89] He says the first testament of God and the first promise offers justification without works. Therefore, that testament—

[85]Rom. 3:20; Gal. 2:16.
[86]Gal. 2:21 [*sic*].
[87]Gal. 3:2, 5.
[88]Gal. 3:10.
[89]Gal. 3:15–17.

confirmed, received, and ratified—is not restrained by the law, which was given long afterwards.

(36) "If a law had been given which could have made alive, then righteousness would indeed be by the law."[90] This reasoning of the apostle is incomplete, for a denial of the antecedent should have been added, namely, that the law cannot give life.[91] As it is said to the Romans, "it was weakened through the flesh,"[92] even though in itself it contained commandments that pertained to life. Thus seeing that it is certain that the law cannot give life, neither can it justify.

(37) "But before faith came, we were confined under the law, kept under restraint until faith should be revealed. So that the law was our tutor until Christ came, that we might be justified by faith."[93] If the law is a kind of tutor, then we would greatly injure God and Christ, who are like parents to us, if we ascribe to the tutor what is proper to them. It is not the tutor who makes us heirs, who adopts us, who gives us all things, but the father. Therefore, let us ascribe our justification to God and to Christ, and not to the law, nor to works, nor our merits.

(38) "Tell me, you who desire to be under the law, do you not hear the law? For it is written that Abraham had two sons, one by a slave and one by a free woman. But the son of the slave was born according to the flesh, the son of the free woman through promise. Now this is an allegory: these women are two covenants. One is from Mount Sinai, bearing children for slavery; she is Hagar. Now Hagar is Mount Sinai in Arabia; she corresponds to the city now called Jerusalem. But the Jerusalem which is above is free, and she is the mother of us all."[94] In these words we should note chiefly that the law produces only slavery as it did for Hagar. But if works could justify, it would create liberty (for what is justification but a kind of freedom from sin?). But since it [law] is both called a slave and brings forth slavery, we should not, therefore, look to it for justification.

(39) In chapter 5 it is written, "If you have been circumcised, Christ will be of no advantage to you." And he gives the reason for this statement: "For he who is circumcised is bound to keep the whole law."[95] Paul removes justification so far from circumcision and works that he says that Christ is of no advantage to them, if they are circumcised after they believe.

---

[90]Gal. 3:21.
[91]I.e., to make a complete syllogism.
[92]Rom. 8:3.
[93]Gal. 3:23–24.
[94]Gal. 4:21–26.
[95]Gal. 5:2–3.

(40) Still more strongly does he confirm what was said: "Christ is of no advantage to you";[96] for if you have justification as the fruit of your works, then Christ's coming, death, and shedding of blood would not have been necessary. "And if I yet preach circumcision, why am I still persecuted? In that case the stumbling block of the Gospel has been removed."[97] The offense and scandal of the cross is that men who are otherwise wicked and sinful are counted righteous by God through Christ crucified and faith in him. Here the flesh is offended, here reason wholly rebels, which does not happen when justification is preached as coming from works, whether ceremonial or moral. But God wishes this offense to remain, "because it pleased him by the foolishness of preaching, to save those who believe."[98]

16. (41) To the Ephesians it is written, in chapter 2, "When you were dead in trespasses and sins in which you once walked, following the course of this world, following the prince of the power of the air, the spirit that is now at work in the sons of unbelief. Among these we all once lived in the passions of our flesh, following the desires of body and of mind" (as in Greek, *kata tôn dianoiôn*), "and were by nature the children of wrath, just as others are."[99] Note in these words that in the beginning, before they came to Christ, men are dead in sins and, therefore, unable to move themselves to live and to be justified. Who has ever said that a dead man could help himself? Those words also show that they were in the power of the prince of darkness, who works effectively in the sons of unbelief. Since they are governed by him, how can they aim at justification by their works? And lest we think he spoke only of some other ungodly people, he adds, "All of us," including even the apostles: "among them," he says, "were we." And what were we doing then? We were following the desires of our flesh. So that we should understand that these desires were not only the evil affections of the baser part of the soul, there follows: "We, doing the will of the flesh and of the mind or reason, followed also the thoughts or inventions of human reason."[100] If we were all like that, where do salvation and justification come from? "But God, who is rich in mercy, out of the great love with which he loved us, even when we were dead through our trespasses, made us alive together with Christ."[101]

(42) What means did he use to give us salvation? "For by grace" (he says) "you have been saved through faith, and this is not your own doing, it is the gift of God—

[96]Gal. 5:2.
[97]Gal. 5:11.
[98]1 Cor. 1:21.
[99]Eph. 2:1–3.
[100]Eph. 2:3.
[101]Eph. 2:4–5.

not because of works, lest any man should boast."[102] Could works be excluded more clearly? Where then shall we place them? Certainly they follow justification, for the apostle adds, "For we are his workmanship, created in Christ Jesus for good works, which God prepared beforehand, that we should walk in them."[103]

(43) They could not be present in us before, something well described thus: "You were at that time without Christ, alienated from the commonwealth of Israel, strangers *[527]* from the covenants of promise, having no hope and without God in the world."[104] Who could pretend that men in this condition could merit justification by their good works?

(44) To the Philippians, chapter 3: "If anyone else thinks he has reason for confidence in the flesh, I have more: circumcised on the eighth day, of the people of Israel, of the tribe of Benjamin, a Hebrew born of Hebrews, as to the law a Pharisee, as to zeal a persecutor of the church, as to righteousness under the law blameless."[105] Seeing that Paul enjoyed so many and such great things before his conversion, and that he had what he could trust and boast of in the flesh, let us hear what in the end he says about them. "These things," he says "if compared to the true righteousness that is through the faith of Christ, I count loss, vile, and dung."[106] If we could obtain righteousness by this means, should such profitable things be counted as losses, such precious and holy things as vile, and matters acceptable and pleasing to God as dung? Let Paul be careful here with what he says, or rather let the readers beware that they do not believe Sophists rather than Paul.

(45) To the Colossians, chapter 1: "And you, who were once estranged and hostile in mind, doing evil deeds, he has now reconciled in his body of flesh by his death."[107] Every word here is to be diligently noted, so that we may see that those who are estranged from God should not regard those things in order to curry favor. The peace that is joined with justification cannot be obtained by those who are hostile in mind; good works cannot come from those who, before they are changed, are said to be full of evil deeds.

(46) What kind of works those were is described in chapter 2, where it is written: "And you, who were dead in sins and the uncircumcision of your flesh, he has made alive together with him, having forgiven all your sins, having cancelled the bond that stood against us."[108]

---

[102]Eph. 2:8–9.
[103]Eph. 2:10.
[104]Eph. 2:12.
[105]Phil. 3:4–6.
[106]Eph. 3:7–9, paraphrase.
[107]Col. 1:21–22.
[108]Col. 2:13–14.

(47) In 2 Timothy, chapter 1:"who called us with a holy calling, not in virtue of our works but in virtue of his own purpose and the grace which he gave us in Christ Jesus."[109] He speaks here of an effectual calling, by which men are justified, not of the general calling through the preaching of the word of God, which is declared unto all. Since this [effectual calling] does not consist of merits or works (as Paul says), neither can justification come from it.

(48) It is written to Titus: "When the goodness and love of God our Savior appeared, he saved us, not because of deeds done by us in righteousness, but in virtue of his own mercy."[110] Also to the Hebrews, there is one sacrifice alone and one oblation, namely, the death of Christ, by which sins are wiped away and satisfaction made for us.[111]

(49) Therefore, justification is not to be looked for from works; it should be enough for us, that the good works we do after justification are sacrifices of thanksgiving (*eucharistika*). Let us not make them propitiatory sacrifices, by which we would do great injury to Christ.[112]

PROOF FROM OTHER SCRIPTURES

The Gospels

17. (50) Setting Paul's letters aside, let us also look for witnesses from other places in Holy Scripture. In chapter 7 of Matthew, Christ says, "Every sound tree bears good fruit, but the bad tree bears evil fruit." And to show more clearly the nature of the unregenerate he adds, "A sound tree cannot bear evil fruit, nor can a bad tree bear good fruit."[113] Therefore, since Christ denies that this can happen, how dare they claim that it may be and assert that men may be justified by works?

(51) Christ uses the same reasoning in Matthew 12: "Either make the tree good, and its fruit good; or make the tree bad and its fruit bad; for the tree is known by its fruit. You brood of vipers! how can you speak good things when you are evil? For out of the abundance of the heart the mouth speaks. The good man out of the treasure of the heart brings forth good, and the evil man out of his evil treasure brings forth evil."[114] Christ's words declare that those who are not regenerate are evil trees, which do not and cannot bear good fruit, that the wicked cannot speak good things,

---

[109]2 Tim. 1:9.

[110]Titus 3:4–5.

[111]See Heb. 9:24ff.

[112]Cf. Martyr, "Sacrifice" locus in *Comm. in lib. Iud.* (Zurich, 1561), 13.22; LC, appendix, pp. 995–99; *The Life, Early Letters and Eucharistic Writings of Peter Martyr,* trans. G. E. Duffield and Joseph C. McLelland (Oxford: Sutton Courtenay, 1989), 310–18. Cf. VWG, 238ff.

[113]Matt. 7:17–18.

[114]Matt. 12:33–35.

much less can they do good works, and that out of an evil heart's treasure evil things will always be expected. Given this, I ask you to consider whether those who are estranged from Christ should be called evil. Without doubt they are evil. Unless they cleave to Christ, no one can be called good.

(52) Moreover, in Luke, chapter 17: "Will any of you who has a servant plowing or keeping sheep, say to him when he has come in from the field, 'Go and sit down.' Rather will he not say 'Prepare supper for me, and gird yourself and serve me, till I eat and drink; and afterwards you shall eat and drink'? Does he thank the servant because he did what was commanded? I trust not. So you also, when you have done all that is commanded of you, say: 'We are unworthy servants; we have done only what was our duty.'"[115] Christ spoke those words to his disciples, indeed his apostles, who were now converted to salvation. If they perform works of duty, what then shall we judge about those who have not yet received the faith of Christ? But the Sophists have made such fools of the world, when they say that works before justification deserve it in one sense, while those works that follow are the most profitable. Therefore, men would in one sense enter into a business transaction with God, and count with beads how many prayers they have said. What else could they mean by this except that they would recite a certain number of Paternosters, or so many Ave Marias, thinking that by such repetition they will surely bring God under obligation to themselves?

[528](53) In chapter 15 of John, Christ is compared to a vine tree, and we its branches. Thus he says, "As the branch cannot bear fruit by itself, unless it abides in the vine, neither can you, unless you abide in me. I am the vine, you are the branches. He who abides in me, and I in him, he it is that bears much fruit.... And whoever does not abide in me is thrown outside, like branches and twigs, and they will gather them and cast them into the fire."[116]

Now that we have cited these words of the Lord, how fitting is it that those who are strangers from Christ and not regenerate, can perform good works by which they may be justified? They are called dry branches that will be thrown into the fire. And it is said that only those can bear fruit who hold to Christ, as branches hold to the vine. In order to understand Christ's will better, it is added, "Without me you can do nothing."

(54) Some try to muddy this statement, saying that nothing can be done without Christ insofar as he is God, since he is the first cause of all things, as if the Lord were discussing the general preservation of natural things and of that power by which God brings forth all things universally. Christ did not come into the

---

[115]Luke 17:7–10.
[116]John 15:4–6.

world to teach this philosophy. Clearly he taught about the fruits of salvation and eternal life, and spoke of those who would hold to his teaching, or else remain strangers from it.

18. (55) Moreover, the Son of God commanded believers to say in their prayers, "Forgive us our trespasses."[117] This shows that the faithful also need forgiveness for the things they do, for our works are not perfect nor are they able to satisfy. Therefore, if our works, which we do after our regeneration, need purging by the merit of Christ, and we pray for this, how can they be propitiatory? Certainly there is nothing to suggest that those works which precede regeneration could be acceptable to God. Further, no one can justly say that he is not in this number, since God has commanded all men to pray in this manner, and it is his will that no one should lie in his prayer.

(56) John also writes, "If we say we have no sin, we deceive ourselves and there is no truth in us."[118] I do not suppose anyone will judge it suitable that many mediators should be introduced, when "there is but one mediator between God and man, the man Jesus Christ."[119] But if our works could justify us in addition to Christ and his merits, they would stand between God and us; nor would Christ be the only mediator.

The Old Testament

(57) Moreover, the prophets everywhere prayed, and David too, that God would wash, cleanse, expiate, and purge their sins, namely, in forgiving and remitting them. But if they could have acquired that by their own works, then they need not strive to obtain it by prayer, or at least without such great vehemence.

(58) In chapter 15 of Job it is written that "the very heavens are not pure in the sight of God."[120] And in chapter 4 he proclaims the angels to be impure.[121] Therefore, what is the state of men before they obtain justification?

(59) David cries out in the Psalms, "If you O Lord should mark iniquities, Lord who could stand?"[122]

---

[117]Matt. 6:12.
[118]John 1:7.
[119]1 Tim. 2:5.
[120]Job 15:5.
[121]Job 4:18.
[122]Ps. 51.

(60) Isaiah calls the thirsty to the waters and commands those without money to purchase, [123] but our opponents want to be justified both by merits and works, and also by money.

(61) Moreover, in chapter 40 of Isaiah, when he heard a voice saying to him "cry out," he answered, "What shall I cry?" And he was told to cry, "All flesh is grass." Now *kabod,* that is, the piety, religion, or mercy with which one comes to the aid of his neighbor, "is as the flower of the field," namely, something vanishing, which certainly fades away and cannot endure. [124]

(62) He affirms the same thing also in chapter 64, where he says that "all our righteousness is as filthy rags." I do not much care whether one applies this verse to works done before or after regeneration, for either way it will support our side. In the same chapter he adds, "Our God, we are clay and you are our potter, and we are the work of your hands." [125]

(63) Paul used the analogy of the potter and clay in chapter 9 of Romans, where it is clearly declared that we are able to contribute to our justification just as much as the clay can influence the potter to shape it in a certain way. [126] We could also mention passages in both Genesis and Jeremiah that show the depravity of our hearts. [127]

I think I have already brought enough testimonies for the confirmation of our proposition. I will now add only this: there have been men who are so rash that they have attributed some merit of justification not only to honest works, which they term morally good, but also to superstitious works, which they have fabricated and invented. For who is ignorant of the rhymes commonly circulated about holy water: "Let your sins be blotted out by holy water, and let it be praise and life to you." [128] They also attribute forgiveness of sins to monks' cowls, to candles, to ashes of olive and palm branches, and to pilgrimages. Therefore, they progress from what they so perversely interpreted in Holy Scripture concerning merits, to these foolish and ungodly things. Certainly no one understands except those who have experienced how difficult it is for a bruised heart, dejected and weary with the burden of sins, to find comfort in the free promises of God through Christ when it is grieved and oppressed. For such a heart earnestly labors so that it may finally establish a firm faith. If, like the Sophists, we commanded someone to have regard for his own works, then he would never find comfort,

---

[123] Isa. 55:1.
[124] Isa. 40:6.
[125] Isa. 64:6–8.
[126] Rom. 9:20.
[127] Gen. 6:5, 8:21; Jer. 17:9.
[128] "Aqua benedicta, deleantur tua delicta, sit tibi laus et vita." Cf. Leo IV *Hom.* (PL 115.679).

would always be tormented and always in doubt of his salvation, and at last would be swallowed up with desperation.[129]

I would not want anyone to think that when we debate this matter we are engaging in a worthless exercise or strife over words. It is something that vindicates the honor of Christ and that belongs properly only to himself, namely, to justify and to forgive sins. We wish to affirm that these things (justification and forgiveness) should in no way be attributed to works or to anything else of ours. We wish to affirm that the promise *[529]* should be firm and that afflicted consciences should receive consolation in the words and promises of God. Last, we wish to affirm that Gospel should be distinguished from law and law from Gospel. But this cannot be done by those who ascribe justification to works, and confuse them. Although I could bring many more reasons to confirm this proposition (indeed an almost infinite number), yet these I have already brought are enough, and I will refrain from others. For those who are not persuaded by these reasons will not be affected by any others.

OBJECTIONS TO PROPOSITION 1

(1) Moral and Ceremonial Works of the Law

19. It is not good, however, to ignore the remedies and deceits which the Sophists employ to avoid and obscure this doctrine we have put forward. First, they acknowledge that as often as the Holy Scriptures take away the power of justifying from works, they do so only with regard to the ceremonies of the old law and not with regard to just and upright works, which they commonly call moral works. This is something about which many are deceived, as the testimony of the Scriptures and especially Paul (whom they claim for support above all) will most plainly demonstrate. Although this apostle says many things that seem to refer both to the rites and the ceremonies of the law, yet in his other discussions he wrote a great deal where he speaks not only of ceremonies, but also of the other laws of righteousness and uprightness. Indeed, to sum up, these things pertain to conduct as well as to the Decalogue.

In chapter 1, when he reproves the Gentiles that they cannot be justified without the faith of Christ, he sets their works in front of their eyes, namely idolatry and shameful lusts.[130] Toward the end of the chapter he reviews a very long catalogue of vices with which they were afflicted, but says nothing about the ceremonies of Moses.[131] Therefore, since those things he recounted are opposed to

---

[129]Cf. the Italian lawyer Francesco Spiera of Cittadella, p. 48 n. 189 above.
[130]Rom. 1:24ff.
[131]Rom. 2:21–22.

the Decalogue and the moral law, one must believe that he also understands what he writes. In chapter 2 he reproves the Jews for the same kind of sins, for he says, "You who teach others, do you not teach yourself? You who teach that a man should not steal, do you steal? That a man should not commit adultery, do you commit adultery? Indeed, you who detest idols, do you rob God of his honor?"[132] Who does not see that these things are contained in the law of the Decalogue?

In chapter 3, he argues the same thing even more clearly when he writes, "None is righteous, no one understands or seeks for God. All have turned aside, together they have gone wrong, no one does good, not even one."[133] We see that these things are of the same kind and relate to conduct. If the apostle wanted to speak only of ceremonial laws, he would never have mentioned these matters. This is more clearly expressed when he also says, "No flesh is justified by the works of the law." He adds, "For through the law comes the knowledge of sin."[134] Therefore, that law by which we know sin, does not justify.

Similarly, he also says in chapter 4, "The law brings wrath."[135] This is far removed from any idea that it should justify. But it is clear enough to all that sins are better known and the wrath of God against transgressions more stirred up by the Decalogue than by ceremonial precepts.

I will pass over that general verse in chapter 4, where it says, "To him who works, a reward is not reckoned as a gift but as his due."[136] Also, God would have the inheritance to consist of grace, that the promise should abide and not be changed, that our glorying might be excluded.[137] This glory comes no less from good moral works than from ceremonies.

It is also written in chapter 5 that "law came in to increase the trespass. Now where sin increased, grace abounded all the more."[138] These things also cannot be derived from ceremonies alone.

Moreover, in chapter 6, when it was objected to him (as they now often object to us) that by minimizing works and the law he seemed to open the door to a loose life, to folly, and to sins, he answered, "We should not abide in sin, since we are now dead to it. By baptism we are buried with Christ, that just as he died and rose again so likewise, we should walk in newness of life."[139] And he admonishes us that "just as Christ died once, and died no more, so also we should consider ourselves dead to

---

[132]Rom. 2:21–22.
[133]Rom. 3:10–12, from Ps. 12:1–2.
[134]Rom. 3:20.
[135]Rom. 4:15.
[136]Rom. 4:4.
[137]Rom. 3:27.
[138]Rom. 5:20.
[139]Rom. 6:2,4.

sin but alive to God."[140] He adds that we must take most diligent care lest sin reign in our mortal bodies, and that we should not yield our members to sin as instruments of iniquity, but yield ourselves to God as men who have been brought from death to life and our members as instruments of righteousness to sanctification.[141]

20. Do these things we have reviewed and the rest which follow generally to the end of the chapter, appear to relate to the ceremonies of Moses or to a just, sincere, and moral life? The matter is so obvious that no question needs to be raised. Yet what is written in chapter 7 is even clearer: "The passions in our members were aroused by the law to bear fruit for death."[142] But what are these passions except desires, lusts, anger, hatred, and envy, which are recounted to the Galatians in that catalogue where the works of the flesh are distinguished from the works of the spirit?[143] There is no doubt that all these things pertain to the Decalogue. That we might better understand this, Paul adds, "What then should we say? That the law is sin? By no means! Yet, if it had not been for the law, I would not have known sin. I would not have known what it is to covet if the law had not said, 'You shall not covet.'"[144] Also it is written, "The commandments are holy, just, and good."[145] And again, "The law is indeed spiritual, but I am carnal and sold under sin, for what I do, I allow not, for the good which I want, I do not; but the evil I do not want is what I do. Therefore, it is no longer I that do it, but sin which dwells within me; for there dwells no good in me, that is, my flesh. I delight in the law of God, in my inmost self, but I see another law in my members resisting the law of the mind. Oh wretched man *[530]* that I am! Who shall deliver me from the law of sin and death? Therefore, with my mind I serve the law of God but with the flesh the law of sin."[146]

Whoever will weigh all these testimonies diligently will easily see that the apostle speaks entirely about the Decalogue, which is also plainly mentioned in these words. The words that follow in chapter 8, however, cannot be explained by the law of ceremonies. "What was impossible to the law, insofar as it was weakened by the flesh, God sending his own Son in the likeness of flesh and for sin, condemns sin in the flesh."[147] These words, I say, cannot be explained as dealing

[140]Rom. 6:10–11.
[141]Rom. 6:12–13.
[142]Rom. 7:5.
[143]Gal. 5:19ff.
[144]Rom. 7:7.
[145]Rom. 7:12.
[146]See Rom. 7:14–25.
[147]Rom. 8:3.

with the law of ceremonies; still less can those words that follow in the same chapter: "We are debtors, not to the flesh, that we should live according to the flesh, for if you live according to the flesh you shall die. But if by the Spirit you mortify the deeds of the flesh, you shall live."[148] This cannot refer to ceremonies any more than what is written to the Galatians: "The law was given because of transgression, for where there is no law there is also no transgression."[149] It is certain that boasting cannot be excluded, nor can the promise be firm if our justification depends on observing the Decalogue and moral precepts. This is the case no matter how much you take away the rites and ceremonies of Moses.

Much firmer is that passage from chapter 11 of Romans: "And if it be of works, then it is not of grace, if of grace, then is it not of works."[150] This is a universal antithesis.[151] Nor can it in any way be applied to ceremonies. I will pass over what Paul says to the Philippians, that in addition to the precepts of Moses, he also lived without blame as to the righteousness which is of the law.[152] For what he wrote to the Ephesians in chapter 2, "Not of works, lest any man should boast," he writes to Gentiles.[153] Therefore, those works he excluded from justification cannot be understood of ceremonies, for Gentiles did not practice them. But what will they say of the letter to Timothy in chapter 2, where we are plainly and absolutely said to be called not according to our works but according to purpose and grace?[154] Also to Titus, "He has saved us not by the works of righteousness which we had done, but according to his mercy."[155]

21. All these things are so clear as to need no interpretation. For no one is so dull but that as soon as he hears these things for the first time, he easily understands how they cannot be twisted into the ceremonies and rites of Moses without injury. I would like to find out from these fellows why they remove the power of justifying from the works of ceremonies and so easily attribute it to our moral works. Is it not good and laudable conduct to worship God with certain fixed rites which he has commanded? Were not the rites and holy services imposed at that time on the nation of the Jews commanded in the Decalogue? Certainly, where the Sabbath is commanded to be observed, all these things are contained. And even these same Sophists, do not they today ascribe the forgiveness of sins and

---

[148]Rom. 8:11.
[149]Gal. 3:19.
[150]Rom. 11:6.
[151]On universals, see Aristotle *An. post.* 1.24, 85a12ff.
[152]Phil. 3:6.
[153]Eph. 2:9.
[154]2 Tim. 1:9.
[155]Titus 3:5.

bestowing of grace to the sacraments, just as in the Old Testament they were attributed to circumcision? What kind of new inconsistency is this, to say that the Mosaic rites had no power to justify, while another confesses that they were the sacraments of the old fathers, and that in circumcision the original sin of infants was forgiven? But we do not affirm this. Indeed, we utterly deny that any sacraments bestow grace. They do offer grace, but it is by signification.[156] For in sacraments and words, and in the visible signs, the promises of God made through Christ are set before us. If we take hold of those promises by faith, we obtain a greater grace than we had before. And with the seal of the sacraments, we seal the gift of God that we embraced by faith.

I cannot marvel enough at these men who both affirm and deny the same thing. Indeed, they respond with their usual lack of prudence, that they do not take away the power of justifying from the sacraments of the old fathers, principally circumcision. But it was only after the time (and from that time only) when the Gospel was proclaimed that Paul's contention arose, namely, that the rites of Moses should no longer be retained. Here, too, as is their habit, they deceived themselves and deceive others. For the apostle teaches that Abraham was not justified by circumcision but received it afterwards, thus being justified by faith. Certainly, when it was first instituted in the time of Abraham, the power of justification was removed from that ceremony. When David proclaimed that blessedness consists in the fact that sins were not imputed (which we now understand is nothing other than to be justified), was he speaking of his own time or of another? And when Habakkuk said, "The just shall live by faith,"[157] excluding works from justification (as Paul splendidly explains), did he speak only of his own time? Undoubtedly, he spoke of our time and also of his own.

Last, when Paul clearly writes to the Galatians in chapter 3, "As many as are of the law are under the curse,"[158] and goes on to prove that thought, from where, I ask, does he derive his testimony? Certainly it is out of the law: "Cursed be he who abides not in all things that are written in the book of the law."[159] Since, therefore, the law speaks like this, and as Paul says, envelops in a curse all those that transgress the commandments, it follows necessarily that no one can be justified *[531]* by those works that pertain to the law.

---

[156]For Martyr's concept of sacramental signification, see OTD, xxiii ff., 121ff., 280–81.
[157]Hab. 2:4.
[158]Gal. 3:10.
[159]Rom. 1:17.

(2) Good Works of Fallen Believers

22. But these fellows had to flee to another position. For they say that all those who are to be justified are not of the same condition. They say that some Hebrews and some Gentiles have come to Christianity. They also say that after they once receive Christ, some fall into grievous wickedness and need renewal. They say that the condition of both parties is no longer the same. For those who have once professed the name of Christian, but then fallen, cannot recover righteousness except by good works, such as almsgiving, shedding tears, fastings, confessions, and other such things. These preparations and merits are not required of those who were first converted to Christ from unbelief. But I want to hear first from these wise men: where in the Holy Scriptures did they find this distinction? And since the ground *(ratio)* of justification is absolutely one and the same, and relates to the one as well as the other, why should one come to it one way and others another? Further, why do they grant to those who are fallen in Christianity the ability to merit for themselves justification by their good works, but do not grant the same to those who come from unbelief? Are those who have not kept the faith when they were in the church better than the pagans? Certainly I think not, for "they which have once tasted the good word of God and afterwards fell from it are in worse state than the other," and, "The servant who knows the will of his master and does not do it is more grievously punished."[160] Also, "He who had not a care over his family and especially over his own household, the same man has denied the faith and is worse than an infidel."[161] But they say they do not deny that those who are converted from unbelief may do some good works. Indeed, if they do such good works, they may deserve justification in some sense, at least in the sense of congruity.[162]

Yet they cannot decide whether these works as well as others are required. But since I have taught elsewhere that all their works are sins, how then can they do good works before God? Moreover, how is it that good works are not required of them before they come to Christ and are baptized? And since none of those who are regenerated by Christ can believe truly unless they earnestly repent of the wretched life they have led, how can good works be required of them? For such a one will greatly lament the sins of his former life and confess that he has greatly erred. If he does not do so, then certainly he does not believe faithfully and truly. Augustine writes about himself in his book *Confessions*, and in the Acts of the Apostles, when the Ephesians had given themselves to Christ, they not

---

[160]Luke 12:47; Heb. 6:4.
[161]1 Tim. 5:8.
[162]For congruity, see Martyr, "Free Will," PW, 281 n. 48.

only confessed their sins but also burned those books that had been used for superstition.[163]

Still, I will declare what has deceived these men. They read perhaps in the fathers that they attributed much to tears, alms, and other godly works of the penitent. But these men do not understand what the fathers meant in those places, for they were concerned about ecclesiastical satisfactions, not our own works, by which God could be appeased or the forgiveness of sins deserved. The church does not see the inward faith of the fallen, for there are many who cannot submit to the shame of excommunication and sometimes give the appearance of conversion and repentance, in order to be reconciled and received into the communion of the other brethren. To prevent this, one should require proof of their faith and conversion. Nor should the fallen be admitted to the community of the faithful unless they had showed tears, fastings, confessions, and almsgiving, as witness of a true and firm change. And because they lack understanding, they confuse everything and build on unworthy hypocrisy.

(3) Good Works of Unbelievers

23. They cast up another position, saying that the works of unbelievers are not sins, although they are done without faith in Christ. For they imagine that there is a certain general confused faith toward God which they have, even though they do not believe in Christ. Nevertheless, they are able to produce many excellent works, which may be acceptable to God and in a sense deserve justification. They say they give many alms, that they honor their parents, that they bear exceeding love to their country. And if they have admitted anything evil, they take on punishment, they live moderately, and do many other similar things of importance because they believe that there is a God who delights in such duties; therefore, they apply themselves to those things to make themselves acceptable to him. Further, they paint and color their invention with an excellent illustration. A stake, for example, or a post is buried in the earth, and although often it does not take root or live, yet it absorbs some moisture from the earth and so brings forth some leaves and buds as if it were really alive. Likewise, they say, although those who are estranged from Christ do not live by the heavenly Spirit, yet by some inspiration of the Spirit they produce those excellent works we have described. But we are taught by Holy Scripture to acknowledge no other faith by which we can please God, except that alone which is in Christ. For "there is no other name under heaven given among men by which we must be saved," but only the name

---

[163]Probably a reference to Augustine *Conf.* 10.1–4 (PL 32.779–82).

of Christ our Savior.[164] As often as Paul mentions the faith that justifies, he always shows it to be that faith by which we are faithfully related to Christ and his Gospel.

Lest Paul alone *[532]* seem to teach this peculiarity, I will return again to the whole matter with more depth. "Abraham believed God and it was counted unto him for righteousness."[165] But what did he believe? Certainly, he saw that he would be given a seed, that is, the unique seed, as Paul interprets it, in which all nations would be blessed, that is, Christ Jesus. This testament was confirmed to him by God in Christ. Indeed, when the Lord himself spoke of him he said, "He saw my day and rejoiced."[166] Job also wrote in chapter 19, "I know that my redeemer lives, and that at last he will stand upon the earth; and after worms have destroyed this body, I shall see the Lord in my flesh, whom I myself shall see on my side and my eyes shall behold and not another."[167] The faith expressed in those words is in no way general or confused. For plainly described in them are the principal points that pertain to Christ. First he is called a redeemer, in whom the forgiveness of sins is proclaimed. Further, he is coming to declare judgment and also the resurrection of the dead, not of other bodies, for the same bodies they had before will be restored to men.[168] There is also mention of the human nature of Christ, which may be seen with the physical eyes. I ask further, what kind of faith is it these men say unbelievers have? For a true and firm conviction and a constant and certain assent to the promises of God draws with it (as I said in the beginning) all the good motions of the mind. How then can they say that these people have faith that still lingers in idolatry and in most foul and crass sins? They may indeed have a certain kind of belief, either by education or by human persuasion or by an opinion they may have conceived in some way. But to have true faith is in no way possible as long as they live like this, unless they want to grant that the Turks also have faith, for they assent to many things we profess and believe.

In that passage in 1 Corinthians where Paul says, "If I have all faith so that I can move mountains and have not charity, I am nothing,"[169] they want it to be understood not only of true faith, but also that this faith may be separated from charity. Indeed, if that is so, they admit that it will profit nothing at all. Therefore,

---

[164]Acts 4:12.
[165]Gen. 15:6.
[166]John 8:56.
[167]Job 19:25–27.
[168]Cf. Martyr's "Resurrection," PW, 113ff.
[169]1 Cor. 13:2.

since they explain that passage in that way, how can they support Paul when they say that a general and confused faith, the attribute of those who are alienated from Christ, can produce good works, which may merit justification by congruity, and please God? How then can they say that the true faith (as they understand it) also profits nothing without love? But the illustration they bring forward of a stake or a post buried in the earth quite overthrows their own opinion. For although it is dead it appears to live; nevertheless, it is not alive. A wise farmer sees that the budding is useless and he discards or destroys such leaves as worthless. God views those works that these people color and adorn in the same way.

(4) Good Works and Common Grace

24. They also invent another fiction, not unlike the former, for they say that the works of unbelievers are not done without grace. They hold that there is a kind of general grace accessible to all and common even to the unregenerate, who are in a sense helped to merit justification and do works which please God. But in saying this, they fall into the heresy of Pelagius. For he also taught that without the grace of Christ, by the strength of nature, and by the doctrine of the law, men could produce good works by which they might be justified. Nor does this in any way help their cause, which they said refers not to nature but to grace, something the Pelagians utterly denied. Their words seem to disagree with them, when in fact they very much agree. For indeed they establish a grace by which they can attain to righteousness without Christ. In this they are against him and the council at Milevum[170] and Holy Scripture.

Further, insofar as they make grace common to all, they turn it into nature. They say that some will want to use it and some not. They call this grace a prevenient grace, but the other, which is absolute, they call subsequent grace.[171] We do not deny this distinction, if it is rightly understood: we admit a prevenient and a subsequent grace. However, it is nothing other than the same favor of God through Christ, which moves us beforehand to rightly exercise our will, and after we are regenerated, helps and stirs us up to live rightly. For whoever doubted that God comes before so that we are changed and renewed in Christ? They are worse than foolish who would say that we were converted prior to the aid of God (*auxilium*

---

[170]The Second Council of Milevum, or Diospolis (Numidia), in A.D. 416 supported Augustine against Pelagius. Augustine wrote a detailed account, *Gest. Pelag.* in 417 (PL 44.319–60). Cf. Martyr's reference in "Free Will," PW, 279.

[171]*Gratiam praevenientem, subsequentem:* see Peter Lombard *Sent.* 2.59a (PL 192.709ff.) on *gratia operante et cooperante.*

Dei).[172] He first loved us before we began to love him.[173] He first incited us by his favor and Spirit, before we can either will or think any good. But it is an error to suppose that men are endowed with the grace of Christ when they are not yet regenerate or renewed in Christ. Indeed, illuminations are sometimes given to them. But if those are not so powerful and so effectual as to change their minds, then they bring about judgment and condemnation, not their salvation. We must think that even the sins of those who are illuminated deserve judgment. Lest anyone be ignorant what these people mean, it must be understood that they assert that Paul excluded *[533]* from justification only such works as are done by their free will alone and by the help of the law.

I would want to know from these people what kind of works they are that are performed by men? Certainly, they are not gross and sordid sins such as murders, fornications, adulteries, thefts, and other such things, for these are not done by the help of the law, but rather by the impulse of the flesh and the devil. Neither are they natural works such as playing, ploughing, harvesting, or sailing. For nothing is commanded in the law concerning these things. Therefore, only virtuous, civil, or moral works remain, such as honoring parents, helping the poor, and sorrow for shameful acts committed. For these things are both commanded in the law, and as these men suppose, can be produced by free will. They say Paul takes away the power of justifying from all these things.

But what other good works remain? I certainly do not see any, unless perhaps they understand those which are done by men already justified. For before justification we have no other works besides those we have already considered. Therefore, since these people exclude both sins, natural works, and these moral works which the law commands, they exclude all works. By which works then would they say men have to be justified? If they had any wisdom, they would always have this saying in front of their eyes, "If of grace then not of works, if of works, then not of grace."[174] Nor can they take refuge in the silly, false, and dull joking that claims Paul must be understood as referring only to those works which are destitute of any faith or grace whatsoever. How can these people speak this way, since they cannot bear it if anyone should say that men are justified by faith alone? In addition, they say that the word "only" is your own invention and not found in Holy Scripture. If they justly throw this against us, why do they themselves commit the same fault? Why will they allow in themselves what they will not permit in

---

[172]The use of the term *auxilium Dei* is identical with that employed by the fourteenth-century Augustinian theologian Gregory of Rimini. Cf. James, "A Late Medieval Parallel," 173; VWG, 173.

[173]1 John 4:19.

[174]Rom. 11:6.

others? Therefore, since Paul takes away from works the power of justifying without adding this word "only," how can they add that word themselves?

We have the firmest arguments drawn from the Scriptures, in which we add the word "only" to faith, and we employ that kind of language which, as we will declare, is received from and used by all the fathers. But let us hear what they babble about on this matter. Paul, they say, had most to do with the Jews, who believed they could be justified by works, and especially the works of the law, so that they had no need of Christ. Therefore, the apostle favors that view exclusively. I am of the mind, however, that whatever he wrote, he wrote to the church, which joined together both Jews and Gentiles who confessed Christ alone. Do they think there were any among all these who promised themselves salvation without Christ? Without doubt, if there had been any such thing the church would not have tolerated them. However, there were some who would have retained, along with Christ, ceremonies to which they granted too much. But to suggest there were any who excluded Christ is not credible. Further, when Paul teaches these things, he instructs not only the Jews but also the Gentiles, as appears most clearly in the letter to the Ephesians where he says, "A man is justified by faith and that not of yourself, lest anyone should boast."[175] In that passage, he calls those to whom he writes Gentiles by name, especially in chapter 2. Therefore, this invention of theirs is vain and ridiculous.

(5) Good Works and Merit

25. Now let us come to their sacred anchor. They say there are two kinds of merit, one congruent and the other condign.[176] And they admit that works preceding justification are not condign merits, but only congruent merits. If one inquires what they mean when they speak of congruent merit, they will answer that they ascribe to it those works which in their own nature do not deserve salvation, except as a promise made to them through a certain goodness of God. And they include those moral acts done by many before justification. But condign merits are all those for which a reward is fully due: this kind of merit they ascribe to those works done by the godly after regeneration. By this distinction they believe they have fully won the victory. But insofar as they do not derive it from Holy Scripture, there is no reason why they should be so pleased.

What if, on the contrary, we teach that the same distinction is clearly and directly repugnant to the word of God? Will they not admit that this noteworthy fabrication was invented and contrived in order to evade our arguments? When

---

[175]Eph. 2:9.
[176]*Meritum congrui, condigni.*

Paul speaks of the justified, even of Christ's martyrs, who at that time endured persecutions and most grievous calamities, he wrote for their consolation: "The sufferings of this time are not worthy of the glory to come which shall be revealed in us."[177] These men say that such sufferings are condign; Paul denies they are condign. How can these things agree? Or rather, how obviously are they opposed one to the other? And since they say that condign merit has in view only the promises of God and not the dignity or nature of the action, let them show what God promised to those works done without the faith and religion of Christ. Who does not see how foolish this kind of language is? Undoubtedly, they who are considered worthy of anything are suited to congruence. And anyone judged to be congruent by an upright and sound judgment, should be judged worthy of it. Therefore, it is sufficiently clear that this distinction was badly framed and wickedly contrived to avoid our doctrine.

(6) Preparatory Works

26. Yet they accuse us as though we disregard *[534]* or rather completely deny those works called works of preparation. This is something we certainly have not done. For although we do not admit such preparations as these, yet we grant and approve other kinds of preparation.[178] For God, the author of our salvation through Christ, employs many and various means, degrees, and ways by which he may lead us to salvation, which may be called preparations because of his providence, wonderful power, and incredible love toward us. But if one considers the nature of things themselves as well as our mind and will in our actions, they have nothing in themselves to explain why our salvation should be ascribed to them. Indeed, they are instead enemies of our salvation. For those splendid actions which they call moral provide the wicked with a cause to puff themselves up, and are occasions to make them pleased with themselves and not to seek the salvation of Christ or sincere piety. On the contrary, we see it happen often that those who have fallen into terrible sins are more easily touched by a wholesome repentance and are more ready to come to Christ. Therefore, Christ said to the Scribes and Pharisees: "The publicans and harlots will go into the kingdom of God before you."[179]

No pious person in fact will say that men are hindered from justification by wicked acts, or moved to it by the strength of civil virtues, but the whole matter consists in this: that these means are sometimes destitute of the grace of God and

---

[177]Rom. 8:18.
[178]Cf. Martyr, "Free Will," PW, 267–68.
[179]Matt. 21:31.

at other times are converted to our salvation by him. Insofar as they concern us, they are sins and according to their own nature, do nothing to help. Yet by the governance of God they are always brought to a good end. Sometimes one will see some men who live well and honorably in the judgment of men. But inwardly they suffer from pride and arrogance and are forsaken by God, so that they rush headlong into the foulest faults and most grievous sins; yet through this, it happens that they more easily acknowledge their sins, amend their ways, and return again to Christ's sheepfold.

This is plainly set forth to us in the Gospel. The prodigal son left his father, and having spent and squandered his patrimony, was at last driven to the point that he became a slave and a swineherd, doubtless something he could not do without great shame. Having been born of such nobility, he should never have lowered himself to such filthy matters. But being in this state, he began to think he would be very happy if he could only eat husks with the swine, since he did not have enough to eat. All these things were certainly to be counted a reproach to him. Yet it came about that he began to think to himself, "Ah! How many hired servants are in my father's house who have plenty of bread and good meat, but I perish here with hunger."[180] And by this means there was aroused in him a proper repentance. Therefore, he prudently and piously returned to his father from whom he had rashly departed. For who knows the secret counsels of God and the deepest abyss of his providence? He often prepares men for salvation by those things that would be hurtful and deadly by their own nature, but by his goodness he makes full use of them for another purpose. I will show this by an illustration so plain and clear that there is no one who will not understand it.

At times a physician sees someone who has an injured leg that can by no means be healed except by cutting. He makes the incision and then applies bandages and medicines to it; at last the man heals. I ask whether that cutting appears to be a preparation to recover health? One can respond that it depends on whether this injury exists by its own nature or as a result of some violence or condition of the sick person. Certainly, it is not by its own nature, for if the sick person who is cut is deserted by the physician, without doubt he will perish. Also, if left in pain and anguish, he will never be able by his own strength to recover his health. Indeed, after the pain and anguish he would die. Therefore, the cutting was a preparation to healing and the same is to be ascribed to the physician and his art. Even so, if God should leave someone in those circumstances (although some are brought to salvation), that man would miserably perish in them. But insofar as God makes full use of those circumstances by his most wholesome skill

[180]Luke 15:11, 17.

and wisdom, they are preparations to justification. For by their own nature they can do nothing, and our defective and corrupt nature brings terrible harm unless the grace of God comes near. But this illustration fails in part because the physician cannot heal the sick person without that cutting. But by an infinite number of other works and methods God is able to bring us to salvation, which I will now show by example. When Judas betrayed Christ, he acknowledged his sin and confessed it publicly. For he openly said that he "had sinned and betrayed Christ's blood."[181] This acknowledgment and confession undoubtedly should have been a preparation to justification if God had wished to employ them. But since God did not use them, what else can we think except that Judas deserved only damnation? It is certain that afterward he hung himself and perished forever. We see this same thing happening to Cain, for he also confessed his sin and yet he was swallowed up by desperation. This is the strength and nature of these things if they are not governed and ordered by God.

(7) Good Works and the Function of the Law

27. Beyond this, our adversaries charge that we contemptuously weaken the law of God and make it useless when we assert that it cannot be observed by men in their natural strength. But these men clearly show that they never thoroughly considered the offices of the law in the Scriptures. For if they had seen them they would never judge them useless, although we cannot easily observe it. The first office, as Paul teaches, is to show sin, for "by the law is the knowledge of sin."[182] Again, it provokes [535] the wrath of God. Moreover, it increases the scope of sin: "For the law entered in that sin should abound." It also brings a curse: "As many as are under the law are under the curse."[183] But to what purpose are these things? That it might be our schoolmaster, leading us to Christ.[184] For those who acknowledge their sins see the wrath of God hanging over them and daily experience the increase of their sins. They are more and more subjected to the curse, and finally, when the Spirit of God breathes on them, they begin eagerly to long for Christ, so that they might be rescued by him from such great evils. And this is the schoolmaster of the law leading to Christ. Since this is the case, can the law seem to be of little use to anyone.

---

[181]Matt. 27:4.
[182]Rom. 3:10. For the triplex *usus legis* see Richard A. Muller, *Dictionary of Latin and Greek Theological Terms* (Grand Rapids: Baker, 1985), 320–21.
[183]Rom. 4:15, 5:20; Gal. 3:10.
[184]Gal. 3:24.

Further, who will say that Aristotle labored unprofitably when, with great skill, he taught the method of a demonstrative syllogism in his *Posteriori analytics?*[185] Yet any methods with such great competence are scarcely found in any faculties or sciences of the learned. For since we are ignorant of the external distinctions of things, we cannot accurately define or fully establish a demonstration. Nevertheless, Aristotle provided an excellent service, for by those superior rules he displayed at least how one should firmly and strongly prove anything. Cicero also, describing an orator for us such as there never has been or will be, yet maintained his standards.[186] At least he shows what should be laid down for those who desire to excel in that method. Thus, God has established his laws so that men should always have an example before their eyes as they arrange their lives. Besides this, to those who are regenerate in Christ, it is not totally impossible to observe the laws of God. For since in one sense they have their strength renewed by the divine Spirit, and the passion of the flesh has been somewhat repressed, they may perform many things that are pleasing and acceptable to God. There is also a sense in which those not yet regenerate may still apply themselves to the laws of God in regard to outward discipline. Where it is practiced, republics prosper and the wrath of God is not inflamed against man; the punishments which God is accustomed to pour out against open sins are avoided for a time.

28. These are not slight or common uses of the law. Those who raise objections against us, seem to be ignorant of this fact, and those who are not content with this, add that the law may be observed even by men who are not regenerate. And if one objects to its loftiness and difficulty, they answer that our righteousness, when compared with the righteousness of God (which is altogether absolute), or if it is compared to the law itself, is not righteousness. But if our righteousness is compared with the law, mindful that God in his goodness condescends to our infirmity, we can observe it and be justified by good works. But you must know that this is a sophistical distinction of Pighius, by which he usurped the authority to moderate the law of God, an authority that certainly is not fitting for a mortal.[187] And we can prove this both by the laws of man and also by the law of God. For it is written in the digests, *De Legibus et Senatus consultis:* regarding

---

[185] Aristotle *An. post.* 1.14, 71b.16ff.

[186] Cicero *De or.* 2.7ff.; the third book of *De Oratore*, setting out the education of an orator, the principles guiding his craft, and the threefold aim of *flectere, probare, delectare* (§69).

[187] For Pighius, see xxvi–xxvii and xxvi–xxvii n. 65, above. Marvin Anderson, PMRE, 270, observes: "More likely Martyr responded to Smith's use of Pighius in the 1550 *Diatribe de Hominis Iustificatione*" whose title page includes *Adversus Petrum Martyrem.…* Anderson suggests that the attack against Calvin by Pighius, *De lib. hom. arb. & div. grat.*, may also have animated Martyr to write against Pighius in the locus on justification in Romans.

those things that are first in a commonwealth, decrees should be made certain, either by interpretation or by the constitution of a good prince, namely, that it be not in the hand of any man or judge to mitigate the laws at his pleasure, or to transgress them under the name of any equity.[188] For such laws would become a flexible rule [*lesbia regula*], and all things would be confused by everyone's lustful desire.[189]

Yes, indeed, this rule is surrendered: that if the supreme law is written in any other law and the equity and moderation of that same supreme law is nowhere expressed, then the judge ought to follow the supreme law and ought not to add equity.[190] Nevertheless, that equity may be followed only if it is expressed in another law. For example, all laws agree that if a debtor does not pay his debt on the due date and the creditor suffers a loss, the debtor is obliged to bear the loss. They call this paying the interest, or as some say, paying the damages. Indeed, we find in the digest, *De Regulis Iuris*, cases where something is assumed to be completed, but it turns out that there is a delay in completing it caused by someone else.[191] In this case, if the debtor can prove that it was not his fault that the debt was not paid, since he had the money and offered it, then the creditor was at fault for the nonpayment, even if the creditor sustained an enormous loss because of a delay of payment. Yet the debtor is not obliged to make compensation in equity. For by written equity it is considered completed when the delay belongs to another person. Therefore, it appears that it is not in the power of a judge or of anyone else to moderate laws arbitrarily.

If this is the case in Roman laws, which are invented and promulgated by men, what shall we think of the law of God? For it should be infinitely more sure than human law. Nor is it permitted for us to represent any equity unless we see it expressly in writing. For example, the law is: "He who shall shed man's blood, his blood shall be shed."[192] Here we have the highest law which we should certainly always follow, unless equity had taught elsewhere that the same important law should be mitigated. In another place it is written: "If two go forth together into the woods to cut down trees, and the axe by chance falls out of the hand of the one and kills another person standing by, let there be cities of refuge for him,

---

[188]Justinian, *Legibus et Senatus consultis et longa consuetudine* [The digest of Roman law], 1.3 in *Corpus Iuris Civilis*, ed. Paul Krueger and Theodor Mommsen, 3 vols. (Berlin, 1928), 1:34.

[189]A *lesbia regula* is a mason's rule made of lead that could be bent to fit and measure curved moldings. Cf. Aristotle *Eth. nic.* 5.10.30ff., 1137b.30 on equity: "when the thing is indefinite the rule also is indefinite, like the leaden rule used in making the Lesbian molding."

[190]On the concept of equity, see Aristotle *Eth. nic.* 5.10.1138a.31ff.

[191]Justinian, *De Legibus et Senatus* 47[sic].2.88, in *Corpus Iuris Civilis*, ed. Krueger and Mommsen, 1:824, "Concerning Theft," 46/2, 88.

[192]Gen. 9:6.

where he can live safely until such time as the matter be tried; *[536]* if he can prove his innocence then let him be freed by the high priest."[193] This equity might be used by the judge because it was written in the laws of God. Indeed, they should also use it as often as they see that the matter in dispute requires it. But to suggest that it might be lawful for them to bend or mitigate the laws of God by their authority cannot be proved by any testimony of Holy Scripture. On the contrary, they were rather commanded that they "should not depart either to the left or the right and that they should neither add anything to the law of God nor yet take away anything from it."[194]

At any rate, we require no long discourse to teach that, with regard to our ability, it is impossible to keep the law, especially before we are regenerated. For the Scriptures plainly testify to this. Paul says in chapter 8 to the Romans, "What the law, weakened by the flesh, could not do...."[195] Also in the same chapter he writes, "The mind of the flesh is hostile to God, for it is not subject to the law of God, indeed it cannot be."[196] And in 1 Corinthians he says: "The carnal man understands not the things which are of the Spirit of God, neither yet can it be, for to him they are folly."[197] Christ also says: "An evil tree cannot bring forth good fruit."[198] Also: "How can you speak good things, when you yourself are evil?"[199] All these texts plainly teach that it is impossible to observe the law of God in human strength, since it is now defiled and corrupt. But concerning these remedies and subtle shifts of the Papists, let this suffice.

(8) Additional Objections from Scripture

29. Now let us come to certain particular objections they favor, with which they take pains to trouble us and to establish their own lies. They say that Ahab, an ungodly king, ripped his garments at the threats of Elijah and put on sackcloth, lay on the ground and fasted, and went barefoot. For that reason the Lord said to the prophet, "Have you not seen Ahab humble himself before me? In his days I will not bring the evil but in the days of his son."[200] They say, see how the works of an ungodly king, one not yet justified, so pleased God, that they brought reconciliation with God. On the contrary, we contend that Ahab was not justified by these deeds, for if he had possessed true faith which justifies, he would not

---

[193]Deut. 19:5.
[194]Deut. 4:2.
[195]Rom. 8:3.
[196]Rom. 8:7.
[197]1 Cor. 2:14.
[198]Matt. 7:18.
[199]Matt. 12:34.
[200]1 Kings 21:17.

have clung to idolatry and other most detestable sins. He was indeed somewhat moved by the threats of the prophet, but what he did only pertained to a certain outward and civil discipline rather than to true repentance. But God revealed that he humbled himself before him.[201] I respond that the phrase "before me" may refer to the words of God which were spoken to Ahab by the prophet, so that the meaning is: "before me, that is, at my words" or else "before me, that is, in the church of the Israelites." And by that deed, Ahab showed that he repented of the wicked act he had committed; that was a good and profitable example before the multitude. But God who beheld the inward parts of his heart saw that the repentance was a pretense and barren, and for that reason promised that he would only defer the punishment so that it, which otherwise should have happened during his life, would happen in the days of his son.

This is not unusual; we should not be ignorant that by observing the outward discipline, plagues are restrained and quite grievous punishments of this present life are avoided. For we teach that not all sins are equal. God would also wait until the sins of the Amorites were full.[202] Finally, his wrath is poured out when lustful and wicked deeds are shamefully done without any restraint. Indeed, where outward discipline is kept, God often grants many blessings, not for the merit of the deeds but in the order he established in nature. For God wants to preserve the good order (*eutaxian*) of things, so that certain consequences should follow from others. I wonder what these persons mean when, drawing from the books of the Chronicles, they say that Rehoboam the son of Solomon "did evil, for he did not set his heart to seek the Lord."[203] They might easily have observed that this serves nothing for this present purpose unless they are, as I call them, "tabular scholars,"[204] who have more skill in indices than in books. For whenever they find in the tables of the holy books this word "to prepare" or "preparation" they immediately seize upon it and think that it (whatever it is) serves their purpose and pertains to their preparatory works. But when sacred history had declared that the king behaved wickedly, it added by exposition, as it often does, that "he did not set his heart to seek the Lord."

Nor is their cause helped at all by what is written in chapter 16 of Proverbs: "The mind belongs to man, but the answer of the tongue is from the Lord."[205] By those words we are to understand nothing else than that men are indeed

---

[201] 1 Kings 21:29.

[202] Gen. 15:16.

[203] 2 Chron. 12:14.

[204] *Doctores tabularii.* Cf. Martyr's jibe at the *patrologi* (instead of the *theologi*), who "collect little sentences out of the writings of the fathers," VWG, 267.

[205] Prov. 16:1.

accustomed to propose many things for themselves to do; however, the event and its success is not in their power but depends on God. Men often decide for themselves what they will say in the senate, in the law court, before the king, to soldiers, and to the people, but what will come to pass lies in the will of God. Certainly they prepare the heart, but God controls the answer of the tongue according to his providence.

They cite another very weighty reason from Psalm 10: "The Lord has heard the desire of the poor, your ear heard the preparation of their heart."[206] But in using this passage, these good masters make two errors. First, they do not understand that of which they speak. Second, they do not cite the text according to the actual Hebrew. For the meaning is that God does not despise the prayer of the poor, but according to his great goodness *[537]* accomplishes those things for them which they had determined in their mind to request of him. This is the preparation of the heart, for no one is godly who requests anything from God without first deliberating in his heart that it is to be asked for. Otherwise, he would blindly approach God and would pray foolishly. But wherever these men find in the divine Scriptures this term "to prepare" they immediately seize upon it, even against its nature, to establish preparatory works.

Now let us see what the meaning is according to the actual Hebrew: *Taauath ananim shamata Iehovah takin libbam tacshif oznecca,* that is, "You have heard the desire of the meek, Lord, you have prepared or will prepare their heart, your ear shall hear." Here we see how David establishes that God hears the desires of the saints, whom he calls meek. He adds a reason, namely, because God prepares their hearts to request those things that may bring about their salvation and please God. Paul teaches about those whom God uses to bring about such a preparation in the hearts of the faithful in his letter to the Romans, writing: "We do not know how to pray as we should, but the Spirit prays for us with sighs too deep for words. But God who searches the hearts, sees what the Spirit will ask for the saints."[207] Thus we see from David and Paul that God hears the prayers of those who pray to him, who are inspired by the impulse of the Spirit. We learn also from pagan philosophers, in more than one place, that those who inconsiderately and blindly claim something from God are reproved. However, those who confess Christ believe that he is the author of their prayers, so they close their prayers in this way: "Thy will be done."

---

[206]Ps. 10:17, Vulg.
[207]Rom. 8:26–27.

30. Opponents point to Ezekiel in chapter 18: "Walk in my ways and make a new heart," and Jeremiah, "Be converted to me, says the Lord."[208] Therefore, they argue, one may in his own strength prepare himself to obtain righteousness. But these men should recognize that it is unfair to cite some Scripture passages and to pass over and conceal others. So let them read what Ezekiel writes in chapter 36: "I will bring to pass that you shall walk in my ways," and "I will give to you a fleshly heart and take away your stony heart."[209] Jeremiah also declares, in chapter 31: "Convert me O Lord, and I shall be converted."[210] Therefore, Augustine said very well, "Give what you command and command what you will."[211]

They also abuse another passage from the prophet Jonah to confirm their error, for there it is written, "God regarded the works of the Ninevites."[212] Consider, they say, the distress of the Ninevites, in which they exhausted themselves with many fastings and cries to the Lord. It is argued that such things prepared their minds and made them ready to seek forgiveness. It is as if the Ninevites should not first have to believe the word of God before they could pray effectively or repent. Since they believed before they did any works, they were justified by faith and not by works, which followed afterwards, and God is said to have regarded their works because they pleased him.

We have never denied that the works of those now justified are acceptable to God. As often as we encounter in the Scriptures such passages that seem to attribute righteousness to our works, we must, according to the teaching of Augustine, consider the foundation from which those works derive. And when we see that they arise from faith, we should ascribe to that root what is added afterward concerning righteousness. We may observe how disgracefully these men err in their reasoning, for they take it upon themselves to transfer those things which are characteristic of one kind of man to another kind. Even human laws do not permit doing this, for as we find in the *Codex* concerning testaments (or last wills): "If unlearned and illiterate men, who dwell outside cities and have no access to the wise and learned, make their last wills without the required solemnity and without the sufficient number of witnesses prescribed, which otherwise would be necessary, such testimonies should be allowed."[213] To transfer this prerogative to citizens who dwell in cities where there is an abundance of intelligent

---

[208]Ezek. 18:31; Jer. 31:18.

[209]Ezek. 36: 26–27.

[210]Jer. 31:18.

[211]Augustine *Conf.* 10.29, 40 (PL 32.796).

[212]Jonah 3:10.

[213]Justinian, *Codex Iustinianus* 6.23.31; in *Corpus Iuris Civilis*, ed. Krueger and Mommsen, 2:257.

men would be a grave error, for if the testaments of those citizens are made in such a manner, they are rejected and have no validity. So we say that the works of the justified may please God; however, this cannot and should not be granted to those who are without faith and are strangers to Christ.

31. Let us observe further the familiar Sophistic assertions of our adversaries, what Logicians term *a non causa ut causa*,[214] for they always appoint good works to be the causes of righteousness, when in reality good works are effects of righteousness, and not causes. It is as if someone should say the fire is hot because it makes heat. But it is precisely the opposite, for the fire makes heat because it is hot. Likewise, it is not because we do righteous things that we are justified; it is because we are justified that we do righteous things. Sometimes they also object, "God will render unto every man according to his works."[215] Therefore, they say works are the cause of our felicity. But here, as is their habit, they are much deceived, for (unless they have devised some kind of new grammar for themselves) without any doubt this word "according" does not signify cause. But, they say, in his last judgment Christ seems to mention these things as causes for which the kingdom of heaven is given. For he will say, "I was hungry and you fed me, I was thirsty and you gave me drink."[216] Yet Christ does not in fact mention these things as causes, but rather as antecedents: "Come you blessed of my Father, possess the kingdom prepared for you since the beginning of the world."[217] The true cause of our felicity is that we are elected and predestined by God to an eternal inheritance. For those who belong to this number are adorned in their time with faith by which they are justified, and have the right of eternal life, but *[538]* since this faith is hidden, it cannot be seen. And Christ would want everyone to understand that none except the just are received into the kingdom of heaven. Therefore, he considers these external works so that it might be clearly understood by them that righteousness is imputed to men by faith. For no one can be so ignorant as not to know there are two principles of things: one by which they exist, the other by which they are known.[218]

Again they object from 1 Samuel: "Those that honor me I honor, and those that love me I love."[219] Here, they say, the promise is made to works. But if they would make a distinction between the promise of the Gospel and promise of the

---

[214]"From what is not the cause as if it were."
[215]2 Cor. 5:10.
[216]Matt. 25:35.
[217]Matt. 35:34.
[218]Aristotle *An. post.* 19.99b.17ff.
[219]1 Sam. 2:30.

law, they would easily understand that this passage says nothing against our understanding of it. For if by ourselves we could satisfy the commandments of the law, then it might be the reason why the promise should be given to us, but since no one is able to fulfill it, everyone ought to take refuge in Christ and so be justified through faith in him. Then with an incomplete obedience we begin to work, and even when not done exactly according to the rule of the commandment, it yet pleases God. And by his sheer liberality he fulfills the promise that had been joined to that work. So those conditions which are joined to the precepts are not unprofitable, for those who are justified attain them.

Neither are these men ashamed to cite these words of Psalm 25, "Consider my humanity and my lowliness, and forgive all my sins,"[220] as though our labors or pains are the causes of the remission of sins. But in this passage David, in a most grievous calamity, entreats God to forgive his sins, and if God was angry on account of his sins, that the cause for the punishment might be removed. The passage is not concerned about labors one undertakes voluntarily, but punishments inflicted by God. We see also that children who are sometimes struck by their teachers, beg for mercy and tenderness. If one gives alms to a leper, the leprosy cannot properly be called the cause of the mercy; otherwise all who pass by the leper would do the same. But the true cause is the kindly affection in your mind.

32. They claim that the Holy Scriptures attribute a great deal to repentance; we do not deny it.[221] On the other hand, we would have them understand that it is the fruit of faith and that no one can profitably produce repentance for his sins unless he first believes. They also wrongly boast of many things regarding confession, but we make the following distinction: On the one hand, it is separated from faith and hope, as it was in Judas, who confessed that he had sinned in betraying just blood,[222] but this is so far removed from bringing any advantage that it is really a preparation for desperation and destruction. On the other hand, it is joined with faith and hope as it was in David and Peter,[223] and so it is not the cause but the effect of justification, for it follows faith, rather than precedes it.

Auricular confession also, derived from the papists, is completely superstitious; therefore, we utterly reject it, for they impose it as something necessary for salvation and a reason why sins should be forgiven, which they are never able to

---

[220]Ps. 25:18.

[221]Cf. Martyr's locus on *poenitentia* in his commentary on the books of Samuel: *In duos Libros Samuelis Prophetae ... Commentarii docitissimii...* (Zurich: Froschauer, 1564), 324–33b; (LC 3.8).

[222]Matt. 27:3–6.

[223]Ps. 51; Matt. 26:75.

prove from the testimonies of Scripture. They seize this also out of the Lord's prayer: "Forgive us our debts as we forgive our debtors," and again, "forgive and it shall be forgiven you."[224] Therefore, they say, the forgiving of wrongs against us is the reason why our sins are forgiven. Their reason, as the saying goes, strokes the head with one hand while the other strikes the jawbone, because if the forgiving of wrongs against us deserves the remission of sins, as they would have it, then that remission would not be a true remission. For after one has paid the price once and for all, there is nothing for which to be forgiven. The time for remission of sins is at the moment when the price has not yet been paid.

In that passage, however, we ask first that our sins might be forgiven, and because benefits are received, the souls of men are encouraged to hope that they will receive other great benefits. Therefore, this is the meaning of that passage: "O Father who, by your goodness, has given us the grace to forgive the injuries of our debtors, forgive us our sins also." Now these words do not signify a cause but a similitude, although it is not perfect and absolute. For no wise person would want his sins forgiven by God on the condition that he has forgiven his neighbor for injuries done to him. Indeed, everyone, because of the flesh and that infirmity that it carries, forgives his brother far less than he should. Some offense always lingers in the mind, even if it does not burst forth. Nevertheless, his own conscience is witness enough that his mind is not honest enough towards those by whom he has been injured. But the former explanation teaches that the likeness does not refer to remission, but to God's liberality, that just as he has given the one so also he will surely give the other. But where it says "forgive and it shall be forgiven," that is a commandment and, therefore, pertains to the law. But you will object that this verse is written in the gospel and not the law. That is irrelevant, for law and gospel are not separate books. The promises of the Gospel are contained in the Old Testament and the law is not only comprehended in the Gospel, but also perfectly revealed by Christ.[225] Therefore, we are commanded by those words to forgive injustice done to us.

Moreover, we should obey according to the rule of the law, which in truth depends on this supreme precept: "You shall love the Lord your God with all your heart, with all your soul, and with all your strength."[226] According to its form, we ought to forgive our enemies, but since no one has fulfilled or can fulfill it, it follows that we must fly[539] to Christ through whom we may be justified by faith. After being justified, we may in some way begin to do what is commanded,

---

[224]Matt. 6:12; Luke 6:37.

[225]"The sum of those things contained in Holy Scripture is the Law and the Gospel, which are contained equally in both New and Old Testaments"; Vermigli, "Theses for Debate," EW, 92, 1.N.4.

[226]Deut. 6:5.

although we are not able to perfectly fulfill it, yet it pleases God. What is more, he liberally bestowed upon us the promise that is added not because of our works or merits, but only for Christ's sake.

Opponents still attempt to deceive us with the words of Daniel when he exhorts the king to redeem his sins with alms.[227] But in that verse, by "sins" we may understand the pains and punishments due to sin, for Scripture often uses such figures of speech, something we never denied. On the contrary, we willingly grant that with respect to works arising from faith, God is accustomed to forgive many things, especially concerning the alleviation of plagues and punishments.

33. They oppose us also from this verse from the first chapter of John: "God gave them power to become sons of God."[228] They reach the opinion that those who have already received Christ, that is, those who believe in him, are not yet justified and regenerate, nor are they children of God, but have only received the power to be made the children of God, which of course they suppose is by their own works. Pighius, the defender and Achilles of the papists, put great trust in this argument, although in vain.[229] For he supposes it is necessarily the case that one to whom power over something is given does not yet possess it. Indeed, here in chapter 1 of John it is as if we ought to treat this matter philosophically, so that potency excludes action. Yet this is not universally true even among the philosophers, for when they define the soul, they say that "it is an act of a physical organic body having potential life."[230] By this definition it would appear that our body has potential life when it actually has life in itself. But here the word "power" (*potestas*) signifies that the body does not have life of itself but from another, namely, the soul. For the present, this is something which we may also affirm, namely, that those who have received the Lord and have believed in him are regenerate and are made children of God, yet this is not from themselves but from another source, that is, from the Spirit and grace of God. This is certainly the meaning of power. However, in that passage the Evangelist does not speak as a Peripatetic philosopher, but simply and most plainly, for just before he had said "his own received him not."[231] By this word "his" he means the Jews, who

---

[227]Dan. 4:24.

[228]John 1:12.

[229]Albert Pighius, *Controversiaru[m] praecipuarum in comitiis Ratisponensis tractatarum, & quibus nunc potissimum exagitatur Christi fides & religio, diligens, & luculenta explicatio*, 3 vols. (Paris 1542) (hereafter Pighius, *Controversiarum*); the reference is to vol. 2, fols. 53v–54r. For Pighius, see p. xxvi n. 65, above.

[230]Cf. Aristotle *De anima* 2.1, 412a.18–19: "a substance in the sense of the form of a natural body, having life potentially within it." See Martyr's "The Image of God" *(De Homine)*, PW, 37–46.

[231]John 1:11.

especially professed the knowledge of the true God. But when they refused the truth offered them, God was not willing to be without a people, so he appointed those who would believe and receive Christ to be his peculiar people. Therefore, he gave to them "power," that is, a right and a prerogative, that when they had received the Lord by faith they would be made, and indeed be, sons of God. Thus Cyril, expounding that passage, says that the power signifies adoption and grace.[232]

Further, although Pighius thinks himself very sharp-witted, he does not see that when he argues he is uttering contradictions, for how is it possible that anyone could have life in himself and yet not be alive? Certainly, if in believing they have received Christ, it must be that they have righteousness at once, for as Paul says in 1 Corinthians: "whom God made our wisdom, righteousness, holiness and redemption."[233] What more is there to say? The evangelist himself declares to us who they are that have received such a power, namely, "who are not born of blood, nor of the will of men but of God."[234] And if they are born of God then it is inevitable that they are justified and regenerated.

Opponents object also that a servile fear somehow precedes love (*caritas*), as though by it we would be prepared for justification and more easily receive love. We answer them: such a fear without love is sin. They reply: Christ commanded that fear, but God does not command sin; moreover, they say, he commanded such a fear when he said: "I will show you whom you ought to fear, fear him who when he has killed the body can also cast the soul into hellfire."[235] They believe that this fear prepares for justification; this can be proved, because when Augustine explains this verse from 1 John, "Perfect love casts out fear," he writes, "This servile fear is not unprofitable, for just as a shoemaker's needle draws the thread after it, so this fear draws with it love."[236]

As to the first objection, I answer that their premise is false. Certainly, nowhere did God command such a fear that lacks love and faith. This is something I know quite well, but they will never discover. As to Augustine, we answer with that passage from 1 John, "In this is love made perfect with us, that we may have confidence for the day of judgment, because as he is so are we in this world. There is no fear in love, but perfect love casts out fear."[237] Here love is not to be understood as our love towards God but the love of God towards us, for he speaks of a perfect love, something we do not have in this life. Moreover, John's meaning

---

[232]Cyril of Alexandria *Ev. Jo.* 1:12 (PG 73.151–54).
[233]1 Cor. 1:30.
[234]John 1:13.
[235]Matt. 10:28.
[236]Augustine *Tract. ev. Jo.* 9.4, on John 4:18 (PL 35.2047), paraphrase.
[237]1 John 4:17–18.

is that after we are persuaded of the perfect love of God by which he embraces us, we have confidence that in the day of judgment we will be safe. And this *[540]* perfect love of God, once we know it, casts out fear because it does not permit us to fear. Therefore, Augustine's interpretation regarding our love towards God has nothing to do with the issue at hand.

Yet suppose John did speak of our love towards God, as that verse is commonly taken? In that sense also Augustine's words may be true, although not universally, that love always follows such a fear (for we know it happened differently in Cain and Judas),[238] but only in men who are to be justified. For God employs this means, first to pierce them with great fear of their sins, and then by it to bring them to faith and charity. Meanwhile, we do not doubt that such a fear is sin. Yet that fear may be called profitable, not by merit or its own nature, but because of the order instituted by God, whose will is to make full use of it for our salvation. We also add that the more love grows in us, so much does it cast out fear more and more, not only servile fear but also the fear which belongs to justified men.[239] Whoever is truly persuaded of God's love towards him can never fear his own damnation, for that doubt by which we fear eternal punishment is sin. Nevertheless, such doubt always lingers somewhat in our minds, for we never in this life believe as we should nor as much as we should. Because of this weakness in love by which we should love our neighbor, and because of the weakness of faith by which we should believe in God as long as we are in this life, we never completely put off all this corrupt fear.

34. They also seize on this passage and object to it against us: "Ask and you shall receive, seek and you shall find, knock and it shall be opened to you."[240] But they should remember that prayer arises from faith and rests on it alone, for otherwise they cannot be heard. But why do they pass this over in such silence: "Whatever you shall ask, believe, and it will be given to you"?[241] For by these words it appears that whatever is given to those who ask, is given to faith.

They also add a verse from Luke: "Give alms and all things will be clean for you."[242] Now these words may be explained in three ways, none of which serves their purpose. The first is to decide that it was ironic language, as if God would have said to the Pharisees: You give alms and think immediately that all things are

---

[238]Gen. 4; Matt. 27.
[239]Cf. Aquinas *S. theol.* 2.2, q. 19 (esp. art. 5), on servile fear.
[240]Matt. 7:7.
[241]Matt. 21:22.
[242]Luke 11:41.

clean to you, which is not so. For we ought first to make clean those things which are within.

A second way is what follows from Augustine in his *Enchiridion ad Laurentium,* that certain people had persuaded themselves that if they gave alms they would be saved, even though they did not cease from sinning. And their chief anchor was these words of Christ. Augustine replies that Christ's words were to be understood as the true and approved alms,[243] of which it is written in Ecclesiasticus 30, "Have compassion on your soul and please God."[244] Therefore, one should properly begin true almsgiving with oneself. Thus having compassion on oneself, one may be converted to God and cease from sins, and afterwards have compassion on others.

The third way, which seems to me to be the most appropriate to the context, is this: When Christ was at dinner with the Pharisees, he began to eat with unwashed hands. When they were offended at this, Christ began to reprove their ignorance [for their law of purification] would have required their dishes, hands, and all outward things to be clean and beautiful, but concerning inward things, that is, in their heart, they cared not at all. Therefore, he exhorted them to first purify the heart, which is inward. This is something done by faith, for it is written in Acts, "by faith cleansing their hearts."[245] Afterwards, Luke adds concerning outward things, "Give alms and all things shall be clean to you."[246] Further, as Theodore Beza, a man of great learning and judgment, has quite prudently concluded in his *Annotations,* Christ did not speak of all kinds of purifications, but only what pertains to food, to which he applies a double commandment.[247] The first is that they should eat nothing obtained by robbery; second, those things that are present, that is, contained in the dishes, should be gathered up as alms for the poor, by which the rest is cleansed and made holy. From all this, there is nothing which may support our adversaries' opinion.

35. Others believe they can establish their error through the ministry of the keys, by which they judge that men are absolved from their sins. But they are greatly deceived, for they do not understand what are the keys that Christ committed to the church. The preaching of the word of God concerning the forgiveness of sins to be obtained by Christ is the only key to open the kingdom of heaven, and if he who hears this Word also joins it with a true faith and fully

---

[243]Augustine *Enchir. lauren.* 1.72 (PL 40.266).
[244]Eccles. 30:24.
[245]Acts 15:9.
[246]Luke 11:41.
[247]Theodore Beza, *Novum Test., Annotationes* (Geneva, 1598), fol. 288b.

assents to these words, then he adds the other key. By these two keys the kingdom of heaven is opened and the forgiveness of sins obtained. Therefore, sending forth his apostles, Christ said: "Go and preach the Gospel," then added, "He who believes shall be saved."[248] By these few words he describes the keys which he delivered to the church. In these words one will find no work done (*opus operatum*), as they call it, for Christ commends only the faith of the hearers and the word of God by which faith is preached.

Finally, how are we to refute this passage that is always coming out of their mouths: "Many sins are forgiven her because she has loved much?"[249] If the text is considered carefully, it will be an easy matter. We ought to know that some reasons are drawn from causes and some from effects. A few words later, Christ *[541]* shows the cause of salvation when he says to the woman, "Your faith has made you well."[250] Because that faith was hidden in her heart, it could not be perceived by those who were present; therefore, by means of a parable he shows that those who love the most receive the greatest gifts from someone. That this woman received a very great gift, that is, justification, is revealed by the effects, namely, that she washed his feet with her tears and wiped them with her hair, that she kissed them and anointed them. Since the Pharisees did not do such things, it may be a strong argument that they had not received the same gift.

Opponents also cite from the letter to the Romans: "Not the hearers of the law shall be justified but the doers."[251] But in that verse, when Paul reproved the Jews because they had received the law and boasted of it, yet lived contrary to the law, he meant nothing else but that if righteousness were to be obtained by the law, it is not sufficient to have it or to hear it only. We should, however, exhibit the deeds and works of the law. We have never denied that someone could be justified by the law if he perfectly satisfies it, but since it is in no way possible, we say that righteousness cannot be hoped for by the law.

They also object from the verse in the letter to the Philippians: "With fear and trembling, work out your salvation,"[252] which does nothing to help them. Undoubtedly, those who understand that everything they have is from God are of a humble and moderate spirit and always afraid of themselves. For they see that there is nothing good in themselves, but help is looked for at the hands of God alone; therefore, Paul commands the believer always to fear and tremble. But those who think it lies within their own power to justify and save themselves

---

[248]Matt. 28:19.
[249]Luke 7:47.
[250]Luke 7:50.
[251]Rom. 2:13.
[252]Phil. 2:12.

(such as those who oppose us in this matter) have nothing of which to be afraid or at which to tremble, for they boast that their salvation is found in themselves. Although they pay respect to Paul when they cite him in this verse, they do not understand justification, for the apostle is writing to those who were already justified; therefore, this verse does nothing for them. But by the word salvation Paul means a renewing, by which we always make better and better progress. Last, as if it were a victory from Colophon,[253] they bring an objection from chapter 3 of the Apocalypse, where it is written: "Behold, I stand at the door and knock, and if any man open to me, I will enter and eat with him."[254] Now we agree completely that these words indicate that from the outset God calls, inspires, and stimulates us to salvation, to which no one by his own strength can be brought without the impulse of God. But we openly deny that of our own accord we can open our heart to God without his grace penetrating and changing the mind, nor can these men confirm it by the Holy Scriptures.

Proof from the Church Fathers

36. Now we have certain adversaries who judge little or nothing at all on the basis of Scripture, but measure all their religion by fathers and councils, so much that they can be called *patrologi* rather than *theologi*.[255] Still more intolerable, they gather together certain sayings out of the writings of the fathers and thrust them upon the people and easily obscure the truth. To simple people they make pretenses and employ subtle language, especially certain ones who think themselves clever orators and have spent the greater part of their lifetime in that kind of study. I wish the impartial reader not to decide anything rashly against the truth, but to consider carefully those things we also will bring out of the fathers. In this way one will easily understand that the fathers do not support our adversaries' side as much as they do ours. Nevertheless, so that we may not refer to any passage from the fathers in a confused or rash manner, we will employ a method that may be easily understood and profitable.[256]

First, we will propose a demonstration, or *apodeiksis*,[257] from those testimonies of the Holy Scriptures to which we have already appealed. Those who perform works according to the precepts of the law, that is, as the law itself requires, are justified by works. But none, and especially before regeneration, do the kind

---

[253]Colophon was a city in Ionia famous for its cavalry. Vermigli's ironic comment is that his opponents view the verse as if it were the cavalry that comes to their rescue and brings victory.

[254]Rev. 3:20.

[255]Martyr uses the same terms in *Exhort. Iuv.* (LC, appendix); see VWG, 267.

[256]See Martyr's "Rules for Patristics," OTD, 76–79; cf. 209.

[257]See Aristotle *An. post.* 1.1, 71a.5ff. on strict demonstration, A; cf. PW, 35–36.

of works the law requires. Therefore, none are justified by works. The first (major) proposition is so clear that it needs no exposition: anyone who does anything contrary to what the law prescribes certainly commits sin. This is a long way from appearing to be just. As to the second (minor) proposition, although it was proved by the testimonies of the Scriptures, we will also expound it out of the fathers, reaching the conclusion that if justification is not of works, then it must be by grace.[258]

Second, we will declare out of the fathers that men are justified freely and without any consideration of merits. Because we do not reject good works, we say that they ought to be held in a place of honor, since a very close connection obtains with the immediate consequences of justification. Last, we will teach this also out of the sayings of the fathers: that good works follow, but do not precede, justification. Especially will we cite from those passages of the fathers that have support from Scripture.

(1) All Works before Justification Are Sins

37. First comes Basil, who in his first book *On Baptism* proposes these words from the Gospel: "Many shall say in that day, 'Lord in your name we have prophesied, we have cast out devils, we have done many miracles.'"[259] Basil says that not only will God cast such people out of his kingdom, he will also call them workers of iniquity.[260] Therefore, those who perform miracles and appear to observe the commandments of God and his just actions, if done *[542]* for their own ends or any purpose other than what it should be, are said to sin. It is clear that they do not follow the precept of God as made known by the apostle Paul: "Whether you eat or drink or whether you do anything else, do all to the glory of God."[261] It is certain that this cannot be done without faith and love, and insofar as unjustified men are without these, it necessarily follows from the words of Basil that their works are sins. He wrote the very same opinion in book 2, question 7, of his *On Baptism*, and he deliberately sought to know "whether anyone, as long as he abides in sin, can do anything that is acceptable to God."[262] This is something he states as impossible, for which many reasons are taken from the Scriptures. First, he says, the Holy Spirit testifies, "He who works sin is a servant of sin."[263] Further,

---

[258]The syllogism: *major premise:* anyone who does something contrary to the law commits sin; *minor premise:* no one who commits sin is justified; *conclusion:* therefore, justification must be by faith alone (QED).

[259]Matt. 7:22.

[260]Basil *Bapt.* 1.2 (PG 31.1567).

[261]1 Cor. 10:31.

[262]Basil *Bapt.* 2.7 (PG 31.1598–99).

[263]John 8:34.

Christ says, "You cannot serve God and mammon, for no man can serve two masters."[264] Paul also says: "Light has no fellowship with darkness, neither has God any agreement with Belial."[265] Basil proves the same thing from the book of Genesis, although he follows the translation of the Septuagint. Thus he says God spoke to Cain: "Cain, if you offer well and divide well you have sinned; be content."[266] The meaning, he says, is that if you offer a sacrifice with respect to the outward appearance and your heart is not right, neither will you respect the purpose as you should; thus your oblation is a sin.

Isaiah also agrees with this opinion when he writes in chapter 66: "He who kills an ox is as if he killed a man, and he who sacrifices a beast is as though he should kill a dog."[267] It is not enough to perform a work that is splendid and admirable; it should also conform to the precept of the law of God, namely, that whatever you do, is done in such a way and under such conditions as the law requires. So he said that Paul indicates, "None shall be crowned but he who wrestled lawfully."[268] Now it is not enough to wrestle unless one "wrestled lawfully." Christ also says in the Gospel, "Blessed is that servant who when his Lord comes he shall find him so doing."[269] By these words it appears that it is not enough to perform, but one must also perform just as God has commanded. Moreover, he [Basil] shows out of the Old Testament that it is a sin where there is a sacrifice to the true God, which is outside of the temple or not in that place where the tabernacle was.[270] For although that which was sacrificed was commanded in the law, yet the condition with respect to the location, which the law also required, was violated. And if anyone killed an offering that had any stain (whether it was killed in the temple or in that place where the tabernacle was), the person has also committed a sin because he neglected a necessary condition. He also cites from the Gospel that derives from the prophet: "This people honors me with their lips but their heart is far from me."[271]

He [Basil] thinks that in the letter to the Romans Paul tends toward the same thing when he writes, "They have indeed the zeal of God but not according to knowledge."[272] Paul also writes about himself to the Philippians, that he counted all his works performed when he lived under the law, which was without complaint, as

[264]Matt. 6:24.
[265]2 Cor. 6:14–16.
[266]Gen. 4:7. Basil *Bapt.* 2.8 (PG 31.1599).
[267]Isa. 66:3.
[268]2 Tim. 2:3ff.
[269]Matt. 24:46.
[270]See Deut. 12:5.
[271]Matt. 15:8 (Isa. 29:13).
[272]Rom. 10:1.

rejections, dung, and losses.[273] Therefore, since the goodwill and intention that should be in them is taken away from works, what else is there to say but that they are sins and displeasing to God? Basil believes that one should serve to the same degree as Paul, who wrote to the Corinthians, "If I deliver my body to be burned and if I distribute all my goods to the poor, and have not love, I am nothing."[274] Therefore, unless they are willing to ascribe faith and love to the unregenerate, they must grant that they can do nothing that is not sin or is not displeasing to God. This is as far as we take Basil.

Gregory of Nazianzus, in that oration he made after he returned from the country and after those things were done against Maximus, says, "There is no work accepted or allowed before God without faith, whether it is done through the desire of vanity or by the instinct of nature, which anyone would judge to be honest."[275] What he says here is worthy of note: work done by the instinct of nature, that is, because it seeks to be honest, is dead, neither can it please God. He has the same idea in his oration *On the Holy Lights,* toward the end.[276] In both places he adds, "Just as faith without works is dead, so a work without faith is dead also."[277] And if it is dead, how can it merit justification (as our opponents would have it)? From these two fathers we understand that, although otherwise they were strong advocates (*ergodióktai*) of works and patrons of free will, yet on this matter they were entirely of the same mind as are we.

38. Most clearly of all, Augustine teaches the same thing in his fourth book, *Against Julian,* chapter 3, where he considers these words of the apostle: "The Gentiles, who have not the law, do by nature those things which are of the law."[278] These words, he says, could be understood of the church converted to Christ, who now fulfilled the law by the grace of the Gospel. So when he says "by nature" it is in no way to be understood that the law is excluded; he means such a nature as is now corrected and amended by the Spirit, who regenerates. Or this passage could be taken another way, says Augustine. If those words are to be understood of the Gentiles who are still unbelievers, one must say that by nature they fulfilled the law in one sense, although not to the extent it required. Such outward and civil righteousness does not benefit them except to be more tolerably punished than

---

[273]Phil. 3:7.
[274]1 Cor. 13:3.
[275]Gregory of Nazianzus *Sep.* (PG 35.1234).
[276]Gregory of Nazianzus *Sanct. lum.* 19–20 (PG 36.358–59).
[277]James 2:17; Gregory of Nazianzus *Sanct. lum.* does not quote James 2:17. This citation seems to refer to Gregory of Nazianzus *Sep.* (PG 35.1234).
[278]Rom. 2:14.

others who utterly abandon all discipline and live wickedly and loosely. For we judge that Fabricius is punished less than Catiline,[279] unless perhaps, he says, the Pelagians have prepared some middle place between the kingdom of heaven and the hell of the damned, for the Fabricii, Reguli, Fabii, Camilli, *[543]* and Scipios,[280] the kind of place they have fabricated for young infants who die without Christ. In sum, he concludes that "since it is impossible to please God without faith,"[281] unbelievers can in no way have true virtues. The Pelagians so mocked this opinion that they said that if the chastity of unbelievers is not true chastity, neither are their bodies true bodies, nor is the grain which grows in their fields true grain. Augustine refutes them and shows that this is not a suitable illustration, because inasmuch as the bodies of unbelievers are made by God, they are true bodies. Their grain also, since it is his work, is true grain, but since their chastity proceeds from their corrupt and defective will, it cannot be considered true chastity. He adds that universal sentence of which we have spoken often before: "Whatever is not of faith is sin."[282]

The same Augustine comments on these words in Psalm 30: "Deliver me in thy righteousness."[283] Who, asks Augustine, is saved by grace? It is he in whom our Savior finds nothing worthy to be crowned, but which is worthy to be condemned. It is he in whom he finds no meritorious good works, but only meritorious punishments. Here we see what the nature of human works is before justification.

The same father in *To Simplicianus*, book 1, question 30, says, "We are commanded to live uprightly and that by a reward set before us, we may attain to live forever blessed. But who can live uprightly and do good works, unless he is justified by faith?"[284] We are taught here that there might be merit in those deserving of a happy and eternal life, if they could accomplish what is commanded. Since that is impossible, we move away from merit.

The same Augustine says in *Enchiridion ad Laurentius*, chapter 121, "The purpose of the commandments is love from a pure heart, a good conscience, and a sincere faith."[285] The goal of every commandment is love and what relates to it. Whatever is done without such love is not done as it should be. Therefore, if it is not done as it should be, it cannot be denied that it is sin.

---

[279]Quintus Fabricius, a rather unknown tribune, made possible Cicero's return to Rome in 57 B.C. Lucius Sergius Catilina, a Roman politician and conspirator, was Cicero's opponent par excellence.
[280]See Augustine *C. Jul.* 4.3.25–26 (PL 44.750–51).
[281]Heb. 11:6.
[282]Augustine *C. Jul.* 4.3.32 (PL 44.755), on Rom. 14:23.
[283]Augustine *Enarr. Ps.* 30 (PL 36.226); Ps. 31:1: In justitia libera me (Vulg.); serve me (Martyr).
[284]Augustine *Ad simp.* 1.2 (PL 40.126).
[285]Augustine *Enchir. lauren.* 121, in re 1 Tim. 1:5 (PL 40.288–89).

39. Chrysostom expounds these words of Paul: "The end of the law is Christ." If the end of the law is Christ, it follows that even if someone seems to have the righteousness of the law, if he does not have Christ he does not have that righteousness in reality.[286] By these words we gather that he who is without Christ may indeed have works that seem to be good, yet in truth cannot be just. Immediately after, he says, "Whoever has faith also has the promise of the law, and whoever is without faith is a stranger from both."[287] Here we gather that those who do not have faith are strangers not only from Christ, but also from the righteousness of the law, which consists in an eager desire to do what is commanded. Then he asks, "for what does the law desire? To make a man just, but it is unable. For no one has fulfilled it."[288] But because someone might argue that while it is true that an unregenerate man cannot fulfill the law, if he strives, endeavors, and makes a great effort, he may acquire righteousness, Chrysostom also excludes this. A little before Chrysostom expounds these words, "Being ignorant of the righteousness of God and willing to establish their own righteousness, they did not submit to the righteousness of God." He [Chrysostom] says that he calls it the righteousness of God, which is by faith because it is wholly by the heavenly grace, in which we are justified, not by our labors, but by the gift of God.[289]

Ambrose wrote the same thing when he expounded these words of David: "Blessed are those whose iniquities are forgiven and whose sins are covered." According to Ambrose, the psalmist calls those blessed who God had decreed would be justified by faith alone, without labor or any observances.[290] Ambrose also comments on these words of Paul: "Being justified freely by his grace," and says that people are justified freely, not because they are working or making recompense, but because they are justified by faith alone, which is by the grace of God.[291] The same Ambrose also comments on these words of Paul: "Wherefore death has reigned over those whose sin was not like the transgression of Adam." The apostle wrote this, said Ambrose, because it is impossible for someone not to sin. Since he perhaps spoke of the regenerate, what are we to think of those who are estranged from Christ?[292]

Cyprian also states in *To Quirinus,* that we should boast in nothing because we have nothing of our own.[293] I suppose it is now clear enough that what we

---

[286]Rom. 10:4; Chrysostom *Hom. Rom.* 18 [*sic*] (PG 60. 563–71).

[287]Chrysostom *Hom. Rom.* 17 (PG 60.565).

[288]Chrysostom *Hom. Rom.* 17 (PG 60.565).

[289]Rom. 10:3; Chrysostom *Hom. Rom.* 17 (PG 60.565).

[290]Ps. 32:1; Ambrose *Apol. Dav.* chap. 9 (PL 14.870).

[291]Ambrose *Comm. Rom.* 3.24, *XIII ep. beati Pauli* (PL 17.79–80).

[292]Ambrose *Comm. Rom.* 5.14 (PL 17.94–96).

[293]Cyprian *Test. Judaeos* 3.42 (PL 4.725).

assert is true, namely, that before justification men are unable to perform their works according to the rule of the law and, therefore, those works are sins and unable to merit justification.

If our adversaries object, saying they do not assert that those preparatory works merit justification, only that there are certain preparations by which we are made more ready to attain justification, we may answer them as follows: If the works are not meritorious, why do you attribute to them congruent merit? Furthermore, why call them good, since they neither please God, as we have already taught, nor are they done according to the rule of the law? Last, insofar as they achieve their aim, they are not only sins but also are rightly called sins. How, then, will you teach that men are prepared for righteousness by those works, when they are more likely to be prepared for punishment by such works? So let them cease at once to adorn those works with splendid titles. For if perhaps God sometimes brings men to salvation by these works, he does it because of his mercy towards them, a mercy so great that he will employ sins and works that are evil *[544]* to their benefit.

(2) Justification is through Grace

40. Now let us see how justification is given, if it is not attributed to works. It is given freely, and depends completely on the grace of God alone. For in no way does it depend on merits. Origen saw this when he expounded these words of the letter to the Romans: "Unto him who works the reward is not reckoned according to grace but according to debt." Indeed, Origen says, "when I wish for an outstanding discourse which says that a person who works is owed a debt, I can scarcely persuade myself that there can be any work which can demand a reward as a debt from God. For whatever we can do or think or speak, we do these by his gift and liberality. What debt then will he owe, since his grace has preceded us?"[294] A little afterward, Origen offers a reason for this, which Augustine often used. He introduces that verse from Paul: "The wages of sin is death but the grace of God is eternal life."[295] Here the apostle did not insert: "But the reward of righteousness is eternal life," as is required by antithesis. For Paul wanted to declare that our wicked works of debt deserve death, an eternal death. But eternal life is not granted except by grace. Therefore, in the second part Paul left out the terms reward and righteousness and substituted the name grace.

Indeed I will not pause for long to note that elsewhere Augustine writes that Paul might have said that the reward of righteousness is eternal life, but would not

[294]Origen *Comm. Rom.* 4:4 (PG 14.971–74).
[295]Rom. 6:23.

say so for fear that he might give occasion for erring.[296] How Augustine could have judged that Paul may have said that, I certainly do not see, unless perhaps by righteousness he understood the works of a regenerated person, since the merits of Christ are joined with those works, for it might be true that eternal life is the reward of such righteousness.

Moreover, Origen proceeds to show that men are justified so freely that previous good works are not required. Expounding this verse: "Blessed are they whose iniquities are forgiven," he says, "the soul whose sins are forgiven must now be in a good state, for it is called blessed. Therefore, it has the righteousness which God imputes to it, although it has not yet done any works of righteousness, but only because of his belief in him who justifies the ungodly."[297] From these words we gather several things. First, that for the sake of works God is not made a debtor to any man. Second, that not only justification but also eternal life is given freely. Last, that righteousness is imputed to the souls of those that believe, although no good works preceded them.

Basil comments on these words of Psalm 116: "Return, O my soul, to your rest, for the Lord has rewarded you." He says, "For eternal rest is laid up for those who in this life have wrestled lawfully, yet it is not granted according to the merits of works, but according to the grace of the most gracious God, which he presents to those who have hope in him. Since these things relating to eternal happiness are said about the works of men already justified, they ought to be viewed as much more true than if they referred to the works of those who are still strangers from Christ. Therefore, just as these people do not merit an eternal reward, neither can they merit justification, for both of these things are given freely."[298]

41. In *The Dogmas of the Church*, chapter 48, Augustine says, "If righteousness comes by the law, Christ died in vain."[299] He said this against the Pelagians, who claimed that human liberty was so great that by nature alone it could do things acceptable to God. Augustine wisely transferred to nature what Paul said about the law, showing that the same absurdity follows both, namely, that the death of Christ is made void. For indeed there is no reason why the law does not bring righteousness, except that our nature is corrupt and weak. Therefore, what is said of the one also may rightly be appropriate to the other. Augustine again expounds these

---

[296]Augustine *Ep.* 194.4.20–21 (PL 33.881–82).

[297]Origen *Comm. Ps.* 31:1 (PG 12.1302).

[298]Basil *Hom. Ps.* 114:7 (PG 29.491–94).

[299]Augustine *Eccl. dogm.* 48 (PL 42.1214–22) does not give this quotation from Gal. 2:21. Augustine *Grat.* 13.25–26 (PL 44.896–97) and *Serm.* 131.9.9 (PL 38.733–34) uses this Pauline text to counter the Pelagians' view on nature.

words from chapter 1 of John: "Grace upon grace."[300] To the question what is grace? Augustine answers, "That which is freely given." To the question what is grace freely given? he answers, "That which is not owed. For if something is owed to you, then it is a payment rendered to you. And if it is owed, you must have been virtuous before. Also in *The Predestination of the Saints,* chapter 7, Augustine writes, "Since it is usually said: 'Let no man extol himself,' he therefore deserved to believe, because he was a good man before he believed."[301] The same thing seems to have been written about Cornelius, that he had faith when he did good works.[302] These words are so clear that they need no explanation.

In his second homily on the 1 Corinthians, Chrysostom says, "Where there is grace there are no works and where there are works there is no grace; therefore, if it is by grace why are you proud? Why are you puffed up?"[303] For the same reason as Paul, he sets grace against works, so that the one excludes the other. So far off the mark is it for anyone that grace could be given because of works.

Commenting on the letter to Philemon, Jerome says: "It is grace by which you are saved and it is in no way by merits or works."[304] He also expounds these words from the letter to the Ephesians: "By grace you are saved through faith and that not of yourselves, for it is the gift of God."[305] He says: "Paul, therefore, said this so that no secret thought would creep into us, that since we are not saved by our works, rather are we surely saved by faith. So it is as though we are saved by another kind of work which is from ourselves. All these testimonies sufficiently declare that justification is granted freely and cannot be acquired by any merits or prior works."[306]

(3) Good Works Are the Fruit of Justification

Now it remains for us to show from the fathers *[545]* how good works are to be obtained. To be sure, they follow justification as fruits, which spring up and sprout from a true faith. Therefore, Origen, in the same place we cited before, expounds these words in Romans: "But to him that works the reward is not reckoned according to grace but according to debt." Origen says, "Therefore, the root of righteousness does not come from works, but works grow out of the root of righteousness."[307] This is the same thing Augustine states to Honorius, saying,

---

[300]John 1:16.
[301]Augustine *Praed.* 7 (PL 44.969).
[302]Acts 10:34ff.
[303]Chrysostom *Hom. 1 Cor.* 44. (PG 61.17); 1 Cor.1:4–5.
[304]Cf. Jerome *Comm. Philem.* (PL 26.645–46), paraphrase.
[305]Eph. 2:8.
[306]Jerome *Comm. Eph.* 1.2 (PL 26.500–501).
[307]Origen *Comm. Rom.* 4.1 (PG 14.965).

"Good works derive from the fact that we are justified, and not that we are justified because of prior good works."[308] In book 1, question 2, of *To Simplicianus*, Augustine says, "But if any work is good, it follows grace, as it is said, it does not precede it."[309] So he adds, "If there is any good," because even the works of the regenerate have much imperfection in them, and unless the righteousness of Christ, which is imputed to believers, is joined with those works, they truly would not be. The same father, in chapter 26, *The Spirit and the Letter*, considers at length that verse in Romans: "Not the hearers of the law shall be justified, but the doers," He proves by many reasons that good works follow justification and do not come first.[310] This also tends to agree with what Basil writes in his second book, *On the Holy Spirit*, chapter 7, about the words of the Lord: "First, the tree ought to be good and then its fruit will be good."[311] Also concerning the Pharisees who were reproved for their dishes and cups that were made clean on the outside, he writes, "Make clean that which is inside and what is on the outside will be clean. Otherwise you will be compared to painted sepulchers which indeed appear to be beautiful on the outside, but on the inside are unclean and full of dead men's bones."[312]

PROOF FROM CHURCH COUNCILS

(1) Early Church Councils

42. Now let us come to church councils; they should not be heard without selectivity and judgment.[313] We ought to receive and reverence only those councils that have kept their doctrine within the rule of the Holy Scriptures. In an oration *Against Androtion*, Demosthenes says: "The decrees of the senate should not be made but according to the precept of those things that are already determined in the laws."[314] Even so, in ecclesiastical councils no new decree ought to be made concerning doctrine; the council should rather address only those things that are either expressly named in the word of God or can be surely and plainly gathered out of the Scriptures. We will begin with the African council where in canon 80 a curse is pronounced against the Pelagians, who said the grace of justification is

[308]Augustine *Ep. (Hon.)* 140 (PL 33.570).

[309]Augustine *Ad simp.* 1, Q. 2 (PL 40:111).

[310]Rom. 2:13. Augustine *Spir. et litt.* 26 (PL 44:228).

[311]This citation does not appear in Basil's *De spir. sanc.* or his *Adv. Eunomium*, where books 3 and 5 come under the rubric of *de spiritu sancto*. Matt. 7:17; cf. Luke 6:43.

[312]See previous footnote.

[313]Cf. Martyr on Councils, OTD 27–28, 209.

[314]Demosthenes *Andr.* 5. See *Demosthenes against Meidias, Androtion, Aristocrates, Timocrates, Aristogeiton*, trans. J. H. Vince, Loeb Classical Library (London: Heinemann, 1935), 159–61.

given so that by grace we may easily fulfill what was commanded.[315] It is as if we could by our free will fulfill the commandments of God even without grace, although with more difficulty. However, when the Lord spoke of the fruits of the commandments he did not say: "Without me you can hardly do any thing"; rather, he said, "Without me you can do nothing."

These words rebuke the papists of our day, who are not ashamed to say that before justification one may do the works commanded in the law that please God and prepare for regeneration. What else is this but Pelagianism, when they say that one may keep the law even before justification, although not as fully and easily as after one is justified? Moreover, there is nothing to what they say when it is asserted that there is a prevenient grace by which an unregenerate person is able to do those preparatory works. In speaking this way, they differ from the Pelagians in name only. For they also taught, no less than do these men, that a certain grace of the law, a knowledge of the will of God, and an illumination come first, so that a person understands what he ought to do. As for everything else, the Pelagians attributed it to free will, something these men also do. And that the Pelagians held that opinion, the Council of Milevis declared in the fourth chapter where this is written: "We curse all those who say that the grace of God through Jesus Christ our Lord only helps us; because by grace it is revealed and opened to us to understand the commandment of God so that we may know what we ought to desire and what to avoid. But we also bind and scorn those who say that grace is not also granted to love so that we are enabled to do that which we know ought to be done. For as the apostle says: 'Knowledge puffs up but love edifies.'[316] It is most wicked to believe that we would have the grace of Christ which puffs up but not have the grace which edifies, especially since it is written in the fourth chapter of the first letter of John that 'God is love.'"[317]

---

[315]Council of Milevis (A.D. 416). See Charles Munier, ed., *Concilia Africae a. 345–a. 525*, Corpus Christianorum, Series Latina, vol. 149 (Turnhout: Brepols, 1974). This north African council, with Augustine in attendance, met in reaction to the Synod of Diospolis, which had upheld the teaching of Pelagius. Augustine followed with several letters to Roman Bishop Innocent I. See Augustine *Ep.* 175–77 (PL 33.819–21). Cf. Bonner, *Augustine*, 329–44. The African council to which Vermigli refers was the Council of Carthage (A.D. 418), and what he identifies as canon 80 of the African Council of Carthage is in fact canon 6. The text of the Council of Carthage is found in Munier, *Concilia Africae*, 71–75, and also *Codex Canonum* 13.5.6 (PL 56.4878). Vermigli's mistake may be explained by the fact that two ancient manuscripts (*Sylloge Dionysio-Hadriana* and *Codex Wirceburgensis*) also cite canon 6 as canon 80. Cf. Munier, *Concilia Africae*, 68.

[316]1 Cor. 8:1. Vermigli's citation from the fourth chapter of the Council of Milevis (A.D. 416) refers to canon 5 of the Council of Carthage (A.D. 418). For the text, see Munier, *Concilia Africae*, 71–75, and *Codex Canonum* 13.5.6 (PL 56.4878).

[317]See Munier, *Concilia Africae a. 345–a. 525*, 149 (1 John 4:8).

43. Moreover, in the Second Council of Orange, canon 4, it is written: "Those who say that the Lord waits for our will resist the Holy Spirit, for Solomon says, 'The will is prepared by the Lord' and also when Paul says to the Philippians, 'It is God who works in us both to will and to do according to His goodwill.'"[318](Canon 5 from this council rejects those who affirm that faith is augmented by the grace of Christ, but that grace does not initiate faith. For the beginning of faith also comes by the inspiration of the Holy Spirit, who corrects our faithlessness, transforming faithlessness to faith and ungodliness to godliness. The proof is drawn from various places in the Scriptures. Paul says to the Philippians, "I trust that he who has begun a good work in you shall accomplish it in the day of the Lord." Again in the same letter, "To you is it given not only to believe him but to suffer for him." And to the Ephesians, "By grace you are saved through faith and that not of yourselves, for it is the gift of God."[319]

Moreover, the council said that they were subject to the curse who said that the mercy and grace of God is granted to the willing, to the believing, to those who desire it, to those who exert themselves, to those who labor, to those who are vigilant, to those who strive, to those who ask, to those who seek, to those who knock, but who would not confess that by the infusion and inspiration of the Holy Spirit and by the gift of God it is granted [546] to us to have a will to believe, to exert ourselves, and to labor. They cite these testimonies from the Holy Scriptures: "What do you have that you have not received? And if you have received it, why do you boast as though it was not received?" And the apostle writes of himself, "By the grace of God I am what I am."[320]

In canon 7 from the council they are condemned who hold that by the power of nature we are able to think or to acquire anything that serves salvation, or that we are able to assent to the preached word of God without the illumination of the Holy Spirit. This may be confirmed by Scripture, for Paul says, "We cannot think anything of ourselves as from ourselves, but our sufficiency is of God." Christ also says, "Without me you can do nothing"; also, "blessed are you Simon Bar-Jona, for flesh and blood has not revealed this to you."[321]

---

[318]Second Council of Orange (A.D. 529). See Henricus Denzinger and Adolfus Schönmetzer, eds., *Enchiridion symbolorum: Definitionum et declarationum de rebus fidei et morum*, 36th ed. (Barcelona: Herder, 1976), 4/374, 132ff. Cf. Charles Munier and Charles de Clercq, eds., *Concilia Galliae*, 2 vols., Corpus Christianorum, Series Latina, vols. 148–148a (Turnhout, Brepols, 1963), 2:511–695. This council, convened by Bishop Caesarius of Arles and affirmed by Pope Felix II and his successor Pope Boniface II, represented the triumph of Augustinianism over Semi-Pelagianism in Gaul.

[319]*Enchiridion symbolorum*, ed. Denzinger and Schönmetzer, 5/375, 132 (Phil. 1:6, 29; Eph. 2:8).

[320]*Enchiridion symbolorum*, ed. Denzinger and Schönmetzer, 6/179, 133 (1 Cor. 4:7, 15:10).

[321]*Enchiridion symbolorum*, ed. Denzinger and Schönmetzer, 7–8/377–78, 133 (2 Cor. 3:5; John 15:5; Matt. 16:17).

Also, the Second Council of Orange cursed those who grant that free will is in some sense weakened and hurt, but not so much that it cannot turn men to salvation. Scripture openly declares against these persons, for the Lord says: "No man comes to me unless the Father draws him." Paul also says in 1 Corinthians: "No one can say 'Jesus is Lord' except by the Spirit of God."[322] This is an excellent thought: God loves us for what we will be by his gift and not for what we are by our own merit.

In the canon 13 of the council's statement it is written: "Free will being lost in the first man cannot be repaired, and because it is lost, it cannot be restored except by him through whom it was given at the beginning. Therefore, the Truth himself says, 'If the Son shall make you free, you shall be free indeed.'"[323]

Further, in canon 17 of the statement it is decreed that the strength of pagans comes from worldly lust.[324] These words declare that their virtues, as we showed from Augustine and other fathers, were not true virtues, since they sprang chiefly from an evil foundation, but human lust includes whatever can be found in unregenerate men. It follows in the same canon that the love of God makes the strength of Christians that is diffused in our hearts, not by free will, but by the Holy Spirit, who is given to us, not by any merits which come before grace.

In canon 25: We ought to preach and to believe that by the sin of the first man, free will is so decayed and diminished that no man afterward can either love God as he ought, or believe in God, or work that which is good for God's sake, unless the grace and mercy of God precedes him. Therefore, Abel the just, Noah, Abraham, Isaac and Jacob, and all the saints in antiquity are said in the letter to the Hebrews to have done those things commemorated in Holy Scripture by faith. This faith, as we have taught before, comes from God. Paul says of himself, "I have obtained mercy that I may be faithful." He did not say: "I have obtained mercy because I was faithful before"; rather, the opposite is true.[325]

In the same canon of the council: "This we also profitably confess and believe, that in every good work it is not we ourselves who first begin and then afterward are helped by the mercy of God. Rather, it is that he first inspires in us both faith and love, and that without any of our merits going before. Therefore, clearly we must believe that both Zaccheus, and the thief, and also Cornelius did not believe through nature, but by the lavish gift of God."[326]

---

[322] *Enchiridion symbolorum,* ed. Denzinger and Schönmetzer, 8/378, 133 (John 6:44; 1 Cor. 12:3).

[323] *Enchiridion symbolorum,* ed. Denzinger and Schönmetzer, 13/383, 134 (John 8:36).

[324] *Enchiridion symbolorum,* ed. Denzinger and Schönmetzer, 17/190, 135.

[325] *Enchiridion symbolorum,* ed. Denzinger and Schönmetzer, conclus. 396 (Heb. 11; 1 Cor. 7:25).

[326] *Enchiridion symbolorum,* ed. Denzinger and Schönmetzer, conclus. 397 (Luke 23:41; Acts 10:31; Luke 19:6).

44. Perhaps I have drawn these things from the Council of Orange to a greater degree than may seem appropriate for this topic. I willingly admit that I did it because I saw that all those things affirmed there are confirmed by the Holy Scriptures, and strongly establish our own view. Such councils, gentle reader, which rest upon the word of God, are to be listened to. For whatever advantage or misfortune the church has, the same ought to be wholly ascribed to observing or neglecting the word of God. For how else did the old and ancient councils overcome Arius, Eunomius, Nestorius, Eutyches, and other destructive heretics, except by the word of God? Certainly they could never be overcome and vanquished by any other means. And in a different way, would the church have begun to succumb to abuses and superstitions unless the Word was neglected? In our times, unless the word of God had been reclaimed and in a sense recalled out of exile *(postliminio revocatum)*, how could we ever have been delivered from the tyranny of popes? Let these few items be a warning to us not to believe every council blindly, but let us receive only those councils that have soundly confirmed the decrees of their doctrine according to the Scriptures. In order to elucidate what I say, I mention the Council of Trent—that by considering the opposite view, the truth may be better understood.

(2) The Council of Trent
Justification is considered in session 6 of the Council of Trent, especially from chapter 5 to chapter 11.[327] There those good holy fathers, that is, hirelings of the pope, decreed that the beginning of justification is by grace. But they immediately make clear what kind of grace they understand, for they say, "It calls and it stirs up. Those who are to be justified are so helped by it, that being called and stirred up they give assent to this grace and work with it and are disposed toward regeneration."[328] But this assent and working together with it [grace] is attributed to free will, as the words show. What else would Pelagius say if he were now alive? For even he certainly did not deny grace, if one takes it as admonition, calling, and stirring up. He also attributed to free will that it had the power to assent and to obey the commandments of God. But the grace *[547]* which the Holy Scriptures set before us renews our understanding and will, and gives us a fleshy heart

[327]Vermigli wrongly states that it was the fifth session. In fact, the doctrine of justification was considered during the sixth session of the council and issued its statement 13 January 1547. The critical edition of the canons and decrees of Trent are found in *Concilius Tridentinium: Diariorum, actorum, epistularum, tractatuum nova collectio*, 13 vols. in 18 (Fribourg: Societas Goerresiana, 1901–85). A more recent edition of the conciliar decisions is H. J. Schroeder, *The Canons and Decrees of the Council of Trent* (Rockford, Ill.: Tan Books, 1978). For an overview of the council see Hubert Jedin, *A History of the Council of Trent* (St. Louis: Herder, 1957–60).
[328]Schroder, *Canons and Decrees*, sess. 6, chap. 5, pp. 31–32.

instead of a stony heart. For it not only consults our reason but also fully persuades, bends, and changes the will. Our men of Trent do indeed grant that God renews the heart of man by the illumination of the Holy Spirit. However, so that a man himself should do something, they add that the man who admits such inspiration may also reject it. Therefore, they fully conclude that it pertains to man to admit or receive grace, although they confess that one cannot do that unless he is called and stirred up by grace.

Unless it has been renewed by the Spirit and the grace of God, how can the heart of man receive those things that are against his nature, which is still corrupt and defiled? Certainly, however much it is stirred up, taught, and moved, unless it is inwardly changed, it will perpetually resist. Therefore, Augustine, in *To Simplicianus*, properly writes, "It is not in our power to make those things which work against us acceptable and pleasant. But we eliminate what is neither acceptable nor pleasant, however much we are urged by admonitions. It is as if a sick man were offered good healthy food, most pleasingly presented, yet because it is not pleasant or acceptable to him, he refuses it, even though many people stand by who say to him that the food is healthy and excellently prepared. The same thing undoubtedly happens to an unregenerate mind, except that concerning the receiving of the grace of God no violence can be done to the mind, whereas the sick person may be compelled to take unpleasant food. Therefore, as long as our will and understanding are not changed by the Spirit of God, the mind will not admit any healthy admonitions. Before he is restored to health, a sick person neither approves of nor gladly receives any food offered to him; so also the mind of man, unless it is changed from faithlessness to faith, from ungodliness to godliness" (as the second Council of Orange says), "will not obey or comply with grace, which calls and stirs up."[329] This is something even the fathers of Trent affirm.

45. So that they would not appear to speak without the Scriptures, they produce two testimonies. One is from the chapter 1 of Zechariah: "Turn to me and I will turn to you."[330] They say this refers to someone who is commanded to do something in justification itself. But Jeremiah says, "Bring us back O Lord and we shall be restored."[331] From these words it is shown that the help of God is also required for that conversion, and by this covenant they divide the whole topic between God and man, but Augustine and many other fathers ascribe the whole business of justification to God alone. As to the passage in Zechariah, it may be explained in two ways. First, these are the words of the law which command us.

---

[329]This citation does not appear to be from Augustine *Ad simp;* the source could not be identified.
[330]Zech. 1:8.
[331]Jer. 31:18.

Yet it cannot be proved from them that a man can be converted unless God converts him. Augustine has written, "The Lord gives what you command and commands what you will."[332] Another explanation is that in justification there are two inward movements. One pertains to reason, which (as we have said) needs not only to be taught, but also to be persuaded and drawn into the purpose of the Holy Spirit; the other motion pertains to the will that is bent to receive all those things the Holy Spirit promises and offers, and this is the faith by which we are justified and by which our sins are forgiven.

Since these things were concealed in the inward parts of the mind, the prophet does not speak of them, but instead speaks of those things that follow. For once a man is justified, he begins to turn to good works. Therefore, those who lived dissolutely and wickedly before, now conduct themselves uprightly and properly, and being renewed with grace and the Spirit, they cooperate with the power of God. The prophet speaks of this conversion when he says, "Be converted to me"; and God promises to heap great benefits upon them, which is indicated by this phrase: "and I will be converted to you."[333] For before, when he withdrew his benefits from them and afflicted them with captivities and other miseries, he seemed to be against them. Therefore, the prophet did not speak of inward justification, but of an outward turning to good works. When Jeremiah said, "Bring us back O Lord and we shall be restored," he was referring to this inward motion of the mind we have already described. But when our men of Trent speak they pretend to distinguish themselves from the Pelagians, yet they can never prove it. They say they do not deny grace, but in fact they put forward a kind of grace that the Pelagians would never have denied.

46. Let us see what stages and preparations the Council of Trent assigns to justification.[334] First, they say that someone who is to be justified is called and stirred up by the grace of God. He begins to believe those things that are written in the Holy Scriptures. Then he is troubled with fear of the sins he has committed. Afterward, looking upon the mercy of God, he begins to have a good hope. Once hope is conceived, he loves God, producing in him an aversion to sins and a desire to live rightly. Finally, he receives baptism or the sacrament of penance. They say that this is justification; all the other things that preceded it were only preparatory. But they do not see that we ought to come to a quite different conclusion about baptism. For the Scriptures teach that Abraham was first justified by faith in uncircumcision and then received circumcision, as a seal (*sphragidas*) of the

---

[332]Augustine *Conf.* 10.29, 40 (PL 32.796).
[333]Lam. 5:21; Cf. LPJ, 209–10.
[334]Schroeder, *Canons and Decrees,* sess. 6, chap. 6, pp. 32–33.

righteousness already received. According to the analogy, this same proportion [*ratio*] is to be kept in baptism, for our baptism corresponds to the circumcision of the ancients.[335] *[548]* When they claim that faith, the fear of God, hope, love, aversion to sin, and the desire to live rightly are but preparations to justification, they determine that a man may be able to be perfect before he is justified.

Then they recite the causes of our justification and begin at the final cause, which they say is the glory of God and our salvation.[336] The efficient cause is God himself with respect to his mercy alone. The meritorious cause (as they call it),[337] they assert to be Christ Jesus, by his death on the cross and the shedding of his blood. So far this is not bad. The formal cause is the justice of God, not that justice by which he himself is just, but that which he communicates to us, by which we are both truly counted just and are just in fact. By these words they understand the renewing of someone already regenerate, and his new formation through grace and the Holy Spirit. That these things are done in one already justified we do not deny, but that justification consists in this we cannot grant. For Paul affirms it to consist in this: "Our sins are forgiven us and that they are not more imputed to us." To confirm this he cites a testimony from David: "Blessed are they whose iniquities are forgiven." Also from that passage in Genesis: "Abraham believed God and it was counted to him for righteousness."[338] So that he might explain the idea more plainly, he often employs in the same passage the word "imputation." Therefore, we say that justification cannot consist in that righteousness and renewal by which we are created anew by God. For it is imperfect because of our corruption, so that we are not able to stand before the judgment of Christ.

Moreover, they say that this righteousness by which they wish us to be justified is distributed to everyone by the Holy Spirit as it pleases him. This indeed may be so, for the Holy Spirit is the judge in the distribution of the gifts of God. But they go further and add *Iuxta modulum praeparationis* (according to the measure of preparation).[339] On the contrary, this can by no means happen. We have shown before from the fathers, and especially from the Scriptures, that all those things done before justification are sins. It is far from the truth to suggest that they can merit and prepare for justification. They also conclude that if justification is received, men can never be sure and certain of it, but ought always to be uncertain

---

[335]Cf. Martyr's teaching on this point: *Comm. in Rom.* 2:25, *Comm. in 1 Cor.* 7:14, *De Votis,* 1373d.

[336]Schroeder, *Canons and Decrees,* sess. 6, chap.7, pp. 33–34.

[337]That is, the material cause.

[338]Rom. 4:5, 6; Ps. 32:1; Gen. 15:6.

[339]Schroeder, *Canons and Decrees,* sess. 6, chap. 7, pp. 33–34.

and anxious.[340] When we object that this is to disparage the truth of the promises of God and the dignity of grace, they deny it to be true. For they say they do not doubt the promises of God, but when they look upon their own "indispositions" (as they call them), they must at last begin to doubt. Certainly this is not to be wondered at, for if one considers his own unworthiness, he will not only doubt the promises of God, but will also be certain that he himself cannot be justified.

The Holy Scriptures teach far differently. They propose to us the example of Abraham and how "contrary to hope, he believed in hope,"[341] and that when he was more than a hundred years old, he had no regard to the barrenness of his own body or the deadness of Sarah's womb. He did not waver because of distrust, but was confirmed by faith and most surely persuaded that God was able to perform whatever he promised. This example teaches us that we should not have regard for those things that can or may attempt to hinder our justification. Our faith should be fixed completely on the words and promises of God. Against this, they want to call us back to what they call our indispositions, and will have us always to be in doubt of our justification. Indeed, we ought not to conceal whatever imperfection or fault lies in us, because it may be daily corrected and amended. However, on that account we ought not to be in doubt and wavering concerning our justification and the grace of God.

Proposition 2: Justification Is by Faith

Proof from Paul's Letter to the Romans

47. Now we must prove the second proposition, namely, that we are justified by faith. We intend first to prove this from the testimonies of Holy Scripture. In chapter 1 of Romans Paul defines the Gospel: "It is the power of God to salvation to everyone that believes."[342] These words touch on the efficient cause of our justification, namely the power of God; the final cause is our salvation; the instrumental cause by which it is received is faith, for he adds "to everyone who believes." He confirms this by a testimony from the prophet Habakkuk, which delighted him so much that he used it in both Galatians and Hebrews in the same sense.[343] Furthermore, he adds: "The wrath of God was revealed from heaven, by reason of the knowledge of the pagans, who withheld the truth of God in unrighteousness and who when they knew God did not glorify him as God but fell into the worship of

---

[340]Schroeder, *Canons and Decrees*, sess. 6, chap. 9, p. 35.
[341]Rom. 4:18.
[342]Rom. 1:16.
[343]Hab. 2:4; Gal. 3:11; Heb. 10:38.

idols."[344] In a different way the righteousness of God is revealed in the Gospel, namely, that righteousness by which men are justified from faith to faith, a phrase of speech we have sufficiently explained in its own place.[345]

In chapter 3: "Now is the righteousness of God made manifest without the law, the righteousness of God by the faith of Jesus Christ in all and upon all those who believe in him."[346] And a little afterward: "Wherefore, being justified freely by his grace by the redemption that is in Christ Jesus, whom God has set forth to be a reconciliation through faith in his blood."[347] This shows not only the grace by which God freely justifies us, but also Christ and his death is displayed so that it may be quite clear that he is the reconciler and the mediator. To this is added the faith by which we receive the fruit of his redemption, which also displays his righteousness in this time, that he himself might be just, justifying those *[549]* who are of the faith of Jesus Christ. If men could provide righteousness for themselves by their works, then the righteousness of God would not be declared like this, but since we understand that it is communicated to us by faith without any preparation of works, it is necessary that it appear very great. Among the other things that God requires of men, this is preeminent: that they should not glory in themselves. If justification consists in works, they could boast of their own zeal and industry, but since we are freely justified by faith, no place remains for boasting; therefore, Paul says, "Your boasting is excluded. By what law? By the law of works? No, by the law of faith."[348] He concluded in this way: "We contend that a man is justified by faith without works."[349] And so that we should not think the proposition is particular, he declares that it is universal: "Is he the God of the Jews only and not also the God of the Gentiles? Yes, of the Gentiles too, for it is one God who justifies the Uncircumcision through faith and the Circumcision by faith."[350] Therefore, just as there is but one God over all, so he justifies all in the same way.

48. In chapter 4, Paul says, "To one who does not work but trusts him who justifies the ungodly, faith is reckoned to him as righteousness."[351] In this verse works are excluded and faith is set forth as the means through which righteousness is imputed to men. Immediately he says of Abraham, "he is the father of all

---

[344]Rom. 1:17–18, paraphrase.
[345]ROM, 22–23.
[346]Rom. 3:21.
[347]Rom. 3:24.
[348]Rom. 3:27.
[349]Rom. 3:28.
[350]Rom. 3:29.
[351]Rom. 4:4.

those who believe without being circumcised, that it might also be reckoned to them. And he is the father of the circumcision, not only to them who are from the circumcision, but also those who walk in the steps of faith which was in the uncircumcision of our father Abraham."[352] Afterward Paul shows that justification is by faith, by the nature of the promise, for he says: "The promise to Abraham and his descendants that they should inherit the world did not come through the law but through the righteousness of faith. If adherents of the law are to be the heirs, then faith is null and the promise is void."[353] In these words two splendid things are to be noted. First, the promise is free and is not joined with a condition of works. Since faith is a correlative, related to the promise, it must follow what kind of promise it is; so it refers to the promise by itself and not to the condition of our indisposition, as the fathers of Trent teach. The second thing to be noted is that if the inheritance and righteousness should depend on the condition of works, then there would have been no need for the promise, for it might be said: why is that freely promised to us, if we are able to claim it by our own zeal and labor? Or why is it so necessary that we should believe, since we are able to obtain righteousness by our own works?

Afterward, Paul adds the final cause as to why justification is by faith: "It is by faith so that the promise might be firm."[354] For if we are justified by our own works and preparations, the promise would always waver, nor would we be able to establish any certainty of it. He then puts forward the example of Abraham, of whom it was said before, "In hope he believed against hope."[355] As to his own role, he did not have any regard for those things that might have hindered the promise of God: "His own body which was as good as dead and a hundred years old, and the age of his wife Sarah."[356] These things declare well enough the kind of faith through which righteousness was imputed to Abraham, so that we may understand the power and nature of the faith which justifies. Paul also adds that through such faith the glory of God is much advanced. For when nothing is attributed to our works and merits, it must be that the whole glory goes to God. Therefore, Paul says of Abraham, "He gave the glory to God, fully convinced that God was able to do what he had promised."[357] In order to express more fully the certainty of faith, he used this participle *plêrophorêtheis*, by which he meant that Abraham embraced God's promise with the fullest assent. So that no one would

---

[352]Rom. 4:11.
[353]Rom. 4:13.
[354]Rom. 4:16.
[355]Rom. 4:18.
[356]See Rom. 4:19.
[357]Rom. 4:20.

think that this was an exclusive and peculiar prerogative given to Abraham, the apostle adds a universal rule and says, "The words 'it was reckoned to him for righteousness' were not written for him only, but also for us. It will be reckoned to us who believe in him who raised up Jesus Christ from the dead, who was delivered for our trespasses and rose again for our justification."[358]

Further, from chapter 5, we have another testimony: "Therefore, being justified by faith, we have peace with God through Jesus Christ by whom we have access through faith into his grace in which we stand."[359] Two points should be noted here. One is that we are justified by faith and through grace. The second is that entrance to this grace is not accessible by preparations or the distribution of our works, but by faith alone.

In chapter 8, certain steps and degrees, as it were, are proposed, by which we must come to eternal salvation. "Whom he foreknew he also predestined to be conformed to the image of his Son, in order that he might be the firstborn among many brethren. And whom he has predestined, those also he has called, and whom he has called, those he has justified, and those whom he has justified, those he will also glorify."[360] Here five stages are recounted: foreknowledge, predestination, vocation, justification, and glorification. For our purposes let us consider what comes between vocation and justification. Nothing else occurs except faith. For when vocation is brought about by the promise of justification and salvation, it is received by faith giving assent.

49. Toward the end of chapter 9, the difference between Jews and Gentiles is discussed, and a reason given *[550]* why Gentiles obtained righteousness and not Jews. Paul says: "What shall we say, then? That Gentiles who did not pursue righteousness have attained it, that is, righteousness through faith; but that Israel, who pursued righteousness did not fulfil the righteousness based on law because they sought it not by faith but as if it were by works?"[361] Nothing could be clearer than these words, for they declare that those who want to be justified by faith obtain righteousness, but those who aspire to it by works, labor in vain.

He proves the same thing at the beginning of chapter 10, where he describes two kinds of righteousness. The one he calls "ours" consists of works, and the other he calls "the righteousness of God," which is taken hold of by faith. Thus he writes, "They being ignorant of the righteousness of God and going about to

---

[358]Rom. 4:23–24.
[359]Rom. 5:1.
[360]See Rom. 8:29–30.
[361]Rom. 9:30.

establish their own, did not submit themselves to God's righteousness."[362] From this it is clear that those who want to establish their own righteousness fall away from the righteousness of God.

Paul goes on to reveal more plainly the nature of these two kinds of righteousness, saying, "Moses says of the righteousness which is by the law, that the man who practices them shall live by them."[363] By these words he shows that the righteousness of the law consists in works. But of the righteousness which is by faith he says: "Do not say in your heart, 'Who shall ascend into heaven' to bring Christ down? or 'who will descend into the deep' to bring Christ up from the dead? But what does it say? 'The word is near you, on your lips and in your heart.' That is the same word of faith which we preach, that those who believe in their heart and confess with their mouth the Lord Jesus Christ, will be saved."[364] By this we see that it is not the righteousness of the law kept by works, but the righteousness of faith that brings salvation. This is clearly confirmed from the latter words, where he adds: "With the heart we believe unto righteousness and with the mouth confession is made unto salvation."[365] The latter clause on confession, which appears to be an outward work, is added so that we would not think that the faith by which we are justified is indifferent, for it is not a vain and barren faith our adversaries dream we thrust upon them. Rather, it has the most plentiful and abundant fruits, among which the profession of piety holds first place, and is most necessary.

Here Paul adds a testimony from the prophet Isaiah: "He who believes in him shall not be made ashamed."[366] Those usually ashamed are those who, contrary to their expectation, are frustrated because of what they hoped to have gained. Therefore, the meaning is that he who believes in Christ and by this faith waits for salvation, will not be put to shame because he will not be frustrated in his hope. He adds another testimony from the prophet Joel: "Whoever calls on the name of the Lord will be saved."[367] In these words the promise of salvation seems to be ascribed to invocation, but Paul profitably teaches, as I have often said, that when promises seem to be joined to works, we must always hasten back from them to their root and foundation, namely, faith. So when Paul says in this verse, "Whoever calls on the name of the Lord will be saved," he immediately adds: "How shall

---

[362]Rom. 10:3.
[363]Rom. 10:5.
[364]Rom. 10:8–9.
[365]Rom. 10:10.
[366]Isa. 28:26.
[367]Joel 2:32.

they call upon him in whom they have not believed?"[368] So he resolves the whole matter of invocation in relation to faith. And lest we think that faith has anything by its own power by which it can justify, he returns once again from it to the objection, saying, "How shall they believe without a preacher? And how shall they preach except they be sent?" Also "Faith comes by hearing and hearing by the word of God."[369] Therefore, the chief points of the resolution are the word of God and the promise concerning Christ, like a fountain from which our salvation and justification is derived.

In chapter 11 there is set forth the antithesis between incredulity and faith which seems very much to confirm what we are now teaching. "The branches were broken off that I might be grafted in." This was an objection of the Gentiles against the Jews. Paul answers, "You say well because of unbelief they were broken off, but you stand by faith."[370] Here the reason for the fall and destruction of men is given, and on the other side the reason for salvation and constancy, namely, unbelief and faith. Concerning the Jews who would one day be restored he adds, "And if they still do not abide in their unbelief, they shall be again grafted in, for God is able to graft them in."[371] Here we see that those that have fallen are restored when they separate themselves from unbelief, which means believing. This makes a strong case against the error of those who state that the first justification is freely given, without any works preceding, yet do not grant that those who have fallen are restored to justification, except by satisfaction and many works of preparation.

Proof from Paul's Other Letters

50. These matters have been gathered from the letter to the Romans; now we will consider the other letters in order. In 1 Corinthians 1, it is written: "Since in the wisdom of God, the world did not know God through its wisdom, it pleased God through the foolishness of preaching to save those who believe."[372] The wise men of this world, Paul says, by their natural seeking were not able to apprehend the wisdom of God by which they might be saved; therefore, God in his goodness has established the opposite way, namely, the preaching of the Gospel. It seems foolish to the flesh that through it salvation should be given to men, not to everyone but only to those who believe. Thus in 2 Corinthians 1, it is written: "by faith

---

[368]Rom. 10:14.
[369]Rom. 10:14–15, 17.
[370]Rom. 11:19–20.
[371]Rom. 11:23.
[372]1 Cor. 1:21.

you stand firm."[373] By these words we understand that the foundation, through which we are confirmed and established in the way of salvation, is faith. Further, Paul writes to the Galatians, chapter 2, where he reproaches Peter for his pretense by which he seemed to lead the Gentiles to observe the ceremonies of the Jews: "If you being a Jew live like the Gentiles and not like a Jew, how can you compel the Gentiles to live like Jews? For we who are Jews by nature and not Gentile *[551]* sinners, know that a man is not justified by the works of the law, and we believe in Christ that we might be justified by the faith of Christ and not by the works of the law, because by the works of the law will no flesh be justified."[374] Here we see that the apostles followed Christ so that they might be justified by faith, which they could not attain by works. Afterward: "The life I now live in the flesh, I live by faith in the Son of God,"[375] which is just as he should have said. Even now sin lingers in my flesh and I carry death in it; nevertheless, I have life not through my own merit but through faith in the Son of God.

In chapter 3 it is written, "Let me ask you only this: did you receive the Spirit by works of the law or by hearing with faith?"[376] He adds at once, "Does he then who supplies the Spirit to you and works miracles among you, do it by works of the law or by hearing with faith?"[377] We understand by these words that it is faith and not works by which we take hold of the gifts of God. He adds, "Be assured that those who are of faith are the sons of Abraham."[378] Certainly, that is for this reason alone, that in believing they imitate him. Therefore, he says, "the Scriptures foreseeing that God would justify the Gentiles by faith, preached the Gospel beforehand to Abraham saying, 'all nations shall be blessed in you.'"[379] This blessing spread to them not because they had their origin in the flesh of Abraham, but because they followed the steps of his faith. In other respects, Abraham lived according to the flesh, but as far as can be determined, he did not propagate this except among the Ishmaelites, Edomites, and Israelites. Then the conclusion: "Therefore, those who are of faith are blessed with Abraham who had faith."[380] "To be blessed," is in the Hebrew phrase nothing else than to receive the gifts of God, among which justification holds first place. Therefore, it follows that "through Christ the promises made to Abraham might come to the Gentiles, that

---

[373]2 Cor. 1:24.
[374]Gal. 2:14–16.
[375]Gal. 2:20.
[376]Gal. 3:2.
[377]Gal. 3:5.
[378]Gal. 3:7.
[379]Gal. 3:8.
[380]Gal. 3:9.

we might receive the promise of the Holy Spirit through faith."[381] So then we see that the promise of the Holy Spirit is not taken hold of by works, as many imagine. Reason sufficiently declares this, for since the Lord, as will be shown, had given his blessing to Abraham through the promise, we must see what is brought to the promise as if as a correlative, which, as we have said, can be nothing except faith, for faith has as its object the promises of God.

51. Paul furthermore adds, "The Scripture has shut up everyone under sin, that the promise by faith in Jesus Christ might be given to those who believe."[382] This is the reason why the Scriptures so diligently show men how guilty they are of sins, that is, that they should be more stirred up to embrace the promises of God by faith, at least when they have no good works by which they could grasp them. We understand this by what is written afterward: "The law is our tutor until Christ came, that we may be justified by faith."[383] These words mean nothing else except that the law thus makes known sins and exposes to men their weaknesses and arouses their lusts, by which sins are more and more increased that, being admonished, they would return to Christ and receive righteousness from him through faith. This is something they certainly did and of whom it is said, "You are all sons of God through faith in Jesus Christ."[384] For what is it to be sons of God unless we have already attained adoption, which we obtain only by regeneration or justification?

And in chapter 4 he says, "Brethren, like Isaac we are children of promise."[385] But to be children of the promise is nothing else than to believe those things God promised, by which we are made his children, just as he promised we would be. Even so, Isaac was born to Abraham not by the strength of nature, but by the blessing of the divine promise.

In chapter 5, he writes, "Through the Spirit, by faith, we wait for the hope of righteousness."[386] In this verse two things are mentioned: first, the Spirit of God by which we are re-created and renewed to salvation; second, the faith by which we apprehend righteousness. Therefore, in this matter of our justification, although there are many other works of the Holy Spirit in our hearts, yet none except faith leads to justification. Thus the apostle concludes, "neither circumcision nor

---

[381]Gal. 3:14.
[382]Gal. 3:22.
[383]Gal. 3:24.
[384]Gal. 3:25.
[385]Gal. 4:28.
[386]Gal. 5:4.

uncircumcision is of any avail, but faith working through love."[387] From this verse it is clear that justification depends only on this faith, which, as I say, is not dead, but thriving and living. For that reason Paul adds, "working through love." Yet this should not be understood as though faith depends on love, or as they usually say, have its form,[388] but if faith should burst forth into actions and manifest itself, it must do so through love. So one's knowledge does not depend on his teaching others, but it is revealed most of all by that activity. But if any perfections of these actions of loving and teaching overflow in faith and knowledge, they would come from another cause, on which they do not depend or have their form, as many Sophists dream.

52. In the letter to the Ephesians, chapter 2, it is written: "By grace you are saved through faith, and that not of yourselves, for it is the gift of God."[389] After that, in chapter 3 it is written, "That he would grant you, according to the riches of his glory, to be strengthened with power through his Spirit in the inner man; that Christ may dwell in your hearts by faith."[390] Whoever has Christ in him, certainly has righteousness. Paul writes of this to the Corinthians, in 1 Corinthians 1: "Who became *[552]* to us wisdom, righteousness, consecration, and redemption."[391] Therefore, here is shown the means by which Christ dwells in our hearts, namely, by faith. Again, in chapter 3 of Philippians Paul writes: "That I might be found in him, not having a righteousness of my own, based on law, but that which is through faith in Jesus Christ."[392] Here he calls that righteousness based on works and law his own, but the righteousness that is from faith, which he desires most of all, he calls the righteousness of Jesus Christ. It is written to the Hebrews in chapter 11: "By faith the saints conquered kingdoms, performed acts of righteousness and obtained promises."[393] These words indicate how much is ascribed to faith, for by it the saints are said not only to have possessed external kingdoms, but also to have cultivated the works of righteousness, namely, to have lived holy and blameless lives, and to have obtained the promises of God.

---

[387]Gal. 5:6.

[388]On *fides caritate formata* (faith formed by love) see Alistair E. McGrath, *Iustitia Dei: A History of the Christian Doctrine of Justification*, 2d ed. (Cambridge: Cambridge University Press, 1998), chap. 3.

[389]Eph. 2:8.

[390]Eph. 3:16.

[391]1 Cor. 1:30.

[392]Phil. 3:9.

[393]Heb. 11:33 (Vulg.).

Proof from Other Scriptures

(1) The Epistles

In his first letter, chapter 1, Peter writes, "You are guarded by God's power through faith for salvation."[394] In these words are indicated the two principal grounds of our salvation. One is the might and power of God that is wholly necessary for us to obtain salvation. The other is faith, that is, the instrument through which salvation is applied to us. In chapter 1 of his first letter, John writes: "Every one who believes that Jesus is the Christ is a child of God."[395] To be born of God is nothing else than to be justified or to be born again in Christ. It follows in the same chapter: "This is the victory that has overcome the world, our faith."[396] This testimony declares that the tyranny of the devil, of sin, of death, and of hell is driven away from us by no other means than by faith alone. And toward the end of the same chapter he adds, "And these things I have written to you who believe in the name of the Son of God, that you might know that you have eternal life and that you might believe the name of the Son of God."[397]

(2) The Gospels

53. Now let us gather from the Gospels what will support the purpose of this inquiry. Matthew writes in chapter 8 that Christ greatly marveled at the faith of the centurion, and confessed that he had not seen such faith in Israel; turning to him Christ said, "Let it be done to you as you have believed."[398] Here some cry out that this history and others like it do not refer to justification, but only the outward benefits of the body, given by God. Such people should know, however, that the sins in us are the causes of the troubles and afflictions of the body. With Christ as the one exception, who died utterly innocent, all others, because they are subject to sin, suffer no adversity without cause. And while God does not consider this in inflicting calamities, he often sends adversities to show forth his glory and to test his people; yet no one, while he is in tribulation, can complain that he is treated unjustly. For no one is so holy that he has not in himself sins that merit similar or even greater punishments. Where the cause is not removed, neither can the effect be removed. Therefore, since Christ delivered men from diseases of the body, he clearly declares that it was he who would justify them from sins.

---

[394] 1 Pet. 1:5.
[395] 1 John 5:1.
[396] 1 John 5:4.
[397] 1 John 5:13.
[398] Matt. 8:10, 13.

To show that this is the case, the same Evangelist teaches it in chapter 9. For when the paralytic was brought to Christ to be healed, he says that Christ answered. *tharsei, teknon,* "Your sins are forgiven."[399] When the Scribes and Pharisees were offended at these words—in order that they might understand that when the cause of evils is removed, so are the evils themselves—he commanded the paralytic to rise, take up his bed, and walk. Therefore, it clearly appears that by the healing of the body, Christ declares himself to be the one who can forgive sins. And just as those healings were received by faith, so also people are justified by the same faith and receive the forgiveness of sins. In the same chapter 9 there is an account of Christ's answer to two blind men who were very persistent and begged to be healed. "Do you believe that I can do this for you?" And when they answered that they believed, he said: "Be it done to you according to your faith."[400] And when our Savior departed to the house of the ruler of the synagogue to raise up his daughter from death, a woman followed him who was afflicted with an issue of blood and who was endowed with such a faith that she thought to herself that if she might just touch the hem of his garment, she would be healed instantly. Therefore, Christ answered her: "Daughter, take heart, your faith has made you well."[401]

The reason Christ joined confidence to faith, we have indicated before in the beginning of this inquiry when we explained the nature of faith. For we taught that the assent by which we apprehend the promises of God is so strong and so vehement that the other motions of the mind agreeable to it, necessarily follow. In Luke also the story of the sinful woman is reported, to whom the Lord answered, "Your faith has saved you,"[402] signifying that he had forgiven her sins because of her faith. The ardent faith of this woman was made clear by its effects: that she loved much, that she kissed his feet, that she washed them with her tears, and she wiped them with her hair.

54. In the Gospel of John, chapter 3, Christ said to Nicodemus: "God so loved the world that he gave his only Son, that whoever believes in him should not perish but have everlasting life."[403] In the same chapter, John the Baptist speaks of Christ: "He who believes in the Son has eternal life but he who does not believe has not life, but the wrath of God rests on him."[404] From this verse we gather information not only relevant to the topic we are presently considering,

[399]Matt. 9:2; printer's error: reading theta for tau.
[400]Matt. 9:28.
[401]Matt. 9:22.
[402]Luke 7:50.
[403]John 3:16.
[404]John 3:36.

but also this, *[553]* that those who are strangers from Christ and do not believe, can do nothing that pleases God; therefore, they cannot gain congruent merit as they call it, nor the grace of God as our adversaries affirm. In chapter 6, Christ says, "This is the will of him that sent me, that everyone who sees the Son and believes in him should have eternal life; and I myself will raise him on the last day."[405] He had previously said, "No one can come to me unless the Father draws him," and also, "Everyone who has heard and learned from the Father comes to me"; afterward, he added, "and he who believes has eternal life."[406]

In chapter 11 when Christ raised Lazarus, he said to Martha, "he who believes in me, though he die, yet shall he live, and everyone who lives and believes in me shall never die."[407] And in chapter 17: "This is eternal life that they may know you, the only true God, and Jesus Christ whom you have sent."[408] Here we ought to observe, that he does not speak of a cold knowledge, but of an effective and robust faith. Therefore, if there is eternal life, there will also be justification. For justification and life are so joined together that the one is often taken for the other. Indeed, justification is nothing else than eternal life already begun in us now. It is written in chapter 20: "These are written that you may believe that Jesus is the Christ, and that believing, you may have eternal life."[409].

(3) The Acts of the Apostles

In the Acts of the Apostles, chapter 15, it is written: "cleansing their hearts by faith."[410] In that verse Peter says that the Gentiles should not be compelled to do the works of the Jewish law. For without them Christ had given them the Holy Spirit and had made their hearts clean from sins by faith. Also, in his oration to King Agrippa, Paul said that he was called by Christ to be sent to the Gentiles who should be illuminated by his ministry, and through faith should receive the forgiveness of sins and a share among the saints.[411]

(4) The Old Testament

So far we have gathered these testimonies out of the New Testament; if I were to recount all the passages occurring in the Old Testament, I would be quite tedious. And if there are any so obstinate in heart that those things we have

---

[405]John 6:40.
[406]John 6:44–45, 51.
[407]John 11:25.
[408]John 17:3.
[409]John 20:31.
[410]Acts 15:9.
[411]Acts 26:18.

already said cannot compel them to confess the truth, then neither would it profit such persons if we added many more. Therefore, a few will suffice, which Paul cited, such as those from Genesis 15: "Abraham believed God and it was reckoned to him for righteousness"; from Habakkuk: "The just shall live by faith"; from David: "Blessed are those whose iniquities are forgiven"; from Isaiah: "Every one of them who believed in him shall not be confounded,"[412] and many others like them. Besides those testimonies, I also cite from the following, Isaiah 53, where Christ is depicted in the most descriptive words.[413] For there he is said to have taken our sorrows on himself, to have borne our infirmities, to have given his soul as a sacrifice for sins, and many other like things that are so plain they can be applied to no one except Christ Jesus our Savior. It is added: "And by his knowledge, the righteous One, my servant, will justify many and will bear their iniquities."[414] These words teach that Christ justifies many, namely, the elect by the acquaintance and perfect knowledge of him, which undoubtedly is nothing else but a true faith, and that he also in a sense justifies those that he takes on himself and bears their iniquities. And in chapter 5 Jeremiah writes: "O God do not your eyes look to faith?"[415] certainly they do. It is as if he had said: "Although you see all things, and nothing pertaining to humanity is hidden from you, yet you chiefly look for faith as the root and foundation of all good actions." This will suffice concerning the oracles of the Scriptures.

OBJECTIONS TO PROPOSITION 2

(1) Contra Pighius

55. Now I will clear up those objections often brought against this second proposition. We will begin with Pighius because our adversaries have him for their Achilles and think that by his subtle acumen he has penetrated into the secret mysteries of the truth. Thus, this man scoffs that we are not justified by something from which this justification may be separated, [416] for it is not possible that the causes should be pulled apart and separated from their effects. Yet faith is separated from justification, for many who believe do live most shamefully, but they are a long way from appearing to be justified. Nevertheless, because he thinks

---

[412]Gen. 15:6; Hab. 2:4; Ps. 32:1; Isa. 28:26.

[413]Isa. 53:4

[414]Isa. 53:11.

[415]Jer. 5:3 (Vulg.; RSV: "O Lord, do not thy eyes look for truth?").

[416]Pighius, *Controversiarum*, vol. 2, fols. 37v–88v, "Controversiarum secunda: De iustificatione hominis, fide et operibus"; the reference is to vol. 2, fol. 78r–v.

that this may be denied, he brings a reason to demonstrate that it is not against the nature and definition of faith, but that justification may be separated from faith. His objection is from 1 Corinthians 13, which says: "If I have all faith so as to move mountains but do not have love, I am nothing." From these words, Pighius concludes that faith may be separated from love and, therefore, from all good works.[417] He also cites from Matthew: "Many will say to me on that day, Lord did we not prophesy in your name, and cast out demons and perform many miracles?' But to them he answered, 'I never knew you.'"[418] These miracles, says Pighius, cannot be done without faith. Therefore, since those who do these things are excluded from the kingdom of heaven, it is clear that they were not justified. So in them faith was separated from righteousness.

He thinks this is even more plainly confirmed by John who writes, "Even many priestly rulers believed in Christ who yet did not confess it openly."[419] But those who shrink back from the confession of the name of Christ are estranged from salvation, for Christ said, "Whoever denies me before men, I will deny him before my Father."[420] Although these arguments at first glance appear to have some validity, yet if one carefully examines them he will come to agree with Epictetus, *[554]* who states in his books, "Therefore, these are but the ghosts of the dreams of hell."[421] So we must diligently consider these reasons and not judge them by first sight. Just as with coins, we are not accustomed so much to directing our attention to the inscriptions or images, as to the quality and weight of the material. So also in arguments ought we to weigh and examine not so much the glitter and outward appearance but the thing itself and its essence. First, we deny that faith can be separated from justification. Although Pighius says this is not repugnant to the nature and definition of faith, we do not admit it, for against that opinion are the Holy Scriptures, a proper understanding of the definition of faith, and the fathers.

As to Scripture, John says: "Whoever believes that Jesus is the Christ, the Son of God, is born of God and he who is born of God, does not sin."[422] For as long as faith flourishes in our hearts, we do not commit those sins which prey upon the confidence and alienate us from God. How then does Pighius say that it is not

---

[417] 1 Cor. 13:2; Pighius, *Controversiarum,* vol. 2, fol. 41r
[418] Matt. 7:22; Pighius, *Controversiarum,* vol. 2, fol. 53v.
[419] John 12:42; Pighius, *Controversiarum,* vol. 2, fol. 81r.
[420] Matt. 10:33.
[421] *Ta de esti oneiron vertheron phantasmata*: Epictetus *Discs* sec. 22.
[422] 1 John 5:1, 18.

against the nature of faith to be separated from justification and good works, especially since John says, "He who sins knows not God"?[423]

This is something the fathers also observe. In his *De Simplicitate praelatorium*, Cyprian complains of the misfortune of his time, how charity, fear, good works, and other such things seemed to have grown quite cold; so he wrote, "No one thinks of the fear of things to come and no one considers the day of the Lord and the wrath of God, and that punishments will come upon unbelievers, and that everlasting torments are appointed for the unfaithful, things of which our conscience would be afraid if it believed them. But because it does not believe, it is quite without fear, for if they believed they would have been on guard and would have escaped."[424] These words declare that true faith is joined with the fear of God, avoiding eternal punishments, and fleeing from sins: Now let Pighius go and say that true faith can be separated from pious motions of the heart and from good works. Together with Cyprian, Jerome affirms this same thing against the Luciferians. He says, "And if I truly believed, I would cleanse that heart with which God is seen. I would beat my breast with my hands. I would moisten my cheeks with tears. I would tremble in my body. I would be anxious in my mouth. I would lie at the feet of my Lord and would wash them with tears and wipe them with my hair. I would certainly cleave fast to the stock of the cross, and I would not let go until I had obtained mercy."[425] From this it is certainly clear that good works and repentance are joined with true faith.

56. Concerning the definition and nature of faith, we can easily prove that it cannot be separated from justification or from good works, that is, from its effects. For faith is not general, but is a firm and vehement assent, which proceeds from the Holy Spirit. If some miserable person who has been condemned to die should receive merely a human promise that he would be freed and believed those words, his mind would at once be completely changed to joy, and he would begin inwardly to love the one who promised him such things, and would do whatever he could to obey him. How much more is to be attributed to true faith given to the word of God and inspired by the Spirit of God? Therefore, if that human faith drew with it wonderful motions of the mind, how are we able to decide that true and Christian faith is naked without good works, forsaken and alone? Consequently, we now see well enough that according to the Scriptures and the fathers

---

[423]1 John 3:6.

[424]This is a precise quotation from Cyprian *Unit. eccl.* 25 (PL 4.535); apparently Martyr employed an alternative title (*De simplicitate praelatorium*).

[425]Jerome *C. Lucif.* 15 (PL 23.155–82). For more on this debate, see I. Opelt, *Hieronymus' Steitschriften* (Heidelberg: Akademie, 1973), 13–27.

as well as the definition and nature of faith, it cannot be separated from righteousness or from good works.

Now let us come to what Paul says: "If I have all faith," and so on.[426] How does Pighius know that Paul is speaking here of that general faith which cleaves to the promises of God and justifies instead of the particular faith by which miracles are performed and which is a charisma or gracious gift of the Holy Spirit?[427] This faith is not applied to everything found in the Holy Scriptures, but only to a certain vehement trust by which we surely believe that God will do this or that miracle. Chrysostom interprets Paul in this verse in terms of this kind of faith.

Since neither part of this distinction should be without an appropriate designation, the one may be referred to as dogmatic and the other the faith of signs (*dogmatum, signorum*). With reference to the latter, Chrysostom applies it to these words: "If you had faith like a mustard seed, you would say to this mountain 'Be uprooted and be planted in the sea' and it would be done."[428] Certainly, it cannot be denied that there is such a faith. For in 1 Corinthians 12, Paul recounts the gifts which the Holy Spirit distributes to whomever he wills, writing, "To one is given the word of wisdom through the Spirit, and to another the word of knowledge through the same Spirit, and to another is given faith through the same Spirit and to another is given gifts of healing by the same Spirit."[429] Here we see that faith is counted among the free gifts of the Spirit, or charismas; it is in the third place because Paul did not speak of a general faith by which we are justified. If we consider these matters diligently we will see that Paul keeps the same order in 1 Corinthians 13. For just as he placed prophecy in the first position here, so he placed the word of wisdom there. Just as he placed knowledge in second place here, he did the same there. In the third position of both texts he places faith. And whereas faith is here followed by the gifts of healing and miracles, *[555]* there it is followed by the moving of mountains. Therefore, those things which Paul declares about individual faith must not be distorted into a general and justifying faith, for that is to make a false argument, which is a *secundum quid ad simpliciter*.[430] It would be as if one were saying that because faith (called faith *secundum quid*) can in one sense be separated from justification; therefore, true and justifying faith (called faith *simpliciter*) can be separated absolutely from justification. If one were to compare the two different kinds of faith in such a way as to ascribe the same property to both, he certainly would be deceived.

[426]1 Cor. 13:3.
[427]Pighius, *Controversiarum*, vol. 2, fol. 41r.
[428]Matt. 17:20; Chrysostom *Hom. 1 Cor.* 32.4 (PG 61.269).
[429]1 Cor. 12:8.
[430]I.e., "to move from what is true in some sense to what is true absolutely."

57. Pighius saw that all his reasoning could be refuted by this simple and plain exposition; therefore, he tried to snatch it away from us, forgetting meanwhile that its author and patron is Chrysostom. Pighius uses the following argument to make it weaker:[431] Paul clearly says: "All faith"; therefore, we are not to understand it as any particular faith. For the apostle makes a universal proposition. However, Pighius should know that universal propositions are to be modified by their context, according to which the meaning of the language is determined. Although many examples could be shown, at present one alone will be enough. In 1 Corinthians 1, Paul says that he gives thanks to God for them, "that in everything you were enriched in all speech and in all knowledge."[432] But it is unlikely that they were endowed by the Spirit of Christ with natural philosophy, with metaphysical and mathematical knowledge, with jurisprudence and other liberal sciences, but only with all the knowledge which pertains to piety and the Gospel. Neither is it likely that they were adorned by the power of the Holy Spirit with all kinds of rhetorical, logical, poetical, and historical discourses, but only with those that relate to building up the church, sound doctrine, and godly admonitions. Therefore, although propositions are universal, they are not always to be accepted simply, but sometimes ought to be restricted to the matter under discussion at the time.

Therefore, when Paul says, "If I have all faith," we understand all that faith devoted to the working of miracles. That such restriction is necessary is shown by the following words, for immediately Paul adds, "So that I can move mountains." Chrysostom also says that within the universal idea, this particular meaning must necessarily be understood, for he says that it may be doubted how Christ can say that a little faith is sufficient to move mountains, when this amount of faith is so small that it resembles a grain of mustard seed.[433] Paul does say, "If I have all faith, so that I can move mountains," as if a remarkable and great faith is required to bring it to pass. He thus resolves the question and says that Christ speaks of the truth and nature of the thing, for the gift of faith, no matter how small, is enough to perform great miracles. But Paul was allowing for the opinion and judgment of people, for when they look at the majesty and vastness of a mountain, they do not think it can be moved without some incredibly efficacious and great faith.

It does not much help Pighius's cause that Erasmus, responding to the Sorbonne theologians, rejected our interpretation.[434] In the first place, his reason is

---

[431]Pighius, *Controversiarum*, vol. 2, fol. 44v. See also PRME, 269–75.

[432]1 Cor. 1:5.

[433]Chrysostom *Hom. 1 Cor.* 32.4 (PG 61.269).

[434]Possibly a reference to Erasmus's defense against the censures of the University of Paris in 1531. See *Desiderii Erasmi Roterodami Opera omnia*, ed. Jean Lequerq (Leiden, 1703–6), 1069D.

very weak, and second, it is false. Erasmus says that the purpose of the apostle was to praise love by analogy; but what praise would there be, he asks, if it were compared with faith, which is one of the free gifts of the Holy Spirit and may fall upon the wicked as well as the godly? It would be dull praise indeed to say of a person that he is better than a dog or a bear. First, it is false to say that Paul does not bring love together with the free gifts of God, for he mentions prophecy, knowledge, and the gift of tongues, placing love before them. Second, it is weak to say that if our interpretation is received, the apostle would bring love together only with free gifts. Indeed we confess that toward the end he does bring it together with true faith, for Paul says there are three things, "faith, hope and love, but the greatest is love." And he brings a reason why: because it endures and the others will cease.[435] Further, it is a full analogy if, as we have said, we begin with the free gifts and then in successive order come to the theological virtues. Indeed, because of that, toward the end of the chapter Paul brings love together with true faith, and it seems likely that he did not do it before.

Even if we were to grant this and vote for Pighius with both thumbs up, as the saying goes, so that the faith of which Paul speaks is a general faith by which people are justified, he still could not maintain his claim. For when the apostle presents love in all kinds of ways, he seeks to amplify it by a fiction, which is a rhetorical device, known even to children. Yet Paul does not declare it to be a false claim, since he uses a conditional proposition that should not be allowed to weaken the categorical; meanwhile, the truth is no less preserved.[436] So if I were to say to someone, "If you had a rational soul without physical life, you would not be adversely affected with emotions," one cannot prove this kind of discourse false. Yet it is impossible that the rational soul in a human being can be separated from physical life. Such statements are also found in Holy Scripture; for example: "If I ascend [556] to heaven you are there, if I descend into hell, you are there, and if I take the wings of the morning and dwell in the uttermost part of the sea, even there your right hand will lead me."[437] These verses are true, yet it is impossible that a man could furnish himself with the wings of the morning. Similarly, we say that if one were to separate faith from love, it would make it useless, although in truth, faith cannot be separated from love.

What Paul said a little before shows well enough that he used such hyperbole or fiction in that verse: "If I speak with the tongues of men and of angels, but do not have love, I have become a noisy gong or a clanging cymbal."[438] Now we know

---

[435]1 Cor. 13:3, 8.
[436]See *New Catholic Encyclopedia*, s.v. "scholastic methods."
[437]Ps. 139:8–9.
[438]1 Cor. 13:1.

that angels have neither bodies nor tongues, yet Paul speaks the truth that if they had tongues and I spoke to them, it would still bring me no profit without love. Basil confirms this explanation in the letter *Ad Neocaesarienses*, for he says that in this verse the apostle intended to commend love, and he used those reasons, because everything recounted here cannot be separated from love.[439] Therefore, concerning the former interpretation we have Chrysostom as an authority, while Basil confirms the latter interpretation. Now let Pighius confidently maintain from this verse of the apostle, if he can, that view about which he has argued so much.

58. On those words of Matthew, "Lord have we not prophesied and in your name cast out demons?" Pighius denies that such things can be done without faith, yet those who have done them are not justified, since they are excluded from the kingdom of heaven.[440] We can respond with the same refutation we have already brought, namely, that those whom Matthew mentions had the faith of signs or a dead faith, but not a true and justifying faith. Moreover, I do not see how this is true, that miracles cannot be done without faith. For God sometimes works miracles without regard to the faith of those through whom they are done, either to advance his glory or to extol the testimony to true doctrine. Certainly, when Moses and Aaron called forth water out of the rock of strife they wavered in faith.[441] Yet through a great miracle God gave water to the people, so that he stood by his promise, then rebuked Moses and Aaron for their unbelief. Naaman the Syrian doubted that he would recover his health in the waters of the Jordan.[442] Indeed, he would have gone away, for he said that the rivers of his country were much better than the Jordan, yet God did not leave his miracle undone. And when a dead body was thrown into the sepulchre of Elisha, by a great miracle life was restored to the corpse when it touched the bones of the prophet,[443] but there was no faith there, neither in the dead body nor in the bones of the prophet nor in those who brought the dead man there.

Still, it is not always granted those who seek to perform miracles when faith is absent. In the Acts of the Apostles we read that when the sons of the high priest Sceva the exorcist tried to cast out devils in the name of Christ, whom Paul preached, the devil answered, "Jesus I know and Paul I know, but who are you? And immediately he leaped upon them."[444] Here we see that God was not willing

---

[439]Basil, *Ad Neocaesarienses, epistolae* 204.1 (PG 32.746).
[440]Matt. 7:22; Pighius, *Controversiarum*, vol. 2, fol. 53v.
[441]Num. 20:12; cf. Ps. 100:32.
[442]1 Kings 5.
[443]1 Kings 13:21.
[444]Acts 19:13–16.

to grant a miracle when it was sought from those who were probably wicked and unbelieving. On the other hand, in Mark 9, we have someone who did cast out demons in the name of Christ, yet did not follow Christ. When John wanted to rebuke him, Christ would not allow it.[445] Pighius should have seen from this that faith is not always required to perform a miracle. Yet if I were to grant that faith is necessarily required, it would be enough to be either the faith of signs or else a dead faith. Therefore, Pighius proves nothing in his second assertion, for it has no genuineness in it.[446]

59. Now let us examine Pighius's third argument. Citing John, who says, "Many of the rulers believed in him, but did not confess him for fear they should be put out of the synagogue," Pighius concludes they were not justified by faith.[447] This reason is puny and not as strong as he supposes. We deny that they had truly believed; indeed, their assent was nothing but a human assent, for when the rulers saw that remarkable works were performed by Christ and that his teaching was confirmed by the clearest signs, they began to agree with him by a certain human persuasion. Even the devil (who certainly knows many things done by God) assents to the truth and believes it. Yet it is incredible that he [devil] is led by this true faith to believe. However, it is clear that these rulers did not have a true and lively faith, for Christ said to them, "How can you believe, when you seek for glory at man's hand?"[448] By these words we understand that those who esteem human glory more than godliness cannot believe truly in God, and those rulers were numbered among such persons, for they made so much of human esteem and judgment that rather than be expelled from the synagogue or be marked by some disgrace among the people, they preferred to forsake the confession of the name of Christ. Therefore, when the Lord says that such persons cannot believe, and John affirms that they did believe,[449] it is clear that they were speaking of different kinds of faith, unless we want to say that two contradictory statements may each be true at the same time. Therefore, John spoke of a human faith and Christ of a sincere and true faith. This true faith should be joined with confession, *[557]* as Paul states: "With the heart we believe unto righteousness, and with the mouth is confession unto salvation."[450] He who sees the connection between righteousness and salvation must also see that a union should obtain

---

[445]Mark 9:38.
[446]This sentence begins §59 in LC.
[447]John 12:42; Pighius, *Controversiarum,* vol. 2, fol. 81r.
[448]John 5:44.
[449]John 12:37, 39.
[450]Rom. 10:10.

between faith and profession. Thus we say that their faith was dead, but a dead faith is not faith any more than a dead man is a man.

(2) Contra Richard Smith

60. Richard Smith, in his little book on justification, which he wrote against me, contends that a dead faith is indeed faith. The chief argument is this: that the body of a dead man, even though it is dead, still is a body.[451] This wise man greatly delights in his illustration, in which he has proclaimed a sophistical argument not unworthy of his genius and wit. Let us examine briefly this admirable illustration. I would want him to explain to me whether a dead body is the body of a dead man or is it simply the body of a man? I do not think he will reply that it is the body of a man, for there is a great difference between the body of a man and a dead body. Certainly, they are more different than two species of the same genus, because they are contained in neighboring but different genera.[452] I grant that the body of a dead man is a body in terms of substance, as are stones, stocks, and other such things, but I flatly deny that it is still truly the body of a man, for death removes the proper form or species from the body of a man, which it had before,[453] but it leaves the general classification, so that it can only be called a body. Even so, when true and justifying faith is lost or ceases to be a true and proper faith, it may even be called, according to its classification, a cold assent born of human persuasion, not something that originates from the Holy Spirit and has the same strength and efficacy it had before. Therefore, if the similarity of the illustration is preserved on both sides of the argument, this marvelous subtlety (*erophologia*) will not count against us, for just as we confess that a dead body is a body, so also we grant that a dead faith is faith, provided that we understand by faith a classification of all kinds of faith, but not the true and lively faith by which we are justified. This argument is false, based on equivocation.[454]

Furthermore, Smith asserts that faith cannot justify because it is dead according to its own nature and receives life from other things, namely love and good works.[455] These objections are vain and futile. No sober-minded person will grant that true faith is dead. Indeed, the righteous man is said to live by his faith.[456] If we draw life from faith, how can it then seem dead to anyone? We do

---

[451]Smith, *Diatriba*, chap. 1, fols. 1r–23r.

[452]Possibly a reference to Aristotle *An. pr.* 1.31. Cf. idem, *Categoriae* 1b.16–24; idem, *Topica* 7.3, parts of animals 642b.7–20, 643a.

[453]Aristotle *De anima* 2.1, 412a.17ff.: the soul is "the form of a natural body"; cf. Martyr, "Image of God, PW, 39ff.

[454]*Paralogismus aequivocationis:* false argument based on ambiguity.

[455]Smith, *Diatriba*, chap. 2, fols. 13r–19r.

[456]Hab. 2:4.

not deny that faith receives life from other things, for it possesses in part those things in which it trusts, namely from Christ, the promises of God, and in part the Holy Spirit by whose breath it is inspired. In this sense we will grant that faith receives life from other things, but not for the reason this man asserts, namely, that faith has life from either love or good works. For what sane person would ever say that either the trunk of a tree or the branches or fruits or flowers give life to the roots? But faith comes before either hope or love. Therefore, one does not receive life from these things, for indeed, faith cannot be the material of which these virtues are composed. Just as that faculty which they call vegetative gives life to the body but does not receive life from the sensible faculties or the rational faculties,[457] so faith gives life to the soul, but does not take that subsequent life from either love or good works. Still, I grant that the life of faith is made so much greater and enlarged as it has more and better works and more fervent love bursting forth from it. Not that it is increased by the frequency of actions, as is said of virtues which they call moral, but because by his grace and mercy, God multiplies the talent which was not idle and by his power brings it about that faith, as it works through love, is itself stronger when it eases off the work.

(3) Pighius Redux

61. Laying aside these things, let us turn again to Pighius. As much as he can, he contends that one cannot be justified by that faith which is for Christ and for the remission of sins, for he says that the faith by which Abraham was justified was not applied to these things. God promised him only many descendants, and possession of the land. It is immediately added, "Abraham believed God and it was reckoned to him for righteousness." In this argument, Pighius triumphs over and insults the truth and sneers at our opinion. [458] This is nothing else than to ridicule Paul himself, for by the most eloquent words Paul affirms that we are justified by faith in Christ and by the remission of sins. There is nothing whatever in Pighius other than sheer madness and a lust to debate, but let Paul stand forth and answer for himself what he feels should be understood by "offspring promised to Abraham." Certainly, in his letter to the Galatians, chapter 3, he calls that progeny Christ: "The promises were made to Abraham and to his offspring. It does not say 'and to offsprings,' referring to many; but, referring to one, 'and to your offspring' which is Christ."[459] I say that this testament was established by God towards Christ. Let Pighius now actually believe Paul, that Christ was

---

[457]The vegetative part of the soul refers to physical life; cf. Plato *Resp.* 4.439d–441a.
[458]Gen. 15:6; Pighius, *Controversiarum*, vol. 2, fol. 86r–v.
[459]Gal. 3:16.

included and declared in that offspring promised to Abraham. Neither let him dare *[558]* say in the future, with such obstinacy and zeal for winning, that the faith by which Abraham was justified was not faith in Christ. Moreover, as to the remission of sins, a blessing promised to us, we should remember that the chief and principal point consists in this, that we are received into favor by God and our sins forgiven us. But Pighius continues secretly to oppose the doctrine of the apostle concerning Abraham's justification, for he says that before Abraham was circumcised and had the witness of Scripture, and before his faith was reckoned as righteousness to him, Abraham believed God, as is made clear in Genesis 12. Therefore, Pighius says that according to the opposing opinion, Abraham was then justified, and yet his righteousness was no different until the narrative in chapter 15.[460] It is astonishing to see how much value he ascribes to his arguments, as if they could take from us all possibility of reply.

What, I ask, prevents the possibility that Abraham had been justified in that first time when God told him to leave his country and his family? For even in the same passage at the beginning of chapter 12, we have the same promises that are in chapter 15. Thus, God promised him, "I will make you a great nation and will bless you and will make your name great and you shall be a blessing; I will also bless those that bless you, and will curse those who curse you and in you shall all the families of the earth be blessed."[461] These words surely contain the promise of Christ and the forgiveness of sins. So there is nothing absurd if we say that Abraham was also justified by believing those words. But because in that chapter Scripture did not plainly state this, Paul, with great wisdom, cited those words from Genesis 15, where it is expressly written that "faith was reckoned to him for righteousness." This verse was quite necessary to confirm the saying of the apostle, namely that "a man is justified by faith." And why God would repeat the same promises is not obscure. Our minds are so weak that unless the words of God are repeated and impressed upon us, we easily resist faith. Indeed, justification is not only taken hold of once, but as often as we truly and effectually assent to God's promises, for since we continually slip and fall into sins, it is necessary that our justification should be repeatedly renewed.

62. Afterward he quibbles that in the letter to the Hebrews many things involving faith and many admirable acts are recounted that were obtained by faith, yet nothing is said about justification being ascribed to it.[462] But this man

---

[460]Gen. 12:4; Pighius, *Controversiarum*, vol. 2, fols. 86–87v. In fact, Pighius supported the doctrine of double justification as articulated at the Colloquy of Ratisbon/Regensburg (1541), which he attended. See James, "Complex of Justification," HRR, 45–58.

[461]Gen. 12:3.

does not weigh the words of Scripture with balanced scales, nor does he sufficiently consider the meaning of these words: "The just have by faith conquered kingdoms, worked righteousness, obtained the promises."[463] These phrases are to be unraveled by considering the last effect before returning to the first. The last is "to conquer kingdoms," the next, "to work righteousness," the first, "to obtain the promises." Among these promises are counted blessing, life, forgiveness of sins, and other such things making for justification. Therefore, this is mentioned first: faith takes hold of the promise and so by faith we are justified. Afterward good works follow, and so it is said, "and they worked righteousness." Last, by the same faith we obtain temporal goods, and for this reason it is said, "they have conquered kingdoms." So then Pighius wrongly claims that in the letter to the Hebrews no mention is made of justification among the effects of faith. Although that word is not found there, still it is necessarily and plainly derived from those things that are written there, for we are not Arians, as some wickedly say, since we will grant nothing except what is plainly and expressly contained in the Holy Scriptures. We also grant those things that are inferred from them by evident and clear arguments.

Later, Pighius demands why we take away from works the power of justifying.[464] We can explain this in a few words: we do it because in the Scriptures the Holy Spirit teaches us truly that men are justified by faith without works. Yet, so that we would not deal with it so briefly, he has placed an obstacle before us, for he responds that the reason for this is that our works are imperfect, neither do they satisfy the law of God or stand sure before God's judgment seat. But in agreeing with this, he also says we ought to come to the conclusion that justification is not by faith, for it also is imperfect.[465] Indeed, in the realm of mortals no one believes as much as he should.

We respond to this by saying, as we often have in other places, that faith, insofar as it is a work, does not justify; for it has that result not by some power of its own, but by its object, for righteousness flows to us from the death of Christ and the promises of God. Like a beggar who receives alms with a leprous, weak, and bloody hand, yet does not have the hand only on condition that it is weak and leprous. But you will ask why other good works are not also grasped equally with righteousness and faith by their object, that is to say, by God, for whose sake they are done? I answer that faith was designed and instituted by God for this use. So also in the human body, although it has different and various parts, yet only the

---

[462]Pighius, *Controversiarum*, vol. 2, fol. 88r–v.
[463]Heb. 11:33.
[464]Pighius, *Controversiarum*, vol. 2, fol. 88r–v.
[465]Pighius, *Controversiarum*, vol. 2, fol. 50r–v.

hand takes hold and receives. Therefore, this everyday falsehood (*paralogismus*) is easily refuted: we are justified by faith, *[559]* faith is a work; therefore, we are justified because of works. In the conclusion this word "because" is stuffed in, but it was not in the premises;[466] therefore, the conclusion is invalid. Further, the form of the argument is accidental (*ab accidenti*). For it is incidental to faith, as if the matter that justifies us may be our work. Therefore, it is a fallacy of the accident, as they call it.[467]

Moreover, Pighius objects that love (*caritas*), instead of faith, justifies, because love is the more noble and excellent virtue.[468] But we earlier rejected as ridiculous the argument that love is nobler than faith and, therefore, it is love that justifies instead of faith, for nobility or dignity bring nothing to justification. In the same way, it is as if a person would argue like this: the eyes are more dignified than the mouth and the hands; therefore, food is to be received by the eyes and not with the mouth or hands. We also see what happens in the natural world, that things that follow are more perfect, although they do not grant life. In the fetus a human being ascends as it were by degrees from the vegetative faculty to the capacity for feeling, and from the capacity for feeling to understanding. Yet it does not follow that the capacities for understanding or feeling, which are more noble than the vegetative faculty, give life to the fetus. To justify belongs to faith rather than love. Besides, Scripture teaches it explicitly, while it can also be demonstrated by good reasons, for the power of knowledge, which pertains to understanding, consists in perceiving; therefore, those who are taught anything, once they understand it, are accustomed to say 'I accept it or I hold it' (*Accipio, Teneo*). Indeed, through knowledge of something it is, in a sense, admitted to the mind.[469] Therefore, it should not seem extraordinary that we are said to take hold of the promises of God and the merits of Christ by faith. But love consists in pouring out, bestowing, and communicating our good deeds to others, which is something that ought to follow justification and not to precede it, for before we are regenerate we are evil and cannot properly, or in any way that God approves, communicate anything good to others.

63. Pighius adds that if justifying faith does not allow itself grievous sins, which devastate the conscience and alienate one from God, it must follow that if a believer falls into some wicked activity, he is immediately destitute of faith and

---

[466]See Pighius, *Controversiarum*, vol. 2, fol. 67r–v.

[467]*Fallacia Accidentis.*

[468]Pighius, *Controversiarum*, vol. 2, fol. 63r–v.

[469]See Aristotle *De anima* 3.7.4; cf. Martyr, "Visions: How and How Far God May Be Known," PW, 140–42.

ceases to believe that there is a God.[470] However, we see that the wicked not only believe there is a God, but also confess all the articles of faith. At first sight, this argument seems to be quite formidable, but do not allow yourself, dear reader, to be deceived by an empty form. Examine and investigate it diligently, and you will find it to be weak and ridiculous. We acknowledge that a person who is alienated from God by sins and wicked deeds may assent to the articles of faith and believe there is a God, but this man should have taught that the same thing is done by the motion and impulse of true faith. There may indeed remain in a wicked person some human belief, either by education or by opinion, because he thinks it to be more probable. So that no one thinks it is my own invention, when I say that a man who grievously sins is destitute of true and justifying faith, let them rather listen to Paul, for he says to Timothy, "He who does not provide for his relatives, and especially for his own family, has disowned the faith and is worse than an unbeliever."[471] Certainly, whoever renounces faith has no faith. To Titus, Paul says, "They profess to know God but they deny him."[472] To profess and to deny are opposites; therefore, when both are spoken about the same person, they must necessarily be taken in different senses. Thus, they may have faith, that is, a certain human opinion, such as it is, but not that firm and powerful assent inspired by the Holy Spirit, which we now consider.

In chapter 2 of his first letter, John says: "He who says that he knows God and keeps not his commandments, is a liar and the truth is not in him."[473] So then the true faith, by which we genuinely believe in God, is not without good works. It would not seem absurd to anyone that the same thing can be known in different ways. For the devil knows and confesses many things about Christ as well as we do, yet I suppose Pighius would not allow him to be endowed with the true faith, which leads us to believe those things we confess of Christ. It is also possible that a mathematician may assent to some conclusion confirmed and proved by demonstration. If perhaps he later forgets the proof, as it were, because of age or some disease, yet for all that he may not cease to affirm the proposition which he held previously, but he will state it as a matter of opinion or of a probable argument, not as a demonstration as before. Therefore, the knowledge of something does not necessarily infer the same basis for that knowledge.[474]

We mention these things only for the sake of argument (*ex hypothesi*), as though we granted the opinion that true faith is lost after any grievous evil deed,

---

[470]Pighius, *Controversiarum*, vol. 2, fols. 65v–66v.
[471]1 Tim. 5:8.
[472]Titus 1:16.
[473]1 John 2:4.
[474]Probably Aristotle *Eth. nic.* 6.3–6 (1139b.14–1141a.8); 7.2 (1145b.21–1146a.9).

and then afterward, by the kindness of God, faith is again recovered in the elect. In general, it may be stated that faith cannot be completely extinguished because serious sins are committed by the justified and those destined by God to salvation. In such cases, faith is lulled to sleep and lies hidden and does not burst forth into action unless awakened again by the Holy Spirit. In such fallen ones, the seed of God remains, although for a time it produces no fruit.

Pighius proceeds to say that faith is only the foundation, and consequently, it is far from a complete building; therefore, it does not justify. Many other preparations, he argues, are required for justification.[475] If by this complete building he means the blessed resurrection and splendid happiness in which we will see God *[560]* face to face, we grant that faith is very far from complete, for we must come into the kingdom of heaven through many tribulations, adversities, and hard labors. In the same way we may say that justification is only the foundation of eternal salvation, and that it is also far from the blessedness for which we long. The first step toward salvation is to be received by God in grace and to be regenerated through Christ. Afterward, we take more steps by which we come to that highest good for which we long. But where Pighius found that faith is only the foundation, this cannot be derived from Scripture unless perhaps he wants to draw it out of the letter to the Hebrews: "Faith is the substance of things hoped for."[476] But nothing else is meant by those words than that the things we hope for are strengthened and confirmed in our minds by faith. Otherwise, they would waver, nor would they hold fast in everything. Now this does not at all serve the purpose. If he should also cite this: "He who will come to God ought to believe,"[477] to which we have already replied. Perhaps we will afterward in due time speak a little more about this.

64. Now that he has attempted in so many ways to overthrow our doctrine, let us hear at last what he himself affirms, and to what things he attributes the power of justification. There are (he says) many preparations and dispositions required in us that we may be justified. First we believe the words of God, afterward we are afraid of his wrath, then we hope for mercy, and then we detest sins. To be brief, he runs up all those things we spoke of before under the name of the Council of Trent.[478] Last, he says that there develops a sincere and pure love of God, which holds complete dominion in our hearts; to this he says justification is

---

[475]Pighius, *Controversiarum*, vol. 2, fols. 53v–54r.
[476]Heb. 11:1.
[477]Heb. 11:6
[478]Schroeder, *Canons and Decrees*, sess. 6, chaps. 5–11, pp. 31–38.

ascribed.[479] I can only marvel at his devices, for he claims that a man is almost perfect before he can be justified, for he who believes, fears, hopes, repents, and sincerely loves God, what does he lack for perfection? This man affirms that man without Christ, being a stranger from God and not yet justified, is able to accomplish those things. Without any doubt, no way does he agree with the Scriptures, for they teach that before a man is justified he is occupied with evil works and the hatred of God. This is clear in Colossians 1, and the letter to the Ephesians, chapter 2.[480] But how can they, by whom such excellent works are performed as this man mentions, be the children of wrath? How can they be sinners? How can they, as is written to the Romans, be enemies of God?

But omitting these things, let us see what are the grounds of his opinion. First he cites from John: "He that loves not, abides in death,"[481] and thereby concludes that justification and life are obtained through love. This is the same as if a man should say "he who cannot laugh is not a man; therefore, by the power of laughter one becomes a man." Anyone may see how absurd this is, for to be human comes from the soul endowed with reason; since the power of laughing is necessarily joined to this soul, this proposition which we have brought is always true: he who cannot laugh is not a man. So what John says is quite certain: "He who loves not abides in death." Yet we do not have life from love, but from faith, with which love is joined of necessity.

Pighius also cites Christ's words: "If God were your Father, without doubt you would love me."[482] Therefore, it is from love we have the adoption by which we are made the children of God, but here also he uses the same form of reasoning. For those who do not love Christ are not the children of God; yet are we not the children of God in regard to that love, except for faith's sake from which love springs? In the same way one might say: "If you were generous you would also be prudent." This is a true proposition, yet it does not follow that a man is made prudent by generosity. Indeed, more often does generosity spring from prudence. To be brief, these arguments and others like them prove nothing else than that justification cannot exist without love and other Christian virtues, yet it cannot be rightly concluded from this that one is justified for those virtues.

Moreover, Pighius adds this saying of Christ: "If any man love me he will keep my commandments, and I and my Father will come to him and dwell with him."[483] By these words (Pighius says) it appears that justification follows love

---

[479]Pighius, *Controversiarum*, vol. 2, fols. 55v–56r.
[480]Col. 1:21; Eph. 1:1.
[481]1 John: 3:14; Pighius, *Controversiarum*, vol. 2, fol. 56r.
[482]John 8:42; Pighius, *Controversiarum*, vol. 2, fol. 56r.
[483]John 14:23; Pighius, *Controversiarum*, vol. 2, fol. 56r.

and the observance of God's commandments, for when observed, Christ promises that he will come with his Father and dwell with us. He means that to receive and retain Christ is nothing other than to be justified. We grant that when Christians are regenerated and justified, they live uprightly and show forth their faith by good works. God comes into them and graciously pours into them greater gifts and more abundant grace. For although God is everywhere anyway, yet it is said explicitly that he comes to those in whom he begins to work new works. Every day he increases and adorns his own, who conduct themselves uprightly and piously, faithfully exercising the talents committed to them; it is well said that he daily comes to them by reason of new gifts, and this is that kind of visitation of which Christ speaks in the Gospel of John.[484] We should learn first the necessity of God and the coming of Christ into our hearts, as Paul teaches the Ephesians, for he writes as follows: "That Christ may dwell in our hearts through faith."[485] So *[561]* Christ's saying does not teach that justification comes from love, for justification comes first, not in time, but in order.

65. Pighius proceeds to make a distinction of covenants (*testamenta*). Some, he says, are absolute and free, according to which the heir may enter at once on the inheritance; others are conditional, making no heir except on certain conditions. He refers God's covenant to the latter kind. So he states earnestly that unless those conditions are fulfilled, no one can be justified. Now we deny what he affirms, namely, that as regards the remission of sins in Christ, the covenant has any condition joined with it.

Paul witnesses to this in Galatians 3, writing: "To give a human example, brethren: no one annuls even a man's will or adds to it, once it has been ratified. Now the promises were made to Abraham and to his offspring. It does not say, 'And to offsprings,' referring to many; but, referring to one, 'And to your offspring,' which is Christ. This is what I mean: the law, which came four hundred and thirty years afterward, does not annul a covenant previously ratified by God (towards Christ), so as to make the promise void."[486] These words state clearly that the covenant God made with Abraham was pure and absolute, and without any condition in law. The very words of God declare the same: "For God once promised the blessing to Abraham." Afterward the law was given, adding conditions of precepts to those promises, so that if men want to be justified and obtain the promises, they should know that they must perform and fulfill all the commandments of God. but while this latter way of justification can by no means be

---

[484]John 14:16ff.
[485]Eph. 3:17.
[486]Gal. 3:15–16.

accomplished, it cannot hinder or make the former void. That first way was nothing else but the Gospel through Christ. In order that we should come to it more willingly, the second way of justification, by works, was also provided. When people understood that they were unable to perform them they would run to Christ, from whom they might freely receive the promises set forth in the law, and being justified, endeavor to live uprightly.[487]

Now let us see what those conditions are that this man adds to God's covenant. In Psalm 103 it is written, "The mercy of the Lord is from everlasting to everlasting, upon those who fear him, and his righteousness to children's children, to those who keep his covenant and remember to do his commandments."[488] Pighius takes these words to mean that the fear of God, the remembrance of God's covenant, and the endeavor to perform his commandments, are the conditions of the promises of God. Here I marvel not a little that Pighius would affirm that a man is justified by love, when he admits that Scripture attributes this to fear, but we will not allow Pighius to contradict himself. If we listen to the Scriptures in Psalm 32, mercy is promised to those who hope; for it is written: "But mercy surrounds him that trusts in God." In another place it is written: "He who believes will not be confounded; and he that calls on the name of the Lord will be made safe."[489] Who does not see that all these virtues exist in someone already justified, and that God has mercy on him?

Here lies the whole controversy: to which of these virtues is justification to be chiefly ascribed? Without doubt by the witness of Scripture it must be attributed to faith. Pighius also says that in that condition David named, it states that they should be mindful of God's commandments to do them. He says, it does not add, "To do all the commandments"; God receives someone who tries to do them, and of his mercy forgives many things. But this that is written—"To do them"—must of necessity be understood of all, for without doubt "all" is written in the law, which he calls covenant. And if God forgives or remits anything it is to those already regenerated, not to those who are strangers from him and children of wrath. This they must be who are not yet justified, but are still preparing themselves and seeking to perform the conditions. To them (I say) nothing is remitted; therefore, they are bound to all. Thus Moses said, as Paul stated, "Cursed is he who abides not in all things that are written in the book of the law."[490]

---

[487]See Martyr, "Theses for Debate," EW, 106–7.
[488]Ps. 103:17.
[489]Ps. 20:1, 32:10; Isa. 28:16.
[490]Deut. 27:26; Gal. 3:10.

66. Further, he contends also about a kind of springing up and bringing forth of faith, and asks where it has its beginning in us. We easily answer in a word: it has its origin in the Holy Spirit. But he pretends to wonder how we grant the Holy Spirit to someone before he believes, for he thinks this absurd. First, I cannot fathom how this man should wonder so much at this, but afterward I see that he clearly teaches and holds with the Pelagians that faith is from ourselves, and that it is obtained by human power. Otherwise, if he believes that it is of God and the Holy Spirit, he should not separate the cause from the effects. But lest he think that we attribute the beginning of faith to the Holy Spirit without good reason, let him take heed to the clearest testimonies of Scripture. In 1 Corinthians, Paul says, "Not in the persuasive words of human wisdom, but what the Holy Spirit teaches, that your faith should not be from the wisdom of men but from God." In the same place he says, "The unspiritual man does not understand the things that are of God, neither can he, for they are folly to him, for they are spiritually discerned."[491] But how can this be spiritually discerned unless the Spirit of God is present? Children also know *[562]* that firm arguments are derived from conjugates, words that are coupled in one yoke, as it were. To the Galatians: "God has sent his Spirit into our hearts by whom we cry Abba, Father,"[492] for by the Spirit we believe, and in believing we call upon God. As Paul says in Romans: "The Spirit himself bears testimony to our spirit that we are the children of God," and to the Ephesians, "Be strengthened by the Spirit in the inward man, that Christ may dwell in your hearts through faith."[493] Here we see that the faith by which we embrace Christ comes from the Spirit of God, through whom our inward man is made strong. When the apostles said: "Lord, increase our faith,"[494] they expressly declared that it sprang not from their own ability and strength, but by the inspiration of almighty God.

In 1 Corinthians 12, Paul says: "To one is given the word of wisdom, to another the word of knowledge, to another faith and to another the grace of healing"; then he adds, "it is one and the same Spirit who works all these things, dividing to every man as it pleases him."[495] If you say that this place and the previous petition of the apostle relates to the particular faith by which miracles are performed, I will not be much against it. Yet if you will have it so, I will reason a *minori*, that is, from the lesser, for if these free gifts are not received except from God's Holy Spirit, much less can that universal and effectual faith by which we are

[491] 1 Cor. 2:4–5, 14.
[492] Gal. 4:6.
[493] Rom. 8:15–16; Eph. 3:16–17.
[494] Luke 17:5.
[495] 1 Cor. 12:8–9.

justified be received from elsewhere.[496] Further, Paul says to the Romans: "To every one as God has assigned the measure of faith," and in 2 Corinthians: "Having the same spirit of faith as that which is written, 'I believed, and so I spoke,' we too believe and speak that God who raised up Jesus from the dead will raise up our bodies also through Jesus."[497] The fruits of the Spirit are recounted to the Galatians: "Love, joy, peace, patience, kindness, gentleness, faith, meekness, and self-control."[498] Here, faith is numbered among the fruits of the Spirit; therefore, it proceeds from the Spirit. But to the Ephesians he says more splendidly, "By grace you are saved through faith, and this is not your own doing, it is the gift of God."[499] It is written in Acts: "The Lord opened the heart of the woman who sold silks to give heed to what was said by Paul," and in chapter 13, "as many as were predestined to eternal life believed."[500] So there is no doubt that faith is engendered in our hearts by the Holy Spirit. For all that, it may be held by those who do not believe, but only as persuading, not as sanctifying them. Although he suddenly pours faith into the elect, yet insofar as he is the cause of faith he is, therefore, before it both in dignity and order.

67. Now let us see what absurdities Pighius gathers out of our statement and judgment. If the Spirit (he says) is the author of our faith and uses the instrument of the word of God, and if it can also be in those who do not believe, how does it happen that when many are at the same sermon, where the Spirit is present and the Word preached, some believe and some do not?[501] We answer in a word, that it comes because the Spirit does not have the same effect in all, nor does the Spirit teach all men inwardly and in the mind in the same way. We cannot give any cause for his will, although we do not doubt that it is quite just. Pighius argues that if this is the case, the hearers will easily content themselves, and will not pursue their endeavor or study, for they know that this is in vain when it wholly depends on the Spirit of God. This is not only a very common objection, but also is spiteful. We answer that all men are bound to believe the word of God; therefore, their duty is to hear it diligently and attentively, and with all their strength to assent to it; if they do not, they will incur the punishments of the law. Nor should they be listened to if they say that they could not obey or that if they had tried to prove

---

[496] *Major premise*: all gifts are from the Holy Spirit; *minor premise*: wisdom, knowledge, etc. are gifts of the Spirit; *conclusion*: therefore, the greatest gift of faith comes from the Spirit (QED).
[497] Rom. 12:3; 2 Cor. 4:13–14.
[498] Gal. 5:22.
[499] Eph. 2:8.
[500] Acts 13:48, 16:14.
[501] Pighius, *Controversiarum*, vol. 2, fol. 68r–v.

what their strength could have done their endeavor would have been in vain and sinful, since they were not yet justified. It is as if a master should bid his lame servant to walk, and he would excuse himself saying that he was lame and could not walk without much trouble; it is not to be thought that he is therefore excused. We are not of a mind to think that all sins are alike; rather we teach that those who omit or neglect those outward works they could perform, and do not attend to their endeavor and study to do well, sin more grievously than those who observe some outward discipline according to their strength and power. As Augustine says, Cato and Scipio will be more tolerably dealt with than Catiline or Caligula.[502]

Now I would have Pighius himself, who is so displeased by our opinion, to declare when he thinks it is that the Holy Spirit is given to men. He will answer: when these preparations have gone before, when a man has believed, feared, hoped, repented, and sincerely loved. What else would Pelagius say? As though to believe, to love, and such like spring from human strength. He also holds this, thinking it serves his purpose: "Come to me all who labor and are heavy laden and I will give you rest."[503] For he thinks that labors, burdens, contrition, confession, and (as they call it) satisfaction, fastings, tears, and similar things make to obtain justification. But this passage is to be understood far differently, for Christ calls those laboring and heavy laden who were oppressed with the law and felt their own infirmity and the burden of their sins, and who had for long labored under human traditions. The Lord calls to him such men, weary and almost without hope, for they are more apt and fit for the kingdom of heaven than are other blessed and quiet men, who by their own works and good deeds think themselves very just. God (Pighius says), requires preparatory works, then *[563]* promises not to fail them with his grace. This is precisely the opinion of the Pelagians. to this the Scriptures are utterly in opposition, for they teach: "It is God who gives both to will and to do according to his goodwill; it is God who begins in us the good work and brings it to completion at his own day; it is God from whom alone we have sufficiency when otherwise we cannot think anything of ourselves, as of ourselves."[504] So it is clear that Pighius confounds the laws of God and mixes up those things that are so well set forth in the Scriptures.

68. Moreover, when we say that it is not sufficient for justification to have a historical faith, he pretends to wonder what we understand by historical faith.[505]

---

[502]Augustine *C. Jul.* 4.3.25–26 (PL 44.750–51).
[503]Matt. 11:28; Pighius, *Controversiarum*, vol. 2, fol. 68r–v.
[504]See Phil. 1:6, 2:13.
[505]Pighius, *Controversiarum*, vol. 2, fols. 71v–74r.

For if, he says, they call all those things written in the Scriptures history, do they wish to bring us another faith by which we may believe those things that are not written in Scripture? But we do not reject a historical faith, as though we would have some new objects of faith besides those that are set forth in Scripture, or are definitely derived from them. We do not require a common or cold assent, such as they have who are accustomed to allow what they read in the Scriptures, being led thereto by human persuasion and some likely credulity, as today Jews and Turks confess and believe many things which we do. But an assured, firm, and strong assent comes from the inspiration of the Holy Spirit, who changes and makes a new heart and mind, and draws with it good motions and holy works. In this way we say that the faith which is effective differs very much from historical assent, and that we are justified by the faith we have just described. For that we have a threefold witness: first is of the Holy Spirit, "who bears witness with our spirit, that we are the children of God."[506] The second is of the Scriptures, the third is of works. On the contrary, those who stand and cry that a man is justified by works do not have a sufficient witness. The Holy Spirit does not urge it and Holy Scripture denies it, only works are brought forth—those lack godliness and faith, as the works of the old pagans in former times, and today the works of many who do not believe in Christ and are strangers from God.

He deserves to be laughed at for also citing Isaiah 66; this alone utterly destroys his case: "God asks, 'To whom shall I look, but to the man who is humble and of contrite heart, to him that trembles at my words?'"[507] Pighius thinks these words signify those works by which God is drawn to justify us. But the matter is far otherwise, for the aim of the prophet was to detest the superstition of the Jews, for, neglecting the inward godliness of the mind, they trusted only in outward ceremonies. Therefore, by the voice of the prophet God condemned this, declaring how odious it was to him: "Heaven is my throne and the earth is my footstool."[508] As if to say, "I say nothing about your temple, which you boast of so much, for 'Heaven is my throne,' such a throne as you cannot pretend to make. 'And the earth,' adorned with all kinds and variety of plants, living creatures, herbs and flowers, 'is my footstool.' Where then shall that house be which you will build for me? And where will my resting place be?" Immediately, to declare that it is not the temple built with hands, he says: "All these things have my hands made and all these things are made, says the Lord." By these words we learn that God delights not in such things and outward ornaments and sumptuous buildings for

---

[506]Rom. 8:16.
[507]Isa. 66:2, Pighius, *Controversiarum*, vol. 2, fol. 44r.
[508]Isa. 66:1.

their own sake, but primarily requires faith and inward goodness of the mind that he may dwell in them.

The believers and the truly godly are identified by certain and proper marks. Whoever is poor and sees himself to lack righteousness, and whoever is contrite of heart, that is, afflicted in this world, whoever is of a mild and humble spirit and not arrogant and proud, whoever with great reverence and fear receives the words of God, he can rightly be numbered among them. These are sure signs, and as it were the proper colors of faith and true godliness. Afterward the prophet declares how much God esteems the works of men that do not believe and are not yet regenerate, though these words be ever so pious in appearance: "He who slaughters an ox is like him who kills a man; he who sacrifices a sheep as if he cut off a dog's neck; he who offers an oblation like him who offers swine's flesh; he who makes a memorial of incense, like him who blesses an idol."[509] All these kinds of oblations and sacrifices were commanded and appointed in God's law, yet when done from an unclean heart and by one estranged from God, they were counted for most serious sins. Thus Pighius gets nothing from this passage with which to defend his error, whereas by the same words we fittingly and truly confirm our own position. What a notable and sharp debater he is, who brings on his behalf those things that are so plainly and clearly against himself!

69. He scratches out this also from the letter to the Hebrews: "He that comes to God should believe that there is a God and that he rewards those who seek him."[510] It seems he wishes to conclude from these words *[564]* that justification is given to those who seek God by good works.[511] But he should have made a distinction among those who seek God, as Paul did, namely, that some seek him by works and others by faith. Paul makes this distinction, and follows it with this, as he writes to the Romans: "Israel who pursued righteousness did not attain to the law of righteousness, because they sought it through works and not through faith."[512] Therefore, those who seek God, to be justified by him through faith, as the apostle teaches, attain what they desire; but those who would be justified by works fall away from justification. We do not deny that God rewards works done by the regenerate, and through which they hasten towards the crown of eternal salvation. But this does not relate to our question, for at present the contention is not about this sort of works, but only about those matters that are done before

[509]Isa. 66:3.
[510]Heb. 11:6.
[511]Pighius, *Controversiarum*, vol. 2, fol. 82r–v.
[512]Rom. 9:31–32.

regeneration. Pighius strives to prove that they have their reward, and that in one sense they merit justification. Nor does it help his cause in the least when he claims that this kind of merit does not redound to God or make him debtor to us, or is equal to what does gain reward. For although such things seem to him to serve only to diminish the dignity of merits, they quite remove the very nature of merit, for whatever good men do, indeed even after justification, it is not properly theirs, for God works it in them. Moreover, all that, whatever it may be, was already entirely due to God, nor can we do anything good or give anything to him that is not his. Therefore, we must take away all merit, not only in those who are not yet justified, but also in those who have been justified.

To persuade us more easily, Pighius presents the simile of a certain master who had many servants; so that they might more diligently and quickly accomplish some work he sets them to, he offers a reward.[513] Who (he asks) will deny that those servants who quickly and diligently have finished their work have deserved the reward that was promised? Let us briefly examine what may be concluded by this simile. If by servants we understand the regenerate in Christ, we will grant that God sets forth prizes and rewards, whereby we are moved to live holy lives. Neither will we deny that they may be said to receive a reward, but we will not grant that they truly and properly merit the crown of eternal felicity. Certain of our writers do declare that this relates to the justified, and use a comparison not of a master and his servants, but of a father and his children. For fathers sometimes, and with some certain condition, promise a gown, a cap, or money to their children; although they would freely give them in any event, yet they do it with certain conditions to stimulate their endeavors, for example that they will have this or that item after they have learned this or that book thoroughly. Here, no one who will speak precisely and properly will say that when these children have finished their work they have deserved the little gifts that were promised to them, for the father openly and of his free liberality gives and bestows the same upon them. Pighius, however, talks about servants, that is, those not yet regenerate. But that God establishes any rewards of goods to such people, what source can he use to show that? How will he prove that the works of such men, which are sins, as we have taught, can please God? Since this is so, to them it is not a reward that is proposed, but a punishment. Yet to make the matter more plain, let us compare children and servants. Although children do nothing, they enter on their father's inheritance, provided that they want to accept it, but though servants labor ever so hard, they have no inheritance with the children. This is so plain that it needs no further explanation.

[513]Pighius, *Controversiarum*, vol. 2, fol. 82v.

70. Pighius tries to refute our argument that if works are required for justification, Christ's honor would be diminished, as though his merit alone could not
be sufficient to reconcile us to God. He says I take nothing away from Christ, but
leave him his honor whole and safe. I ask you, how do you take away nothing
when you require works for our justification, and require them in such a way, as
you say, that God regards them more highly than faith? But he expounds his own
subtle riddle, in that order of his, Christ is a sufficient cause, as if to say: "If we
speak of reconciliation and that sacrifice by which we are reconciled to God,
Christ alone is sufficient. But we cannot be prepared and made ready for that
benefit except by many works." I can only marvel where the judgment of this great
Sophist has gone. As though those against whom the apostle disputes ever said
that works are required for justification as outward principles or ground. Certainly they also thought the same as Pighius, that works are some kind of purging
and preparing of the mind. Further, who does not see that if a general proposition
is true, it is legitimate to apply what is affirmed or denied in it to all its particular
propositions? So, since Paul denies that one is justified by works, he excludes all
kinds of works, in whatever order you line them up.

Pighius also says that God requires these works in order to freely impute justification to us. Whoever studies the Scriptures even a little will easily see that this
man is directly opposite to Paul, for in the letter to the Romans he says, "To him
who works, a reward is not reckoned according to grace."[514] But Pighius says, "to
him who works, God reckons righteousness freely." *[565]* Every child may see that
to reckon freely and not freely are contradictory.

But, gentle reader, ponder this dilemma: These works which he speaks of
either contribute to justification or else do not. If they are of no benefit, why does
he call them preparations? For among causes there are also reckoned preparatory
causes. Or if he says that they profit and are indeed preparatory causes, can he
boldly affirm that he snatches nothing away from Christ's honor, but appoints
him to be the whole and absolute cause of our justification? Perhaps someone will
turn this dilemma against us, regarding these works that follow justification? For
one will say either they contribute to obtain salvation or they do not contribute. If
they do not, why are they required and why are promises made to them? But if
they are, why do we not allow merit to be ascribed to them? I answer that such
works are profitable to the regenerate, for by living uprightly and orderly they are
renewed and made perfect. Yet that is nothing else than a sort of beginning and
participation in eternal life. Further, it has seemed good to God by such means to
bring men to eternal felicity. But we cannot call these works merits, for Paul

---

[514]Rom. 4:4.

expressly teaches that "the reward of sins is death, but eternal life is grace."[515] But what is given freely, excludes merit completely. Meanwhile, we should remember that there is a great difference (as we have often taught) between their works who are as yet strangers from Christ and from God, and who are now by grace grafted in Christ and made his members.

71. Afterward he proceeds to refute our claim that one is justified by that faith which pertains to the promises of Christ and the remission of sins, as though we hold this faith to be the proper correlative of such promises. For he says that faith has an equal respect to all the things set forth in the Scriptures. Indeed, he says he does something equally acceptable to God in believing that he created the whole world, or believing in the three persons of the divinity, or in the resurrection to come, or believing that Christ was given to be our mediator and that remission of sins is to be obtained through him. For that faith is no less worthy than any other. He affirms that if we are justified by faith, that faith pertains no less to other articles than to the remission of sins through Christ.[516]

He thinks this may be proved by what Paul says in Romans 4: "And not for him only were those things written, but for us also, to whom it shall be imputed; so that we believe in him who has raised up Christ from the dead."[517] "Behold" (Pighius says), faith is imputed to us for righteousness by which we believe that God raised up Christ from the dead, not that faith by which we believe that sins are forgiven us by Christ. First, we affirm here that our faith assents to all the things contained in the Scriptures. But since there is among them only one principal and excellent truth, to which all other truths are directed, namely that Christ the Son of God suffered for us, that by him we might receive forgiveness of sins, what wonder is it if our faith regards this one thing above all? Paul proves what we say, for he states: "Christ is the end of the law."[518] Therefore, since he is the end of all the Scriptures, he is also the sum and principal object of our faith, although otherwise by our faith we also embrace all other things contained in the Scriptures.

When he adds that faith in the other articles is no less acceptable to God than this faith which concerns Christ and the remission of sins, we may say at once that if one rightly weighs the dignity of the action of faith it is not true, for the dignity of faith, as with the dignity of other similar kinds of powers and qualities, is measured by the objects. For as those objects differ one from another in excellency

---

[515]Rom. 6:21–22.
[516]Vermigli seems to be referring to Pighius, *Controversiarum*, vol. 2, fol. 86v.
[517]Rom. 4:23–24.
[518]Rom. 10:4.

and dignity, so the assents of faith should be considered lower or higher as their objects differ among themselves in importance and dignity. Since God would have his Son to die, and men to be reconciled by him in this way, for this reason he has instituted all the other things to be believed, that are set forth in Scripture; we cannot doubt that this pleases him much more than other matters, for those are directed to this as to their end. This is a common rule among Logicians: the thing itself is greater in condition and quality than the means by which something else has that condition and quality.[519] Thus this act of faith by which we assent to this most noble truth should excel all other acts of faith. So it is not equally acceptable to God whether a man believes this or that. If we were to use this answer, I know that Pighius could never refute it.

Moreover, we say that he contends in vain about the greater or lesser dignity of faith regarding this or that article; we are not justified by the dignity of faith, since it is weak and feeble in everyone. We say, therefore, that we are justified by faith because we apply Christ to us and grasp the forgiveness of sins through it, as through an instrument given to us for this purpose and appointed by God. Hence its worthiness or unworthiness is of no consequence. But what Pighius brings out of Romans 4, he brings cut and maimed; for if one reads the full and perfect sentence he will easily see that clear mention is there made of the death of Christ and the remission of sins we have obtained through it. *[566]* For Paul says, "It shall be reckoned to us as it was to Abraham, if we believe that God raised up our Lord Jesus Christ from the dead, who was delivered for our sins and rose again for our justification." Is it not said clearly here that we should believe that Jesus Christ whom God raised up, was dead and rose again, that we should be justified and have all our sins forgiven? Doubtless it is most unfitting for a theologian not to see something that is so clear.

72. Afterward Pighius cavils about the particular faith by which we say that whoever believes truly in Christ should hold it with absolute certainty that his sins are forgiven. He denies that there is any such faith found in the Scriptures and that, therefore, this is only our device and invention.[520] Here indeed I cannot restrain myself, but must say that Pighius lies baldly; I would have him tell me what Abraham believed when he was justified, except that one day those promises of God to him would be fulfilled? For whom else except him were they likely to be fulfilled? The same thing may be said of Moses, of David, and many others of whom it is certain that they believed that the promises God made to them would

---

[519]Cf. Aristotle *An. post.* 1.2.72a.29ff.
[520]Pighius, *Controversiarum,* vol. 2, fol. 87r.

be fulfilled for them individually. What else, I ask, did Christ mean when he said to the man with palsy, "Son, your sins are forgiven," and when he said to the woman, "Your faith has made you well?"[521] Did not Paul write to the Galatians, speaking of Christ, "Who loved me and gave himself for me?"[522] What can be more manifest than these words?

Now let Pighius go and boast that we were the first to discover this proper and singular faith, and let him shout that every Christian should believe that the promises are made only indefinitely, and that it is not fitting that every one of us should apply them individually to himself. For we should believe them about ourselves and not about others; in regard to others we may be deceived as to whether they believe; but as to ourselves, we may be sure and certain of it. Let everyone believe the promises of God regarding others indefinitely, for we know not who is predestined and who is reprobate. Yet no one who is faithful should have any doubt about himself, but believe that the promise is particular in regard to himself, when he perceives himself to believe truly. Further, when promises are set forth in a general proposition, we may most surely deduce from it a particular proposition. Christ says in John: "This is the will of my Father, that every one who sees the Son and believes in him should have eternal life."[523] Therefore, we infer this: I believe in the Son of God; therefore, I have now and shall have what he has promised.

73. Pighius still goes on, to prove that the faith of every other article justifies, besides what refers to Christ or the remission of sins. He uses the example of Noah, for he says that he believed only those things that pertained to the safety of his family and the destruction of the world.[524] He says Noah was justified by this. No mention (he says) is made here of Christ or the remission of sins. But it seems to me that this man has not very diligently read what Peter wrote in 1 Peter 3, for he says:, "When God's patience waited in the days of Noah, during the building of the ark, in which a few, that is, eight persons, were saved through water (baptism, which corresponds to this, now saves us also), not as a removal of dirt from the body but as an appeal to God for a good conscience well answering to God."[525] What Peter saw was signified by the ark and by those things that Noah did—can we think that the patriarch himself did not see them? Clearly this would detract from him; if he saw those things Peter mentions, he believed not only those things that

---

[521]Matt. 9:2, 22.
[522]Gal. 2:20.
[523]John 6:40.
[524]Heb. 11:7; Pighius, *Controversiarum,* vol. 2, fol. 87r–v.
[525]1 Pet. 3:20–21.

happened, but also what was expected to be accomplished by Christ. Therefore, it is well said to the Hebrews, "He became an heir of righteousness by such faith."[526]

Pighius says nothing about this; in order to oppose us he is not afraid to take on even the apostles themselves, for he dares to affirm that our first father, Adam, was justified, yet not with that faith we speak of, concerning the remission of sins through Christ.[527] For Pighius says that Adam had no promise about that, so far as may be gathered from the Scriptures. Certainly he is greatly deceived, and has also forgotten his fathers whom he would seem to make so much of. Was not the same thing said to Adam, whom God promised to Eve, his wife, namely, that his seed should bruise the head of the serpent? Christ was that seed, and he has so broken the head and strength of the devil that now neither sin nor death nor hell can hurt his members in the least. Almost all the fathers interpret this passage like this.

Yet Pighius is even less to be endured, for he is not even afraid to say that justification is not given to us by the promise. In this he is clearly against Paul, who wrote to the Galatians: "God gave unto Abraham by the promise,"[528] and there is no doubt that it is now given us in the same way that it was given to Abraham. Now we should know that this word "promise" is taken in two ways. One is for the thing promised, and so we must not doubt that we are justified by the promise, that is, Christ and the forgiveness of sins promised to those who believe. Or else it is taken for the very words of God in which through Christ he promised remission of sins to us. In this way also we may be said to be justified by the promise, for although the cause of justification is the will and mercy of God alone, yet it is not offered to or *[567]* signified to us, except by the words of promise and by sacraments, for we have these as sure testimonies of God's will toward us. Thus unless that faith is lacking, through which we apprehend the things that are offered, we are justified by the promises.

74. In order to prove that God attributed more to works than to faith, Pighius cites a passage from Genesis 22. In that place the excellent work of Abraham is described, when he did not refuse to slay his only son and offer him to God; therefore, God spoke to him from heaven: "Because you have done this, by myself I have sworn that in blessing I will bless you, and in multiplying I will multiply your descendants as the stars of heaven and as the sand of the sea. He shall possess the gates of his enemies and in you shall all the nations be blessed."[529] See, says Pighius, here are promises given for works' sake, and added

---

[526]Heb. 11:7.
[527]Pighius, *Controversiarum*, vol. 2, fol. 88v.
[528]Gal. 3:18.
[529]Gen. 22:17–18; Pighius, *Controversiarum*, vol. 2, fol. 86r–v.

to it is the most faithful oath, but no mention is made at all of faith; therefore, God has more regard for works than for faith. He says this with a grin, but according to the proverb, the mountain will be in labor and out will spring a silly mouse.[530] For if you ask what I think concerning this matter, I will answer that it is a notable and most excellent history, but what this man claims cannot be gathered from it. First, no mention is made of justification; how does it then serve the matter we are dealing with now? As often as something is cited in controversy, we must run to those certain and sure places where the same subject is treated, not to those where it may be replied that they treat another matter. This is the nature of that passage Paul cites about our subject: "Abraham believed God and it was reckoned to him as righteousness."[531]

Concerning this history, I willingly grant that Abraham by that work obtained a certain more ample benefit than that which he had previously from faith. Yet not in substance or number or quantity of the promises, but in a sound and firm certainty. For although he did not doubt that whatever he believed, God would faithfully give him, yet afterward when he had done those excellent deeds he was more fully persuaded of the verity of his faith, the constancy of the promise, and the strength of the righteousness imputed to him. I do not deny that by such excellent work Abraham obtained these things. Then what is here that Pighius should boast of? What new thing is promised here? What covenant not heard of before or new oath is set forth? Nothing is recounted here that was not mentioned before, for the covenant which is made here was already obtained partly when circumcision was appointed, and partly in that sacrifice where it was commanded that animals should be cut in two, some on the right and some on the left, as though those who were to swear and make covenant should pass through the midst.[532] That custom was also present among the people of Athens, as Demosthenes declares in his oration against Aristocrates.[533] Moreover, we cannot deny that Abraham was already justified, for it was said before, "Abraham believed God and it was counted to him for righteousness." Since this is the case, although a promise was added later, that still does not count against us, for we do not deny that those works which follow justification are both good and pleasing to God, and are rewarded with great and ample gifts by him, although freely.

Now it remains only to declare another way to understand this cause: "Because you have done these things." This pertains to the certainty we mentioned above,

---

[530]Quotation from Horace *Ars poetica* line 139: "Parturient montes, nascetur ridiculus mus."
[531]Rom. 4:9.
[532]Gen. 15:5ff.
[533]Demosthenes *Aristocr.* 67ff.

which as we have said is from the effects and (as they say) a posteriori, that is, from what comes after. Lest you think this is my own invention, go and read Augustine in his questions on Genesis, for he diligently explains these words: "Now I know you fear God." Augustine asks whether God was ignorant of this before. Had he any need of this trial since he is the searcher of the inward man and the heart?[534] Not at all, for this word "I know," is nothing else than "I have made you to know" or "I have made plain and open." Therefore, this does not provide a reason for the promises through a cause, but rather in the same way it was said of the sinful woman: "Many sins are forgiven her because she has loved much." We have dealt fully with this before so that there is no need for repetition.

75. Pighius has scraped together another objection from Ezekiel 18, where the prophet says: "If the wicked man repents of all his iniquities, and obeys all my commandments, I will no more remember all his iniquities."[535] Here Pighius says that we see that justification which is the forgiveness of sins is not promised to faith but to perfect repentance and the observation of God's law. Here his bristles arise as though we must yield. But if you consider his argument more closely it is both empty and trifling, for we easily grant that if a man perfectly repents of all his iniquities and obeys all the commandments of God, he will have justification by works. None of us ever denied this. But the whole subject lies here, where it is hard work to find such a one who, while not yet justified, has performed this. Where, I ask you master Pighius, is your interpretation where you said before that God does not require us to perform all the commandments, but that because of his mercy he remits much? For here you have brought the clearest testimony against yourself.

But let us return to the topic. Since one neither performs *[568]* nor can perform those things that are set forth, both by the prophets and the law, what remains then but that he should come humbly to Christ and after freely receiving justification through faith should, by grace and the Spirit now given him, perfectly repent (so much as this life will allow) and obey God's law with obedience (such as in this life we may begin). Advancing this argument, there came to my mind the old philosopher Antisthenes. A certain vain youth who was one of his pupils boasted that he had a ship loaded with choice merchandise and when it arrived he would give Antisthenes an excellent gift. This was quite a familiar song in his mouth, and was troublesome to all who heard him, so much so that Antisthenes led him into the marketplace and in a particular shop asked for a few measures of

---

[534]Gen. 22:17; Augustine *Quaes. Hept.* 1.58 (PL 34.563).
[535]Ezek. 18:21–22; Pighius, *Controversiarum,* vol. 2, fol. 45v.

cloth. When Antisthenes had the cloth in his hand, not having paid the money, he made a move to go his way; the merchant called him back again. "Here, good fellow," he said, "before you leave pay me my money." Then pointing to the young man, Antisthenes said, "this man will pay you as soon as his ship arrives."[536]

Even so will I answer Pighius: when you show me one who is not regenerate but by his own strength repents of all his sins and observes all God's commandments, we will say that he is justified by his works. But when will this ship arrive? Therefore, let him cease to boast of the words of the law, for whatever those words are, whether they pertain to promises or precepts, we will interpret in this way. Moreover, he says that Christ also said, "He that does the will of my Father will enter the kingdom of heaven."[537] According to Pighius the Lord did not say "he who believes." Yes, but I say that in another place he did and makes no mention of any work: "This is the will of my Father, that he who sees the Son and believes in him has eternal life."[538] Let not Pighius deny from now on that the Lord ever said this. But lest anyone think that the Scriptures speak contrary things, I answer that these two sentences are not repugnant, but agree very well together. Pighius understands by the will of the Father a great heap of good works, but Christ says, "This is the work of God, that you believe."[539] And after this action of believing, many other good works follow, so that the Scriptures do not contradict one another, and Pighius's argument is left weak and of no effect.

Yet because Pighius sees himself driven by God's Word, because so often we read the Scriptures that "man is justified by faith"; therefore, he says that this should be understood of a lively and strong faith that has other virtues joined with it, as though we ever spoke of any other faith.[540] If he spoke this from the heart, he believes the same thing that we believe. Therefore, lay aside the contention, and with the controversy ended let us all agree as one! But Pighius cannot accept that this agreement should take place; for afterward, when he would expound how we are justified freely, he says that is nothing else but that God will freely impute righteousness to us, the works of faith, hope and love. What will we do? It seems clear to me that this man does not read Scripture with sound judgment, but with a corrupt attitude wrests them at his pleasure. For where works are, there Paul denies that there is a free imputation, for these two are opposites.

[536]Antisthenes (ca. 445–ca. 360 B.C.E.), follower of Socrates and presumed founder of the Cynic school. This story does not seem to come from Diogenes Laertius's compendium on the lives of the philosophers.

[537]Matt. 7:21.

[538]John 6:40.

[539]John 6:29.

[540]Rom. 3:28; Pighius, *Controversiarum,* vol. 2, fols. 63v–77r passim.

Therefore, because Pighius proceeds to join them together, does he not seem quite plainly to be against the apostle?

(4) Smith Redux

76. So much for Pighius, to whom our Smith, the eighth wise man of Greece and the first wise man of England, joined himself as companion, as Theseus did to Hercules.[541] But in fact he [Smith] brings nothing else than what he has drawn out of the sinks of Pighius and others like him. First, he says that faith is not for the remission of sins and that, therefore, we fondly pretend that justification can be obtained by it. For he says that the faith by which Christians are distinguished from non-Christians is [faith] in Jesus Christ. As if this were much to the point, he goes about to prove it by the Scriptures and by a testimony of Jerome.[542] I would have him tell me, if he ever learned Hebrew, what is the signification of this name "Jesus"? Certainly among all the Hebrews this word *Iasha* signifies "to save." So in Latin "Jesus" may rightly be termed *Servator*, that is, "Savior." Now if (as I think) he is ignorant of the Hebrew language, he still should at least have believed the angel who interpreted that name in this way: "You shall call his name Jesus, for he shall save his people from his sins."[543] How then can faith be in Christ Jesus, unless it also concerns the remission of sins through Christ?

Afterwards he is not afraid to cite the following from the letter of Peter: "Love covers a multitude of sins."[544] Now, he says, here the forgiveness of sins is ascribed not to faith but to love.[545] The person who wishes to use a suitable axe to cut these knots should pay attention.[546] Let him consider the Scriptures and diligently see where those places cited in the New Testament are taken out of the Old. This sentence of Peter is taken from Proverbs 10; it is written there: "Hatred stirs up reproachful speech."[547] For as much as he can, one tells and publishes abroad the faults of someone he hates. On the contrary, love finds and covers the sins of his brother. For those who truly love one another always defend one another and cover one another's faults so much as they think they may according to their conscience.

---

[541]The legends of Theseus and Hercules are intertwined; Theseus emulated Hercules, joined him in the expedition against the Amazons, and was ultimately rescued from Hades by a hero (*Oxford Classical Dictionary*).

[542]Jerome *Comm. Matt.* 1.2 (Matt. 1:21): "Jesus Hebraico sermone *Servator* dicitur" (PL 26.25); Smith, *Diatriba*, 2: fol. 77r–v.

[543]Matt. 1:21.

[544]1 Pet. 4:8.

[545]Smith, *Diatriba*, vol. 2, fol. 100.

[546]As Alexander the Great cut the Gordian knot.

[547]Prov. 10:12.

This is a true sentence of Solomon; therefore, when Peter proceeded to exhort Christians to love, he wisely and aptly borrowed this sentence from Solomon. But not understanding or considering this, Smith supposes that Peter thought that remission of sins is gained through love, although *[569]* he is terribly deceived, as he often is.

But passing over these men, let us remember that if at any time the fathers seem to attribute righteousness to works, this is not to be understood of that righteousness which God freely imputes to us through Christ, but that inward righteousness which is rooted in us, which we obtain and confirm by leading a continually upright life. Or if those things they say clearly pertain to imputed righteousness, that is, to the remission of sins, we must always, as we have taught, run to the foundation of good works, namely, to a lively faith in Christ. If our adversaries would consider these rules and others like them, they would never so impudently and obstinately defend so many lies. If I have to say anything about Pighius, since I see him as neither dullwitted nor unlearned, I cannot say that he wrote on this subject in earnest and from the heart; but when he had once taken the matter in hand, he took those things for pastime and pleasure.

Proof from the Church Fathers

77. Now to tackle that order which I have begun, let us come to the fathers and see how much they make for our side. To accomplish this we will not need any great number of witnesses. For just as to understand the taste of seawater it is not necessary to drink up the entire ocean, even so to understand what the fathers think about this, we need not go through all their sayings.

Irenaeus, a most ancient author, in his *Against Valentine*, book 4, chapter 30, writes somewhat on this matter, although briefly. I suppose that he wrote so briefly about it because in those early times this truth was so professed and certain that it was not for anyone to doubt. Yet by that little portion it may sufficiently be understood what his judgment was— as the saying is—that Protogenes recognized Apelles by the drawing of only one line.[548] Irenaeus, therefore, says that the old fathers, including those who lived before the law, were justified by faith. First, when he had spoken of Abraham, he proceeded from him to Lot, to Noah, and to Enoch. Afterward he gave the reason why in their times the law was not written. Irenaeus says because they were already just the law was not given them, because the just have the law written in their hearts.[549]

---

[548]Rival painters in fourth-century-B.C.E. Greece. Apelles visited Protogenes, and finding he was out, drew a single fine line on a wall, saying it would tell who had called. Protogenes bisected it with a finer line; Apelles in turn drew an even finer one, leading Protogenes to declare himself surpassed.

[549]Irenaeus *C. Valent.* 4.30.

Perhaps you will scarcely admit this testimony, because when Irenaeus speaks of Enoch in that place, he says that he was sent as delegate to the angels, which may seem apocryphal. But I think it is cited not so much from some apocryphal book as out of some old tradition, for many things were delivered by hand, as it were, to the ancient fathers and are not to be rejected, especially if they are not repugnant to the Scriptures. Otherwise, if we reject this testimony for that reason, why do we not also reject the letter of Jude? For he also cites a sentence of Enoch, that "God will come with a thousand angels to judgment." But whereas Irenaeus says that Enoch was a legate to the angels, I suppose it may be understood as saying that those angels were such men as princes and great kings, or such as were born of the family of Seth, as in Genesis: "The sons of God are said to have seen the daughters of men that they were fair."[550] Perhaps Enoch was sent to them by God to reprove them. This is enough of Irenaeus.

In his book on baptism, Tertullian says that faith entails a perfect assurance of salvation.[551] Thus it is not we alone who have introduced a particular faith for the remission of sins. Nor should it bother anyone that in that book he defends the most obvious errors regarding baptism, and exhorts men to defer baptism until they come to a ripe age, and not to rush to it before they marry. Even if we disallow these things, yet meanwhile when he treats it he has many things that should not be condemned, since at that time they were received in the church. Thus when Cyprian deals with the rebaptism of heretics when they returned to the church, he has many true and weighty testimonies along the way, which we cannot reject, although in the actual state of the question we completely disagree with him.[552] What father is there, I ask you, among them all who in some one place does not defend some subject that is not to be allowed; yet should all their works be condemned? For there is no pomegranate so fair that has not in it some rotten kernel.

78. Now let us come to Origen. In his first book on Job (if it is indeed Origen's work) he writes, "All the things men do whether in virginity or abstinence, in chastity of the body or burning of the flesh, or in the distribution of one's goods, they do all these things *gratis*, if they are not done from faith.[553] In this passage, when he says "*gratis*" everyone understands that he means "without effect." Certainly, this is something Pighius and his followers will not admit. They

---

[550]Jude 14–15; Gen. 6:2.
[551]Tertullian *Bapt.* 13 (PL 1.1323).
[552]Cyprian *Laps.* (PL 4.463ff.).
[553]Origen *Sel. Job* (PG 17.413–14), now regarded as spurious. In his *Hexapla*, Job 1:9 is "Numquam gratis timet Job Deum?" (PG 16/1.291).

want these things to be preparations for justification. But Origen expressly opposes them, as is clearly declared by the words which follow, for he writes, "All the holy and righteous acts anyone does without faith, are done in vain and to their own destruction." Then he cites this verse of Paul: "Whatever does not proceed from faith is sin."[554] Pighius cannot deny that Origen in this place supports our view of this verse, and that he understood Paul's words, *[570]* "Whatever does not proceed from faith is sin," in the same sense. Yet he cries out that we constantly abuse these words, although not only Origen but also Augustine, Basil, and other fathers explain those words in the same way, as we have shown before.[555] Therefore, he accuses us unjustly and shamelessly. But if he says that we must not look to the interpretations of the fathers so much, but must notice the context in which the verse can be understood, then we will commend his judgment. We gladly accept the appeal beyond the fathers to the word of God, but he should have remembered that it is not honest to reprove in others what one does oneself. Therefore, he should permit us also, when the matter requires it, to appeal beyond the fathers to the Scriptures.

Concerning this very matter, we have elsewhere declared that this verse of Paul, as written in his letter, is to be explained in such a way that we may infer from it that the works of unregenerate men are sins. Origen afterward adds, "from whom will he receive a reward? Do you think someone for whom he did not fight? Whom he has not acknowledged? In whom he has not believed? He will not say he received from him a reward but judgment, wrath and condemnation."[556] If these things are derived from such works, who will deny that they are sins? Afterward he brings an illustration: "Just as he who builds without a foundation loses his labor and has only travail and sorrow, so it is with him who builds up good works without faith. Just as all things are possible to one that believes[557] so that he finds refreshment at the hand of him in whom he has believed, just so to him that does not believe nothing is possible. As the earth without the sun brings forth no fruit, so unless the truth of God through faith shines forth in our hearts, the fruit of good works will not spring up. Thus that entire year (he says) when Noah was saved from the flood, since the sun did not shine the earth could bring forth no fruit."[558] Thus Origen has much to say in that passage we have cited, from which we can conclude that faith forms and perfects all good works which follow,

---

[554]Rom. 14:23; Origen *Comm. Rom.* 10.5 [*sic*] (PG 14.1255).

[555]See sec. 37, p. 144 above.

[556]Origen *Comm. Rom.* 10.9 (PG 14.1269?).

[557]Mark 9:23.

[558]This illustration does not appear to come from Origen's *Comm. Rom.* The source could not be identified.

but does not, as these men have somehow imagined, take or borrow its form from good works.

Origen again, commenting on Romans 4, reasons, "If he who believes that Jesus is the Christ is born of God, and he who is born of God sins not, then it is certain that he who believes in Christ Jesus sins not."[559] This kind of argument is called *sorites,* and is permitted by Logicians; the Stoics were often inclined to use it.[560] The former propositions of this argument cannot be denied, for they are taken out of the Scriptures. But he adds afterward, "And if he sins, then it is certain that he does not believe." This follows of necessity from the former conclusions, for if every one who believes does not sin, then doubtless whoever sins does not believe. Let Pighius now go and laugh when we say that because of grievous sins, true faith slips (*amitti*) or is so lulled to sleep that it is no longer active. And let him enlarge the matter as much as he can by saying that one who sins grievously neither believes that there is a God, nor the other articles of faith. Origen thinks and writes the same thing we do, but he also adds that "a token of true faith remains where sin is not committed, whereas where sin is committed, it is a token of unbelief." Again, he adds in the same chapter, "if perhaps what the apostle says, 'To be justified by faith,' seems the opposite of that which says 'we are justified freely' (for if faith is offered first by someone, then it does not appear he is being justified freely) we must remember that even faith itself is given by God; he proves this by many testimonies."[561]

But this is something our Pighius cannot accept, for he derides us every time we say that faith is acquired by the grace and the inward working of the Holy Spirit. He says that it is astonishing that the Holy Spirit should abide and work in those who do not yet believe. The same Origen, commenting on Leviticus, in his book 3, chapter 3, writes: "The holy shekel represents our faith. For if you should offer faith to Christ as a price for the ram without spot, given as a sacrifice, you will receive forgiveness of sins."[562] Here also we have expressly stated that forgiveness of sins is obtained by the faith which is directed to Christ, who was delivered to death and sacrificed for us. Nothing can be clearer than these testimonies which Origen has brought to us. But the opponents are so obstinate that they will not be led from the opinion, which they had once taken in hand to defend, even if you carry the sun in your hands, lest they should seem to any of their allies to have defended a foolish cause.

---

[559]Origen *Comm. Rom.* 4.1 (PG 14.961); cf. 1 John 5:18.

[560]Sorites: a series of categorical propositions in which each conclusion is the premise of the next.

[561]Origen *Comm. Rom.* 4.1 (PG 14.962).

[562]Origen *Lev.* 3.3 (PG 12.428).

79. Besides those things we said above regarding the union of faith with a good life, Cyprian also writes in his *To Quirinus,* book 3, "That faith alone profits and that we can do as much as we believe."[563] The first part of this sentence pertains to article 3 of this question, but the latter serves very much what we are now concerned with. It is without doubt a wonderful saying that so great is the force of faith we are able to do what we will through it. Yet Cyprian did not think it sufficient to state this absolutely, but has also confirmed it by many and sundry testimonies of the Scriptures.

As to Basil and Gregory of Nazianzus, what I cited above will be enough. In his sermon which he entitled *De fide lege natura et Spiritu,* Chrysostom says "even faith is able to save a man by itself."[564] As an example he brings forth the thief who only confessed and believed; but works alone cannot save the workers without faith. After that he compares works without faith with the relics of dead men, for dead corpses (he says), even if clothed with costly and excellent garments, do not obtain heat from them; so those who lack faith, although decked with glorious works, are not helped by them.

The same father, on the letter to the Romans, comments on these words of Paul, "But the righteousness which is of faith." "You see" (he says) "that this is chiefly peculiar to faith, that treading underfoot the complaint of reason we should inquire after that which *[571]* is above nature, and when the weakness of our thoughts is removed by the virtue and power of God, we should embrace all God's promises."[565] Here we see that by faith we obtain the promise of God; while we assent to all that is contained in the Scriptures through it, it still has a special regard to the promises of God. We should also consider that he says "that the weakness of our thoughts, in believing, is removed by the virtue and power of God"—this counts against those who contend that this is done by human power and strength, as though we had faith from ourselves, and that it comes before justification. Chrysostom again, Genesis 29, in his homily 54, writes, "This is the true faith, not to give heed to those things that are seen even though they seem to be against the promise, but to consider only the power of him that promises."[566] Let them ponder this well, who wish us to regard not only the power and promises of God, but chiefly also our own preparations. And expounding these words in Genesis, "Abraham believed God and it was reckoned to him as righteousness," he writes, "Let us also learn, I beseech you, from the patriarch of God, to believe his sayings and to trust his promises, and not search them out by our own reasoning, but show

---

[563]Fidem in totum prodesse…; Cyprian *Test. adv. Judaeos (ad Quirinum)* 3.42 (PL 4.725).
[564]Chrysostom *Fide nat.* 1 (PG 48.1082), spurious.
[565]Rom. 4:3; Chrysostom *Hom. Rom.* 8.2 (PG 670.456).
[566]Chrysostom *Hom. Gen.* 54 (PG 54.477).

deep gratitude, for this can make us just and also cause us to obtain the promises."[567] Here also are two things to be noted: one is that we are made just by faith, the other that by the very same we obtain the promises. Our adversaries strongly deny both.

[Chrysostom] comments on Paul's words to Timothy: "Of whom are Hymenaeus and Alexander who have made shipwreck as concerning faith." "Thus he who once falls away from the faith has no place where he may rest himself, or where to go, for if the head is corrupted and lost, what use can the rest of the body be? For if faith without works is dead, much more are works dead without faith."[568] Note here that this is an argument a minori, that is, from the lesser to the greater, for he says that works are more dead without faith than is faith without works.[569] The same author, in his sermon *On the Words of the Apostle,* expounding these words of the apostle, "Having one and the same spirit of faith,"[570] says, "it is impossible, certainly is it impossible, if you live impurely, not to waver in faith."[571] By this we see how great a connection Chrysostom thought there is between faith and good works. This father, expounding these words of the apostle: "Do we then destroy the law by faith? God forbid, rather we uphold the law,"[572] says, "As soon as one believes, he is at once justified; therefore, faith has upheld the will of the law, while it has brought to an end even that for which the law performed all things."[573] How then does Pighius say that faith is only the foundation and consequently very far from the perfection of justification? Or to what purpose is it, that after faith he puts so many steps and means by which we come to justification? For Chrysostom speaks far differently, that one is justified immediately, as soon as he believes.

Further, he also attributes to faith the fact that it makes men just when the law was not able to perform that, even though it attempted to do so in many ways. Moreover, when he expounded these words of Romans, "Being ignorant of the righteousness of God, and seeking to establish their own righteousness, they did not submit God's righteousness," he says: "this righteousness of God he calls the righteousness of faith which is wholly given by grace from above and not in regard to our labors."[574] And on these words, "Behold I am laying in Zion a stone of offense," he says: "you see then that faith has with it confidence and

---

[567]Gen. 15:6; Chrysostom *Hom. Gen.* (PG 54.340).
[568]1 Tim. 1:20; Chrysostom *Hom. 1 Tim.* 5.2 (PG 54.477).
[569]It is false to argue from a minor premise to the major premise in a syllogism.
[570]2 Cor. 4:13.
[571]Chrysostom *Hab. Spir.* (PG 51.280).
[572]Rom. 3:31.
[573]Chrysostom *Hom. Rom.* 7.4 (PG 60.447).
[574]Rom. 10:3; Chrysostom *Hom. Rom.* 17 (PG 60.464ff.).

security."[575] Here he clearly appoints a particular faith and a certainty about the remission of sins, things our adversaries speak against so much.

Moreover, when Chrysostom expounds that saying in chapter 11, "And if they do not persist in their unbelief, they will also be grafted in," he says: "If when you were a wild olive tree faith could graft you to a good olive tree, it can restore them to their own good olive tree."[576] Here also the power to be grafted into Christ by justification and the power to restore those who are cut off, is attributed to faith.

I could now pass to Jerome if there was not something that calls me back again to Chrysostom, for he writes that faith alone is not sufficient for salvation.[577] Such sentences are often read in the fathers which our adversaries continually twist against us, although (to speak the truth) such an objection is not the gauntlet of Entellus, nor so fearsome,[578] since it may easily be answered in a word. He does not say that faith is not enough for justification, only to salvation, for faith itself is enough for justification, but after we are justified it is not enough to obtain salvation to say "I believe." We must also set ourselves to a holy life and good works, for by them as by certain steps, so to speak, God brings us to happiness. In this way may we interpret all the sentences of the fathers that seem to tend in this direction. If as it sometimes happens, their words will not bear such an exposition, then when they write carelessly we will appeal from them, as seems right, to the same fathers writing elsewhere in a more sound and orthodox way. It is like that woman in ancient times who appealed from Philip when drunk to the same Philip when sober.[579]

80. Jerome, on the letter to the Galatians, comments on these words: "And we knowing that man is not justified by the works of the law but by the faith of Christ Jesus."[580] He says that all the forefathers were justified by the same faith in Christ by which we are now justified today; he confirms this statement by bringing in many examples. *[572]* He counts Abraham first, for he says Christ spoke of him as follows: "He saw my day, he saw it and was glad."[581] After him he mentions

---

[575]Rom. 9:33; Chrysostom *Hom. Rom.* 16.10 (PG 60.564).

[576]Rom. 11:23; Chrysostom *Hom. Rom.* 19.5 (PG 60.590).

[577]Chrysostom *Hom. Rom.* 19.6 (PG 60.591).

[578]*Caestus Entelli*: When Aeneas reached Sicily he held funeral games in honor of his father. In a boxing match, the Trojan Dares issued a challenge; at last the old champion Entellus threw down his huge and famous gauntlets (he won the match): "With fear and wonder seiz'd, the crowd beholds / The gloves of death." See Vergil *Aeneid* 5.387ff.

[579]Perhaps Philip II of Macedon, notorious for his heavy drinking.

[580]Gal. 2:16; Jerome *Comm. Gal.* 1.2 (PL 26.368ff.).

[581]John 8:56.

Moses, for of him (he says) is it written in the letter to the Hebrews: "He considered abuse suffered for the Christ greater wealth than the treasures of Egypt," and refusing to be in Pharaoh's court chose rather to embrace the cross of Christ.[582]

He adds that John the Evangelist, in chapter 12, teaches quite clearly that all those things Isaiah has put into writing about the glory of God, when he saw the Lord sitting on a high throne lifted up, are to be understood of the Son of God.[583] He adds, from the letter of Jude, that the Lord Jesus Christ delivered the people of Israel out of Egypt and afterwards destroyed the unbelievers.[584] In this place I am much amazed that Jerome, a man otherwise excellent in the Greek language, rendered it as "the Lord Jesus Christ," when in our text it has only the word "Lord," unless we assume that his copy differed from the one we use now.[585] I do not speak as if I doubted whether what happened at that time was done by Christ the Son of God, for John says: "No man has seen God at any time, but the Son, who is in the bosom of the Father, has declared him."[586]

Therefore, whatever is spoken to men about things divine is spoken by the Son of God who had most truly given himself to mankind, a faithful interpreter of God his Father.[587] In 1 Corinthians 10, Paul says: "They drink of the spiritual rock following them, and that rock was Christ." Again, "Let us not tempt Christ as certain of them tempted him."[588] Commenting on the letter to the Galatians, where he reckons up the fruits of the spirit when he comes to faith, Jerome writes, "If love is absent, faith also departs with it."[589] These words clearly declare that his judgment was that true faith cannot be divided from love, something we also teach and defend, but Pighius and his colleagues scorn it and cry out against it. Yet let him growl as much as he will; it is enough for us that this doctrine agrees with both the Scriptures and the fathers.

Ambrose also, expounding these words from the letter to the Romans, "For it is the one God who justifies circumcision by faith,"[590] says, "because there is one God, he has justified all in the same way," since nothing causes merit and dignity but faith. Afterward he comments on these words, "Therefore, it is by faith, that

---

[582]See Heb. 11:24–26.

[583]Isa. 6:9; Jerome *Comm. Gal.* 1.2 (PL 26.369ff.).

[584]Jude 5.

[585]Some manuscripts did read "Jesus" or "the Lord" or "God." Jerome *Comm. Gal.* 1.2. (PL 26.369).

[586]John 1:18.

[587]Cf. Martyr, "Whatever was said to have been spoken by God in the Old Testament, was revealed by Christ … as often as we read that the word of God came to this man or that, I think this should always be attributed to the Son of God"; *In Iud.* 2:1, 6:22; see VWG 86ff. Cf. John 1:18.

[588]1 Cor. 10:4, 9.

[589]Jerome *Comm. Gal.* 3.5.22 (PL 26.420).

[590]Ambrose *Comm. Rom.* 3.30 (PL 17.81).

the promise may rest on grace and be firm to all the descendants." He says: "The promise cannot be firm to all descendants, that is, to all sorts of men, of whatever nation, except by faith. For the beginning of the promise is from faith and not from law, because those who are under the law are guilty; the promise cannot be given to the guilty; therefore, they should first be purified by faith that they may be made worthy to be called sons of God, and that the promise may be firm."[591]

Near the beginning of chapter 5, commenting on these words, "Being justified by faith, we have peace towards God," [Ambrose] says, "Faith and not the law causes us to have peace with God, for it reconciles us to God when our sins are removed; they had made us enemies to God in the past."[592] Afterwards he comments on these words, "The law of the Spirit of life." He says: "It is faith that justifies those who fly to it, that it may forgive them whom the law holds guilty, that living under faith they may be free from sin."[593] In book 2 of his commentary on the Gospel of Luke, he [Ambrose] says that Peter did not weep until the Lord had looked back on him, adding that the Lord produced in him both repentance and the power to weep.[594]

81. When Augustine deals with this matter he seems to be in his own field, so that to hunt in him for testimonies about this controversy is (as the common saying goes) to look for water in the sea. Yet it is not far from our purpose to pick something out of him also. On the words of the Sermon on the Mount in the Gospel of Matthew, near the end of sermon 7, Augustine says: "If you presume it is your own work, a reward is given you, it is not grace. I ask now: do you believe, O sinner? I believe. What? Do you believe that your sins may be freely forgiven by him? Then you have what you believed."[595] In his preface on Psalm 31 he writes: "You have done nothing good and yet remission of sins is given to you. Your works are examined and found wanting. If God should render to those works what is their due, doubtless he should condemn you."[596] In his book *On the Spirit and the Letter,* chapter 12, he says "We gather that a man is not justified by the rules of good life but by faith of Jesus Christ."[597] And in his book *Two Letters against the Pelagians,* book 7, chapter 5, he writes: "Our faith that is the catholic faith discerns the just from the unjust, not by the law of works but by the law of

---

[591] Ambrose *Comm. Rom.* 4.16 (PL 17.97).
[592] Ambrose *Comm. Rom.* 5:1 (PL 17.88).
[593] Ambrose *Comm. Rom.* 8:2 (PL 17.117).
[594] Ambrose *Exp. Luc.* 8, on Luke 22:62 (PL 15.1826).
[595] Augustine *Serm. 100* (PL 38.604).
[596] Augustine *Enarr. Ps. 31,* Enarr. 2: Serm. Plebe (PL 36.262).
[597] Augustine *Spirit. et litt.* 13 (PL 44.215).

faith."[598] Also Augustine and Alypius, in letter 106, write: "Righteousness is of faith by which we believe that we are justified, that is, that we are made just by the grace of God through Jesus Christ our Lord."[599]

The same father against Pelagius and Coelestius in book 1, chapter 10, writes: "It is not enough to confess whatever grace you wish, but only that grace by which we are persuaded, by which we are drawn, and by which what is good itself is given to us."[600] This makes things clear against those who appoint I know not what general grace, and will have it lie within everyone's power either to accept or to refuse it. But this grace by which we are so persuaded is nothing else but faith, the faith in fact necessary to justify. Those works which are done before we are justified count for nothing, for the same Augustine in his *Two Letters Against the Pelagians*, book 3, chapter 5, writes: "Just as works that seem good are to unbelievers turned into sins," and so forth.[601] And in his book *On the Spirit and the Letter*, chapter 28, he writes: "Just as there are certain venial sins without which the properly just man cannot live, yet they do not hinder *[573]* our salvation; so there are some good works without which even the most wicked men can barely live, yet they do not count for anything for their salvation."[602]

Lest we think that this faith by which we are justified is common and aimless, he adds afterward in chapter 34: "Why is this man so instructed that he is utterly persuaded and another not? There are but two things I think good to answer: 'O the depths and the riches...' And 'What? Is there injustice on God's part?'[603] He that is displeased with this answer, let him seek someone more learned, but let him beware of presumptuous persons."[604] If we give credit to our adversaries, this would be a very crude and blind doubt, for they would immediately have answered with a word, that one was persuaded because he wanted to be and the other because he did not. But considering the matter more deeply, Augustine cites the Scriptures: "It is God who works in us both to will and to perform according to his goodwill."[605] Seeing that Paul himself was overcome with admiration of this matter and made such an exclamation, he thought it best to refer the whole subject to God who distributes to every man what seems good to him—no doubt justly, even if we do not see the reasons for his justice. Nor is it proper for us to search them out, unless we would have that happen to us which usually happens

---

[598]Augustine *C. Pelag.* 3.5 (PL 44.597).
[599]Augustine (and Alypius) *Ep.* 186 (PL 33.818).
[600]Augustine *C. Pelag. et Celes.* (PL 44. 365?).
[601]Augustine *C. Pelag.* 3.5 (PL 44.598).
[602]Augustine *Spir. et litt.* 28 (PL 44.230).
[603]Rom. 9:14, 11:33.
[604]Augustine *Spir. et litt.* 34 (PL 44.241).
[605]Phil. 2:13.

to a certain kind of fly that is allured by the light of a candle and flies too close to it, being often burned by its flame.

In his book *The Predestination of the Saints*, chapter 5, Augustine reproves Pelagius for dreaming up a common grace to all the saints, which he would have to be nothing else than nature.[606] This is the very thing our adversaries do now when they claim that grace is set forth openly to all as it were, and that it lies in everyone's power to receive it, if he chooses. The same author in *To Vitalis*, letter 107, writes: "To those whose cause is like theirs to whom grace is given, yet it is not given to them, so that those to whom it is given may understand how freely it was given them."[607] In the same place he plainly declares that "it is God who of our unwillingness makes us willing and takes away our stony heart and gives us a heart of flesh."[608] This clearly shows that it is faith by which we are justified, and that God distributes it according to his goodwill. The same father in *The Dogmas of the Church*, chapter 4 (whoever wrote that book, it bears the name of Augustine): "In our being purged from sins, God does not wait on our will,"[609] and in chapter 44, "The Holy Spirit makes us choose, think, and consent to every good thing pertaining to salvation."[610] In book 13, chapter 17, of *The Trinity*, he writes: "The Word of the Son of God took on him human nature, without any kind of merit, and in the same way also is the grace of God given to us."[611] This comparison is taken from the greater premise (*a maiori*), for if that man who was made the Son of God obtained it without any merit, much more are we received into adoption without any merit, whether congruent or condign.[612]

The same Augustine in *To Simplicianus*, book 1, question 2, writes, "Who can live uprightly and work justly unless he is justified by faith? Who can believe unless he is touched by some calling, that is, some witness of things? Who has it in his own power to have his mind touched with such a sight by which the will may be moved to faith?"[613] In sermon 61 on John he writes, "All sins are comprehended under the name of infidelity"[614] and adds, "if faith cannot exist without hope and love," which he also teaches quite plainly in Psalm 31.[615] The same

---

[606] A summary of Augustine's argument in *Praed.* 5.10 (PL 44.968).

[607] Augustine *Ep.* 107 *(Ad Vitalem)*, 6.24 (PL 33.987).

[608] Augustine *Ep.* 217, 6.8 (PL 33.988).

[609] Augustine *Eccl. dogm.* 4.21 (PL 42.1217).

[610] Augustine *Eccl. dogm.* 4.4 (PL 42.1211?).

[611] Augustine *Trin.* 13.17.22 (PL 42.1031), paraphrase.

[612] *Major premise:* the Son of God was incarnate without merit attached; *minor premise:* grace is given through the incarnate Son; *conclusion:* therefore, we are adopted through grace without merit attached (QED).

[613] Augustine *Ad simp.* 1.2.2 (PL 40.111), paraphrase.

[614] Augustine *Tract. Ev. Jo.* Hom. 61 (PL 35.333?).

[615] Augustine *Enarr. Ps. 31*, esp. 5–8 (PL 36.260–63).

father in his first book, *Two Letters against the Pelagians,* chapter 19, treats at length the way in which we are drawn by God; among other things he says that the Pelagians would greatly triumph over the Christians if they had not the word for drawing in the Scriptures. But insofar as that word is expressed in the Gospel itself, they have no place at all to fly to.[616] There are an infinity of other places in Augustine that confirm this opinion; at this time I think it well to pass over them for the sake of brevity.

82. In *Against Julianus,* book 1, page 14, Cyril says, "The faith of Abraham and our faith is completely one and the same."[617] The same author, commenting on John in book 3, chapter 31, expounding this sentence, "This is the work of God, that you believe in him whom he has sent," writes, "Faith brings salvation and grace justifies, but the commandments of the law rather condemn; therefore, faith in Christ is the work of God."[618] In these words we should note that faith is that through which salvation comes; we are justified by grace. He declares these things more plainly in his work on John, book 9, chapter 12, commenting on these words, "And where I go, you know, and the way you know." He writes, "For we are justified by faith and are made partakers of the divine nature by the participation of the Holy Spirit."[619]

In sermon 13 on the passion of the Lord, Leo writes, "The fathers believed along with us that the blood of the Son of God should be shed. Therefore, dearly beloved, there is nothing in the Christian religion different from what was signified of old; neither was salvation hoped for at any time by the righteousness of men who have lived before us, except through the Lord Jesus Christ, for whom they looked."[620] This and many other similar testimonies strongly confute those who dare say that Abraham was indeed justified, yet not through faith in Christ, but through faith regarding earthly promises. Yet this author may seem to make against us in that we say that true faith is not found without love; for in his sermon *On Collecting and Almsgiving* he writes of Satan, "Knowing that God is denied not only in words but also in deeds, he [Satan] has taken love away from many, from whom he could not take away faith; he has filled the field of their heart *[574]* with the roots of covetousness, and has spoiled the fruit of good works of those whom he has not deprived of the confession of their lips."[621] If

[616]Augustine *C. Pelag.* 19.37 (PL 44.568).
[617]Cyril of Alexandria *C. Jul.* 1.14 (PG 76.34).
[618]John 6:29; Cyril of Alexandria *Ev. Jo.* 3.5 (PG 73.495).
[619]John 14:4; Cyril of Alexandria *Ev. Jo.* 9.766 (PG 74.186).
[620]Leo I, *Serm. 64, De Passione Domini 13* (PL 54.357).
[621]Leo I, *Serm. 9, De collectione et eleemosyna* 4 (PL. 54.161).

these words are considered deeply, they do not in the least count against us, for we speak of a true, sound, and lively faith. But Leo understands only a certain outward profession of faith, for when he would render a reason by which it might appear that faith was not taken from them, he mentions only an outward confession of the lips. We also grant that this may exist without love and is often boasted of by many who nevertheless are most evil. I suppose similar statements could be explained like this when they occur.

Gregory, bishop of Rome, in his homily 19 on Ezekiel writes, "We come to faith not by works, but by faith we attain to virtues, for Cornelius the centurion did not come by works to faith but by faith he came to works, for it is said: 'Your prayers and alms' and so forth. But how did he pray if he did not believe? Because he did not know that the mediator was incarnate, by works he came to a fuller knowledge."[622] By this I would have our adversaries know that faith necessarily goes before all good works, for they affirm that moral works that are performed by pagans who do not yet believe in Christ are good. That is refuted in this passage of Gregory. The same author in book 2, chapter 25, of his *Morals*, speaking of the same matter: "Unless faith is first obtained in our hearts, all other things whatever cannot indeed be good, even though they seem good."[623] Bede, commenting on James 2, writes: "Only he believes truly who by working practices what he believes, for faith and love cannot be separated."[624] This will be enough from the fathers.

PROOF FROM THE CHURCH COUNCILS

We have already dealt at length in the former article with what the councils held at Milevum in Africa and at Orange teach concerning justification, faith, grace, and works.[625] I will now add this, that when our adversaries say that God offers his grace to all and gives his gifts to those who desire them and take hold of them, and forgives sins to those who do what they ought to do, such utterances are clearly against those councils just noted, because they meanwhile omit the inspiration of the Holy Spirit and the power of God that draws us, the inward persuasion of the mind, and also those things that are paramount in this matter. Still, I cannot leave it unsaid that in the Council of Mainz, celebrated under Charlemagne, chapter 1 cites

---

[622]Acts 10:4; Gregory the Great *Hom. Ezech.* 2.7.9(19) (PL 76.1018).
[623]Gregory the Great, *Moral.* 2.46 (vet. 333) (PL 75.588).
[624]Bede *Expo. Jacob.* 2.17 (PL 93.21); James 2:17.
[625]See §42–44 p. 154 ff., above.

Gregory, who writes as follows: "He believes truly who by working practices what he believes."[626]

Proposition 3: Justification Is by Faith Alone

83. Since we have now spoken to this article, namely, that men are justified by faith in Christ, and have confirmed it by Scriptures, and overturned the objections of our adversaries and alleged testimonies of the fathers to confirm our proposition, let us now come to article 3. We hold that justification exists by faith alone. This saying is proved by all those places of Scripture which teach that we are justified freely, as well as those that affirm that justification comes without works and also those that draw an antithesis between grace and works. I say that all these places truly prove that we are justified by faith only, even if this word "only" is not read in the Scriptures; but that is not of much weight, since its signification is derived from them by necessity. Further, this also is to be noted, as we have already taught, that we do not say that faith through which we are justified is in our minds without good works, though we do say that the same "only" is that which takes hold of justification and the remission of sins. The eye cannot be without a head, brains, heart, liver, and other parts of the body, and yet the eye alone apprehends color and light. Therefore, those who reason against us in this way commit the error of a false argument: faith (as they say) justifies; but faith is not alone; ergo faith alone does not justify. It is as if one concludes: only the will chooses; but the will is not alone in the mind; ergo the will alone does not choose. Here even little children may see the fallacy of, as they call it, Composition and of Division.[627] And is it not a scandal that such great divines should not see it?

Contra Richard Smith

Just here Richard Smith (the very light of divinity) sets himself against us. Recently[628] he complained, until he was hoarse, that we falsely affirm that those places in Scripture stating that we are justified freely (*gratis*) mean the same thing as by faith alone (*sola*). For *gratis*, he says, is not the same as *solum*.[629] O

---

[626]One of the synods held after Charlemagne granted privileges to the city; he had a castle nearby.

[627]The fallacy of composition argues that something is true of a part that is true of the whole; the fallacy of division argues from a premise that something is true of the whole to the conclusion that the same is true of the parts of that whole. See Aristotle *Soph. elench.* 166a.ff.

[628]Vermigli employs the term *iamdudem* (ROM, 574), which seems to suggest a more recent encounter with Smith. This may be evidence that this locus was composed primarily in Oxford instead of Zurich—a city Smith never visited as far as we know. Smith's *Diatriba* already had been published in Louvain in 1550.

dull Grammarians that we are, who without this good master could not understand this adverb so much in use! Yet this Aristarchus the grammarian, lest he
should seem to play the fool without some reason, says that it is written in Genesis that Laban said to Jacob, "Because you are my kinsman, will you therefore
serve me *gratis*?"[630] Here, he asks, put *solum* and see what an absurd kind of
speech it will be. In the book of Numbers the people said that in Egypt they ate
things *gratis*; and in the Psalm, "They have hated me *gratis*."[631] He says that this
adverb cannot be put here, and so we but rashly and weakly conclude that
because in the Scriptures one is said to be justified *gratis*, he is, therefore, immediately justified by faith only.[632] But this sharp-witted man, so well exercised in
the concordance of the Bible, should have remembered that this word *gratis* signifies "without a cause" or "without reward and price"; therefore, we rightly say
that justification comes by faith alone (*sola fide*), because it is said to be given
freely (*gratis*). If works were required there would be a cause or reward or price
to obtain righteousness. But since *gratis* [575] excludes all these things, it is
rightly and truly inferred from that word, "by faith alone." Those passages this
man has alleged are not hard to refute. Laban says, "Will you serve me *gratis*?"
that is, without this covenant that I should give you something, which is only to
take and not to repay. And when the Israelites said they ate fish *gratis*, they meant
that they ate them without paying a price. And that saying, "they hated me
gratis," is nothing else than without a cause or without any deserving. So that if
this word *gratis* removes price and merit, insofar as Paul says that we are justified
gratis, we must understand that it is done without any cost or merit; no doubt
this would not be true if works were required as causes and merits.

We once cited a passage out of the letter to the Galatians, "But since we know
that a man is not justified by works of the law, but through faith in Jesus Christ,"[633]
and judged from this particle "except" that justification consists of faith alone; this
man must, therefore, according to his wisdom rage, saying that this word "except" is
not the same as "only." He says that in Genesis Joseph said to his brothers, "You shall
not see my face unless you bring your youngest brother," and Christ says, "Except
you eat the flesh of the son of man, you shall not have life in you,"[634] He asks, Who
will say that life is obtained only by eating the sacraments? Therefore, these things

---

[629]Smith's wide-ranging discussion begins at *Diatriba*, 125r.
[630]Gen. 29:15. Martyr refers to Aristarchus of Samothrace (ca. 217–145 B.C.E.), famous poly-
math and critic, head of the Alexandrian Library, styled *ho grammatikôtatos*.
[631]Num. 11:5; Ps. 69:4 ("who hate me without cause").
[632]Smith, *Diatriba*, 138v.
[633]Gal. 2:16.
[634]Gen. 43:5; John 6:53.

cannot be expounded by this word "only." Yes indeed, they may, for in Genesis what did Joseph mean except to admonish his brothers so that they would return to him, only on this condition, namely, if they brought their younger brother with them? And in John 6, Christ did not deal with eating the sacrament, for he had not yet instituted it; so by this word "to eat," he signified "to believe." And he says that those who are of full age have life only in this, if they eat of his flesh and drink of his blood, that is, if they believe that the Son of God was delivered for them for the remission of their sins; that is the only way they may be saved.[635]

84. Smith adds that justification must not exclude hope, love, and other good works.[636] I grant indeed that those are not to be excluded from one who is justified, yet I do not attribute the power of justifying to them. For what Paul says, that "a man is not justified by works," would not be true if we were justified by any kind of works. If one should say that a craftsman does not work with his fingers, and afterward should agree that he does use his fingers in the work he does, he would be worthy of being laughed at. If cornered, he would like to say that he meant only the little finger and not the thumb, forefinger, or middle finger, for he who used three fingers certainly uses fingers. But why does this man say that hope and love are not excluded? Because (he says) even you yourselves will have us to be justified by a lively faith, which certainly is not lively without them. We grant that these virtues are always joined with true faith, yet we do not attribute our justification before God to them. There is a fallacy of accident in this argument, because what belongs to the substance is attributed to those things that are added to it, as if a man should say: the sun is round and high; therefore, the roundness and height of the sun made us warm.[637] What works then does Smith exclude from justification when he includes hope and love? I suppose he excludes outward works, fastings, alms, and so on. But how can he boldly say so or teach it, seeing that he posits and defends preparatory works?

This sharp-witted man thinks he has escaped beautifully, for he says that these things are not necessarily required for justification, that they are helpful for justification only if they are present. But he deserves to be laughed at, for we have already taught quite clearly that all works done before justification are sins, so far is it off the mark that they can serve for justification in any way. If by any means they promote justification, our self-glorification would not then be excluded. For we might glory that we had done these things by whose help and tiny assistance

---

[635]Smith, *Diatriba*, 143v–144r.

[636]Smith, *Diatriba*, 149r ff., 103v–117v.

[637]The "fallacy of the accident" adds a conjunct to an undistributed middle term, e.g., arguing from "Some P [faith] is R [justifies]" to "Some PQ [faith with love] is R."

we were justified. But Smith says of this that we cannot boast, because they were done by a certain prevenient grace of God. This is the chief thing to be marked, that these men attribute a greater part of such works to free will and, therefore, on that score at least, we may glory. Nor will it be true what the apostle says, "What have you that you did not receive?" and again, "Why do you boast, as though you have not received it?"[638] Some of them answer that we cannot glory in such liberty of will since we do not possess it on our own, for it is God who has endowed us with this faculty and given us free will when he created us. Yet this is not sufficient to take away glorying. First, this is to fly to the common grace of creation as the Pelagians did, and by that means there would at least be left in us a good use of free will of which we might boast. For although we have it from God by creation, yet its proper use is ours, namely, to assent to God when he calls us and to apply ourselves to good works, which God sets before us.

Therefore, to remove all glorying we must always bear this in mind, something that Augustine advises us in his book *The Spirit and the Letter*, chapter 24, saying: "The will and choosing to act well is of God, not only because by creation he has given choice and free will, but also because by the persuasion of seeing things he has made us both to will and to believe, not *[576]* only by the outward preaching of the Gospel, but also by inward persuasion, for he does not only stir up the heart, but also persuades, draws, and bends it to believe."[639] I willingly admit that it is the office of the will, to will and to embrace that which God offers, for we do not will by understanding or by memory, but by will. And yet for all that, I doubt not but that it is God who causes us to will and to follow good things.

85. Further, our adversaries think that although works rush towards justification, what Holy Scripture teaches is nonetheless true, that we are justified freely, because as our adversaries say, those works are given by God and performed by grace. If this refuge might help, Paul would not have done well when he took away the power of justifying from ceremonies, for a Jew might say: "Our fathers who in the old time were circumcised and performed other observances of the law did not do them by their own natural strength but by the grace of God both helping them and encouraging them." So if other works commanded in the law could lead towards justification, to merit it (as you say) by congruity, why could ceremonial works not do the same? Nor will it help at all to say that Paul only removes the power of justifying after the coming of Christ, for he clearly speaks of Abraham,

---

[638]1 Cor. 4:7.
[639]See Augustine *Spir. et litt.* 24.40 (PL 44.224).

who was justified by faith and not by circumcision, and uses a statement of David, of whom it is well known that he lived under the law.[640] But whereas Smith says that love and hope cannot be excluded, I would really like to know from him whether the works of these virtues are just or not? I know he will grant that they are just. What will he then answer Paul, who wrote to Titus, "Not by works of righteousness which we have done"?[641] I know their fond devices—they answer that such works are excluded, if they are done by the law and by free will without grace, but what need is there to exclude what cannot be, for who will either love God or hope in him without grace? Further, no matter how they are done, they cannot serve for justification, for we are justified by grace as appears clearly by the Scriptures. So great is the opposition between grace and works that Paul says, "If of grace then it is not now of works, and if of works, then it is not of grace."[642]

They should not be so displeased when we use this word "only" (*solum*), for we derive it of necessity from what Paul says, first, "We are justified by faith," adding, "without works."[643] I will show by a simile how fitting is our conclusion. In Deuteronomy 6 (if we follow the truth of the Hebrew text) it is written, "You shall fear the Lord your God and him shall you serve."[644] Here you see that the particle "only" is missing, yet because there follows, "You shall not go after strange gods," the Septuagint rendered the passage like this: "You shall fear the Lord your God, *kai auton monô latreuseis* [and him only shall you worship]." Since the first proposition is affirmative, that God is to be worshipped, and the other negative, that strange gods are not to be worshipped, these men concluded that God alone is to be served. Their authority would not be so weighty with me except that Christ himself cited that passage like this, for he rebuked the devil: "Depart from me Satan, for it is written, 'You shall worship the Lord your God and him only shall you serve.'"[645] Here we see that to disprove the worship given to a creature, this particle "only" is necessary; even though it does not appear in the Hebrew, yet it is necessarily gathered out of it. Now when we also reason in this way, why should they be so much offended?

86. Let them consider also that the best and most ancient fathers did not dislike that word. It is ridiculous to see how Smith tries to oppose them with stale and wretched tricks and quibbling. First he says that they meant nothing else but

---

[640]Rom. 4:3, 7; Ps. 32:1–2.
[641]Titus 3:5.
[642]Rom. 11:6.
[643]Rom. 3:27.
[644]Deut. 6:13.
[645]Matt. 4:10.

to repress men, that they should not become insolent.[646] But let Smith answer me in a word, according to his wisdom, whether the fathers said this truly or falsely. If they spoke truly, they are on our side; then why does this man criticize it so much? If falsely, their good intention to repress human insolence does not help them, for, "evil must not be done so that good may come";[647] therefore, false doctrine must not be accepted in order to refute other false doctrine. But this man is undoubtedly so far beside himself that he says this was lawful for the fathers to do. For in his little book *On Vows* (which he published a few years ago) he says that Augustine writes in *De bono viduitatis*, "The matrimonies of those who have taken a vow of virginity or of a celibate life are true marriages and not adulteries."[648] He wrote this for no other purpose than to persuade Juliana the widow (to whom he wrote the book) that marriage in general is not evil. Therefore, he confesses, if the gods be pleased, that Augustine sets forth one false doctrine to overthrow another false doctrine.

With similar wisdom he pretends in the same book that Clement of Alexandria wrote that Paul had a wife (which he thinks quite false), only to prove that marriage is good and honorable.[649] And if it is acceptable to mingle true things with false like this, and to confuse all things, when will we believe the fathers? What can ever be certain to us so that we may not be deceived by them? Further, he pretends that Paul excluded from justification only the works of the law, but we have already refuted this abundantly, teaching that Paul's reasons are general. Indeed the fathers saw this as well, for Augustine in many places affirms that Paul deals not only with ceremonial works but also moral. Because *[577]* the authority of Augustine is for some reason suspect among our opponents, let us see what Jerome says.

In his book to Ctesiphon against the Pelagians, he [Jerome] comments on these words, "By the works of the law no flesh shall be justified." He says: "Because you think this is spoken of the law of Moses only and not all of the commandments contained under this one name of the law, the apostle says: 'I confess to the law of God.'"[650] There are other fathers who teach the same thing, but now I pass over them. Let it be enough to show that this other imagined invention of Smith is empty and trifling.

---

[646]Smith, *Diatriba*, fols. 125r–159r, passim.

[647]Rom. 6:1.

[648]Richard Smith, *Defensio sacri Episcoporu[m] & sacerdotum Coelibatus, contra impias & indoctas Petri Martyris Vermelij nugas, & calumnias, quas ille Oxoniae in Anglia, duobus retro annis in sacerdotaliu[m] nuptiarum assertionem temerè effutiuit* (Paris: Reginaldi Calderii, 1550); Augustine *Vid.* 3.5 (PL 40.433).

[649]Richard Smith, *De votis monasticis*, reference to *Stromata* 4.20.

[650]Rom. 3:20; Jerome *Pelag.* 1 (PL 23.543?).

87. Third, Smith says that they meant to exclude penal works (as he calls them); I suppose those are the works that the repentant do,[651] but it requires no lengthy argument to show how ridiculous this is as well. First, such works were required of men not so they should be justified before God through them, but only to prove themselves to the church, that is, lest by a sham and affected repentance they should seek to be reconciled. Further, it is unlikely that Paul spoke of any such works, since they were not then in use. Indeed, when Ambrose excluded works from justification he referred to them once or twice, but we should not spend time on what one or two of the fathers say but on what agrees with Scripture.

Smith adds, moreover, that it is certain that God requires much more of us than faith; in Mark it is written, "Repent and believe." He says, "here repentance is joined to faith."[652] In another place it is written, "He that believes and is baptized will be saved."[653] Smith adds a passage from the letter to the Ephesians, "The church is said to be sanctified by the washing of water in the word." Also Peter in chapter 3 of his first letter writes, "Baptism has saved us."[654] And Jerome writes on Isaiah 1, "The washing of regeneration alone remits sins. Behold, justification and remission of sins are ascribed not only to faith but also to the sacraments."[655]

As to the first, we grant that Christ requires more of us than faith, for who doubts that he wants those who are justified to live uprightly and to practice virtue of all kinds; otherwise, they shall not come into eternal salvation? Yet these are fruits of faith and effects of justification, not causes. As to the sacraments, we have often taught how justification is to be attributed to them, for they stand in relation to justification as does the preaching of the Gospel and the promise of Christ offered to us for salvation. Very often in the Scriptures what belongs to the substance is ascribed to a sacrament. Since baptism promises remission of sins by Christ, and signifies and seals it in those who are washed, Jerome, therefore, attributes this to it alone of all other sacraments. So the words of the fathers should not bother us when they write that faith alone is not sufficient for salvation, for they understand it of that eternal salvation to which we do not come unless some fruit follows our faith. But we should not gather from their sayings that one is not justified by faith alone. Even if the fathers sometimes seem to refer their words to justification, yet they are to be understood as wishing to express the nature of the true and justifying faith, for it indeed is never alone but always has hope and love and other good works as companions. Sometimes also by justification they understand that righteousness

---

[651] Smith, *Diatriba*, fols. 39v–68r passim.
[652] See Smith's discussion of Mark 1:15, *Diatriba*, fol. 45r–v.
[653] Mark 16:16; Smith, *Diatriba*, fol. 46r.
[654] Eph. 5:26; 1 Pet. 3:21; Smith, *Diatriba*, fols. 46r–v, 48v.
[655] Jerome, *Comm. Isa.* 1.1 (PL 24.35); Smith, *Diatriba*, fol. 51r–v.

which dwells in us, which beyond all doubt does not consist of or depend on faith alone.

88. They also think this counts against us when Paul says to the Romans, "In hope we are saved."[656] They do not see that hope there is taken for the last regeneration,[657] which we hope we shall one day obtain in our fatherland, for the apostle spoke of it a little before. And without doubt we possess that salvation only in hope, not yet in actual fact. If there is perhaps any for whom this most just and most true answer will not do, let him follow the interpretation of Origen for he comments on that place saying, "Hope stands for faith, which is not a rare thing in the Scriptures."[658] Our opponents have discovered yet another fond device by which, as much as they can, they proceed to qualify this word "only," so often used by the fathers. That is, that faith alone has the beginning and as it were the first step to justification, which afterward is made perfect and full when other good works come into it. But how empty this is, Paul himself teaches well enough, for he not only says that "we are justified by faith alone," but also adds "without works."[659] What is written in the Book of Wisdom 15 also makes against them: "To know God is full of righteousness."[660] It is some sport to see here how Smith flings himself about. First he dares not deny the sentence, for he considers that book canonical; but as he is a sharp wit, he finally contrives that God is not known by faith alone, but also by love. Now who ever would say so except this man? Certainly we do not know through love, rather, we love.

What the Book of Wisdom says (although it is not of so great authority for me) Christ himself said most clearly in the Gospel, "This is eternal life that they know you the only true God."[661] Recently, Winchester devised I'm not sure what about this saying of our Savior, namely that to know God *[578]* is not properly eternal life, although it helps somewhat towards it.[662] But since neither the fathers

---

[656]Rom. 8:24.
[657]I.e., the last resurrection.
[658]Origen *Comm. Rom.* 7.5 (PG 14.1118).
[659]Rom. 3:28.
[660]Wisd. of Sol. 15:3.
[661]John 17:3.
[662]Stephen Gardiner, bishop of Winchester (1497–1555), adversary of Archbishop Cranmer and Vermigli. At the request of English Protestants, Vermigli composed a thorough (and very large) refutation of Gardiner's sacramental doctrine, which he completed after Cranmer's death in 1556. It was published as *Defensio Doctrinae veteris & Apostolicae de sacrosancto Eucharistiae Sacramento … adversus Stephani Gardineri* (Zurich: C. Froschauer, 1559). During Vermigli's sojourn in England (in the reign of Edward VI), Gardiner was imprisoned in the Tower of London and deprived of his bishopric, but was restored by Mary Tudor and became lord high chancellor. The reference to Gardiner may also suggest this locus was written in Oxford, not Zurich.

nor Paul nor Christ himself can satisfy these men, there is no hope of our prevailing with our reasons. They also add that the fathers say that only faith justifies— that is, it is the principal thing by which we are justified. I agree that "only" sometimes means "principal." But this sense cannot meet Paul's intention, for if love is compared with faith, love (as Paul says) is more excellent and better. Thus if both of them justify, as they will have it, then love should have the chief part, not faith. It is also a great obstacle to these men of whom I have often said that Paul ascribes justification to faith so much as to say, "Without works." But they say that in his *To Simplicianus* Augustine writes: "by faith we begin to be justified."[663] To this we may reply in two ways. First, that beginning is such that in actual fact it has full and complete justification. Thus Augustine's meaning is that we are justified as soon as we have faith. Or if this does not please them, we will say, as is quite true, that Augustine meant the righteousness that dwells in us.

They also cite Ambrose's commentary on chapter 5 of Galatians, "In Christ," and so on. Ambrose says, "For we need faith alone, in love to justification."[664] You see, say our opponents, for justification we need love no less than faith. But they are quite deceived, for by those words Ambrose meant nothing else than to make a distinction between true faith and empty opinion; so he says that we need faith alone, namely, that which is joined with love. But commenting on chapter 5 of Galatians, Jerome says, "It is love alone that makes the heart clean."[665] What else should we answer here, but that his words, if put forward strongly and sincerely, are false? For it is faith that purifies the hearts, as it is written in the Acts of the Apostles.[666] Writing to Timothy, Paul says: "Love from a pure heart and a good conscience," etc.[667] By these words it is clear that of necessity the heart must first be pure before love can come. Therefore, we will interpret that sentence by the effect and in relation to our knowledge, for then it is most certain that we are regenerated and have a clean heart if we are endowed with love. In this way also have we expounded this passage before, "Many sins are forgiven her because she loved much."[668]

---

[663] Augustine *Ad simp.* 1.2.7 (PL 40.115).
[664] Gal. 5:6; Ambrose *Comm. Gal.* 5.6 (PL 17.366): "sola enim fide, inquit, opus est, in charitate iustificationem."
[665] Jerome, *Comm. Gal.* 5.6 (PL 26.463?).
[666] Acts 15:9.
[667] 1 Tim. 1:5.
[668] Luke 7:47.

89. We may answer that saying of Augustine in his book *Nature and Grace*, chapter 38, in similar fashion, "It is the love of God alone by which whoever is just is just."[669] It seems best to me to understand such sayings of the fathers as meaning that righteousness that dwells and remains in us, for it consists not only of faith but also of all virtues and good works. Now because among all virtues love is the principal, the fathers sometimes attribute righteousness to it alone. And what our opponents have most unjustly usurped by expounding this word "alone," as "principal" or "chief," may in this place serve us more properly, for here we do not treat of that justification which is had by imputation, but of that we attain after regeneration. So in our proposition we do not exclude hope, love, and other good works from someone who is justified; we say only that they lack the power or cause or merit of justifying. And when we say that one is justified by faith alone we obviously say nothing else than that one is justified only by the mercy of God and by the merit of Christ, which we cannot grasp by any other instrument than by faith alone.

We must not yield to our adversaries by dropping this word "alone," no matter how much they exclaim that great offense comes of it, while minds are somewhat weakened in the pursuit of virtues by this persuasion. For we easily remedy those difficulties by sound doctrine, for we always teach that it is not true justification or true faith if it lacks the fruits of good life. But we notice their subtle and crafty devices, for if we should say that one is simply justified by faith, leaving out this word "alone," they would at once add of their own accord that one is indeed justified by faith and yet he is no less justified by hope and love and other good works. For this very reason Catholics in times past would not grant the Arians this word *homoiousios* [of like substance]. For they would immediately have said that by appellation or name, the Son is God, almost equal to the Father, yet not really of the same nature and substance. Thus with tooth and nail they defended and still keep this word *homoousios* [of the same substance] as a word most fitting to express the truth of that controversy.[670] They could do so with every right, chiefly because they saw that the word was implied in the meaning of the Scriptures. From this our word "alone" is also quite clearly deduced. We consider it a most appropriate term to refute the error of those who would have justification come from works.

Moreover, Gardiner, bishop of Winchester, considered our proposition to be absurd; against it, among other arguments, he used this one (it is very strange to me that it is so greatly esteemed by some of his papist parasites): "the righteousness

---

[669] Augustine *Nat. Grat.* 38.45 (PL 44.268ff.).

[670] The Arian controversy over "the iota" was settled by the Council of Constantinople, A.D. 381.

given us by God, by which we are justified, pertains to all the faculties and powers of the mind, or rather to the whole man. Therefore, we are not justified by faith alone, for that pertains only to the higher part of the soul."[671] Here (gentle reader)—lest you be deceived—lies hidden a double fallacy. First, grant that the righteousness which is given to us pertains to the whole man and to all the powers and faculties of the mind: does it follow that the righteousness which is offered by God *[575]* is not grasped by faith alone? Surely the meat that we eat is distributed to all the members and into the whole body, and yet it is received with the mouth only and not with the whole body. Moreover, the dispute is not about any righteousness that clings and stays in us, which is indeed dispersed in the whole man, but about justification which is the forgiveness of sins. This righteousness has no place nor seat in our minds, but only in God by whose will alone are our sins forgiven.

Proof from the Church Fathers

90. Now that this article has been sufficiently defended against the cavils of troublesome men, we will ignore them, and declare briefly that the ancient fathers did not dislike this word "only," which our adversaries so greatly shun. Origen, commenting on these words of the letter to the Romans, "Your boasting is excluded. On what principle? On the principle of works? No, by the principle of faith. For we hold that a man is justified by faith apart from works of law."[672] Justification by faith alone is sufficient, so that someone who only believes should be justified even though he has done no good deeds at all. For example, he brings forward the thief who was crucified together with Christ, and that woman to whom Christ answered, "Your faith has made you whole."[673] Afterward he raises for himself the objection that someone hearing the same things might be made self-confident and despise good works. He answers that whoever does not live uprightly after justification throws away the grace of justification. "No one," Origen says, "receives forgiveness of sin to use as a license to sin, for pardon is not granted for faults still to come but for sins past."[674] No statement could fit in better with our doctrine. Cyril, writing to Quinimus, chapter 42, says "faith can be only profitable and the more we believe, the more we are able to do."[675]

In his sermon *On humility*, Basil writes, "A man is justified by faith only."[676] Hilary also, commenting on Matthew 8, says: "faith alone justifies."[677] Ambrose,

---

[671] Probably Stephen Gardiner's *In Petrum Martyrem florentinum malae tractionis querla Sanctissimae Eucharistiae* (1550?). See OTD, xxxv.

[672] Rom. 3:27; Origen *Comm. Rom.* 3.9 (PG 14.952).

[673] Luke 23:43; Matt. 9:22.

[674] Origen *Comm. Rom.* 3.9 (PG 14.953).

[675] Cyprian *[sic] Test. Lib.* 42 (PL 4.747).

commenting on chapter 3 of Romans, on these words "being justified freely," says, "because they do nothing and give nothing back in return, by faith alone are they justified by the gift of God."[678] The same author writes on the words "according to the purpose of God": "So Paul says, 'it was decreed of God that with the law ceasing, only faith should be required for salvation,'" and a little later, "God has ordained that men should by faith alone, without labor and any observation, be justified before God."[679] Commenting on 2 Corinthians 1, the same father says: "It is appointed by God that he who believes in Christ is saved without works by faith alone."[680] He also has similar statements in his book *The Calling of the Gentiles*.[681]

I could bring many places to confirm this sentence out of Chrysostom, but I will select only a few of them. Commenting on chapter 3 of Romans on these words, "Boasting is excluded," he says: "Here there is set forth the might and power of God in that he will have saved, justified, and created our religion by faith only, without works." And at the beginning of chapter 4, "It may perhaps appear to be good that someone without works should be justified by faith, but that one adorned with virtues and good works is nevertheless not justified by them but by faith alone. This surely is wonderful."[682] Our adversaries may understand from this that although faith is accompanied by hope, love, and other good works (which was undoubtedly true of Abraham) yet they do not contribute to attaining righteousness. Commenting on Romans 10:3, "They being ignorant of the righteousness of God and going about to establish their own righteousness, were not subject to the righteousness of God," he writes: "He calls the righteousness of God that righteousness which is of faith because without labor we are justified by faith alone through the gift of God."[683] I will say nothing about Augustine, for he is fully involved in this matter against the Pelagians, and anyone can easily confirm his teaching from his writings.

Hesychius, commenting on Leviticus, in book 1, chapter 2, says, "Grace is grasped by faith alone not by works." He said almost the same thing in book 4, chapter 14.[684] Theophylact, commenting on chapter 3 of Galatians, expounding

[676]Basil *Humil.* 3 (PG 31.530).
[677]Hilary *Matt.* 7.6 (PL 961).7 (PL 9.961).
[678]Rom. 3:24; Ambrose *Comm. Rom.* (PL 17.19).
[679]Ambrose *Comm. Rom.* (PL 17.127).
[680]2 Cor. 1:4; Ambrose *Comm. 1 Cor.* [*sic*] (PL 17.275–81).
[681]Ambrose *Voc. gent.* (PL 17.1073ff.).
[682]Rom. 3:27; Chrysostom *Hom. Rom.* 4 (PL 60.446).
[683]Rom. 10:3; Chrysostom *Hom. Rom.* 17.1 (PL 60.565).
[684]Hesychius *In Lev.* 1:2(2) and 4:14(9) (PG 93.805, 956).

these words, "Because by the law no man is justified before God," says, "Now Paul plainly declares that even alone, faith itself has within it the power to justify."[685] Phocius, commenting on chapter 5 of Romans, says, "Justification consists of faith alone."[686] Acacias in *Oecumenius*, commenting on chapter 1 of Romans writes, "He has by faith alone raised up and quickened us, who had been killed by our sins."[687] Bernard in sermon 22 on the Canticles: "By faith alone he that is justified shall have peace." And in the same sermon he says, "Whatever you ascribe to merits lacks grace. Grace makes me justified freely."[688]

Anyone who finds that these things are not enough should read Gennadius on chapter 1 to the Romans; Cyril in his book 9, chapter 3, on John; Theodoret on chapter 5 of Romans; Didymus on chapter 2 of James; Eusebius in his *Ecclesiastical History*, book 3, chapter 27; Cyprian, or whoever it was, in his exposition of the creed; Lyra on chapter 3 to the Galatians; the *Ordinary Gloss* on the Letter of James; Haymo on the gospel of circumcision; Sedulus on chapters 1 and 2 of Romans; Thomas on chapter 3 of Galatians; Bruno on chapter 4 of Romans; Arnobius on Psalm 106.[689] Now I think I have spoken enough on this question.

Finis

---

[685]Gal. 3:11; Theophylact of Ochrida, *Gal.* (PG 124.987).

[686]Rom. 5:14; Photius, Patriarch of Constantinople, *Fr. Pauli* (PG 101.1234).

[687]Acacius of Berea (b. ca. A.D. 322), active in ecumenical councils and in the union formula for the Council of Ephesus, A.D. 433.

[688]Bernard of Clairvaux *Serm.* 22 on the Canticles (PL 183.881).

[689]In Vermigli's last litany of citations, some could be verified and some could not. The following citations were identified: Theodoret *Comm. Rom.* 9.3 (PG 82.95–103); Sedulius [*sic*] Duns Scotus *Collectanea in omni b. Pauli epistolas* 1–2 (PL 103.9–33); Bruno Carthus *In ep. ad Rom.* 4 (PL 153.42–48); Arnobius the Younger *In Psalmos* 106 (PL 53.488ff.); Didymus, *Jam.* 2 (PG 39.1752); Eusebius of Caesarea *Hist. Eccl.* 3.27 (PG 20.273, Greek col., and 274, Latin col.); *Glossa Ord. ad loc*; Cyprian *Symb. Apost.* (by Ruffinus) (PL 21.377); Haymo of Halberstadt *Expositio in epp. S. Pauli* (PL 117.679, 686); Thomas Aquinas, *In Gal.* 3 (*Expositio in S. Pauli ep. Sup. Ep. ad Galat. lect.* 2 and 3). The Thomas citation is from S. Thomae Aquinatis Doctoris Angelici, *Super epistolas S. Pauli lectura*, ed. P. Raphaelis Cai, O.P. (Turin: Marietti, 1953), 1:593–94 (lecture 2), 595–96 (lecture 3). Two of Vermigli's citations could not be verified: Cyril of Alexandria *Ev. Jo.* 9.3, and Nicholas of Lyra *Gal.* 3, *Postilla*. The citation of Gennadius of Marseilles *Rom.*, is not extant.

About the Editor and Translator

Frank Allison James III was awarded the D. Phil. in history from Oxford University in 1993 for his dissertation on the intellectual and historical origins of Vermigli's notion of *gemina praedestinatio* (double predestination) and the Ph.D. in historical theology from Westminster Theological Seminary in 2000 for his dissertation on Vermigli's theological doctrine of justification. He received a Lilly Theological Research Grant (1999), was elected by the faculty of Keble College, Oxford University, to membership of the Senior Common Room (1994). Other awards include an Overseas Research Students Award (1991–92), the Isaiah Berlin Bursary, Oxford University (1990-91), the Leonard J. Theberge Memorial Scholarship, St. Peter's College, Oxford University (1991–93), an Oxford University Research Grant (1991), the Christina Drake Research Award for Italian Studies, Taylor Institution, Oxford University (1991), and the St. Peter's College Graduate Award, Oxford (1990–92).

James is the coeditor and contributor (with Charles E. Hill) of *The Glory of the Atonement in Biblical, Theological, and Historical Perspective* (2003); coeditor (with Emidio Campi and Peter Opitz) of *Peter Martyr Vermigli: Humanism, Republicanism and Reformation,* Travaux d'Humanisme et Renaissance, 365 (2002); coeditor (with J. Patrick Donnelly and Joseph C. McLelland) of *The Peter Martyr Reader* (1999). He is the author of *Peter Martyr Vermigli and Predestination: The Augustinian Inheritance of an Italian Reformer,* Oxford Theological Monographs (1998); coeditor (with Heiko Augustus Oberman) of *Via Augustini: The Recovery of Augustine in the Later Middle Ages,* Renaissance and Reformation, Studies in Medieval and Reformation Thought, vol. 48 (1991). Since 1996, he has served as a general editor (with Joseph C. McLelland and J. Patrick Donnelly) of the Peter Martyr Library series and senior editor of *Ad Fontes: Digital Library of Classical Theological Text* (with Alister E. McGrath, Richard A. Muller, and Herman Selderhuis).

James was assistant professor of systematic and historical theology at Westmont College (1987–89); lecturer in philosophy and history, Villanova University (1986–87); and contributing editor at *Christian History Magazine* (1986–89). Since 1993 he has been professor of historical theology at Reformed Theological Seminary in Orlando, Florida, and in 2002 was appointed vice president for academic affairs of that institution.

Scripture References

Genesis
2:8 26
4 140
4:7 145
6:2 206
6:3 76
6:5 114
8:21 114
9:6 130
12:3 182
12:4 182
15:5ff 201
15:6 . . . . 90, 122, 159, 172,
    181, 210
15:16 . . . . 26, 132
18:17 76
22:17–18 . . . . 200, 202
25:21 4
29:15 219
43:5 219
45:8 83

Exodus
2:12 68
9:16 . . . . 16, 25, 56
12:1 29
13:17 26
23:31 83
32:21 68
33:19 . . . . 56, 105

Numbers
11:5 219
20:12 178

Deuteronomy
2:5 145
4:2 131
4:37 14
6:6 6
6:13 222
19:5 131
27:26 189
67:5 137

Joshua
6:6 83
10:12 69

1 Samuel
2:30 135
9:21 67
12:22 38
16:7 41
19:24 42

2 Samuel
11 68
12:10 14

1 Kings
5 . . . . 95, 178
10:1 69
11:4 67
13:21 178
17:1 69
19:4 31
21:17 131
21:29 . . . . 67, 132

2 Kings
12:2 67
20:1ff 75
20:5 . . . . 13, 75

2 Chronicles, 12:14 132

Job
1:9 206
1:21 83
4:18 113
15:5 113
19:25–27 122

Psalms
2:11 89
10:17 (Vulgate) 133
12:1–2 116
14:1 76
14:3 64
20:1 189
22:5 89

Psalms, *continued*
25:18 136
31:1 (Vulgate) 147
32:1–2 . . . . 100, 148, 159,
    172, 222
32:10 189
51 . . . . 11, 136
51:10 57
69:4 219
83:37 14
100:32 178
103:17 189
115:3 . . . . 46, 71
116:36 57
139:8–9 177
145:14 64

Proverbs
1:26 46
8:17 36
10:12 204
16:1 132
16:4 16
16:11 7

Ecclesiastes, 30:24 141

Wisdom of Solomon
1:13 46
1:14 47
15:3 225

Isaiah
6:9 . . . . 55, 212
6:10 24–25
7:4 95
7:9 95
8:14 29
10:7 83
26:2 92
26:3 89
28:16 189
28:26 . . . . 164, 172
29:13 145
40:6 114
42:16 28
46:9 21

Isaiah, *continued*
49:15. 66
53:4. 172
53:11. 172
55:1. 114
64:6–8 114
65:2. 66
66:1–3 193–94
66:3. 145
66:23. 64

Jeremiah
1:5. 14
5:3 (Vulgate) 172
17:9. 114
18:8. 75
25:8. 76
25:11. 13
25:12. 76
31:18. . . . . .134, 157
31:33. 64
31:34. 60

Lamentations, 5:21 158

Ezekiel
11:18. 57
11:19. 30
14:9. 24
16:6. 39
18:21–22 202
18:24. 67
18:31. 134
33:11. 46
36:26–27 134

Daniel
3 .69
4:24. 138

Joel
2:28. . . . . .60, 64
2:32. 164

Amos, 3:7. 76

Jonah
3:4. 75
3:10. . . . . .75, 134

Habakkuk, 2:4. 89,119,
   160, 172, 180

Zechariah, 1:8 157

Malachi, 1:2. 4

Ecclesiasticus
8:21 57
15:12 47
17:29?. 67

Matthew
1:21 204
4:10 222
5:45 43
6:12 . . . . 82, 113, 137
6:24 145
6:32 13
7:7 140
7:16 28
7:17–18 111
7:18 131
7:21 203
7:22 . . . . . . .93, 144, 173, 178
8:10 169
8:13 169
9:2 . . . . 170, 199
9:22 . . . . .170, 199, 228
9:28 170
10:22 64
10:28 139
10:29–30 . . . . 13, 18
10:33 173
11:21 . . . . 32, 63
11:21–24 59
11:23 32
11:25 . . . . 34, 55
11:25–26 6
11:27 55
11:28 192
12:32 71
12:33–35 111
12:34 131
13:1–23 93
13:11 55
13:23 34
13:69 6
15:8 145
16:17 . . . . 34, 154
16:35 83
17 140
17:20 175
20:15 43
20:15 (Vulgate). 24
20:16 56
20:19 70
21:22 140
21:31 126
22:14 . . . . 6, 43
23:37 64
24:24 . . . . 14, 55, 71
24:46 145

Matthew, *continued*
24:55 71
25:34 6
25:35 135
26:14 47
26:53 74
26:74 68
26:75 136
27. 140
27:3–6 136
27:4 128
28:19 142
35:34 135

Mark
1:15 224
9:23 207
9:38 179
16:16 224

Luke
1:48 41
2:6 60
2:29 71
3:6 64
6:37 137
7:47 . . . . 142, 227
7:50 . . . . 142, 170
9:53 8
10:20 4
11:41 140–41
12:47 120
15:11 127
15:17 127
17:5 190
17:7–10 112
19.6 155
22:37 71
22:62 213
23:41 155
23:43 228

John
1:1 9
1:7 113
1:8 212
1:9 63
1:11 138
1:12 . . . . 61, 138
1:13 139
1:14 9
1:16 1521
2:4 13
3:8 55
3:16 170
3:27 55

John, *continued*
3:32. 64
3:36. . . . . .89, 170
4:18. 139
5:15. 53
5:18. 208
5:44. 179
6:29. . . . . .203, 216
6:37. 55
6:40. . . . . .171, 199, 203
6:44. . . . .6, 31, 53–55, 155, 171
6:45. . . . . .60, 64, 171
6:46. 54
6:51. 171
6:53. . . . . .53, 219
7:42. 12
8:34. 144
8:36. 155
8:42. 187
8:56. . . . . .122, 211
10:11. 83
10:28. . . . . .14, 54
10:29. . . . . .6, 54, 71
10:35. 71
11:25. 171
12:37. 179
12:39. 179
12:42. . . . . .173, 179
13:18. 6
14:1. 6
14:4. 216
14:16ff. 188
14:23. 187
15:4–6 112
15:5. 154
15:16. . . . . .4, 6, 35, 59
17:3. . . . . .171, 225
19:11. 53
20:31. 171

Acts
1:23. 42
2:23. . . . . .5, 14, 70
4:12. 122
4:27. 83
4:28. 16
7:51. 38
8:22. 56
10:4. 217
10:31. 155
10:34ff. 151
13:48. . . . . .14, 33, 191
15:9. . . . . .141, 171, 226
16:14. . . . . .33, 56, 191
16:18. 171
17:28. . . . . .18, 81

Acts, *continued*
19:13–16 178

Romans
1:7 119
1:16 160
1:17–18 161
1:18ff. 97
1:20 65
1:21 52
1:24 24
1:24ff. 115
1:25 52
1:28 24
2:5 25
2:6 68
2:13 . . . . .142, 152
2:14 146
2:17–24 98
2:21–22 115–16
3:3 90
3:8 68
3:10 128
3:10–12 116
3:10–18 98
3:17 222
3:19 99
3:20 . . . . .107, 116, 223
3:21 . . . . .99, 161
3:24 . . . . .161, 229
3:27 . . . .99, 116, 161, 228–29
3:28 . . . . . . .99, 161, 203, 225
3:29 . . . . .65, 161
3:31 210
4:1–4 100
4:3 . . . . .209, 222
4:4 . . . . .116, 161, 196
4:5 159
4:7–8 100
4:9 201
4:11 . . . . .100, 162
4:13 162
4:13–15 100
4:15 . . . . .116, 128
4:16 . . . . .101, 162
4:18 . . . . .101, 160, 162
4:19 162
4:19–21 88
4:20 162
4:23–24 . . . . .163, 197
5:1 163
5:5 89
5:6 101
5:8 . . . . .35, 101
5:10 101
5:12 102

Romans, *continued*
5:14 . . . . .102, 230
5:17 62
5:20 . . . . .116, 128
6:1 223
6:4 116
6:10–11 117
6:12–13 117
6:21 . . . . .102, 116
6:21–22 197
6:23 149
7:1–4 102
7:5 . . . . .103, 117
7:7 117
7:12 117
7:14–25 117
7:15 82
7:15–18 103
7:18 58
7:22–23 82
8:3 . . . . . . .108, 117, 131, 193
8:6–7 104
8:7 131
8:11 118
8:15–16 190
8:16 193
8:17 89
8:18 126
8:24 225
8:26–27 133
8:27–28 36
8:28 . . . 10, 16, 20, 51–52, 104
8:29 . . . . .10, 14, 21
8:29–30 163
8:30 . . . . .30, 104
8:31 36
8:31–35 42
8:33–34 104
8:35 . . . . .10, 21
9:7 33
9:10 4
9:11 . . . . .15, 20, 33, 51
9:11–12 . . . . .11, 29
9:11–13 . . . . .14, 37, 104
9:12 52
9:13 30
9:14 214
9:15 . . . . .14, 30, 56
9:15–18 105
9:16 57
9:17 . . . . .26, 59
9:18 . . . . .25, 30, 51
9:19 44
9:20 114
9:21 . . . . .14, 28–29
9:22 25

Romans, *continued*
9:23. . . . . 16, 26
9:23–24 24
9:30. 163
9:31–32 . . . . 105, 194
9:33. 210–11
10:1. 145
10:3. . . . . . .105, 148, 164, 229
10:4. . . . . .148, 197
10:5. 164
10:5–6 105
10:8–9 164
10:10. 179
10:11. 66
10:14. . . . . 65, 164
10:17. 165
11:5. 31
11:6. . . . . .118, 124, 222
11:19. 21
11:19–20 165
11:23. . . . . .165, 211
11:33. . . . . .31, 105, 214
11:33–34 44
11:34. 5
12:3. . . . . .33, 191
14:22–23 106
14:23. 207
17:22. 56

1 Corinthians
1:5. 176
1:21. . . . . .109, 165
1:23–24 38
1:26. 38
1:30. . . . . .29, 139, 168
2:4–5. 190
2:9. 15
2:14. . . . . .131, 190
3:2. 9
3:5. 30
3:6. 59
4:4. 106
4:7. . . . . .58, 154, 221
4:13–14 191
6:11. 38
7:25. . . . . .30, 33, 155
8:1. 153
9:27. 75
10:4. 212
10:9. 212
10:31. 144
11:4–5 151
11:19. 74
12:3. 155
12:8–9 . . . . .93, 175, 190
12:11. 56

1 Corinthians, *continued*
13:1 177
13:2 . . . . 93, 122, 173
13:3 . . . . 146, 175, 177
13:8 177
15:10 . . . . 57, 154

2 Corinthians
1:4 229
1:12 9
1:24 166
3:5 . . . . 57, 154
4:13 210
5:10 135
6:14–16 145

Galatians
1:15 . . . . 4, 15, 59
2:14–16 166
2:16 . . . . 107, 211, 219
2:20 . . . . 166, 199
2:21 . . . . 107, 150
3:2 . . . . 107, 166
3:5 . . . . 107, 166
3:7 166
3:8 166
3:9 166
3:10 . . . . . 107, 119, 128, 189
3:11 . . . . 160, 230
3:14 167
3:15–16 188
3:15–17 107
3:16 181
3:18 200
3:19 118
3:21 1–8
3:22 167
3:23–24 108
3:24 . . . . 128, 167
3:25 167
4:6 190
4:21–26 108
4:28 167
5:2–3 108–9
5:4 167
5:6 . . . . 168, 226
5:11 109
5:17 82
5:19ff.. 117
5:22 191

Ephesians
1:1 187
1:4 . . . . . 7, 11, 14–15, 20, 22,
    26, 30, 34
1:5 . . . . 9, 20–21, 30, 37

Ephesians, *continued*
1:6 52
1:9 30
1:10 22
1:11 . . . . 17, 20, 37, 59
2:1–3 109
2:3 109
2:4–5 109
2:8 . . . . 33, 110, 151, 168, 191
2:9 . . . . 110, 118, 125
2:10 . . . . 9, 26, 30, 52, 110
2:12 . . . . 38, 110
3:7–9 110
3:16 . . . . 168, 190
3:17 . . . . 188, 190
4:14 95
5:26 224
6:16 91
6:23 33

Philippians
1:6 . . . . 6, 59, 192
1:27ff. 6
1:29 33
2:12–13 . . . . 6, 57, 142
2:13 . . . . .30, 56–57, 73,
    192, 214
2:21 64
3:4–6 110
3:6 118
3:7 146

Colossians
1:21–22. . . . . 110, 187
2:13–14. 110

2 Thessalonians, 2:13. 7

1 Timothy
1:5 . . . . 147, 226
1:20 210
2:1–2 63
2:4 . . . . 8, 62
2:5 113
2:6 62
3:1 42
4:10 66
5:8 185

2 Timothy
1:9 . . . . . . 20, 31, 34, 111, 118
2:3ff. 145
2:17–18. 28
2:19 . . . . 20, 27, 71
2:20–21. 27
2:21 28

2 Timothy, *continued*
2:25 56

Titus
1:16 185
3:4 31
3:4–5 111
3:5 . . . . 118, 222
3:7 89

Hebrews
6:4 . . . . 71, 120
9:24ff 111
10:38 160
11:1 . . . . 90, 155, 186
11:6 . . . . 186, 194
11:7 199–200
11:24–26 212

Hebrews, *continued*
11:33 (Vulg.) 168, 183

James
1:17 21
2:17 . . . . 93, 146, 217
2:26 93

1 Peter
1:5 169
3:20–21 199
3:21 224
4:8 204

2 Peter
1:10 100
2:22 7

1 John
2:4 185
3:6 174
3:14 187
4:10 37
4:17–18 139
4:19 . . . . 37, 124
5:1 . . . . 169, 173
5:4 . . . . 91, 169
5:10 88
5:13 169
5:18 173

Jude
5 212
14–15 206

Revelation, 3:20 . . 56, 66, 142

Classical, Patristic, and Medieval References

Acacius of Berea 230
Ambrose
  Apologia Prophetae David 148
  Comm. Gal. 226
  Comm. Rom. 74, 148, 212–13, 229
  Comm. 1 Cor. 229
  Expositio evangelii secundum Lucam. . 8, 213
  De fuga saeculi 82
  De vocationem gentium 229
Ambrosiaster, *Ep. Rom.* 33
Ambrosius, *De fide*, 5.83. 33
Antisthenes 203
Aquinas
  Summa theologiae 30, 140
  Super epistolas S. Pauli lectura 230
Aratus, *Phaenom.* 81
Aristotle
  Analytica posteriora 26, 90, 118,
    129, 135, 143, 198
  Analytica priora 180
  De anima 138, 180, 184
  Categoriae 180
  Ethica nichomachea [Nichomachean
    Ethics] 130, 185
  Topica. 180
Arnobius the Younger, *In Ps.* 230
Augustine
  Ad. simp. . . 19, 38, 54, 57, 59, 147, 152, 215,
    226
  Contra Julianum 44, 63, 147, 192
  Contra secundam Juliani 36
  Contra duas epistulas Pelagianorum
    ad Bonifaticum 36, 73, 214, 216
  De bono viduitatis 223
  De civitate Dei. 10, 18, 72, 76, 78–79, 83
  Confessions 9, 121, 134, 158
  De correptione et gratia. 5, 36, 63, 102
  De diversis quaestionibus ad
    Simplicianum 44
  De dogmatibus Ecclesiasticis 150, 215
  Enarratio in Psalmos 147, 213, 215
  Enchiridion ad laurentium 46, 141, 147
  Epistolae. 63, 65, 150, 214
  Ad Honoratum 152, 215
  Expositio quarumdam quaestionum
    in epistula ad Romanos 33
  De gestis Pelagii 40, 123

Augustine, *continued*
  De gratia et libero arbitrio) 80, 150
    41, 23
  De natura et gratia 227
  De dono perseverantiae . . . 5, 7, 8, 36, 65, 82
  De praedestinatione Sanctorum. . . 4, 19, 36,
    41, 58, 63, 151, 215
  In Evangelium Johannes tract. 91, 93, 215
  Quaestionum n Heptateuchum 202
  Retractionum libri II 36
  Sermones de scripturis 19, 93, 150, 213
  De spiritu et littera . . . 93, 152, 213, 214, 221
  De Trinitate 91, 215

Basil
  De baptismo 144, 145
  Homiliae in Psalmum 150
  Homiliae de humilitate 229
  Ad Neocaesar., ep. 178
Bede, *Expositio Jacob* 217
Bernard of Clairvaux, *Sermo 22* 230
Bruno Carthus, *In ep. ad Rom.* 230

Chrysostom, John
  De fide et lege naturae 1, 209
  In cap. Genes.: Homiliae 209, 210
  Hom. Rom. 33, 148, 209-11, 229
  Hom. 1 Cor. 74, 93, 151, 175
  Hom. 1 Tim. 210
  De verbis apostoli, Hab. eundem Spiritu. 210
Cicero
  De Amicitia. 90
  De Divinatione. 76
  De natura deorum 76
  De Oratore 129
Cleanthes the Stoic 72
Cyprian
  Comm. in symb. Apost. (by Ruffinus) . . . 230
  De cath. ecclesiae unitate 174
  De lapsis 206
  Ad Quirinum testimonia adversus
    Judaeos) 36, 40, 148, 209, 229
Cyril of Alexandria
  Contra Julianum. 216
  Comm. in Ev. Ioannis. 139, 216, 230

Demosthenes
   Adversus Androtionem 152
   In Aristocratem 201
Didymus, *James,* 2. 230
Duns Scotus, *De divisione naturae.* 50

Epictetus, *Dissertationes,* sec. 22 173
Erasmus, *De libero arbitrio.* 35
Eusebius, *De Praep. Evangelica,* 7. 77
Eusebius of Caesarea, *Hist. eccl.*. 230

Gennadius of Marseilles, *Rom.* 230
Gregory of Nazianzus
   Oratio in laudem Basili
      Dialogus 83
      in Pentecosten 8
      In sancta lumina 146
      n sepisum. 146
Gregory of Rimini 124n
   Gregorii Arminensis OESA Lectura 50
Gregory the Great
   Homiliae in Ezechiel 217
   Expositio in Librum Job xiv
   Moralium libri . . . . xxv, 218

Haymo of Halberstadt, *Exp. in epp.*
   S. Pauli. 230
Heychius, *In Lev* 230
Hilary (of Arles) 4, 229
Homer, *Odyssey.* 72
Horace, *Ars poetica* 201
Hostiensis (Henry de Segusio), *S. trin.*
   & fide cath. 91–92nn

Irenaeus, *Adversus Valentinos.* 205

Jerome
   Adversus Pelagianos dialog . . . 21, 31, 40, 223
   Altercatio Luciferiani et orthodoxi
      seudialogus contra Luciferianos 174
   Comm. Eph. 151
   Comm. Gal. 211–12, 226
   Comm. Isa.. 224

Comm. Matt. 204
Comm. Philem.. 151
Comm. Rom. 151
John of Damascus 21
Justinian
   Codex Iustinianus. 134
   Legibus et Senatus 130

Leo I
   Homiliae. 114
   Serm. 9, De collectione et eleemosyna . . . 216
   Serm. 64, De Passione Domini 13 216

Nicholas of Lyra, *Gal.* 230

Origen
   Comm. Ps.. 150
   Comm. Rom. 149, 207, 208, 225
   Contra Celsum 12, 74
   Deprincipiis (Peri archon) 60
   Hexapla. 206
   Homilae in Leviticum 208
   Selecta in Job. 206

Peter Lombard, *Sentences* 19, 62, 93M 123
Photius, *Frag. in epistolam ad S. Pauli* 230
Plato, *Respublica.* 98, 181
Prosper of Aquitaine 4

Seneca the Younger, *Epistulae morales* 72
Sophocles, *Oedipus rex (Antigone)* 77

Tertullian, *De baptismo* 206
Theodoret, *Comm. Rom.* 230
Theophylact, *Hom. 1 Cor.* 93
Theophylact of Ochrida, *Exp. Gal.* 230

Vergil, *Aeneid* 211

William of Occam 21, 80n

Index

Abraham
  covenant and law, 107–8
  descendants of, 182
  faith of, 88, 100, 122, 160, 162–63, 166, 172,
    198–99, 209, 216, 222
  and justification, 181–82, 188, 205
  and mercy of God, 41, 99–101
adoption
  and justification, xxxvi, 139, 187
  and predestination, 21
Ahab, humility of, 131–32
almsgiving, and faith, 140–41
Ambrose
  on faith and predestination, 33, 212–13
  on free will, 82
  on justification, 229
  on regeneration, 148
amen, defined, 95
angels, 113, 206
anger, of God. See wrath of God
Antisthenes, 202–3
apocrypha, 206
apodeiksis (strict demonstration), 143
Aquinas, Thomas, on predestination, xxx
Arian controversy (AD 381), 127n
Aristarchus the grammarian, 219
Aristotle
  on fourfold causality, 26
  on syllogistic method, 129
Asper, Hans, portrait of Vermigli, xiv, xv
assurance, 45, 89–90, 185–86, 199, 201, 206,
    210–11
astrology, 72
Augustine
  on almsgiving, 141
  on causality, 79
  on celibacy and marriage, 223
  on Cicero, 75–76
  city of God vs. city of the devil, 64
  on election, 38
  on faith, 33, 91–93, 213–16
  on fate, 18

Augustine, continued
  on foreknowledge, 79–80, 82, 202
  on free will, 79
  on grace, 227
    and justification, 149–50
    and mercy, 57
    sufficiency of, 58–59
  on humanity of Christ, 41
  on justice of God, 44
  on justification, 157–58
  on love of God, 140, 147
  on natural law, 146–47, 150–51
  on Pelagianism, 123, 150, 214, 229
  on predestination, 8–9, 19, 33, 151, 215
  on reprobation, 27
  on salvation
    universal, 62–63
    and works, 36
  on supralapsarianism, 49
  on the will, 221
  on will of God, 46, 83
  on works, 134, 151–52
Augustinianism
  of Bucer, xl–xli, xlnn
  and election, xxviii
  and Pelagianism, xxvii–xxviii, xxxv
  predestinarian views, xxx
  vs. semi-Pelagianism, 254n
  of Vermigli, xii, xxvii, xxxv–xxxvii, xl–xli

Bapasme, Hubert de, xx
baptism
  and remission of sins, 224
  and works, 117, 120, 158–59
Basil
  on eternal life and grace, 150
  on humility, 229
  on love, 178
  on works and justification, 144–45
belief
  and assurance, 89, 199
  means of, 93, 94

believers
  fallen, and good works, 120–21
  marks of, 194
Beza, Theodore, 141
Bible, Wisdom noncanonical, 46
Bibliander, Theodore, attacks Vermigli, xxiv–xxv
Bucer, Martin, xvii, xviii, xix, xxxix
  on justification, xlii
    debate with Young, xxxii–xxxiii
    threefold, xxxvii
  on predestination, xxx
  recommends Tremelli to Cranmer, xvii*n*
budding post motif, 121
Budé, Guillaume, 90*n*
Bullinger, Heinrich, xvii, xix
  on justification, xlii
  Vermigli's correspondence with, xxiv

Cain motif, 095
Calvin, John, xvii, xix
  answer to Pighius, 94*n*, 129*n*
  on justification, xlii
  and *simul iustus et peccator* concept, xxxvi
  Vermigli's correspondence with, xxiv
Calvinism, and despair, 48*n*
Catholic Reform, influence on Vermigli, xii
Catilina, Lucius Sergius, 147, 147*n*
causality
  an justification, 159
  and effects, 27, 99–100
  eternal vs. efficient cause, 34
  faith and predestination, 33–34
  and fall of Adam, 101–2
  fourfold
    Aristotelian, 90*n*
    of predestination, 26
    vs. intentionality (Augustinian), 79*n*
  Logicians on, 30
  and predestination, 25–51
  vs. rationality, 25–26
  and salvation, 142
  and sin, 23–24
  St. Paul on, 31–32
  works vs. predestination, 36
Chrysippus the Stoic, on free will and necessity, 77
Chrysostom, John
  on faith, 176, 209–11
  on faith and predestination, 33

Chrysostom, John, *continued*
  on grace, 151
  on justification, 229
  on necessity of prediction, 74
  on works, 148, 151
church fathers, on justification, 143–52, 205–17, 228–30
Cicero
  on foreknowledge and free will, 76–78
  oratorical method of, 129
circumcision
  and justification, 108–9, 159, 162, 221–22
  of Paul, 110
  as a seal, 100
Cleanthes the Stoic, 72, 72*n*
Clement of Alexandria, on St. Paul, 223
Colophon (city), 143*n*
Commonplaces *(loci communes)*, xxii–xxiii
compassion. *See also* mercy of God
  and conversion, 141
condemnation, vs. reprobation, xxviii
confession
  auricular, 136–37, 164
  unto salvation, 179
congruity, 120, 221
conscience, as faith, 106
conversion, *auxilium Dei*, 123–24
Cooke, Anthony, xix
councils
  Carthage (AD 418), 153, 153*n*
  criteria for validity of, 152
  Mainz, 217–18
  Milevis (AD 416), 153*n*
  Milevum (2d), or Diospolis (Numidia), 123, 123*n*, 217
  Orange, 2d (AD 529), 153–57, 154*n*, 217
  proofs for justification, 217–18
  Trent (1545–63), xvii, xxxiii
    on justification, 156–60, 186–87
covenant(s)
  conditional, 189
  distinguished by Pighius, 188
  and faith, 162
  and law, 107–8, 119
  and works, 162
Cranmer, Thomas
  last letter of, to Vermigli, xviii
  Tremelli recommended to, by Bucer, xviii*n*
  and Vermigli, xvii, xviii
creeds, Athanasian, 93*n*

Crucifixion of Christ, and grace, 1–7
Cyprian
    on faith, 209
    on justification, 229
    on salvation and works, 36, 148–49
Cyril, 139
    on faith, 216
    on justification, 230

damnation
    Pighius's view of, 42
    and reprobation, 27
Dampmartin, Catherine (wife of Vermigli), xvi
David, 14
    imputation of righteousness, 100
    sins of, 68
Decalogue, 116–18. *See also* law
Democritus, on free will and necessity, 77
Demosthenes, 152, 201
depravity, and will of God, 46–47
despair, of the alienated vs. the justified, 48, 48*n*
dignity, and regeneration, 61–62

Eck, Johannes, xxxiv, 94, 94*n*
ecumenical councils. *See* councils
Edward VI, xvii, xix
election. *See also* predestination; reprobation
    and effectual calling, 111
    of Gentiles, 65–66
    by grace, 105
    and humility, 7
    and justification, 104
    and mercy, 41, 60
    Pighius's view of, 41–42
    and predestination, xxviii, 19
    to salvation, 59
    secure, in Christ, 54–55
    temporal vs. eternal, 3–4
    Vermigli's view of, xxix
    and will of God, 37–38, 44–45
    and works, 41
Empedocles, on free will and necessity, 77
England
    church reform, xviii
    Vermigli in, xvi–xxi, xxxix
Erasmus, Disiderius, on faith, 176–77
eternal life, and grace, 34, 57–58, 149–50, 171
Eusebius of Caesarea, on philosophers, 77
excommunication, and false repentance, 121

Fabricius, Quintus, 147, 147*n*
faith. *See also* belief
    of Abraham, 100
    and assurance, 185–86, 201, 206, 210–11
    and belief, 93
    as conscience, 106
    and conviction, 91
    defined, 88, 88*n*, 90–92, 219
    distinguished from charity, 122–23
    and fear of God, 174
    given by God, 175, 214–15
    and grace, 57, 154
    historical, 192–93
    and hope, 92
    and *hypostasis,* 91–92
    imputed for righteousness, 197
    vs. incredulity, 165
    justifying vs. temporary, 93–94, 122, 173–
        75, 180, 183
    and the law, 108
    living vs. dead, 180
    and love, 168, 176–77, 212, 216
    and miracles, 173, 179–79, 190
    moving mountains motif, 175–76
    mustard seed parable, 175
    nature of, 170
    origin of, 190–91
    parable of the sower, 93–94
    vs. patience, 91–92
    and predestination, 33–34, 135
    as prerequisite of love or works, 181
    and profession, 179–80
    and repentance, 136
    and righteousness, 148, 197
    and salvation, 165–66, 169
    sequence of, 92
    and trust, 94–95
    varieties of, 196–200, 203
    and works, 95–96, 105, 122, 135–36, 185,
        200–201
fallacies
    of the accident, 220
    of composition, 218*n*
fallen Christians, 120
fall of Adam, xxxvi–xxxvii, 47
    free will lost, 155
    and infralapsarianism, xxix
    and justification, xxxviii, 102
    and regeneration, 62

fall of Adam, *continued*
    and supralapsarianism, 49
    and will of God, 52–53
fate, vs. predestination, 12–13, 18–19, 72–73
favor, as a work, 95
fear
    and faith, 174
    vs. love, 139–40
    as a work, 95
flesh
    defined, 98–99
    and salvation, 109
    works of, 103–4, 124
foreknowledge, 163
    benefits of study of, 7
    and contingency, 74, 81–82
    and free will, 72–74, 79–81
    and justice, 82–84
    and predestination, 16–17
    and providence, 71–73
    and works, 7
forgiveness, 137–38
    and love, 204
free will, 146. *See also* will of God
    bondage of, 82
    canon on, 2d Council of Orange, 154–55
    and compulsion, 70
    and consequent will of God, 63, 65
    and good works, 30, 32, 58
    and grace, 54–58
    lost in the fall, 155
    and necessity, 70–71, 73–82
    and predestination, 11–12, 35, 81–82
fruit motif, 112–13

Gardiner, Stephen, 225*n*–226*n*, 228, 228*n*
Gennadius, 230
Gentiles
    and Abrahamic covenant, 166–67
    and the Decalogue, 116
    elect among, 65–66
    and justification, 166
    and righteousness of God, 163
    works of, 97
glorification, 163
God. *See also* love; mercy of God; will of God
    as author of sin, 45
    will of, 46
good works. *See* works
Gospel, vs. law, 115

grace
    defined, 219
    as defined at Trent, 156–57
    efficacy of, 66
    and election, 105
    and faith, 154, 208, 214, 218–19
    and free will, 54–55
    general/universal, 60–68, 123
    and justification, 144, 149–51
    particular, 53–59
    and regeneration, 102–3
    vs. rewards, 149–50
    sufficiency of, 58–59, 65
    and works, 45, 123–25
Grammarians, 219
gratis (in vain), 107
gratitude, for justification, 209–10
Greenslade, S. L., xxii, xxxii
Gregory of Nazianzus
    on prayer, 83
    on works and faith, 146
Gregory of Rimini, xxxi, 124*n*
    predestinarian views of, xxx
Gregory the Great, on faith, 217
Grynaeus, Simon, xvii

hatred, between God and Judas, 47
heaven, 135
Hebrew (language), 87*n*–88*n*
Hesychius, on grace, 230
Hilary of Arles, 4, 4*n*
history, and faith, 193
holiness. *See* righteousness
Holy Spirit
    and faith, 107, 167–68
    fruits of, 191
    and grace, 157
    as origin of faith, 190
    Pighius on, 191–92
    role of, in salvation, 154
Honorius, 151–52
hope. *See* faith
Hostiensis, on faith and hope, 91–92
humanity. *See also* free will
    two classes/groups, 63–64
human nature, as unrighteous, 98–99
Hume, David, theodicy dilemma, 18*n*
humility, 194
    of Ahab, 131
    and election, 7, 142–43

humility, *continued*
    and justification, 202
    of the Virgin Mary, 41
hypostasis (substance), and faith, 91–92

idolatry, 160–61
imputation
    defined, 100
    and justification, xxxv–xxxvi, xlii–xliii, 100
infallibility, and necessity, 70, 74
infants, and free will, 32
infralapsarianism. *See under* predestination
iniquity. *See* sin(s)
invocation. *See* prayer
Irenaeus, on justification, 205–6
Isaac and Ishmael motif, 33
Israel, and works righteousness, 105

Jacob and Esau motif, 11, 14, 29, 33, 37, 51, 59, 74, 219
Jerome
    on faith, 211
    on free will, 31
    on grace vs. works, 151
    against Pelagianism, 223–24
Jews
    and consequent will of God, 65–66
    and justification, 166
    and predestination, 38–39
    and righteousness of God, 163
    superstitions of, 193
    works of, 98
John the Baptist, 55, 170
Judas motif, 95, 128
justice
    and foreknowledge, 82–84
    and predestination, 35, 43
    and reprobation, 25
    and sin, 24
    and will of God, 83–84
justification
    and adoption, xxxvi
    cause and effects, 159
    by congruity, 122–23, 221
    defined, 87–88
    development of doctrine, xxxix, xli–xlii
    and election, 104
    and faith, 92–93, 134, 160–205, 213
    by faith alone, 218–30
    as forensic verb, xxxv, xxxviii, 87–88

justification, *continued*
    and forgiveness, 87–88
    and grace, 1–7, 149–51
    and human perfection, 186–87
    imputation of, xxxv–xxxvi, 100, 196
    and law, 102–3
    as liberty, 108
    and love, 184, 187, 204
    and merit, 195
    nature of, and providence, 104–5
    in old and new covenants, 119
    and original sin, xxxviii
    outward benefits of, 169
    as a Pauline doctrine, xxxiii
    and piety (sanctification), xxxiv–xxxv
    preparations for, 158–59, 196
    and regeneration, xxxvii
    renewal of, 182
    and repentance, 136, 202
    restoration to, 165
    and righteousness, 135–36
    and salvation, 163
    and sanctification, xxxvii, xli–xlii
    vs. self-glorification, 221
    and *simuliustus et peccator,* xxxviii
    threefold, xxxvii
    Vermigli's views, xxxii–xxxix, xl–xli
    and works, 97–107, 110, 144, 158, 160–65, 183, 194, 203

keys, to the kingdom, 141–42
Kimhi, David (rabbi), 88*n*, 95
Kirby, Torrance, 73*n*

law
    Christ as end of, 148
    and civil order, 129–30
    as a curse, 107, 119
    Decalogue, 117–18
    and faith, 1–8
    and fall of Adam, 52–53
    and forgiveness, 137
    function of, 120, 128–30
    vs. Gospel, 115
    and justification, 102–3, 131–32
    lesbia regula (mason's lead rule), 130*n*
    moral vs. ceremonial, 115–18
    natural, 146–47
    offices of, 128–31
    pre-Noahic, 205

law, *continued*
of purification, 141
and righteousness, 105, 142, 150
righteousness of, 148, 164
and salvation, 104
as schoolmaster, 128
and sin, 145
supreme vs. human, 130
and works, 96–103
Leo I (pope), on passion of the Lord, 216
Loach, Jennifer, xxiii
loci communes (commonplaces), xxii–xxiii
Logicians, 15, 135, 208
on causality, 30
Lombard, Peter. *See* Peter Lombard
Lord's Prayer, 137
Lord's Supper, 219–20
love
and adoption, 187
expression of, 184
and faith, 176–78
vs. fear, 139–40
and forgiveness, 226–27
of God, 124, 139–40, 153
and predestination, 19
and good works, 146
as grace, 57
and justification, 184, 187–88
as a work, 95
Lucius Sergius Catilia, 147
Luther, Martin, xvii, xxxix*n*
Lutherans, xxiv, xxv, xli–xlii

Marbach, John, opposes Vermigli, xxiv, xxv
marks of believers, 194
Martyr, Peter. *See* Vermigli, Peter Martyr
Mary Tudor (queen of England), xviii
Massa perditionis defined, 102*n*
McGrath, Alister, xli
McNair, Philip, xx, xxvii, xl
means and ends, for salvation, 23, 49, 93, 126–27
medical motif, 127–28
Melanchthon, Philip, xvii, xix, xxii, 94
mercy of God
and election, 41, 60
and grace, 57
and imputation of righteousness, 99–101
and reprobation, 25
and works, 105

merit
congruent vs. condign, 125–26, 221
and justification, 195
and works, 114, 125–26
miracles, and faith, 173, 178–79, 190
morality. *See* righteousness
Muller, Richard, xxix, xlii
murder, 12, 130

necessity
of certainty, 70–71
of consequence, 70–72
defined, 69, 69*n*
and free will, 73–82
imposition of, 69–73
and infallibility, 70, 74
intrinsic, extrinsic, and hypothetical, 69–70, 69*n*, 82–84
and justice, 82–84
of prediction, 74
and prophecy, 85
new birth, 139
Nicodemus, 160

Oberman, Heiko A., xii
Ochino, Bernardino, xviii
Oecolampadius, John, xxxix, xlii
Oenomaris the Cynic, on free will and necessity, 77
Origen
on fate, 12
on grace, 206–8
on justification, 228
on justification and grace, 149
on necessity, 74
on universal restoration, 60
on works, 151
Oxford Disputation, xviii
Oxford University, xii, xxi
regius professorship, xix*n*, xx
theological curriculum, xxiii, xxiii*n*
Vermigli's lectures at, xix, xxvi

pagans, and free will, 65
parables, spoken to the elect, 55
Parcae (Fates), 72*n*
Paul (apostle), on causality, 31–32
Pelagianism, 229
of Catholic church, 153
on natural law, 146–47

Pelagianism, *continued*
   of Pighius, xxvii
Pellican, Conrad, xxiv
Peter (apostle), on election, 42
Peter Lombard, 19, 93
Phidias (sculptor), 95*n*
philosophers, on free will and necessity, 77
physician motif, 126–27, 170
piety
   and justification, xxxiv–xxxv, 114
   as a work, 126–27
Pighius, Albert
   attack on Calvin, xxvii, 129*n*
   characterization of, xxvi–xxvii, xxvi*n*–xxvii*nn*
   Controversiarum, xxxiv, 138, 173*n*, 175–80, 178*n*, 179*n*, 181–207 passim
   De libero, 11*n*, 40, 40*n*–42*n*, 43, 44*n*, 48*n*, 50*n*, 67
   on double justification, xxxiv
   on faith and justification, 138
   on the Holy Spirit, 191–92
   on justification, 172–73
   on law and righteousness, 129
   on origin of Virgin Mary, 41*n*
   on prayer, 13–14
   on predestination, 11
   on providence, 12–13
   on "signs" of God's acts, 49–51
   on universal salvation, 62
   Vermigli's objections to, on works and predestination, 40–51
pity, as a work, 95
Pole, Reginald, relationship with Vermigli, xvi
possibility, and foreknowledge, 74
potter motif, and predestination, 14, 22, 28, 37, 114
prayer
   author of, 133, 140
   and foreknowledge, 7, 83
   by the justified, 113
   Lord's Prayer, 137
   morning collect, 73, 73*n*
   and predestination, 13–14
   for salvation, 164–65
   and will of God, 133
preaching, universal, and particular salvation, 60
predestination, 163. *See also* election; reprobation; will of God

predestination, *continued*
   causes of, 25–51
   defined, 15, 19–23
   double, xxxiv, xxvii–xxviv
   effects of, 51–68
   and election, 19
   existence of, 10–15
   and faith, 33–34, 135
   and fate, 4–5, 12–13, 18–19
   and foreknowledge, 16–17
   and free will, 11–12, 35
   and human reason, 106
   as infralapsarian, xxix
   and justice, 35
   locus on, four principal parts, 3
   and love, 19
   nature of, 15–19
   necessary relatives, 22–23
   necessity of, 69–73
   and obedience, 75
   and original sin, 49
   as a Pauline doctrine, xxvi
   Pighius's view of, xxxiv, 49–51
   potter motif, 14, 22, 28
   and properties of God, 23
   and providence, 17–18
   and purpose/good pleasure, 29–31
   and regeneration, 22
   and reprobation, 45
   and righteousness, 45
   as supralapsarian, xxix
   and time, 11–12
   Vermigli's lectures on, xxv–xxvi, xxv*n*
   Vermigli's view of
      context, xxiii–xxv
      countours, xxv–xxix
      origins, xxx–xxxi
      significance, xxxi
      and works, 27–41
   Zwingli's view of, xxviii–xxix
preparation
   defined, 133
   for justification, 158–59, 196
   for salvation, 134
prodigal son motif, 127
promise. *See* covenant(s)
prophecy, 11–12, 75–76
Prosper of Aquitaine, 4, 4*n*
Protestantism
   in England, xvi–xx

Protestantism, *continued*
  of Vermigli, xxxviii–xxxix
  views on justification, xxxvii, xlii
providence, 18*n*, 71, 78–79
  defined, 18
  nature of, and justification, 104–5
  and predestination, 17–18
  and preparatory works, 126

Quintus Fabricius, 147*n*

rationality/reason
  vs. causality, 25–26
  of God's purpose, 44
redemption, 137–38
  sufficient vs. effectual, 62
Reformed theology
  on justification, xxxvi–xxxvii, xlii
  of Vermigli, xxix
regeneration
  and dignity/privilege, 61–62
  and good works, 29
  and justification, xxxvii, xlii
  and predestination, 22, 138
  and sanctification, 102
  and works, 95
repentance
  vs. auricular confession, 136–37
  and faith, 224
  and forgiveness, 137
  as fruit of faith, 136
  and good works, 120
  of Judas, 128
  means of, 127
  vs. self-discipline, 132
reprobation
  vs. condemnation, xxviii
  and damnation, 27, 47
    (*See also* election; predestination)
  defined, 23–25
  effects of, 51–53
  in God's purpose, 67
  as infralapsarian, 49
  Pighius's views of, 51
  and predestination, 45
  and supralapsarianism, 49
  Vermigli's view, xxviii
  and will of God, 47–48, 52
restoration, universal, 60
reward simile, 195, 197

righteousness. *See also* works
  and civil morality, 129–30
  comparative, 129
  and faith, 89, 161–62, 194, 197
  and grace, 159–60
  of Jesus Christ, 168
  and justification, 88–89, 194
  and law, 105, 142
  and the law, 103, 108
  a non causa ut causa principle, 135
  and predestination, 36, 45
  of the regenerate, 87
  simul iustus et peccator, xxxvi
  threefold, xxxvii, xli
  two kinds of, 163–64, 204–5
  and works, 95, 151, 194

sacramental signification, 120
sacrifices, 145, 194
salvation
  and assurance, 45
  cause and effect, 142
  in Christ only, 216
  and election, 59, 104
  and faith, 169
  five states of, 163
  by grace, 109–10
  limited atonement, 62–63
  means and ends, 23, 49, 93, 126–27
  universal call to, 66
  and works, 35–36, 109–10, 164–65
Samuel, and election, 41
sanctification, and justification, xxxiv–xxxv,
  xxxvii, xlii, 102
Santerenziano, Giulio, xviii
Schmidt, Charles, xxiii
Scholasticism
  on necessity, 69–70
  on predestination, 16
  on redemption, 62
  syllogistic reasoning of, 28*n*
Scotus, Duns, 50
Scriptures, infallibility of, 71
Seeberg, Reinhold, xxix
servant vs. child motif, 195
Simler, Josiah, xxx, xxxii, xxxix
sin(s). *See also* fall of Adam
  and alienation from God, 185
  causes of, 23–24
  and depravity of nature, 46–47

sin(s), *continued*
    of the faithful, 113
    God as author of, 52–53
    good intentions, 146
    levels of, 132
    original, 44, 48, 155
        and grace, 62
        and justification, xxxviii
        and reprobation, 49, 52
    of the predestined, 68
    as punishment, 52
    and repentance, 127
    and reprobation, 25, 68
    revealed by Scripture, 167
    and *simul iustus et peccator* concept, xxxvii,
        xxxviii
    and true faith, 106
    of the unregenerate, 207
    and will of God, 73
    as will of God, 45–46
    and works, 45, 144, 220
Smith, Richard, xxxiii–xxxiv, 94, 94n
    arguments against, 218–28
    Defensio sacri, 223
    De votis Monasticis, 223n
    Diatriba, xxxiii–xxxiv, 180, 204, 219–20,
        223–24
    on faith, contra Vermigli, 94
    on justification, 180–81
    paralleled with Pighius, 204
    as regius professor at Oxford, xxxiii
Smyth, C. H., xvi
society, godly vs. ungodly, 63–64
Solomon, 37, 46
Sophists, 110, 118, 135, 196
sorites argument, 208
soul, defined, 138
Spiera, Francesco, of Cittadella, 48, 48n, 115
Spirit. *See* Holy Spirit
Staedtke, Joachim, xxv
Stoics
    Cleanthes, 72, 72n
    on free will, 77
Strasbourg, Vermigli in, xx–xxi, xxv, xxix
Strype, John, characterization of Vermigli, xxxi–
    xxxii, xxxiin
supralapsarianism. *See under* predestination
syllogisms, 23n, 28n, 103n, 108n, 144, 144n,
    191, 210, 215n

teaching, of predestination, 42
Tertullian, on faith, 206
test, 24
theodicy dilemma (Hume), 18n
Thomas Aquinas. *See* Aquinas, Thomas
time, and predestination, 11
treasure motif, 78
Tremelli, Emmanuel (1510–80), recommended
    by Bucer to Cranmer, xviiin
trust, and faith, 94

unbelievers, works of, 121–23
universal restoration, 60
universals, 118

Valdés, Juan de, xii
    on justification by faith, xxxix–xl
    predestinarian views of, xxx
Vergerio, Paolo, 48n
Vermigli, Peter Martyr
    biblical orientation, xiii
    commentaries, xv–xvi
        Genesis, xxxvii
        1 Samuel, xxvn
        Romans, xx–xxii, xliii–xliv
        1 Corinthians, xxxvii
    defines predestination, 19–23
    doctrines/views of, xl
        Augustinianism, xii, xxvii, xxxv–xxxvii
            (*See also* Augustinianism)
        on justification, xxxi–xxxiv, xli
            (*See also* justification)
    lectures
        Genesis, xxv–xxvi, xxxii
        1 Samuel, xxvn
        Romans xix, xx, xxvi
    on Pelagianism, xxxv
    on predestination, xxiii–xxiv, xxxi
        (*See also* predestination)
    Protestantism, xxxviii–xxxix, xl–xli
        in England, xvi–xxi, xxxi–xxxii
    regius professorship, at Oxford, xxii,
        xxxii
    self-perception as Reformed, xxi
    wife (Catherine Dampmartin), xvi
    and other Reformers
        Bucer, xxxix, xl–xli
        Bullinger, xxiv
        Calvin, xxiv
        Cranmer, xvii–xix, xviii, xxxix

Vermigli, *continued*
  and other Reformers, *continued*
    Gregory of Rimini, xii
    Marbach, xxiv
    Melanchthon, xxii
    Oecolampadius, John, xxxix
    Valdés, xxxix–xl
    Zwingli, xxviii–xix
vileness *(tapeinôsin)*, contrasted with virtue, 41
Virgin Mary, Pighius's view of, 41, 41n
virtue *(tapeinophrosym)*, contrasted with vileness, 41
vocation, 163

Westminster Theological Seminary, xii
Whittingham, William, xviii
wickedness, defined, 88n
will. *See* free will
will of God. *See also* free will
  absolute vs. hidden, 46
  consequent, 63, 65
  effective, 64
  and fate or destiny, 72–73
  of his good pleasure, 46, 56
  and self-determination, 133
  signified, 46
  and sin(s), 73
wills, last, of humans, 134
wisdom, and salvation, 165–66
works. *See also* righteousness
  as antecedents of righteousness, 135–36
  and boasting, 99
  and common grace, 123–25
  confession, 164
  defined, 95
  as effects of righteousness, 135
  and eternal life, 57–58
  and faith, 95–96
  of fallen believers, 120–21

works, *continued*
  and foreknowledge, 7
  and function of the law, 128–31
  of Gentiles, 115–16
  good vs. superstitious, 114
  and grace, 45, 149, 155
  inward and outward, 95
  and justification, 113–14, 124–25, 143–44, 151
  of the justified, 110–11, 113, 124, 129, 134
  and knowledge of God, 145–46
  and the law, 96
  and mercy of God, 105
  and merit, 114, 125–26
  moral vs. ceremonial, 95, 115, 124, 126
  natural, 124, 146
  a non causa ut causa principle, 135
  penal, 224
  and predestination, 21–22, 27–41, 52
  preparatory, 126–28, 149, 153, 159, 192, 196
  properties of, 100, 105, 113
  and providence, 104
  of the reprobate, 67–68
  and righteousness, 151–52
  and salvation, 19–110
  and sin, 45
  source of, 134
  of unbelievers, 121–23
  of the wicked, 111–12
  and will of God, 73
wrath of God, 116, 160–61

Young, John, justification debate, with Bucer, xxxii–xxxiii

Zanchi, Girolamo, xx, xxv
Zurich, xxiv, xxv
Zwingli, Ulrich, on double predestination, xxviii–xix
Zwingli, Ulrich, on justification, xlii